Concepts and Reason in Political Theory

Iain Hampsher-Monk

© Iain Hampsher-Monk 2015

First published by the ECPR Press in 2015

Cover: ShutterStock 190800344 © agsandrew

The ECPR Press is the publishing imprint of the European Consortium for Political Research (ECPR), a scholarly association, which supports and encourages the training, research and cross-national co-operation of political scientists in institutions throughout Europe and beyond.

ECPR Press
Harbour House
Hythe Quay
Colchester
CO2 8JF
United Kingdom

All rights reserved. No part of this book may be reprinted or reproduced or utilised in any form or by any electronic, mechanical, or other means, now known or hereafter invented, including photocopying and recording, or in any information storage or retrieval system, without permission in writing from the publishers.

Typeset by Lapiz Digital Services

Printed and bound by Lightning Source

British Library Cataloguing in Publication Data

A catalogue record for this book is available from the British Library

ISBN: 978-1-907301-70-4
PDF ISBN: 978-1-785521-32-4
EPUB ISBN: 978-1-785521-31-7
KINDLE ISBN: 978-1-785521-33-1

www.ecpr.eu/ecprpress

The ECPR Press Series Editors
Dario Castiglione (University of Exeter)
Peter Kennealy (European University Institute)
Alexandra Segerberg (Stockholm University)

More in the ECPR Press Essays series

Choice, Rules and Collective Action: The Ostroms on the Study of Institutions and Governance (ISBN: 9781910259139) Elinor Ostrom (Author), Vincent Ostrom (Author), Paul Dragos Aligica (Editor) and Filippo Sabetti (Editor)

Immigration, Integration and Mobility: New Agendas in Migration Studies. Essays 1998–2014 (ISBN: 9781907301728) Adrian Favell

On Parties, Party Systems and Democracy: Selected Writings of Peter Mair (ISBN: 9781907301780) Peter Mair (Author) and Ingrid Van Biezen (Editor)

Varieties of Political Experience (ISBN: 9781907301759) Gianfranco Poggi

Please visit www.ecpr.eu/ecprpress for information about new publications.

To my colleagues at the University of Exeter

Contents

List of Figures and Tables	vii
Acknowledgements	ix
Foreword	xi
Sources	xiii
Concepts and Reason – Introduction	xv

PART ONE

Chapter One – Politics, Political Theory and its History	3
Chapter Two – Speech Acts, Languages or Conceptual History?	21

PART TWO

Chapter Three – Classical and Empirical Theories of Democracy: The Missing Historical Dimension	45
Chapter Four – Is There an English Form of Toleration?	57
Chapter Five – Political Liberty and the Concept of Citizenship in Early Modern English Political Discourse	73

PART THREE

Chapter Six – The Individualist Premise and the Practice of Politics	97
Chapter Seven – Two Arguments Against Rawlsian Equality	119
Chapter Eight – Rational Choice and Interpretive Evidence: Caught Between a Rock and a Hard Place?	135

Chapter Nine – Prices as Descriptions: Reasons as Explanations 155

Chapter Ten – The Market for Toleration: A Case Study in an Aspect
   of the Ambiguity of 'Positive Economics' 177

Bibliography 193

Index 213

List of Figures and Tables

Figure 8.1: Percentage of articles using rational choice theory, 1984–2005   141

Table 8.1: Articles providing interpretive and empirical evidence   142

Acknowledgements

I would like to thank the commissioning editor, Dario Castiglione, the ECPR Press Production Controller, Laura Pugh, and Production Editor, Simon Ward, for their assistance (and patience), the publisher's readers, Albert Weale and Terence Ball for their support and suggestions, Stuart Ingham for his help in transcribing and formatting the texts as well as commenting on them, and Andrew Hindmoor for stimulating discussion over the years on many of the issues raised in part three of the book.

I should like to thank all my colleagues at Exeter in the Department of Politics and beyond, who, over the years have provided the stimulating environment in which these essays were written. The book is dedicated to them.

Iain Hampsher-Monk
April 2015

Foreword

The pieces collected here all illustrate or discuss the historicity of our concepts and the implications of this for political science. In the first section two essays situate the discussion by considering the relationship between the study of politics and the history of political thought considered as a topic in its own right. There follows a section in which specific concepts – democracy, toleration, liberty and citizenship – are subject to historical analyses, showing how awareness of their histories might contribute to current or recent debates about them or in which they feature. In the final section the focus is on the concept of reason and the way in which a particular modern, individualist version of it has been deployed in political theory and political science. The linking theme in all these essays is the claim that any political science which deploys concepts in a way which is historically naive or hermeneutically restricted is liable to impoverish and distort our understanding of social and political reality, our normative theorising, and our policy thinking.

Following a suggestion by Albert Weale, one of the readers for this volume, the introduction situates these essays in a lightly sketched intellectual autobiography. This also advances a summary positive case for a political science which recognises both the constitutive element of the hermeneutic in our political practices and institutions, and the deeply historical character of the concepts which inform both practice and our reflections on it.

Editing principles

Although silently correcting small grammatical errors and infelicities of expression, I have suppressed the (often considerable) temptation to substantially change the texts – even where my thinking might have changed. I have however tried to render uniform the format, referencing and sectionalisation of the pieces. I have altered or added comments and footnotes where the piece has been removed from its original context, or the passing of time and subsequent developments has seemed to require it. Such changes to the original have been placed in square brackets.

Sources

Chapter One 'Politics, Political Theory and its History' was written for a seminar series organised at Oxford by Jonathan Floyd and Marc Stear, 'History and Political Philosophy: On the Political and Ethical Significance of the Past'. Versions were also given at the Political Theory Seminars at the universities of Exeter and Oxford. It was previously published in the book of essays that resulted from the original seminar series *Political Philosophy versus History?* J. Floyd and M. Stears (eds) (Cambridge, Cambridge University Press, 2011).

Chapter Two 'Speech Acts, Languages or Conceptual History?' was written for the Dutch Conceptual History Group and first given to the Conceptual History Seminar at the Netherlands Institute for Advanced Study, Wassenaar, in 1995. It was published with other papers produced by that group in *History of Concepts: Comparative Perspectives*, I. Hampsher-Monk, K. Tilmans and F. van Vree (eds) (Amsterdam, Amsterdam University Press, 1998). It has been translated into Chinese, published by the East China Normal University Press.

Chapter Three 'Classical and Empirical Theories of Democracy: The Missing Historical Dimension' originally intended as part of a doctoral dissertation, was first published as 'Classical and Empirical Theories of Democracy: The missing historical dimension?', *British Journal of Political Science*, X, no.1 (1980) pp. 241–51, and reprinted as 'The Historical Study of Democracy', pp. 25–35 in *Democratic Theory*, G. Duncan (ed.), (Cambridge, Cambridge University Press, 1984), pp. 296 and viii. Later versions of the argument were given at the conference 'Democracy' sponsored by the Chinese Academy of Sciences in Beijing (2004) and at the conference in Lucca on 'Democracy's Journey', the latter published as 'The Conceptual Formation of Democracy', in *Viaggio nella democrazia: il cammino dell'idea democratica nella storia del pensiero politico,* M. Lenci and C. Calabro (eds) (Edizioni ETS, Pisa, 2010) pp. 31–42.

Chapter Four 'Is There an English Form of Toleration?' was commissioned by and first published in *New Community: European Journal on Migration and Ethnic Relations*, 21, no. 2 (April, 1995), pp. 227–240.

Chapter Five 'Political Liberty and the Concept of Citizenship in Early Modern English Political Discourse' was presented at the 'citizenship' workgroup of the Dutch Conceptual History project, in Wassenaar in 2008, and to the conferences (2008–10) funded through Quentin Skinner's 2006 Balzan Foundation Prize. First published in Q. Skinner and M. van Gelderen (eds) *Freedom and the Construction of Europe*, 2 vols., Cambridge, CUP (2013), vol 2., chapter 6. A Russian translation is published in *Sovremennaya Respublikanskaya Teoriya* (*Contemporary Republican Theory*) E. Roshchin (ed.) (St. Petersburg, St. Petersburg Free University Press 2015).

Chapter Six 'The Individualist Premise and the Practice of Politics' was first published in *Defending Politics: Essays on politics and pluralism in honour of Bernard Crick*, in I. Hampsher-Monk (ed.) (British Academic Press, London, 1993). A slightly revised version was published in P. King (ed.), *Socialism and the Common Good* (London, Frank Cass, 1996).

Chapter Seven 'Two Arguments Against Rawlsian Equality' was written for the British Academy-CNRS sponsored seminar 'The Legacy of Hobbes' 2000–02 and was also presented at the Conference for Socio-Legal Philosophy. It has not previously been published.

Chapter Eight 'Rational Choice and Interpretive Evidence: Caught Between a Rock and a Hard Place' was sketched by the authors, with contributions by their hill-walking and academic colleague Keith Zimmerman, whilst climbing Ben Dorain in the Scottish Highlands (during a June snowfall). Versions were presented at Griffith University (Australia) and the Universities of Newcastle and Exeter (UK) and Queensland (Australia). It was first published in *Political Studies*, vol. 58, 1, (2010). It was co-authored with Andrew Hindmoor.

Chapter Nine 'Prices as Description: Reasons as Explanations' was first presented at an interdisciplinary seminar organised at the University of Exeter by the editors of the proceedings: *Culture in History: Production, consumption and values in historical perspective*, J. Melling and J. Barry (eds) (Exeter, University of Exeter Press, 1992).

Chapter Ten 'The Market for Toleration: A Case Study in an Aspect of the Ambiguity of "Positive Economics"' was first published in the *British Journal of Political Science* 10, 1 (1991). It was developed during a sabbatical leave funded by the Acton Society Trust. Earlier versions were given at the Morrell Trust Conference on Toleration at the University of York, and at the Graduate Political Philosophy Seminar at the London School of Economics and Political Science.

Concepts and Reason – Introduction[1]

A would-be political theorist emerging from a degree in PPE in the UK of the late 1960s was faced with an extraordinarily stimulating range of influences.[2] Towards the end of the previous decade Peter Laslett had famously declared normative political theory dead.[3] 'Conceptual Analysis', which largely replaced it in the undergraduate curriculum, involved reflections on the 'use patterns' of key terms, with a nod or more to Wittgenstein's 'meaning of a word is its use in normal speech'.[4] The study of *historical* texts in political theory was presented to me as a series of jumping-off points for such conceptual analysis, or for critical (spot the value judgment/illicit move/ unexpressed premise) appraisal of the integrity of arguments. I exaggerate, but only slightly: Professor Anthony Flew opened our first year Introduction to Philosophy Lecture course in characteristically flamboyant style: 'Today we begin our study of Philosophy which will focus this term on Plato's Republic. And let no one ask when we are going to do some contemporary philosophy, because we are doing it NOW!'[5]

At the same time, as I shortly became aware, a more historically considered and not philosophically ungrounded approach was re-emerging. Although often identified as the 'Cambridge' school, it was part of a wider change in sensibilities beautifully captured in E. P. Thompson's reference to 'the enormous condescension of posterity' so often displayed in writing about past actors and thinkers.[6] When I moved to Sheffield in 1969 to write

---

1. I thank Albert Weale for suggesting the biographical format of this introduction and for his, Dario Castiglione's and Christopher Fear's comments on drafts of it.
2. I took Keele's wonderful original four year degree in PPE, 1965–69. This involved a pre-degree first year covering the range of human knowledge (as construed and professed at Keele at the time), and subsidiary subjects chosen so that the spread of specialisms included at least one subject from each of humanities, social and natural sciences.
3. Although his prescient caveat: 'for the moment, anyway', is less often remembered. Peter Laslett, 'Introduction' in *Philosophy, Politics and Society*, P. Laslett (ed.), (Oxford, Blackwell, 1957) p. vii. Isaiah Berlin was more sanguine: 'Does Political Theory Still Exist' in *Philosophy, Politics and Society*, P. Laslett and W. G. Runciman (eds), (Oxford, Blackwell, 1962).
4. Wittgenstein (like Laslett) had been more careful: 'For a *large* class of cases – though not for all – in which we employ the word 'meaning' it can be defined thus: the meaning of a word is its use in the language', *Philosophical Investigations* §43. (Oxford, Blackwell, 1963) (author emphasis).
5. Ironically, it was, I subsequently realised, John Rogers' course in *20th Century Philosophy*, that was actually being taught most historically.
6. E. P. Thompson, *The Making of the English Working Class*, (London, Gollancz, 1963, revised ed. Harmondsworth, Penguin Press, 1968 and 1980), p. 12.

an SSRC[7] funded PhD (on – inconceivably as it now seems – 'The Concept of Democracy') under the supervision of Bernard Crick, I met doctoral students from very different intellectual backgrounds to my own. Andrew Lockyer[8] and Chris Taylor[9] were products of a Leicester Department headed by one of the last surviving British Hegelians, Christopher Hughes. They both challenged my slick and shallow linguistic analyses. Bernard himself – if he needed to – had already caught the wind: 'Don't hit them with modern weapons' he wrote in the margin alongside one of my anachronistic criticisms of Leveller democracy. Bernard had set me on to three substantive areas – Leveller democracy in the English Civil War, the radicalism of the 1790s, and twentieth-century debates about the meaning of 'democracy'. They were each intrinsically interesting enough to continue generating work throughout a career. But they were different enough to force reflection on the relationship between the history of, and contemporary, political thought, and the relationship between both of them and what was emerging as a more methodologically self-conscious 'political science'– influenced by an American tradition about which Bernard himself had famously written a history.[10]

By the time I was appointed to a post in political theory at Exeter in 1971 (again, unbelievably nowadays, barely eighteen months after graduating) what that subject constituted was in a state of full-blown transition, and the major methodological challenges mounted by Quentin Skinner, John Dunn and J. G. A. Pocock to any historically naïve textual analysis had all been set out.[11] Although I had had no serious training in history, I found these arguments *philosophically* convincing; and I set out to turn myself into what I regarded as a proper historian of political thought. Exeter's Politics Department was in the process of revising its curriculum to include a compulsory two year sequence in the history of political thought, covering major texts from Plato to Marx, followed by a (also compulsory) third year course entitled *Analytical Political*

---

7. Under the first Thatcher administration, following a move to disband it altogether, Sir Keith Joseph, the Minister of Education, rebadged the 'Social Science Research Council' as the 'Economic and Social Research Council', on the grounds that the Social Sciences were not really 'sciences', a move which was as revealing of the prejudices – and indeed ignorance – of those who made the changes, as it is of their intention to denigrate the disciplines concerned. The USA still recognises the original terminology; most European academic cultures of course possess a more generous conception of 'science' as any organised body of knowledge.

8. Lecturer and latterly Stevenson Professor of Citizenship at the University of Glasgow.

9. Lecturer in Political Theory at the University of Kent.

10. B. Crick, *The American Science of Politics: Its origins and conditions* (Berkeley and LA, University of California Press, 1964).

11. J. G. A. Pocock, 'The History of Political Thought: A methodological enquiry' in Laslett and Runciman (eds), *Philosophy, Politics and Society*, 2nd ser. (Oxford, Blackwell, 1962) pp. 183–202; Q. Skinner, 'Meaning and understanding in the history of ideas', *History and Theory* 8 (1969); John Dunn, 'The identity of the history of ideas', *Philosophy*, XLIII (April 1968), and in *Philosophy, Politics and Society*, (VI ser.) Laslett, Runciman and Skinner (eds), (Oxford, Blackwell, 1972).

Theory, all of which I taught. Switching between these required running rather different intellectual software. Indeed the very identity of the latter became increasingly problematic. I remember Maurice Goldsmith trying to explain to a puzzled visiting Hungarian academic exactly what 'analytical political theory' was. After a couple of failures, Maurice – who was certainly no Marxist but delighted in the puckish *aperçu* – said: 'It's ... bourgeois political ideology'. And in an important sense of course, a lot of it was.

How this analytical – and, following the publication of John Rawls' *A Theory of Justice* – increasingly normative mode of political theorising into which I had been first inducted, related to the historically nuanced understanding that I was trying to develop, remained – and remains – a puzzling, if always extraordinarily stimulating, question. And although the relationship between *analytical* approaches to political theory and the rest of political science was relatively clear, the relationship between both of them and the study of historical texts – or even contemporary political philosophy texts such as Rawls' – became more problematic, the more deeply historical one's understanding of texts became.[12] Whilst professionally identified largely with the *History of Political Thought*,[13] I have, as I hope this collection demonstrates, tried to keep my interests broad. One important institutional vehicle for this has been the Political Thought Conference, held early each New Year in Oxford since 1971, which manages to sustain stimulatingly diverse programmes to this day. And when Exeter gave me a personal chair in 1995 I very deliberately chose as a title, not the expected 'History of Political Thought', but instead, the more ecumenical, 'Political Theory', and structured my inaugural around the tensions between the two.[14] 'Theory' in the Exeter Department has always been committed to sustaining a diversity of approaches.

This tension between the historical and the conceptual exists not only within the field of 'political theory' but is also an issue across the study of politics itself and hence for any department of politics. In the UK, the study of politics is commonly situated in faculties, colleges or schools of social science construed in a broadly positivist tradition, even if that tradition's (now widely challenged) philosophical underpinnings are often not explicitly recognised or addressed. The unfortunate division of the study of politics into 'theory' (whether historical or philosophical) and 'institutions' is a widespread response to this. Exeter once hired a resolutely empiricist international relations lecturer from a distinguished military background who was to teach alongside Peter Butler – a product of Aberystwyth's path-breaking combined honours degree in Philosophy and IR. Following a discussion, the Major General disarmingly announced that their

---

12. Chapter One is a sketch of how I have come to understand the relationship between political philosophy, the history of political thought and the practice of politics.
13. Most prominently through the journal *History of Political Thought*, started by myself and my colleague Janet Coleman, at Exeter in 1980, and edited by us ever since, and my *History of Modern Political Thought* (Oxford, Blackwell, 1994).
14. Unpublished Inaugural Lecture.

complementary backgrounds would enable our undergraduates to benefit from an exemplary division of intellectual labour: 'Peter will do the theory and I'll do the facts'.

History can be construed as an assemblage of facts, no less than 'institutions'. But to generate understanding they must both, I maintain, include 'facts' about the concepts and beliefs of the agents performing the roles constituting those institutions. There was only one department I was aware of in which this principle was applied pedagogically, and that was the department assembled by Professor Jack Greenleaf at Swansea where each lecturer was appointed to teach the institutions *and theory* of particular national polities.

These tensions, not only between history and philosophy, but between the human sciences construed hermeneutically and their construction as empiricist enterprises, had received, I came to realise, a classic articulation in the thought of Hegel. In Keele's (only just) post logical-positivist environment, I had been actively discouraged from reading Hegel,[15] but I was required to teach his *Philosophy of Right* at Exeter. Before long I tackled the *Phenomenology*, a work since taught as an option almost annually to generations of initially perplexed, but (for the most part) subsequently grateful third year students. Hegel of course meets both the philosophy/history (and hence time-and-meaning) and institutions/ideas issues head on – since his concepts are evolving entities which he depicts as differentiating, refining and articulating their content over time; and institutions are nothing but ideas in the minds of those operating them. But Hegel also highlights the evolving character, not only of its content, but of consciousness itself – and what its different incarnations are capable of cognising. Bracketing the metaphysics, Hegel provides an account of how both the logical analysis (properly understood) and the history of a concept can be combined and are both essential to an understanding of it (as well as how this is deeply implicated in understanding political reality). Whilst for the analytical theorist, contradictions are transgressive, and to be abjured, for the historian of concepts contradictions can be explored as the very stuff of the history of meaning (and practice).

The then current conceptual analysis – which was in fact usually linguistic – often revealed the 'exhaustion' of the meaning of a word through the accumulation of a range of 'standard' uses so wide as to make quite impossible the identification of any core – or 'family' – of meanings, or even criteria by which to identify blatant misuses of it. The articulation of the notion of 'essential contestability' had provided a technical account of terms that had reached this stage – characteristically as a result of their overly-adventurous rhetorical deployment.[16] At this point, purely use-based linguistic analysis had not much more to say than

---

15. One professor, whose posthumous blushes I shall spare, warned me 'You shouldn't read Hegel; it will ruin your mind'. I leave the reader to judge the veracity of this prediction.

16. W. B. Gallie, 'Essentially contested concepts', *Proceedings of the Aristotelian Society*, vol. 56, (1956), pp. 167–198 and J. Gray, 'On liberty, liberalism and essential contestability', *British Journal of Political Science*, vol. 8 (4), (1978), pp. 385–402.

to point to the *naiveté* of making essentialist claims about the meaning of, for example, 'freedom' or 'democracy'.[17] But the *history* of the use of a term, let alone the history of the *concept* – which was a rarely-recognised distinction in Anglophone work and raised a raft of further problems – was not merely a history of its acquisition of increasingly diverse meanings, but also a history of how and why it acquired the positive or negative evaluative potential that users sought to recruit for those various meanings. Such analysis – which is both historical *and* conceptual – enables us to clarify which meanings are able (and did in fact) give rise to which evaluative meanings, and more precisely which *kind of* evaluative meanings they were capable of giving rise to. And this in turn makes the contestability not essential, but tractable – at least for the analyst.[18]

In 1970, when Chapter Three was first drafted, approaching controversies about the meaning of 'democracy' in political science through an historical frame seemed to me to enable us to get further than 'empirical' theorists of 'democracy', their 'essentialist' critics, or even those prepared to give up on the concept altogether. It was surely only certain *kind*s of institutional arrangements or their theoretical description that could generate or be associated with specific values? Ascribing the legitimating participatory values plausibly associated with certain classical democratic theories to an account of democracy construed as elite competition and a largely passive electorate is, to say the least – ideologically if not logically – odd. How could *that* kind of political order lay claim to *those* kinds of values? It was too late, of course, to legislate for lay use of the term. But an historical account of how – and for *which* values – 'democracy' came to be a commendatory term, could surely rescue contemporary conceptual – and normative – academic discussion from cynicism?[19]

In February 1989 the *Fatwa* against Salman Rushdie was issued. The liberal left's sometimes fulsome embrace of an optimistically universalist multiculturalism was forced to appraise the reality of cultures that had no truck with the kind of secular individual rights so dear to them. I had accepted an invitation to respond to the initial Rushdie furore.[20] But, away from the polemical heat, it seemed

---

17. As Quentin Skinner concluded in his discussion of 'Empirical theorists of democracy and their critics: a plague on both their houses', *Political Theory*, vol. 1 (3), (1973), and more recently Janet Radcliffe-Richards whose examination of 'Equality of Opportunity' concluded: 'The obvious moral ... is ... that the term should be dropped ... Nothing would be lost except potential for confusion, oversimplification and political sleight of hand', J. Radcliffe Richards, 'Equality of opportunity', *Ratio* (new series), X (3), (1997), pp. 254–79; p. 279.
18. 'Classical and empirical theories of democracy: the missing historical dimension?', *British Journal of Political Science*, X (1), (1980), pp. 241–51. Chapter 3 in this volume.
19. For a fine collection of recent work on the historical relationship between the evaluative and denotative uses of the term *see Re-Imagining Democracy in the Age of Revolutions: America, France, Britain, Ireland, 1750–1850*, in J. Innes and M. Philp (eds), (Oxford, Oxford University Press, 2013). More widely, some of the literature on 'institutional design' began to take on issues of the relationship between values and institutions in a prospective perspective.
20. 'Salman Rushdie, the Ayatollah and the limits of toleration', in A. Ehteshami (ed.), *The Islamic Revolution and the West*, (London, Routledge, 1991), pp. 162–172.

worth following through the tension between a universalist, and supposedly culture-blind conception of toleration, and an evident desire to maintain a concept of the intolerable. And one important aspect of this lay in the historical fact that this aspirantly universalist 'toleration', bore a deeper relationship to the West's indigenous varieties of toleration than those who invoked them might care to admit. However much modern political liberalism owed, as John Rawls had famously claimed,[21] to a secularisation of the concept of religious toleration, indeed precisely *because* it owed it so much, it seemed that the modern discussion of liberalism would benefit from being more historically informed about the structure of the arguments through which toleration had been advanced in early modern England or France.[22]

In an early-modern world where the imperative to act on religious truth was considered irresistible, the category crucial to the very possibility of toleration was the notion of *adiaphora* – those things indifferent to salvation. Paradoxically to moderns, the identification of matters indifferent initially licensed the distinctly illiberal Anglican view that, far from marking out a candidate realm of toleration, *adiaphora* identified one within which the then state church would be entirely entitled to be *intolerant*, to enforce uniformity – for the sake of liturgical unity, without transgressing the essential religious freedoms of the individual. After all, no-one could justify disturbing religious peace over a matter of religious *indifferency*. Only later (and amongst radical non-conformists) did it give rise to the view that the concept of *adiaphora* could be used to demarcate a sphere from which the state church should *withdraw*, and in which individuals could be *allowed* freedom to follow their consciences. Both these views, moreover, were premised on the notion that there was some non-controversial way of deciding authoritatively what was or was not a matter of indifference – which, of course, was often precisely the issue at stake. The distinction originally marked within religion by indifferency is carried across to the distinction between the whole realm of the religious and the secular, for example in Locke's claim that religious toleration does not allow the doing of anything in the name of religion that would not be permitted by the civil magistrate. For it still required an authoritative, if now secular judgement, about what is and is not the proper province of religion itself, (about which, of course, different belief-communities were very likely to have different views) and which could therefore be matters of state-indifference. Rawls' difficulty in identifying what claims were or were not dependent on a particular comprehensive conception of the good, or later, what could or could not be asserted on the basis of public reason seemed indeed to be intellectual descendants of the problem of ruling authoritatively – or finding agreement on

---

21. J. Rawls, *Justice as Fairness: A restatement* (Cambridge, Mass., Belknap Press, 2001) p. 1; *Political Liberalism* (New York, Columbia University Press, 1993), pp. xxiv ff.

22. Which is what I set out to provide a sketch of in Chapter Four 'Is there an English form of toleration?', *New Community: European Journal on Migration and Ethnic Relations*, 21 (2), (1995), pp. 227–240.

adiaphora, and in doing so revealed historically particular features of the English, or Anglophone, concept of toleration.

What is an historical understanding of the concept of 'toleration' contributing here? The merely conceptual analysis of any concept is invariably accompanied by unexpressed and perhaps unconscious premises (or suppression of premises), the admission of which may affect the logical properties of the concept. In the case of toleration, this leads moderns to the expectation that establishing the existence of 'things indifferent' should logically lead to a principle of toleration for individuals within this area. But the suppressed premise – which would not occur to moderns – is that it is pleasing to God and better for communities, to worship in an orderly fashion; and once this premise is exposed, the Anglican conclusion is readmitted. The secular corollary of this might well be the liberal political premise itself – the need for all in the same political community to be equally subject to the same laws.

In the late 1980s my colleague Janet Coleman had been invited to chair a panel on 'The State and the Individual' as part of a major European Science Foundation project on *The Origins of the Modern European State*.[23] Her invitation to participate – for which I have always been grateful – had a huge impact, opening up to me both intellectually and at the level of personal contacts, a range of European approaches to the kind of work I was interested in doing. One particularly important association resulting from that project has been with Martin van Gelderen, who rang me up one day in 1993, to ask whether I would like to spend a year in a Dutch village. The 'village' in question was Wassenaar where the Netherlands Institute for Advanced Study was located. NIAS, unlike many other advanced schools, had, apart from the Director, no permanent academics. Scholars come for a year, either as individuals – in The Netherlands university sector sabbaticals are gained through scholarships won at NIAS or other institutions – or, as was increasingly encouraged, as members of research groups. The group to which I was being invited had been set up as a national project on the conceptual history of Dutch social and political concepts. The model for this was a German genre – *Begriffsgeschichte* – conceptual history. In this work the historical subject under investigation, the '*Begriff*' or 'concept', was construed in a specific and distinctive way.[24] The concept was not to be identified with a

---

23. 'The State and the Individual, Seventeenth–Eighteenth Centuries: Theorising the challenge of subjective individualism in Britain', pp. 243–267 in J. Coleman (ed.) *The Individual in Political Theory and Practice* (Oxford, Clarendon Press, 1993–4); vol. 6 of *The Origins of the Modern State in Europe 13th–18th Centuries*, in W. Blockmans and J. -P. Genet (eds), 7 vols., (Oxford, Clarendon Press and the European Science Foundation, 1996) and in French, (Paris, Maison des Sciences de l'Homme, 1996).

24. German intellectual historians and historians of philosophy had been producing dictionaries or handbooks of their subject matter going back over a century and a half. The particular variant *Begriffsgeschichte* emerged as a project in the 1950s at the University of Bielefeld under the collective direction of Otto Brunner, Werner Conze and Reinhart Koselleck, resulting in the *Geschichtliche Grundbegriffe* (Stuttgart, Klett-Cotta, 1972–90) and the *Handbuch politisch-sozialer Grundbegriffe in Frankreich 1680–1820*, R. Reichardt, H. J. Lüsebrink (eds.), (Munich, Oldenburg, 1985).

specific term or linguistic unit, and indeed could be carried by a social practice. Marriage, for example, can be identified as a social practice independently of it having any stable lexical marker – and could therefore form the subject of a *conceptual* and not merely a lexical history. The Dutch team wanted a practitioner from a different genre of the history of ideas to sit in constructive criticism of their deliberations (a kind of licensed court jester, it occurred to me) and I was that critic. Also present was Hans Bödeker of the Max Plank Historical Research Institute at Göttingen, who had been a student of Koselleck's and intimately involved with the first generation of German *Begriffsgeschichte*. One of the nice ironies of that year was that whilst Hans moved to a position increasingly sympathetic to Anglophone practice, I, initially critical, moved towards a greater appreciation of the German enterprise.

One product of that year was an edited book on varieties of conceptual history[25] to which I contributed a discussion and comparison, reproduced here in Chapter Two, of the two major Anglophone exponents of the history of political thought as it was there called, and the German genre. The encounter between these intellectual traditions had been pioneered by Keith Tribe and Melvin Richter, and was subsequently to be pursued in various confrontations and discussions by the three *virtuosi* themselves, Quentin Skinner, John Pocock and the surviving member of the original triumvirate, Rheinhardt Koselleck.[26]

The encounter with *Begriffsgeschichte* had exposed me to a highly articulated account of how one might, as a matter of practice, move beyond the history of language usage and go about studying the long-term development of concepts – even where they had not yet found stable lexical markers.[27] A further product of the year in The Netherlands was a successful *European Science Foundation* network funding bid, originating from the three of us at Wassenaar – Martin van Gelderen, Hans Bödeker and myself – joined by Ivo Comparato at Perugia, and Catherine Larrère at Bordeaux and chaired by Quentin Skinner. This enabled us to hold a two-year series of seminars exploring the varieties of 'Republicanism' as a 'shared European heritage' and resulted – thanks to the enthusiasm of Richard Fisher at Cambridge University Press – in the magnificent eponymous

---

25. *History of Concepts: Comparative perspectives* in I. Hampsher-Monk, K. Tilmans and F. van Vree (eds) (Amsterdam, Amsterdam and Michigan University Presses, 1998); and subsequently translated into Chinese.

26. *See* Melvin Richter, *The History of Social and Political Concepts: A critical introduction* (Oxford, Oxford University Press, 1995); for Pocock on *Begriffsgeschichte see* 'Concepts and Discourses: A difference in culture? Comment on a paper by Melvin Richter', in *The Meaning of Historical Terms and Concepts: New studies on Begriffsgeschichte*, H. Lehmann and M. Richter (eds), (Wash., DC, German Historical Institute, 1996), pp. 47–58; for Pocock on Skinner: 'Quentin Skinner: The history of politics and the politics of history', *Common Knowledge*, 10, 3 (August 2004), pp. 532–550.

27. In Quentin Skinner's wonderful example, when John Milton, in *Paradise Lost* (I, I.16) announced his intention to accomplish 'things unattempted yet in prose or rhyme' he clearly possessed the concept, even though the English language did not yet possess the word, 'originality'.

two-volume publication.[28] Quentin Skinner subsequently generously devoted a large part of his Balzan Prize to funding a further such project on 'Freedom and the Construction of Europe'.[29] Included here as Chapter Five is my contribution to the latter which I hope exemplifies the way in which exploring a conceptual field, both as a set of practices and by recognising that its identity need not be tied to a single lexical marker, enriches our understanding of it.

The methodological imprecations of Skinner and Pocock and possibly also those of the school of *Begriffsgeschichte*, can be read as methodology in a purely practical sense, what Mark Bevir (himself an Exeter graduate) has called an 'heuristics' of historiographical practice. That is to say they can be read as providing intellectual devices and procedures that practising historians of thought can use in their research and in constructing their narratives. Knowing the prevailing practices/conventions/languages of a culture is a condition for identifying and understanding those innovative interventions that constitute the dynamic of any kind of history. A great deal of my writing – which could have constituted a very different volume – has been historical in this substantive sense. But this present collection does not, primarily, concern substantive histories of specific concepts so much as the historicity of concepts in general, and the implications that a recognition of this might have for the study of political and social science.[30] The various versions of the 'historical revolution'[31] can indeed provide a toolkit for practitioners; but they can be much more than that. Whether we regard them as such depends on a particular view of social or political ontology.

If we regard the history of ideas (or concepts) as a history of essentially surface-like, or epiphenomenal features of an underlying social and political reality, constituted or determined by other processes – economic or material in a wider sense – then the heuristic view may be sufficient for that limited purpose. But if we see the realm of human meaning as more than merely epiphenomenal then these methodologies are more than merely heuristic and take on a different status. On

---

28. *Republicanism: A shared European heritage*, Q. Skinner and M. van Gelderen (eds), 2 vols., (Cambridge, Cambridge University Press, 2002). My contribution 'From Virtue to Politeness' (vol. I, pp. 85–105) was lightly reworked, translated and published as: 'Die kultivierte Höflichkeit: eine Form kollektiver Freiheit im England des 18. Jahrhunderts', [Refined Politeness: A form of collective freedom in Eighteenth Century England] pp. 491–511 in *Freiheitsvorstellungen im frühneuzeitlichen Europa (1400–1850)*, G. Schmidt *et al.* (eds), (Berlin, Verlag Peter Lang, 2005).

29. *Liberty in Europe*, (2 vols.), Q. Skinner and M. van Gelderen (eds), (Cambridge, Cambridge University Press, 2013); 'Liberty and Citizenship in Early Modern English Political Discourse', in vol. II, pp. 105–127.

30. For suggestions of the ways in which very different versions of the historical revolution can affect contemporary and normative political theory *see* K. Palonen, 'The history of concepts as a style of political theorizing: Quentin Skinner's and Reinhart Koselleck's subversion of normative political theory', *European Journal of Political Theory*, 1 (2002), pp. 91–106.

31. Versions of which were surveyed by Dario Castiglione and myself in *The History of Political Thought in National Context* (Cambridge, Cambridge University Press, 2001).

this view they are effective *if and because* they engage with certain fundamental aspects of social and political reality. If we take human actions to be intimately and constitutively grounded in their perceptions and beliefs about the world, as I do, then any histories or explanations of the events, processes or institutions that are constituted by – or cumulatively result from – human actions, must *at the very least* take into account, or more maximally, regard as fundamental to an understanding of those actions, the beliefs that inform them. From this perspective, the being, and therefore the history and understanding of human society and politics, is fundamentally constituted by the beliefs of the members of those societies. These include beliefs about what is the case, how the world is causally ordered, and what moral or other normative demands individuals feel themselves bound by, or at least called upon to consider. This is not to deny that there may be 'objective', natural or 'brute' facts that constrain human action – for me at least, there are things 'outside the text' – but it is to insist that those objectivities *always* impinge on agents' understanding and action through the mediation of their beliefs. Shortages of food, volcanic eruptions, plagues and epidemics, inflationary influxes of precious metals, are all events or episodes to which we may wish to accord 'objective' status. We may even wish to deploy our contemporary understanding of them in order to describe their local historical aetiologies. But the historical role ascribed to such 'objective facts', must always operate via, and therefore be understood through, the concepts and categories available to those on whom they impinged, and whose responsive actions comprise the history or social institutions we seek to understand and explain.

This is all the more true for social institutions and practices. For these are ideational in a much more thorough-going way. Institutions and practices, unlike natural phenomena, are ideational *all the way down*; they are in ontological terms, ideationally *constituted*, and not merely a cognitive take on a pre-existing if unreachable, noumenal world. That a tutorial is understood as a tutorial by its participants is not an additional fact about something which is already constituted as a tutorial, it is that very understanding of it by its participants that makes it a tutorial. Whilst we can imagine a society lacking any concept of famine or an epidemic nevertheless undergoing such phenomena, we cannot imagine a society with a king that did not possess the concept of one – or something like it. A society cannot *have* the rule of law, or marriage, or kingship, without possessing the concepts constituting such institutions, since there is nothing to such institutions and practices beyond their presence as ideas in the minds of their role-bearers and practitioners.[32]

If something like the above is true, the relationship between the study of political thought and its history on the one hand and 'politics' construed in broadly institutional, empirical or 'behavioural' terms on the other, is much more

---

32. My first encounter with the academic formulation of this relatively common sensical position was through Peter Winch's *The Idea of a Social Science and its Relation to Philosophy* (London, Routledge, 1958). Something like it seems recently to have been 'discovered' by excited constructivists of various stripes.

intimate than the current state of the discipline commonly acknowledges.[33] The imprecation that we study the beliefs, and concepts, as revealed in the institutional self-descriptions, practices and vocabularies of the societies whose politics we are trying to understand, is linked to their existential status as more than a happy heuristic that turns out to deliver good results. It is a very presupposition of understanding and explaining any society, because it is intrinsically and uniquely connected to their ontological status as social existents. And given that we have this unique insight into the ontological status of such realities, it seems perverse to retreat from this hermeneutic dimension in order to follow a positivist tactic, treating social realities as facts to be defined in a purely external way, and to then try to establish external, 'causal' links between them, a critique advanced in Chapter Eight.[34]

The concept of reason occupies the contested and equivocal terrain between political science construed as a natural science on a broadly positivist model, and an approach that regards the hermeneutic features of social institutions as foundational. Whilst hermeneutic approaches must regard conceptions of reason as themselves objects of interpretive and historical investigation, one influential model of positivist political science has deployed a particular conception of reason as independent of culturally local conceptions of it. Such a concept of reason, it has been claimed, emancipates political science from the historical and hermeneutic claims of its rival.[35] That model is the one built on the axioms of rational calculation imported from a de-historicised version of the discipline of economics. The notion of rationality here is supposedly neutral as between different ends or values that might be sought, and it is this neutrality that supposedly guarantees the universal applicability of the 'rational choice model'. Historians of political thought are very aware of the variations in 'reason', not only over time (Aquinas to Hobbes say) but in different vocabularies at the same time ('Reason of State' as against 'right reason'). It will seem odd to them that all these might be reduced to a single operation. They will be more disposed to suspect that the different conceptions of reason might actually reflect different mental operations performed by individuals at different times, and in different cultures or contexts. The rational choice theorist will characteristically be undeterred by such claims as to the historicity of reason;

---

33. And much closer to that put forward by R. G. Collingwood in *The Idea of History* (Oxford, Oxford University Press, 1946) or exemplified in M. Oakeshott's 'Vocabulary of a modern European state', *Political Studies,* vol. 23 (2–3), (1975), pp. 319–341, reprinted in Oakeshott, *Selected Writings*, vol. I, L. O'Sullivan (ed.), (Exeter, Imprint Academic, 2004). Acknowledgedly, the 'history of political thought' as a history of largely *philosophical texts*, bears a problematic relationship to the history of 'concepts in action' that I have been sketching, and there is much more to be said about the relation between the two than can be done here, or in Chapter One where that relationship is outlined.

34. Rational Choice and Interpretive Evidence: Caught between a Rock and a Hard Place?

35. The hegemonic claims of Rational Choice theory over the study of politics were chillingly enunciated by D. Mueller, 'The future of public choice', *Public Choice* 77, (1993), pp. 145–50, who claimed that within a generation the approach would become pervasive, extinguishing all alternatives, p. 147.

or indeed to claims that any specific, historic-cultural beliefs could disconcert the universality of the operations of the 'rational chooser'.

Nevertheless the foundational claims of philosophical economists generally acknowledge that the issue is more complex than this. Most of them recognised that the abstract universality of an ascribed 'reason' can only be secured by giving up any claim about its content, or the context in which it might be applied. The axiom of 'economising' is apodictic, claimed von Mises. It is not an empirical hypothesis about human psychology, and hence not susceptible to proof or disproof. It is a premise from which testable claims can be derived, but not itself a testable claim.[36] But those applying an explanatory model derived from these axioms commonly forget, in their enthusiasm, this empirical price that has to be paid for the universality of the economising axiom. The claim that an agent economises on *some particular thing* (price, time, reputation, etc.) is always an empirical claim – and hence requires evidence and is subject to falsification.

Nevertheless the historical origins of rational choice theory in psychological egoism leave a persistent trace contributing to the equivocal status of reason in 'rational choice'. This has implications for its application not only in explanatory, but also in normative work in political theory. The huge debate surrounding John Rawls' modelling of 'decision-making' in the original position hung on many of these. The crucial issue in such theorising is often thought to be with how thick or thin a theory of 'the good' such choosers should be accoutred. But one could as well argue that it is how 'thick' or 'thin' a conception of *reasoning* they are allowed. Rawls' original choosers were precluded from allowing others' preferences, or relative social positions, to enter into their deliberations, on the ground that such 'nosey' preferences permitted 'envious' motivations. But a little-remarked consequence of this is that the exclusion of such 'nosey' preferences, also precluded altruistic ones. And a consequence of this seemed to be the prescriptive exclusion of any concern with substantive equality as a candidate social good, since it is difficult to formulate any such conception without reference to such 'other-regarding' motivations. For anyone with a background in the history of political thought this is a fairly astounding exclusion. In an unpublished paper from the early 1990s I argued against this 'rational' limitation on equality as a value.[37] This argument was sketched in tandem with another argument against the limitations of 'Rawlsian equality' which, by contrast, accepted the premises of the original position but exploited empirical findings about unequal societies to urge that even Rawls' 'rational choosers' might be forced to regard a degree of substantive equality as a good – if not in itself, then as an instrument by which 'rational choosers' might maximise their expected utilities. Both arguments, the one from within, the other by challenging Rawls' model of the rational chooser,

---

36. Thus Amartya Sen's ironic characterisation of the position of the 'revealed preference' version of the theory: 'no matter whether you are a single-minded egoist or a raving altruist or a class-conscious militant you will appear to be maximising your own utility in this enchanted world of definitions.' Sen, 'Rational fools', *Philosophy and Public Affairs*, 6 (4) 1977, p. 323.
37. Chapter Seven.

licensed serious concern for an equality more extensive than that allowed by his 'difference principle'.[38]

The restrictions imposed by such 'rational chooser' premises, I claimed, distorted arguments not only in moral philosophy, but in politics and public policy too. In a contribution to Bernard Crick's Festschrift, *Defending Politics,* I had tried to expose the way in which the increasingly salient 'individualist premise' closed off considerations of policy issues that might otherwise have seemed plausible.[39] This restricted vision imposed by the 'rational chooser' model in prescriptive work has a parallel defect when it is deployed in social or historical explanations. This restriction licenses the presumption that 'explanations' based on what rational choosers would/must have done can be confidently deployed, when in fact such accounts can never be secure unless grounded in some independent evidence about the agent's perceptions, values and intentions. Without these, the historical subject can be 'fitted up' with all sorts of plausible motivations and choice scenarios. Such a rational choice 'explanation' will always be merely an *ascription*, one among other plausible ones. Thirty-five years ago academic life was sufficiently relaxed to enable me to continue an earlier habit of spending parts of my vacation as a field archaeologist.[40] In such work the difference between the material remains confronting the scholar and the ascription of meaning to them was recognised as a perilous and ever-present problem.[41] The ascription of particular reasonings to prehistoric peoples (how they 'must have' responded to this or that empirical feature of their world), an academic parlour-game common – indeed unavoidable – in the popular genre of evolutionary psychology, is, in pre-history, *definitionally* incapable of receiving support from the necessary written evidence about agents' beliefs. The archaeology of (prehistoric) knowledge is irreducibly speculative. Conversely, *secure* claims about individuals' reasonings, being grounded – as, to be secure they must be – in independent, hermeneutic evidence about their beliefs, values etc., cannot claim to be much more than formalised models of what is already known. Rational choice models sometimes claim to *reveal* prices (agent's relative valuations of one outcome/good/value over another), but they do not, unless we already know what they have been thinking about and how they have been thinking about it.[42] But then they are merely *re*-descriptions of things

---

38. Rawls retreated from the claim that his principles could be strictly deduced from the version of economic reasoning ascribed to individuals in the original presentation of *A Theory of Justice*, but not from his defence of the difference principle which was derived from it. See *Justice as Fairness*, p. 133.

39. Chapter Six.

40. For some of the remains *see*: Hampsher-Monk, with T. Phillips, and P. Abramson, 'The excavation and reconstruction of the recumbent stone circle at Strichen, Aberdeenshire, 1979–82', *Proceedings of the Society of Antiquaries of Scotland,* 136 (2006), p. 23.

41. I was intrigued to realise that the English historian who most insisted on this aspect of historical interpretation was R. G. Collingwood – the only other political theorist I know of with a background in archaeology.

42. Again Sen: '...choice may reflect a compromise among a variety of considerations of which personal welfare may be just one.' 'Rational fools', p. 324.

we already know about the agents. Whilst it is normally held that hermeneutic work produces only understanding, I claim social *explanation* – as opposed to description – requires, irreducibly, an hermeneutic element.

This line of thinking is explored in the last section of the book. *Prices as Descriptions, Reasons as Explanations* meets the issue head on and discusses it in the context of a paper[43] on prehistoric economic history by the celebrated historian of the world economy, Douglas North.[44] North was the subject of a stimulating series of seminars organised by the Department of Economic History in Exeter in the late 1980s. North's 'prehistoric' economic history involved ascribing to prehistoric peoples both objective choice situations, and their responses to those situations, for either of which the only firm evidence we have are the material outcomes. But this involves a double ascription – ascribing to them a particular choice (which was said to produce the known outcome), and ascribing to them a view of the world which presented that choice to them in that particular way. But *we can never know what individuals were seeking – or even what they thought were their options – from the mere apparent fact of their having chosen*. During the apartheid era I remember being about to buy some oranges and refusing them on finding that they were South African. 'Quite right sir', offered the obsequious but fatally miscued assistant, 'I don't like the idea of those blacks handling them myself.' The bare facts of market exchange can never provide grounds for the ascription of motives or beliefs, for which only hermeneutic knowledge can supply evidence.

The other essay in this final group criticises a normative application of economic rationality, which commonly exploits its ambiguous status between axiom and substantive claim.[45] A prominent defence of the market is (I think still) that it is a medium through which preferences are expressed and goods exchanged that is entirely neutral as between the different preferences that individuals bring to the market place. But it has also been claimed (since at least Voltaire) that there is a connection between free markets and the growth of toleration.[46] The suggestion being broadly that the market encourages some (tolerant) dispositions at the expense of others (involving prejudice or bias against some class of agents). One version of the mechanism by which this happens (advanced by Milton Friedman) is that it does so through imposing costs on the discriminators, through narrowing their market/range of employees/suppliers etc. But this is only true if one assumes that maximising money-holdings is the overriding aim of the market actor, and

---

43. Chapter Nine.

44. The seminal work in this aspect of North's output was *The Rise of the Western World: A new economic history* (Cambridge, Cambridge University Press, 1973), (with Robert Thomas). However, although deploying rational choice explanations, this work did so within an historical period in which, at least in principle, corroborative hermeneutical evidence was available. It was the extension of such explanations to prehistory, where it was not, (in *Structure and Change in Economic History* New York, Norton, 1981) that exposed their purely ascriptive character.

45. Chapter Ten.

46. *Lettres philosophiques sur les Anglais* (1734).

the only goods being exchanged are the physical objects that pass (as it were) across the counter. Of course such motives may obtain across wide areas of human life and interaction, but this is a contingent fact about those areas (and their boundaries), a feature indeed of a particular culture, and there is no reason to presume that they apply elsewhere, or even ubiquitously in such cultures. There is nothing irrational about an individual who chooses to pay a little more for class or racial exclusivity (if that is what they want), indeed the apodictic status of the economising premise reserves this possibility. This particular defence of the market wants to have it both ways – markets are neutral processors of preferences *and* markets select positively for some kinds of preferences. The two ways it wants to have it reflect the two different statuses that can be ascribed to economising reason, and indeed two different conceptions of the market – as a culturally thick specific social formation, and as a culturally empty set of equivalences between different resources – time, uses, money holdings, etc. which can be modelled to formally represent the outcomes of agents' activities.

Hindsight is a wonderful thing. This introduction is not meant to persuade the reader that these writings represent the execution of a prospectively conceived, coherently executed, life long research programme. Far from it; whether or not evidence for the cunning of reason, it is clear that chance, serendipity and the wisdom and generosity of colleagues all played a part. (Many of my generation wish that the 'managers of research' better understood the importance of such circumstantial elements in any fertile academic environment.) Nevertheless, the themes that run through these writings were real and clear enough preoccupations for me from early in my career; the study of politics sustains an enormously creative tension between historicised and philosophical understanding, between the claims of sympathetic understanding and rationalist reconstruction that has, and continues to prove for me, a source of huge and ongoing stimulation. I hope that it will continue to do so for our discipline.

PART ONE

Chapter One

Politics, Political Theory and its History

This chapter seeks to reflect on the differences and relationships between political philosophy, the history of political thought, and the conduct of politics itself. It seeks to sketch out political discourse as a kind of force field constituted by three nodes, identified by three idealised intellectual practices: history, philosophy and rhetoric. The kinds of intellectual enterprises that we conduct in the field of politics are characterised by blends of these, inasmuch as perhaps no one ever entirely succeeds in emancipating itself from the other of these categories. Yet each enterprise has its own distinctive properties, an understanding of which is important to their proper and effective conduct.

If we take the study, or writing of the history of political thought (hereafter HPT) to be a historical exercise, and theorising about politics (hereafter PP) to be a philosophical one, then the relationship between the two becomes an instance or exemplification of the distinction between history and philosophy. Sharpening and idealising for a moment that distinction, the subject matter of history, we might say, comprises unique particulars, individuals, and individual sequences of actions (which might be utterances), and possibly, on the largest scale, the story of whole peoples and societies.[1] The history of political thought (HPT) is the history of particular utterances (ultimately written or recovered from other sign-bearing artefacts). The subject matter of philosophy, by contrast, is constituted by universals, or by whatever can be said to be universally true, or, at a meta-level, the necessary and universal conditions under which propositions can be advanced about, or within a particular subject area.

These are idealised types. I realise it is more contentious to map these onto historical figures, but let me try. To start at the beginning, history and philosophy were both '*istorie*' – enquiry.[2] Herodotus' claim is to reveal the truth about what has been done, to 'set down and preserve the memory of the past by putting on record the astonishing achievements both of our own and of other peoples.' And for

---

1. It is of course true that, as practised, history involves all sorts of activities imported from other hermeneutic and the social sciences.
2. Herodotus' background is Ionian, and his immediate predecessors and contemporaries include Thales and Hippocrates. But the Ionian philosophers focused their thought on the physical world and it is only in Herodotus that these intellectual qualities become focused on humankind in an ethnographical and historical way. P. Cartledge, *Ancient Greek Political Thought in Practice* (Cambridge, Cambridge University Press, 2009), pp. 69–70.

Herodotus, part of the past is what is, or has been, believed.[3] It is part of his genius to stand apart from his sources ('the Egyptians say...', 'The Phoenicians say ...') and leave his listeners to judge, or on occasion to offer his own assessment. But this distantiation is not only critical scepticism. His authorial voice paradoxically both creates his presence in the narrative and depicts the rules of a genre (that he himself is inventing) as imposing duties on him as to how he conducts his enquiry: 'My business is to record what people say, but I am by no means bound to believe it – and that may be taken to apply to this book as a whole.'[4] In this sense Herodotus is already a historian of thought, and the history of thought, if not what all history is, is at least the *prima materia* of it.[5]

But this claim (the claim to discern what lies at the basis of reality) is also a claim made by philosophy – at least what we now construe as philosophy. Pre-Socratic philosophers were preoccupied with identifying the enduring reality (if indeed there was one) beneath or inherent in the surface features of experience. Philosophy's claims – ever since Plato – have involved, at least in part, claims about the necessary and enduring (timeless?) character of philosophical truths. It is not of course, that philosophers wish to say that history's claims are untrue, rather that they are formulated to refer to, and to hold true only of particulars in time. That Plato taught a theory of the forms in Athens around 375 BC, although an enduring truth, is a historical truth about philosophy, but not a philosophical truth. It is an enduring truth precisely because it is formulated as a historical claim about the propositions advanced by a particular individual at a particular time in a particular place. The historical truth is that the theory as a set of propositions was taught, not the truth or falsity of the propositions themselves, which is the province of philosophy. The philosophical claims advanced in the theory of forms by contrast lay claim to universal and timeless validity. For Herodotus the historian, the question is: 'what was said written or believed?' For Plato the philosopher, the question is: 'were the beliefs true?'

Nevertheless it is not so easy to separate history and philosophy. I want to go on to explore as it were the disciplinary claims each might make on the other; but before doing so it is worthwhile at least gesturing to the peculiar status of political thought or philosophy. (False) beliefs about natural phenomena do not belong at

---

3. Herodotus, *The Histories* (London, Penguin Classics, 1996), Bk. I.1.1 ff. *Cf.* 'so much for what the Persians and the Phoenicians say; and I have no intention of passing judgement on its truth or falsity...', *ibid.* 1.7. The distinction I make here is not that discussed by B. Williams, *Truth and Truthfulness* (Princeton, NJ., Princeton University Press, 2002), p. 155 ff., which relates to whether or not Herodotus distinguished between events in historical time and mythical happenings. My point is Herodotus' claim that the historian can (indeed must) record the fact of human's claims and beliefs without necessarily having to ascertain their truth or falsity.

4. Herodotus, *The Histories* 7.152.3. Also 2.123.1 (let he who will believe the Egyptians) 'As for myself, my task in the whole work is to write down what everybody says, as I hear it.' On Herodotus' construction of the constraints inherent in his self-created genre, *see* N. Laraghi 'Metahistoriē: Method and genre' in C. Dewald and J. Marincola (eds) *The Cambridge Companion to Herodotus* (Cambridge, Cambridge University Press, 2006).

5. The claim that all history is the history of thought is famously made in R. G. Collingwood, *Autobiography* (Oxford, Oxford University Press, 1970), p. 110.

all to the (true) content of say, physics (but only to its history⁶). Philosophical beliefs in the field of politics (even when 'false') can be constitutive of political reality for those communities, and constitute a part of political reality (in terms of the political culture, or the *long durée*) for their successors. If we think political communities are essentially hermeneutical and historical products (as opposed to, say, rational-choice products), the history-philosophy (as belief) distinction is much more tricky to negotiate than in the natural sciences, where the contemporary properties of copper, say, are quite unaffected by previous beliefs about it.

As disciplines, there is a tension between history and philosophy for two reasons, one contingent and the other not so. It seems to be a contingent feature of histories that alongside the particular story that any history tells, the aspiration to discern persisting features of human action and circumstance has emerged, either as a historical aim, or as a condition of historical explanation.⁷ Thus Herodotus' terribly politically incorrect explanatory aside on the origin of the Trojan Wars involves a generalisation that purports to be a universal truth about young females: 'Abducting young women ... is not a lawful act; but it is stupid after the event to make a fuss about it ... for it is obvious that no young woman allows herself to be abducted if she does not wish to be.'⁸ Conversely, claims advanced as philosophical truth can come to look extraordinarily parochial in the light of later assumptions and beliefs. Indeed whole areas of investigation, such as the identity of natural slaves, or the vexed question of how many angels could occupy the head of a pin, can simply drop out of philosophical repertoires.

These observations about contingent reasons for the failure of historical and philosophical claims to vindicate their own characteristic qualities, as, respectively, particular and universal, suggest two more generic demands that each discipline can make, from within itself, on the other. Thus the historian can always claim that the status of any philosophical proposition is historically situated, and so liable to revision. And it is a claim that philosophy can always make about any historical explanation (or indeed claim) that it rests on certain (unexamined) philosophical presuppositions. So, whilst we may have here two modes of enquiry aspiring to truth, each mode is dependent on and vulnerable to propositions formulated in its alternative.⁹ The philosopher on the one hand can always ask the historian for a philosophical account of her enterprise – what is the status of this claim, what is the principle of inclusion, what is the nature of the subject, how and under what

---

6. And the history of sciences, unlike the history of political thought, does not form part of their pedagogy. Part of the process of economics becoming a 'science' has been its (attempted) emancipation from its history.

7. Indeed on one model of explanation the historical enterprise is impossible without adverting to some universally true features of humans' being; as does any understanding of explanation that invokes a covering law conception of causality.

8. Herodotus, *The Histories*, 1.3.42 ff.

9. As sketched for example by M. Oakeshott, in *Experience and its Modes* (Cambridge, Cambridge University Press, 1933). *See* further the chapter in this volume [i.e. Chapter 1 in *Political Philosophy versus History?*, J. Floyd and M. Stears, Cambridge, Cambridge University Press, 2011].

conditions does her explanation explain? The historian, on the other hand, can always point out that the philosopher's questions are a product of a discipline at a particular point in time, of a particular historical set of preoccupations, beliefs about the nature of reality, causation, significance etc.

Now it is sometimes claimed by those who wish to preserve the independence of philosophy from history, that whilst *political* philosophy (or at least those examples of it that are interventions in a historically constituted problem or context) is indeed bound to be particular and historically situated, philosophy itself (and maybe those examples of political philosophy, if there are any, that are not constituted as responses to immediate contexts) *is* immune to the counter-claims of history; since philosophers commonly do discuss (or at least take themselves to be discussing) – across time – problems formulated by their predecessors. This could then be held to constitute a trans-historical debate, or repertoire of positions that anyone, at any time, might participate in or utilise. Yet I take it that if we treat the historian's objections really seriously, this will not do. For the historian's point is not to deny that political (and indeed other) philosophers sometimes *claim* to be evading the hermeneutic horizons of time and place. It is rather that even where they *aspire* to this, they do not – and cannot in principle – succeed. It is not just that political philosophy (as opposed to, say, metaphysics), by being an intervention in a political situation, is historically anchored, as it were; it is that because meaning is intrinsically historically constituted, *any* philosophy draws on, and presupposes, a particular historical configuration of meaningfulness.[10] The historian's claim is that all attempts to transcend the limitations of one's own hermeneutic environment are bound to fail, simply because they must necessarily be formulated from within that hermeneutic, and even the most abstractly formulated philosophical claims cannot escape their historical origins. That the historian's claim is effectively a philosophical one (i.e. a claim about the universally parochial conditions of philosophical speech) is of course, ironic, and is surely damagingly so when formulated in a language particular enough to be identified as itself a claim within a parochial philosophical position.[11] And of course the philosopher can counter at a similarly abstract and general level about the dependence of any historical story on philosophical presuppositions. In the absence of some kind of Hegelian account of the ultimate culmination of historical process and philosophical development in an absolute knowledge, these two competing claims do not look to be resolvable, although of course one could always simply *claim* hegemonic authority for one or the other.[12]

---

10. 'Understanding is, essentially, a historically effected event', H. G. Gadamer, trans. W. Glen-Doepel, *Truth and Method* (London, Sheed & Ward, 1989), p. 300.

11. Thus Quentin Skinner's formulation of this claim in the idiom of mid-twentieth century speech act theory might be thought to hoist the historian's claim with its own petard. But the fact that similar claims to historical hegemony have been made in a variety of other philosophical idioms (e.g. by Collingwood, Oakeshott, Gadamer), suggests the claim itself might still be true.

12. Thus Gordon Schochet characterises Quentin Skinner's work as 'an attempt to resolve a conflict between history and philosophy that by its nature cannot be settled', G. Schochet, 'Quentin Skinner's method', *Political Theory*, 2 (1974), p. 269.

The range of propositions for which philosophy's timeless truth-status could be claimed has waxed and waned over time. Plato seems to have held out the hope that all propositions, at least about the ideal-type of things in the world, could achieve this status – including propositions in ethics and politics. Augustinian-influenced Christian thinkers, on the other hand, seemed to think that there were vanishingly few such propositions, or at least few available to human intellects. In the high Middle Ages a view emerged that whilst certain, philosophical, knowledge of the primary items of creation was in principle available, only prudential knowledge of human creations was possible, and prudential knowledge was as corrigible as were its objects – institutions, practices, moral rules of thumb, etc.[13] (a kind of division of the world, interestingly, that was largely replicated by some logical positivists[14]). On this view, any reflections on political institutions or conduct would be bound to fall short of philosophy, since there could simply be no enduring truth about such contingent phenomena. Thinking about politics was therefore necessarily prudential, casuistic and subject to *raison d'etat*. There might be political theory, but there could be no political philosophy, although there were those who sought (thus far unsuccessfully) to construct enduring political maxims (the characteristic genre in this circumstance) derived from such reflections. These may be prudential: that it is better to be feared than loved, for example, or hover between the definitional and the empirical: that sovereignty is the power to decide the exception, for example.[15]

This looks as though it might set the bar too high to admit any political theory as philosophy at all. Although Rawls' second thoughts about the reach of his theory of justice were more modest than his first, many modern practitioners – including the late lamented Gerry Cohen – have not so moderated their claims. For Ronald Dworkin the task of political philosophy was 'to find some inclusive formula that can be used to measure social justice in *any* society'.[16] It may, however, be that the range of statements that can be counted as philosophical in this sense are very small and have the character of Locke's ground clearing activities or other such epistemological preliminaries. Nevertheless, even such preliminaries have led thinkers to adopt particular political positions. The political implications of cognitive indeterminacy for Hobbes formed an important part of his argument for the extensive reach of the sovereign's powers, and led Burke's thought in an ineluctably historical and conservative direction.

---

13. 'Time, History, and Eschatology in the Thought of Thomas Hobbes', in J. G. A. Pocock, *Politics, Language and Time* (London, Methuen, 1972).

14. A. J. Ayer once said: 'Philosophical propositions, if they are true, are usually analytic.' But he adds in a curiously concessionary footnote: 'some empirical propositions, such as those that occur in histories of philosophy, may be counted as philosophical ... But in so far as they are not merely (!) historical I think that the truths discoverable by philosophical methods are analytic.' A. J. Ayer, *Language, Truth and Logic*, 2nd ed. (London, Dover, 1946), p. 26.

15. N. Machiavelli, *The Prince* (London, Penguin Books, 1999), ch. xvii; C. Schmitt, *Political Theology* (Chicago, Chicago University Press, 2005), p. 5.

16. *New York Review of Books*, 17 April 1983, my emphasis.

But no matter how much or how little material a political philosophy adhering to this position would generate, and no matter how confident it would find itself, there remain epistemically foundational claims to be made differentiating propositions in PP from claims in HPT. This is because, as I have been insisting, even in non-normative political philosophy predications in PP would be universal, not unique and particular, or culture bound, whereas in HPT we report claims made by others in particular contexts without (necessarily) endorsing or even appraising their truth status. And once we take into consideration normative political philosophy there is at least one further difference. HPT *describes* normative beliefs, whereas normative PP seeks to *evoke* them. There is a dramaturgical quality to normative theory (not that its more austere practitioners would want to see it that way) which is, at least on first blush, lacking in HPT.[17] I say on first blush because history can instruct, even when not overtly didactic, and we may want to bracket – for later consideration – how some appreciation of HPT may indirectly affect our political practice. And it is to the conduct of politics itself, as opposed to the philosophy or history of it, that I now turn.

Political practice and rhetoric

Up to now we have been considering the relationship between HPT and PP largely in terms of the way they function as exemplars of history and philosophy. But as we have begun to focus on their specifically *political* character, we are led to consider the relationship between each of these activities and the world of political practice.

Until the rise of a mass and politically mobilised electorate, examples of both of what we now see as the history of political thought and political theory, where they were intended to relate to politics, were contributions to a controversialist or polemical debate conducted amongst the relatively small and educated elites whose opinions counted in political decision-making. Commonly these elites were relatively culturally self-contained to the extent that a particular mode of argumentation predominated, privileging legitimating claims formulated in legal, philosophical or religious discourse, or specific variants of these.[18] Periodically though – in

---

17. The reluctance is revealing of the Kantian background to most contemporary political philosophising. The moral will is to be moved by recognition of the moral law, not (if moral) by naturalistic (enthusiastic or empirical) motivations. There is more to say about this in the last section.

18. Pocock's concept of a political language and his deployment of it in constructing histories of political thought is paradigmatic here. His *The Ancient Constitution and the Feudal Law*, exploring the dominance and breakdown of the language of the common law, relies in part on the isolation of a particular elite – the common lawyers – from alternative accounts of English pasts. *The Machiavellian Moment* pursues a specific language – that of republicanism – as a 'tunnel history' through the matrix of past political discourse, and its response both to changes in political and social practice and exposure to alternative accounts of political reality. *See* J. G. A. Pocock, *The Ancient Constitution and the Feudal Law: A study of English historical thought in the seventeenth century* (Cambridge, Cambridge University Press, 1987); *The Machiavellian Moment: Florentine political thought and the Atlantic republican tradition* (Princeton, N. J., Princeton University Press, 2003). For further discussion, *see also* A. Pagden, *Languages of Politics in Early Modern Europe* (Cambridge, Cambridge University Press, 1987).

classical Athens, in the self-governing communes and cities of the renaissance – and in the emergence of a modernity in which epistemic elites could no longer enjoy an unreflective isolation – such elite linguistic hegemony broke down altogether. Emancipated from these insulated discourses, political argument takes place within an unspecialised, demotic, linguistic field.

Under these conditions we can identify a third force, tugging at political expression in addition to the rival claims of philosophy and history – that of rhetoric. Rhetoric is the activity of persuading audiences to adopt or reject action or policies, or of the guilt or innocence, praiseworthiness or contemptibility of individuals.[19] The intention of deliberative (and forensic) rhetoric is to generate action, it is not (like history or philosophy) contemplative, nor does it necessarily presuppose a commitment to truth. It is concerned (amongst other things) to discover and recruit pre-existing beliefs in the hearers, beliefs which can be mobilised by the orator to shape the hearers' commitments in the desired way. The result is what is important – what is persuasive is what – evidently – persuades, although as an intellectual discipline there are both techniques to be learned and – in Aristotle at least – moral limitations on the means to be used in bringing about persuasion. Rhetorical proof is by words: no weeping relatives in the courtroom or stage props – material evidence like sworn depositions or bloodied daggers.

Politics, where it exists – which is only in deliberative communities – is conducted through rhetoric. Politicians have to persuade, and only what is persuasive persuades. In democratic societies politicians have to persuade a majority. If scientific evidence – or other propositions drawn from specialist discourses, such as theology – is not persuasive to the public, then so much the worse for the evidence. Aligning policy with the evidence may be a fine aspiration, but it cannot be achieved if it requires the public to become scientists before they can be persuaded to adopt such policy. The politician seeking to promote evidence-based policies might well need to find other means of persuasion than the mere evidence on which the policies are based.

Political rhetoric is related in particular and indirect ways to both history and philosophy. The rhetorician's sources, the topics from which he draws his persuasive arguments, are drawn from the history of the beliefs of the community – or at least the version of that history held by the political community. This may, needless to say, be a history far removed from those histories constructed by historians of political thought. Indeed, it exposes a potential bifurcation in what we have been calling HPT. That is, HPT can be the history of political philosophies, or it can be the history of political discourses more widely construed – the history of the languages in which politics has been conducted. And the internal relationship between these is not unproblematic, of which there will be more to say.

---

19. Rhetoric is deliberative, forensic or appraisive. Aristotle, *Rhetoric* (London, Penguin Classics, 2005), 1.3.3. In this and what follows I draw, as do almost all subsequent formal treatments, on Aristotle.

Rhetoric relates also to philosophy, Aristotle claimed, in being conducted by an inferior kind of dialectic or formal argument – the enthymeme.[20] An enthymeme is an incomplete syllogism, usually lacking the major premise – which is a truth assumed and provided by the listener; this engages the listener with the argument. Such a premise must be one they already hold – a *topos*, or commonplace of political life.

Consider again, for example, the 'tabloidish' story quoted earlier from Herodotus. Here the listener is presented with an incomplete syllogism, the major premise of which is a commonplace thought, initially suppressed, but in this case added as an afterthought: Herodotus' thoughts run something like this:

Abducting young women is not lawful.
It is stupid to make a fuss about it afterwards.
Helen was a young woman.
The Trojan wars followed from her abduction.
The Trojan wars were stupid.

As an argument, this is full of holes. One of the holes is the universal proposition which Herodotus provides afterwards: 'No young woman allows herself to be abducted if she does not wish to be.' This claim – that for young women, abduction against their will is an empty category – is actually the logical underpinning for the 'enthymeme-ish' (i.e. incomplete) argument: Although the abduction of young women is unlawful, it is not worth making a fuss about.

We could tidy up Herodotus' argument to make it more formal, making the major premise explicit (which in rhetoric it would not be). It would then run something like the following:

No young women permits abduction against her will. Helen was a young abducted woman. This was not against her will.
It is always stupid to object, after the event, to things that people are not made to do against their will (even if they are against the law).
The Trojan wars were an objection after the event to Helen's abduction.
The Trojan Wars were stupid.

We might of course want to object to the foundational premise, but that would take us into the realms of (social) science or philosophy proper. For the rhetorician it is enough if the principle is held to be true by the intended audience, for they will then assent to the premises implicitly deduced from it, and as a result the (incomplete) argument will prove persuasive. Indeed, it might well be rhetorically important to suppress the universal premise, since if it is made explicit it might excite objection. In philosophy this would be a good thing, since in philosophy we seek the truth and we want to make explicit and meet all possible objections. In rhetoric, however, we seek to persuade: if we can evade objections, rather than

---

20. Aristotle, *Rhetoric*, 1.2.8.

having to overcome them, then this is a good thing. This is, if you like, the realm of Plato's cave, and it is because cave-dwellers are unconvinced by philosophy that philosophers do not rule (just as tabloid readers are unconvinced by evidence, which is why cabinet ministers are constantly tempted to substitute policy-biased evidence for evidence-based policy).

If the above, or something like it, is correct, then this sets up a trio of polarities (or possibly – dare one say – a trilarity?) through which to characterise politics and our reflections on it. We could think of these as three nodal points defining the argumentative and discursive space occupied by political language which at its extremes is deployed:

> to tell its history;
> to identify necessary features of it or conditions of its employment;
> and to persuade hearers to action.

These polarities – history, philosophy, rhetoric – are identified in antiquity as distinct intellectual activities. But their identity as distinct activities, it seems to me, is not a contingent feature of that local culture, and certain confusions follow from failing to recognise the epistemic and social properties to be found within each, and of claiming them for, or confusing them with, another activity. Shortly I will go on and explore these features and some of the relationships between these, but first I want to add a 'wrinkle'.

During the last century and a half, the emergence of professionalised academics conducting both HPT and PP in a context that was more or less – and arguably increasingly – distanciated from politics and public life itself has further altered the situation.[21] HPT and PP are now kinds of meta-political discourses that do not map seamlessly – if indeed at all – onto even intelligent bar-room, dinner party, or even party conference discourse about political events. Who amongst us has not experienced the moment of glacial panic on the face of even the most accomplished social interlocutor that greets the news that you are a political philosopher, or a historian of political thought? But this is not merely a sociological observation. The distance between academic discourse and political life is revealed by the way it affects the meanings or import of statements drawn from one area and articulated in another. In particular, academic truths about public policies change character when intruded into public debate.

For example, the academic observation that economic recession and cuts in public expenditure may be likely to bring about industrial and political unrest can be considered a claim in social science to be evidenced in whatever way the discipline deems appropriate. However, such a claim made in the course of public debate by a trades union leader, is likely to be perceived – and denounced – as a threat. Similarly, an economist's claim that statutory limitation of bankers' bonuses may lead to sub-optimal hiring and an exodus of talent may be an investigable

---

21. S. Collini, 'Afterword' in Iain Hampsher-Monk and Dario Castiglione (eds) *The History of Political Thought in National Context* (Cambridge, Cambridge University Press, 2001).

hypothesis. But such a claim made by a banking CEO might, again, appear as a threat. Indeed, I can remember Gerry Cohen disqualifying the latter kind of argument from consequentialist reasoning to establish egalitarian principles in moral theory precisely because it was not a fact about the world, but a moral threat.

The professionalisation of the academy, then, adds a wrinkle to my three nodes, as it were of political theoretical discourse – politics/rhetoric, political philosophy and the history of political thought – recognising the tension in the latter between the history of PP and the history of the political rhetoric. Let me now consider some possible relationships between them.

HPT and PP

How might HPT stand then in relationship to current PP? It is a commonplace that the Historical or Cambridge Revolution disrupted any easy assumptions about the relationship between the two. Taking history seriously would often, indeed normally, reveal how different from its supposed descendants were theories of the past. Indeed it has been claimed by Quentin Skinner that an awareness of this strangeness was one of the main benefits of historical study, since it emancipated the student from a certain kind of myopia about possibilities different from those currently being articulated.[22] Here was one way, it was thought, in which HPT could influence PP and indeed politics itself, by educating – enlarging the views of – political philosophers or citizens, and by helping them to understand the parochial ways in which different political societies – including their own – constitute themselves or their political thinking.[23]

This is a broad and dispositional effect, but on this view HPT, precisely *because* it reveals the strangeness of historical political thought, might be incapable of producing knowledge applicable directly to PP. Understanding the theological underpinning of Locke's thought broadens our understanding of how legitimacy has been thought of in Western societies. But we surely then cannot – to cite a still disarmingly common aspiration amongst certain academics – seek to apply Locke's theory of legitimacy to liberal society in a Godless world – or at least in a political theory that eschews theistic premises. Such indeed was the explicit message of the founders of the Historical Revolution.[24] But equally problematic might be some of the benefits that *were* held out – the recovery of a particular concept – of liberty say – in hopes of re-introducing it into contemporary PP. I say *might* be, because given the ultimately open-ended character of the *paroles* made possible in a *langue*, these are all contingent matters – contingent, that is, on the logic of the theory or the concept's relationship to the argumentative or intellectual context into which it is hoped to insert it.

---

22. Q. Skinner, *Visions of Politics,* vol. I (Cambridge, Cambridge University Press, 2002), pp. 88, 125–6.
23. Indeed many of the essays in this collection can be construed as attempting to perform precisely this.
24. J. Dunn, *The Political Thought of John Locke: An historical account of the argument of the 'Two Treatises of Government'* (Cambridge, Cambridge University Press, 1982).

That is to say, I take it that it is always conceivable that a concept or argumentative move taken from one historical context might be inserted successfully in a different one. The little phrase, *'quod omnes tangit, ab omnes approbatur'*,[25] extracted from its very specific role in the Roman private law of trusts, was successfully inserted into the completely different public world of political legitimation in the late medieval and early modern period.[26] But these are in a way exceptional cases (and cases that the intensification of scholarship surely renders less likely). HPT is full of examples of enthusiastic movements to appropriate past thought – the early modern revival of Roman law being the most famous – in which the increasingly sophisticated application of scholarship designed to assist its recovery merely served to expose the historical distance between past and present and in the end revealed the impossibility of the exercise.[27]

HPT and politics

Turning now more specifically to the relationship between HPT and politics, it seems true that not only does the scholarly historical appreciation of a past theory or concepts contained within it often reveal the incongruity of their current applicability within contemporary political *philosophy*, it also commonly reveals their lack of *rhetorical* appeal to wider contemporary political audiences. The idea of the social contract enjoyed a brief revival in the attempts to rein in inflationary wage demands in the late sixties and seventies, but it was merely a rhetorical appeal to social unity in a divided society, and proved incapable of generating articulations of a morally or politically operationalisable kind. It failed to hook into the political reality it addressed.

It seems implausible, however, to suggest that its appeal would have been any greater had the meanings and valences of the term been more precisely focused through the lens of historical scholarship. Whilst the academy can uncover a more or less authentic version of Rousseau's or Hobbes' or Mill's thought, the more 'authentic' it is, the less plausible it is likely be to a (non-academic) modern. Considered as public political arguments, the recovery of historical authenticity surely damages, rather than enhances, the political – that is rhetorical – appeal to modern ears. As Hans Keller, the celebrated music critic, remarked of the authentic

---

25. 'That which concerns all should be approved by all'.
26. '(The maxim) was only applied towards and guardians in Roman law, but during the Middle Ages it supported a theory of consent that was a basic element of corporate theory and representative government.' K. Pennington, 'Law, Legislative Authority and Theories of Government, 1150–1300', in J. H. Burns (ed.), *Cambridge History of Medieval Political Thought* (Cambridge, Cambridge University Press, 1988), p. 440 ff.
27. 'The more they worked upon the sources the more convinced the humanists became that much of Roman Law was peculiar to its time and place.' J. H. Franklin, *Jean Bodin and the Sixteenth Century Revolution in the Methodology of Law and History* (New York, Greenwood Press, 1963), p. 27, and *see* at greater length D. R. Kelley, *Foundations of Modern Historical Scholarship: Language, law and history in the French Renaissance* (New York, Columbia University Press, 1970).

performance movement: 'We have period instruments but we do not have period ears!'[28]

At a certain level, the extent to which the above remarks apply depends on the political cultures of particular societies. In some political cultures the very pastness of ideas – irrespective of the appeal of their content – can render them and arguments in which they are embedded unviable. As societies have ceased to be traditional and have become innovative, a process still incomplete in my professional lifetime, the mere fact of a theory or a concept – or a thinker – having a significant status in our past is no longer sufficient to endow them with authority. The invocation (however misguided) of Adam Smith by Margaret Thatcher, and of the Levellers by Tony Benn, were already isolated instances in the 1980s, and I can think of no further British examples since. The predisposition of the democratic public (always drawn, as Aristotle remarked, to novelty) requires political actors – conservative as well as progressive, to vie with each other to present themselves as more innovative. As a consequence, apart from the periodic invocation of a generalised chocolate-box nostalgia, the more precise we are in delineating the local meanings of past theories, the less persuasive purchase they are likely to have on the contemporary mind. In contrast to early modern innovators – who often sought to rhetorically dress their theories up with a historical pedigree, modern revivalists present their offerings from our tradition as innovation, the better to ensure their rhetorical persuasiveness. So, the Conservative moderniser David Cameron's new 'big idea' turns out to have been an unacknowledged recycling of the distributivist social teaching of the Catholic Church as expressed in the ideas of Hilaire Belloc and G. K. Chesterton.[29]

Yet there are other political cultures in which the historical appeal is more rhetorically persuasive and so available to the political actor. In the USA the importance of Founders' Intent in legal philosophy and the presentism of the Founding Fathers in public life exemplifies the ease with which history can be invoked. And a skilled orator such as Barack Obama makes full and unembarrassed use of its resources. But this is already very much a public and not an academic history. It is difficult to imagine a politician being able to make political use of some historical discovery that disconcerted an idealised public history. Most academic historians of political thought find claims about the applicability of Founders' Intent to contemporary society intensely problematic as political philosophy, despite its being an undoubted matter of fact about American political culture.[30]

---

28. My case might be thought to be weakened by the observation that since Keller's remark, period performance has become very popular, as modern ears become attuned to period sensibilities and timbres. But if we were to think what the parallel would be in political life, it will be seen that this would be difficult to hold – to recreate a society susceptible to the political arguments of a Locke, would be to recreate seventeenth century society itself.

29. Jonathan Raban, review of P. Blond's *Red Tory: How left and right have broken Britain and how we can fix it*, London Review of Books, 22 April 2010, p. 22.

30. T. Ball and J. G. A. Pocock (ed.) *Conceptual Change and the Constitution* (Lawrence, KS., University Press of Kansas, 1988), Introduction, Section III.

In sum, whether viewed as 'arguments' or as 'concepts', the more historically constructed, the less plausible the material provided by the history of political thought seems to be. Where political cultures are susceptible to appeals to history, it is the *topoi* to be found in a publicly held history, not in the academy, which are available for political deployment.

There is however another way of reading this relationship between HPT and politics. If certain views of the relationship between a political community and its political-linguistic history obtain, there is another way of thinking about the HPT – politics link which suggests it could be considerably stronger. And this possibility relates to the history of political discourses, rather than the history of political philosophy.

For example, rather than providing discrete items for appropriation – concepts or arguments, say – the history of political thought can be construed as providing an understanding of the hermeneutic and cultural-historical roots and structure of the discourse in which our contemporary politics is conducted. Inasmuch as political reality is constituted by the language in which its practitioners describe it and the beliefs it supports, such an understanding, it could be claimed, is not merely of interest to academic hermeneutics, it is an understanding of the very ontology of political modernity itself.[31] Conversely, since political reality comprises sets of beliefs and institutions constructed and perpetuated only through language, and since these beliefs and institutions are historical products, a deep understanding of our politics (and what can be accomplished within it, and how) must presuppose an understanding of the history of its public discourse. This, of course, must be the history of its public discourse, rather than the history of its star political philosophers, who enter into the picture only to the extent that they figure in the former. As has been argued:

> The trick is to encapsulate all this in a story that makes sense to those who hear it, for politics is not inherently or self-evidently coherent. To the extent that it is itself historically continuous, the public discourse of a society performs precisely this function. Its goal is to create, and even sanctify a tradition that tells a people who they have been and are and allows them to ponder who they might become. At this point discursive continuity and academic history can stand as partners in the same enterprise.[32]

---

31. Such a view seems to inform J. G. A. Pocock's rigorously historical analysis of the way the English and other inhabitants of the British archipelago have characterised themselves and their internal and external relationships. Focusing both on their conceptions of sovereignty and their historiography, *see* the essays in *The Discovery of Islands* (Cambridge, Cambridge University Press, 2005), especially 'Sovereignty and History in the Late Twentieth Century'.
32. G. J. Schochet 'Why Should History Matter', in J. G. A. Pocock, G. J. Schochet and L. G. Schwoerer (eds), *The Varieties of British Political Thought, 1500–1800* (Cambridge, Cambridge University Press, 1996), p. 323.

This need not be a totalising or monopolistic story, but it is one that has to be carried on for political identity to be sustained. As Pocock himself has later argued:

> ... it is possible for a sovereign state, a self-governing community, to open up its sovereignty to debate, to render that debate open-ended and ongoing, to debate the history in and on which it is founded, and to proceed to a confrontation and negotiation between two concepts of sovereignty and of history, all this without dissolving the state or abolishing its sovereignty.[33]

But for this to be so, the claim still has to be that the 'history' of political thought that we are dealing with comprises thinking which is constitutive of, rather than external to, the political society that it describes. It is a history of public discourse that a public would have recognised, even if it had its origins and periodic *précis* in political philosophy.

Given this, to grasp for example 'the vocabulary of a modern European state'[34] is not to engage in some arcane lexicographical exercise, remote from reality. It is to understand – indeed to delineate the very features of – that reality in which we live. Historically informed political philosophising of this kind – although still a second-order activity – is not something potentially distanciated from political reality, it is rather a formalisation or 'abridgement' of that experienced reality. It is moreover potentially extremely useful to the active politician who, in a democratic culture, is required to deploy the resources of that linguistic culture in order to generate support for his or her policies.

I am not saying that politicians can only do this through conscious intellectual routes. There are instinctive politicians who accomplish the same through a practical grasp of such resources, through the contingent coming together of a personality with a particular assimilation of experience and a set of circumstances congruently matched to those two chance events – a Machiavellian *occasione*. I once asked a very senior civil servant in the entourage of Margaret Thatcher whether she was conversant with the academic work on economic or political libertarianism on which she seemed so often to be drawing. 'Not a bit of it', he replied, 'it was all pure instinct'. This is not to deny, of course the well-documented roles of Joseph, Letwin *et al.* in elaborating these instincts and providing them with an academic pedigree (something, of course, that could have been done with other policy orientations as well). My point (and, I think, that of my nameless senior official) was that Thatcher's instincts were already there focusing policy – the intellectual shoring-up arrived after the event. Parts of it had indeed been around a long time,[35] but it was not as a self-conscious exercise in historical recovery that Thatcher herself adopted it.

---

33. Pocock, *The Discovery of Islands*, p. 259.
34. M. Oakeshott, 'The vocabulary of a modern European state', *Political Studies*, 23 (2) (1975), pp. 319–41.
35. *See* most recently B. Jackson, 'At the origins of neo-liberalism: 1930–1947', *Historical Journal*, 53 (1) (2010).

HPT and PP revisited

Could such a relationship – HPT as the broad linguistic repertoire within which specific speech acts are articulated – obtain between HPT and PP? One is tempted to say no. Political philosophers in the contemporary anglophone tradition characteristically consider themselves to be operating innovatively, and according to strictly logical, deductive canons. They nevertheless often deploy arguments, the validity of which depends on an unacknowledged construal of meanings in ways deeply shaped by local academic convention. Continental philosophers, on the other hand – thinking here particularly of francophone work (Ricoeur, Deleuze) – often pride themselves on growing out of and relating to the history of political philosophy, and yet often do so in a way that seems unconcerned with recovering those figures' historical meanings.[36] To the degree that political philosophy has become an academic discipline, the standards by which it is judged have become internal to the discipline. Full-time, career political philosophers recognise features of their productions – elegance, coherence, integration to an existing body of literature – that would have been irrelevant to political argumentation considered rhetorically as part of a public debate, just as those standards do not necessarily map onto the concerns of the historian of political thought.

From the consequences of this narrow-minded professionalism, it is sometimes claimed, the history of political thought can rescue us. This sits oddly with the earlier claim that what the history of political thought reveals to us is the utter strangeness of our historical origins, that the benefit of studying it is akin to that of anthropological study in revealing human (and hence our own) particularity. There is indeed some tension between these two claims, which has not stopped them being advanced at the same time. And there is some tension between the second and the persuasive deployment of arguments drawn from the history of political thought in our own politics. However, this presages another, different and more diffuse, possible relationship between HPT and PP.

That is to say that rather than providing the political theorist directly with categorical and controversial material for contemporary deployment, HPT's contribution to PT operates through affecting us dispositionally, through challenging the otherwise narrowly based confidence characteristically evinced by the political philosopher, through affecting our sense of the indeterminacy of reasoning. HPT feeds a certain scepticism about the claims of PP, without (as do some other scepticisms) entirely undermining it. Political philosophy often cites its own emancipation from the past, and yet if the former view of history as a dispositional corrective to the stridency of PP is correct, such emancipation may render it more narrowly grounded, as well as less – not more – likely to be persuasive beyond its professional membership.

---

36. Ricoeur's *Rule of Metaphor*, for example, devotes a considerable amount of space to the history of metaphor in Western writing, P. Ricoeur, *The Rule of Metaphor: The creation of meaning in language* (London, Routledge, 2003) Deleuze's later, substantive work was preceded by, and draws on a number of studies of individual historical thinkers undertaken in his earlier career: including *Nietzsche et la philosophie,* (London, Athlone, 1963) and *La philosophie critique de Kant,* [*Kant's Critical Philosophy*] (London, Athlone, 1983).

PP and politics

I turn lastly to consider the relationship between PP and politics. Political philosophers often consider themselves to be operating in a political environment – indeed some of them have redefined the political in order to vindicate the claim. The claim that the political world is discursively constructed seems often to be accompanied by a further claim: that there is an unproblematic discursive continuity between the meta-language of political philosophy and the quotidian world of every-day politics. This assimilates the theoretical world that philosophers created in the academy to the political one they would influence, and blurs the distinction between rhetoric and philosophy.

Thus, for example, Chantal Mouffe, in a work devoted to the reinvigoration of democracy, writes: 'Democratic societies today are confronted with new challenges they are ill-prepared to answer …'. One of the main reasons for this 'lies in the rationalist framework which informs the main currents of political theory.' In order to 'consolidate and deepen our democratic institutions' we need to adopt a way of political philosophising that is more informed by Wittgenstien.[37]

Now the assumption that there is a seamless causal link between problems of contemporary democracy and the mode in which a tiny group of academics conduct the distinctly *recherché* activity of political philosophising is surely as breathtaking as the assumption that those problems would disappear if that tiny group conducted their activity under a different set of assumptions from the one they do. It is the slipperiness of the 'we', moving as it does from the community of political theorists to the political community at large, that reveals the dubious supposition of discursive continuity between what philosophers do and what is done – or indeed doable – politically.

Another way in which political philosophy seems to bleed across into politics itself is in the various ways that it seeks to model or emulate what representative citizens could be persuaded to endorse, without actual recourse to persuading them. Yet original choosers, public reason and idealised interlocutory situations cannot substitute for the empirical test of what a given public can actually be persuaded to endorse (can they?). The rhetorical task of persuading people is an irreducible feature of politics, for which no degree of theorising can substitute. What is persuasive is only what persuades (not what would persuade if …).

Philosophers only try to understand the world, but to change it you do not need a different kind of philosophy, you need – as Marx recognised – a different kind of activity – rhetoric, and rhetoric is defined not only in terms of its characteristic mode of persuasion – enthymeme, rather than the syllogism – but also in terms of (1) the arena in which it is practised, (2) its aim, and (3) its audience. The arena of rhetoric includes the political assembly, public debate, and, in modernity, the various forms of print and electronic media. Its aim is persuasion and the audience is those who constitute the political community to be moved to a decision – to exercise its or

---

37. C. Mouffe, *The Democratic Paradox* (London, Verso, 2000), pp. 60–1.

their power.[38] Philosophy – the aim of which is truth – cannot destroy or supplant rhetoric (unless the political community becomes philosophers). Philosophy is to be found in the academy, and the condition of the integrity of its practice is its refusal to seek power. Philosophy may, as did Socrates and Diogenes, speak truth to power, but if it seeks power for its truth, it will always be drawn into the realm of rhetoric. Plato and Aristotle, it seems to me, were on to something in insisting on distinguishing between philosophy and rhetoric.

Why and how have we moved away from retaining this distinction? Two axes along which important distinctions have been conflated can be identified. One is the political-private. If the political is not some identifiable public forum, but extends even to the most private and intimate emotional and intellectual corners of our lives, then, of course, even the most private or intellectualised of actions can be dignified as political. Academic actors can delude themselves – and their few readers – into believing that they are performing works of great political moment by urging (or 'calling for', as the modish locution characteristically has it) the adoption of a different methodology in philosophical reflection, or claiming to have identified a just foundation through modelling what a citizen would (and by implication, should) decide is foundationally just.

To the sceptical speech-act theorist the illocutionary question that the former exercise raises is 'to whom is the "call" addressed?', whilst the further perlocutionary question that arises is 'who is going to hear or take notice of it?'[39]

Implicit in such questions is the second axis, which has collapsed and contributed to the obscuring of the distinction between rhetoric and philosophy. This is a failure to think through carefully enough the implications of the undoubtedly true claim that social and political entities are discursively constructed. I have no wish to dissent from this, but it does leave unanswered the further question: within which, and whose, discourse is the entity constructed? If it is true – as it seems to be – that late modernity's political academy operates with a discourse, or discourses, that are dislocated from those of the general population, and with which our political world is constructed, how exactly are interventions in the former supposed to be effectual in the latter? The relationship between the (at least two) discourses is an empirical/historical one, not a logical or philosophical one. It requires at least some token effort on the part of the theorist to demonstrate the means by which the one is supposed to affect the other. Berlusconi's discursive construction of a favourable political environment for himself had surely more to do with his control of newspapers, television and other public spaces – which he achieved through political and rhetorical means – than with the happy choice of the foundational philosopher favoured by his right-wing ideological theoreticians.

---

38. Ricoeur, *The Rule of Metaphor*, p. 11.

39. Which is not to say that it cannot be done, as the consciousness-raising exercises of the feminist movement showed in the last century. But this was a widespread movement which took seriously, in intellectual and organisational terms, the business of bringing together intellectual insight and personal experience.

I have tried to identify three ideal kinds of political-theoretical talk. First, political philosophy, which attempts positively or normatively to discern constitutive truths about the political realm. Second, the history of political thought, which seeks to construct a narrative about such enterprises, and about the more quotidian languages in which politics takes place. And third, rhetoric, the animus of which is to change the commitments of members of a political community by the manipulation of existing beliefs. Although these are idealised specifications, which I concede are never fully realised or separated from each other in practice, being self-conscious about their identity – about which activity we are engaged in and being aware of their socio-linguistic properties and context – can, I think, help us to practise each of them better, as well as avoid the not always obvious pitfalls of confusing one with the other.

Chapter Two

Speech Acts, Languages or Conceptual History?

This chapter[1] discusses the work of the two most prominent names in Anglophone history of political thought, and offers some comparison between their work and the project of *Begriffsgeschichte* as approaches to the history of political concepts broadly conceived.[2] J. G. A. Pocock and Quentin Skinner both studied at the University of Cambridge where Skinner [became] Regius Professor of History. Pocock has held permanent posts at Canterbury University in New Zealand, at Washington University, St. Louis and at Johns Hopkins University, Baltimore, where he is now professor emeritus. Each has published major methodological and substantive historical work of their own, but each has also initiated and directed major collaborative works which, whilst not as minutely concerted as the German *Lexikon*, certainly bear comparison with them in terms of scope and ambition. Together, as I hope to show, they represent competing programmes of how to understand historical changes in social and political concepts.[3]

Quentin Skinner has been a moving force in two major publishing initiatives undertaken by Cambridge University Press which have come to dominate Anglophone scholarship in this field. The first of these was the 'Ideas in Context' research monograph series which now has some thirty titles in print. The declared aim of the series was to present studies of the development of new 'procedures, aims and vocabularies' within the then existing intellectual context. It expressed the hope that such an approach would dissolve 'artificial distinctions between

---

1. [Written for the volume *History of Concepts: Comparative perspectives*, I. Hampsher-Monk, K. Tilmans and F. van Vree (eds), (Amsterdam, Amsterdam University Press, 1998).]

2. Whilst writing this essay I have benefitted greatly with discussions with Martin Van Gelderen, Hans Bödeker, Dario Castiglione and my two co-editors, and from the comments at the Netherlands Institute of Advanced Study, Wassenaar and at the Universities of Amsterdam and Leiden.

3. The major substantive works are Q. Skinner, *Foundations of Modern Political Thought*, 2 vols., (Cambridge, Cambridge University Press, 1978); and J. G. A. Pocock, *The Machiavellian Moment: Florentine political thought and the Atlantic Republican tradition* (Princeton N. J., Princeton University Press, 1975). Methodological works are cited in the body of this chapter as appropriate. Major representative statements of each author are: Quentin Skinner 'Meaning and Understanding in the History of Ideas', reprinted in J. Tully (ed.), *Meaning and Context: Quentin Skinner and his critics* (Polity, Cambridge, 1988); and J. G. A. Pocock, 'The State of the Art', in Pocock, *Virtue, Commerce and History* (Itself one of the 'Ideas in Context' series), (Cambridge, Cambridge University Press, 1985). Assessments and bibliographies can be found for Skinner in J. Tully, *Meaning and Context...*, and for Pocock in I. Hampsher-Monk, 'Political languages in time: the work of J. G. A. Pocock', *The British Journal of Political Science*, XIV(1) (1984) pp. 89–116.

the history of philosophy, of various sciences, or society and politics, and of literature'.[4] The second publishing venture promoted by Skinner has been the publication of a massive range of cheap yet high quality editions of original works of political theory, many of which were unavailable in modern editions, or indeed, in many libraries, at all. The 'Cambridge Texts in the History of Political Thought' now comprises some eighty-three titles, and reflects, as the series description claims, the needs of modern scholarship for access to less well known texts in order to make sense of the major.[5] Although Skinner has not hitherto been involved in systematically collaborative research work, he is now chair of the co-ordinating committee of the European Science Foundation Network on Early Modern European Republicanism which will, under his editorship, produce a major internationally collaborative publication.[6]

It is in this collaborative field that Pocock has excelled: He chaired the steering committee of the Center for the Study of British Political Thought, established at the Folger Library in Washington in 1984. An original series of six huge seminars covering British Political Thought from the end of the Wars of the Roses to the American War of Independence ('From Bosworth to Yorktown') ran from 1984—87. This involved scholars from all over the world and was later supplemented by further seminars, recapitulating certain periods and extending the historical range down to the period of the French Revolution. The Folger seminar series produced an impressive five-volume *Proceedings* and a fertile synoptic volume of essays by the conveners of the individual seminars, as well as a number of works relating to their own historical periods or interests.[7]

---

4. Quotations are drawn from the series description found in all volumes, facing the title page, e.g. P. N. Miller, *Defining the Common Good: Empire, religion and philosophy in eighteenth century Britain*, (Cambridge, Cambridge University Press, 1994), p. *ii*.

5. The number of volumes is now considerably greater. For a recent retrospect and assessment of the various initiatives in the field conducted by Quentin Skinner under the aegis of CUP *see*: R. Fisher, 'How to do things with books: Quentin Skinner and the dissemination of ideas', *History of European Ideas*, 35 (2) (2009).

6. *Republicanism: A shared European heritage*, Quentin Skinner and Martin van Gelderen (eds), 2 vols., (Cambridge, Cambridge University Press, 2002); and now *Freedom and the Construction of Europe*, 2 vols., Q. Skinner and M. van Gelderen (eds), (Cambridge, Cambridge University Press, 2013).

7. The origins of the Centre are described in 'The history of British political thought: the creation of a centre', J. G. A. Pocock, *Journal of British Studies*, 24 (3) (1985) pp. 283–310; *Proceedings of the Center for the Study of the History of British Political Thought*, G. Schochet (ed.), 5 vols. (Washington D.C., Folger Institute, 1990–1993); and J. G. A. Pocock with G. Schochet and L. G. Schwoerer (eds) *Varieties of British Political Thought 1500–1800*, (Cambridge, Cambridge University Press, 1991). Other more specialist works relate intimately to particular portions of that seminar. Amongst those which are closest to the interests of conceptual history are T. Ball and J. G. A. Pocock (eds) *Conceptual Change and the Constitution*, (Lawrence, Kansas, University of Kansas Press, 1988); L. Levy Peck, *The Mental World of the Jacobean Court*, (Cambridge, Cambridge University Press, 1991); R. A. Mason (ed.) *Scots and Britons: Scottish political thought and the Union of 1603*, (Cambridge, Cambridge University Press, 1995) and J. C. Robertson (ed.) *A Union for Empire: The Union of 1707 in the context of British political thought*, (Cambridge, Cambridge University Press, 1996).

Unlike the editors of *Begriffsgeschichte*, neither Pocock nor Skinner attempted to impose uniformity of sources, treatment or structure on their contributors, whose work characteristically comprised the free-standing academic essay or monograph. Nevertheless there is a shared intellectual approach and sense of common enterprise in both sets of work which, together which the sheer scale of the enterprises, makes comparison with the great collaborative German enterprises not inappropriate.[8]

Since other contributors[9] make reference to the context within which *Begriffsgeschichte* arose and the positions it was opposed to, it might help also to make some prefatory remarks about the Anglophone context in which the 'historical revolution' arose and with which Skinner's and Pocock's work have become identified. For the academic audience that both Skinner and Pocock addressed at the start of their careers were political theorists, practitioners who, whilst they often studied political theorists of the past, did not do so in a self-consciously historical fashion.[10] Whilst such historical work had been conducted in the British and American history departments (often by European *émigrés*) it was rarely central to Anglophone historiography. 'Political theory', however, was a subject taught in English-speaking universities across a range of departments – political science and philosophy as well as history. In the academic study of 'political theory', critical attention was paid to a wide variety of texts produced under a huge range of historical circumstances from ancient Greece to industrial modernity. Such study could assume that the object of the authors of all these had been to provide some (often comprehensive) and certainly enduring philosophical account of political concepts and it was commonly conducted – particularly outside history departments – as though all these authors were alive and well, and working just down the corridor. Although in philosophy and political science departments it was common to separate 'political theory' into the study of a chronological sequence of 'authors' on the one hand, and an a temporal study of 'concepts' on the other, no disciplinary distinction was commonly made in approaching these two exercises. Just as the history of philosophy, for twentieth century Anglophone philosophers has often been a training ground, a repertoire

---

8. Few such comparisons have come to my notice. The major exception and persistent Anglophone champion of *Begriffsgeschichte*, in a number of articles published between 1986 and the present, has been M. Richter. His 'Pocock, Skinner and the *geschichtliche Grundbegriffe*' appeared in *History and Theory*, 19 (1990), pp. 38–70 and is now superseded by his critical introduction to *The History of Political and Social Concepts* (Oxford, Oxford University Press, 1995), which appeared after the writing of the conference paper on which this chapter was based. Chapter Six contains an extended comparison of *Begriffsgeschichte*, Pocock and Skinner, however even Richter's comparison focuses on their methodological prescriptions rather than their intellectual entrepreneurship. *See also* 'Editorial' by M. Freeden, *Journal of Political Ideologies* 2 (1) (1997), pp. 3–11.
9. P. Den Boer and H. Bödeker in the volume *History of Concepts: Comparative perspectives*.
10. J. G. A. Pocock 'The History of Political Thought: A methodological enquiry' in *Politics, Philosophy and Society*, ser. 2, (Oxford, Blackwell, 1962), and Q. Skinner's 'Meaning and understanding in the history of ideas', *History and Theory,* 8 (1969), reprinted in J. Tully (ed.) *Meaning and Context: Quentin Skinner and his critics* (Cambridge, Polity, 1988).

of problems and arguments, a jumping-off point for the *practice* of philosophy and not an historical subject matter in its own right;[11] so political theorists too – working to philosophical criteria of coherence, consistency, comprehensiveness, as well as considerations of perceived political relevance – sought to use past theorists, just as much as a-historical, conceptual analysis, as a basis for their own theorising activity.[12]

Exhilarating as such a philosophical treatment was, it was often outrageously unhistorical in two important senses. Firstly, in the synchronic dimension, the critical emphasis meant that in approaching any individual thinker insufficient attention was commonly given to recovering the intended meanings (or indeed the agenda) of the texts as written. This was particularly exacerbated by a prevailing Cold War Manichaeism which deemed it imperative to assign to authors (for whom such terms could have had no meaning) championship, or even responsibility for the emergence of the then prevailing totalitarian and liberal ideologies. Thus writers as diverse as Marsilius of Padua and Hobbes were identified as articulating the foundation of liberalism, whilst Plato and Rousseau were held to be advocates of totalitarianism … or at least of those patterns of thought, whose logical outcome was the camps of Auschwitz and the Gulag.[13]

Writers were commonly criticised for failing to address certain problems or concepts, as though, if they were competent political theorists, they ought to have known that such 'eternal problems' ought to have been addressed.

---

11. When I was an undergraduate my notoriously controversial Professor of Philosophy Anthony Flew, began his first year lectures with the following announcement: 'Today I begin our Introduction to Philosophy course. I shall be lecturing on Plato for the first term, and I don't want to hear anyone complaining that we aren't doing contemporary philosophy because we are!'

12. Thus Pocock remarked in 1969: 'the history of political thought has a constant tendency to become philosophy.' Curiously, Pocock sees this as driven not only by misplaced philosophical standards, but also by historical demands of narrative coherence. Pocock, 'History of political thought', *Politics, Philosophy and Society*, p. 187. Cf. the not entirely dissimilar position of Koselleck in 'Terror and Dream: Methodological remarks on the experience of time during the Third Reich' in R. Koselleck (tr. Keith Tribe), *Futures Past: On the semantics of historical time*, (Cambridge, Mass., MIT Press, 1985), p. 215; original *Vergangene Zukunft. Zur Semantik geschichtlicher Zeiten*, (Frankfurt am Main, Suhrkamp Verlag, 1979). A provoking and sensitive discussion on the relationship between this kind of political theory and various strands of within the 'historical revolution' is provided by Dario Castiglione 'Historical arguments in political theory', *Political Theory Newsletter*, 5 (1993) pp. 89–109.

13. This is not to say that these claims were not often advanced with considerable erudition and scholarship. On Marsilius and Hobbes as liberals *see* A. Gewirth, *Marsilius of Padua – the Defender of the Peace*, 2 vols., (London and New York, Columbia University Press, 1961), and Leo Strauss, *The Political Philosophy of Hobbes: Its basis and genesis* (Chicago, University of Chicago Press, 1936), Plato's totalitarianism is famously unmasked in Karl Popper: *The Open Society and its Enemies*, 2 vols., *Volume I: The Spell of Plato* (London, Routledge and Kegan Paul, 1945); and the *locus classicus* for Rousseau is the surprisingly short chapter by J. L. Talmon in his *Origins of Totalitarian Democracy* (London and New York, Praeger, 1952). See my 'Rousseau and Totalitarianism – with Hindsight?' in R. Wokler (ed.), *Rousseau and Liberty* (Manchester, Manchester University Press, 1995), pp. 267–88.

Skinner's path-breaking article 'Meaning and Understanding' mercilessly exposed the mythologies generated by such a-historical expectations.[14] The mythology of 'doctrine' – by which expectations that a certain subject matter had to be addressed lead commentators to construct a position to be ascribed to writers, or to criticise writers for 'failing' to have addressed it. The mythology of 'coherence' – by which writers were presumed to have aspired to present closed and coherent systems which it was the task of the exegete to reveal, lead to a failure to countenance the possibility that the author in question may – as a matter of historical fact – have contradicted themselves, changed their minds, or failed to notice some tension or contradiction in their thought. In the mythology of 'prolepsis', the meaning or significance a work could have had for its author is conflated with that subsequently ascribed to it by present-day commentators. In the myth of parochialism, the commentator, faced with some truly alien thought – world or conceptual framework, construes it as one that is familiar and meets their expectations.[15]

The second important sense in which 'political theory' was not historical – even when it did treat texts in an historical sequence as 'the history of political thought' – concerned the diachronic dimension. A sequential canon of texts selected for philosophical interest, tended both to obscure important historical connections (where *historically* important works were missing from the canon),[16] and to foster

---

14. Amongst the works cited by Skinner as engaging in this and related practices which involve 'reifying' doctrines, many but by no means all, emerging from Political Science Departments, are the following: Ernst Cassirer, *The Philosophy of the Enlightenment* (Princeton, Princeton University Press, 1955); G. E. G. Catlin, *A History of Political Philosophers* (London, Allen and Unwin, 1950); J. W. Gough, *John Locke's Political Philosophy* (Oxford, Clarendon, 1950); Andrew Hacker, *Political Theory: Philosophy, ideology, science* (New York, Macmillan, 1961); Peter H. Merkl, *Political Continuity and Change* (New York, Harper and Row, 1967); Christopher Morris, *Political Thought in England from Tyndale to Hooker* (Oxford, Oxford University Press, 1953); Hans J. Morgenthau, *Dilemmas of Politics* (Chicago, Chicago University Press, 1958); J. Plamenatz, *Man and Society*, 2 vols., (London, Longman, 1963); Bertrand Russell, *History of Western Philosophy* (London and New York, Allen and Unwin, 1946); G. H. Sabine, *A History of Political Theory* (London and New York, Holt Rinehart and Winston, 1951 (1937)); L. Strauss, *History of Political Philosophy* (Chicago, Chicago University Press, 1963); T. D. Weldon, *States and Morals* (London, John Murray, 1946).

15. This paragraph summarises the structure of Skinner's argument in sections I and II of 'Meaning and understanding', *Meaning and Context*, pp. 30–50. A number of these points – particularly the tendency to reorganise thought to a higher level are also to be found in Pocock's 1969 article.

16. The most salutary example of this was the virtual ignoring of the English Civil War thinker James Harrington, whose work was neither philosophical, in the sense of engaging in metaphysical or epistemological preliminaries, nor it must be said a model of clarity. As Pocock has shown, however, he is the pivotal figure both for the transmission of civic republican thought and for English historiographical self-understanding in the later seventeenth and eighteenth centuries. *See* the seminal 'Machiavelli, Harrington and English political ideologies in the Eighteenth Century', *William & Mary Quarterly*, 3rd ser., vol. XXII/4 (1965) reprinted in J. G. A. Pocock, *Politics Language and Time* (Chicago, Chicago University Press, 1971), as well as Chapters 11 and 12 in *The Machiavellian Moment*. Pocock's edition of *The Political Works of James Harrington* (Cambridge, Cambridge University Press, 1977), contains a 150 page introduction which includes a substantial chapter on 'Harrington's ideas after his lifetime'.

the ascription of historical connections between canonical texts where none were in fact present.[17]

It was the recognition of these two important deficiencies that largely fuelled, from the late 1960s, an 'historical revolution' in the Anglophone study of political theory, and with which the names of J. G. A. Pocock and Quentin Skinner are rightly associated.[18] They thus shared with *Begriffsgeschichte* at least two major aims, namely that of recovering – from the Lovejoyan transhistorical ideas in the case of English, from Historicism in Germany – the meanings which historical actors and writers brought to their activity; and secondly that of looking beyond the 'great texts' to a wider usage in order to recover histories of meanings. Beyond this agreement – important as it was – however, lay deep divergences to which we turn after the positions of the two Anglophone writers are outlined.

John Pocock and political languages

Pocock's offensive against un-historical political theory started from an attempt to clarify what a genuine *history* of political thought might be, and to distinguish the sequence of philosophical meditations on historically unsituated texts that often passed for it,[19] from the genuine attempt to identify historical meaning and the detailed shifts and changes that actually took place in it. Using the metaphor of topography also favoured by Lovejoy, Koselleck and Rolf Reichardt, he claimed that what had passed for the history of political thought had involved a progression from one mountain top of abstraction to another (Grotius to Hobbes to Locke, say), assuming that the shape of the connecting ridges in between could be deduced from the disposition of the peaks. By contrast, the true historian must empirically

---

17. The classic case here was the assumption that Locke, simply because he came after Hobbes, was in some sense 'responding' to him. That Locke was virtually oblivious of Hobbes, and the vital importance of recognising Filmer as the adversary in order to understand Locke's argument was demonstrated by Peter Laslett in his crucial edition of Locke's *Two Treatises of Government* (Cambridge, Cambridge University Press, 1960) – a work which exerted a seminal influence on Skinner's early understanding of context, Skinner, 'Reply to my Critics', *Meaning and Context*, p. 327 fn 12.

18. Although this essay focuses on only the first two, John Dunn's early methodological essay 'The identity of the history of ideas', in *Philosophy*, XLIII (1968), reprinted *Politics, Philosophy and Society IV*, P. Laslett, W. G. Runciman and Q. Skinner (eds), (Oxford, Blackwell, 1972), and in J. Dunn, *Political Obligation in its Historical Context* (Cambridge, Cambridge University Press, 1980), was one of the trio of works invariably cited as initiating the historical revolution. The other two were Pocock's 'History of Political Thought: A methodological enquiry', in *Politics Philosophy and Society II* (Oxford, Oxford University Press, 1962), and Skinner's own 'Meaning and understanding in the history of ideas', first published in *History and Theory* 8 (1969) and reprinted in J. Tully (ed.), *Meaning and Context* (Cambridge, Polity Press, 1988). Skinner generously credits Dunn with the insight that Austin's theory of speech acts might be relevant to the interpretation of texts in the history of political thought. 'A Reply to my Critics', *Meaning and Context*, p. 327 fn 12.

19. Pocock, 'History of Political Thought: A methodological enquiry', p. 187.

investigate these contours to ensure whether the peaks were indeed related to one another in the ways claimed.[20]

To continue the analogy, the medium for this landscape or topography was identified with a linguistic repertoire which might include very abstract and high-level works as well as relatively specific and mundane ones. His claim was that, at least in stable societies, relatively discrete vocabularies of politics comprised concepts grouped together in an internally ordered domain with a grammar and syntax, even a literature and repertoire of associations (*topoi* even!), which mimicked that discoverable in a natural language.[21] Often, particularly in early modernity, such languages were deployed by distinct occupational or status-groups which re-enforced sociologically the discrete character of the language.[22]

Pocock's recent remark that 'the history of political thought has been becoming ... less a history of thought than of language, literature'[23] is both a truth of his personal intellectual biography and of the determinedly linguistic character of Anglophone philosophy in the last forty years. Since we cannot identify thoughts except as they are articulated, the history of political thought must collapse into the history of their articulations. The postulation of thoughts as entities distinct from the articulations of them parallels, the postulation of *noumena* as distinct from *phenomena*, and is vulnerable to the same criticisms.

The work done by the concept of language in Pocock's thinking – with a short detour via the paradigm[24] – has accordingly increased over time, acquiring a Saussurian vocabulary to distinguish not only the diachronic from the synchronic dimension) but the characterisation of the language *(la langue)* as a whole from the particular performances *(les paroles)* undertaken in it.[25]

---

20. Thus Locke turns out not to be related to Hobbes at all, but, antithetically to Filmer (as shown by Laslett), and by way of his construal of the language of sovereignty to George Lawson (Julian Franklin), possibly the Levellers and ultimately Calvinist resistance theorists (Quentin Skinner).

21. 'When we speak of "languages", therefore, we mean for the most part sub-languages: idioms, rhetorics, ways of talking about politics, distinguishable games of which each may have its own vocabulary, rules, preconditions and implications, tone and style.' 'The Concept of a Language and the *Metier d'Historien*: Some considerations on practice', in A. Pagden (ed.), *The Languages of Political Theory in Early-Modern Europe* (Cambridge, Cambridge University Press, 1987).

22. This was particularly true in Pocock's first work, *The Ancient Constitution and the Feudal Law* (Cambridge, Cambridge University Press, 1957, reissued 1987), where Common Lawyers, Royalists and Antiquarians formed different and eventually ideologically conflicting conceptions of the past.

23. Pocock: 'The Owl Reviews his Feathers: A valedictory lecture', xerox, Johns Hopkins University 11 May 1994: 'the history of political thought has been becoming all my life less a history of thought than of language, discourse, literature', p. 18.

24. *See* most enthusiastically, *Politics Language and Time*, preface to reprint, (Chicago, University of Chicago Press, 1989), p. x, and the first and last essays therein 'Languages and their Implications' and 'On the Non-Revolutionary Character of Paradigms', but note in 'The Concept of a Language', p. 21: 'we may think of them as having the character of paradigms, in that they operate so as to structure thought and speech in certain ways and to preclude their being structured in others, we may not describe them as paradigms if the term implies that preclusion has been successfully effected'.

25. 'Languages and their Implications', p. 25; 'The Concept of a Language', p. 23; 'The State of the Art', p. 7.

Pocock saw the primary interpretive task of the historian as that of identifying and reconstructing the languages in which politics had been discussed, and their mutation over time. The most famous example is the recovery of the language of civic humanism in early modern Britain. But language could also perform an explanatory role with regard to an individual thinker's thought which could be understood by identifying its relationship with the language – or languages – being deployed by the writer. For example, Edmund Burke's peculiar conception of reason could be illuminated by reconstructing the common-law language and associations from which it derived.[26] Explanation was thus a two-way, Janus-faced enterprise, in which either the *langue* or the *parole* could be used to explain the other. A *langue,* and indeed its history, could be reconstructed from reading a variety of the *paroles* performed in it, and a particular *parole* could be illuminated by a fuller appreciation of the *langue* in which it was couched, or *langues* it attempted to combine or synthesise.

Pocock was aware of the potentially trivial character of such explanations, and stressed the importance of maintaining a distinction between *langue* and *parole*. The author's *parole* is one performance amongst many possible in any given *langue*. If the language cannot be identified independently of the text which exemplifies it, it can exercise no explanatory power.[27] The investigator must satisfy him or herself that the language they have identified was indeed an existent and discrete cultural resource for the writer and 'not merely a gleam in the historian's interpretive eye'.[28] At one point, Pocock even identified a series of verification criteria to test for the independent existence of a language:

a. different authors carried out a variety of acts within it;
b. they discussed one another's use of it, sometimes giving rise to meta-languages;
c. investigators are able to predict the implications, and intimations, entailed by its use in particular circumstances;
d. they can discover its use in unexpected places; and
e. they successfully exclude languages from consideration on grounds of non-availability.[29]

The historian's articulation of a language – or a statement articulated in it – always involved the temptation to render coherent a position which was not, and Pocock was initially concerned to draw attention to the (for Anglophone political theorists) irresistible temptation to confuse the *doing* of political theory (the attempt to create a coherent account of the political world), with the writing of histories of it (the construction of an historically accurate account of such

---

26. 'Burke and the Ancient Constitution', in *Historical Journal,* 112 (1960) and in *Politics, Language and Time.*
27. This is not quite the idiom in which Pocock puts the point *see* 'The Concept of a Language', pp. 26–7, but it seems concisely appropriate.
28. 'State of the Art', *Virtue, Commerce and History,* p. 10.
29. 'The Concept of a Language', pp. 26–27; and less formally 'State of the Art', p. 10.

an attempt or attempts). Escaping such pitfalls involved correctly assessing the level of abstraction at which any given composition was intended to operate, as well as the extent to which the author intended a reflective or reconstitutive philosophical activity or a rhetorical exhortation to action.[30] Thinkers at a high level of abstraction uncovered and sometimes sought to restructure basic linguistic relationships fairly self-consciously (one thinks of Hobbes' self-proclaimed intention to 'set before men's eyes the mutual relation between protection and obedience' and his more covert and subversive one of defining outward acts and faith in such a mutually exclusive way as to virtually preclude the possibility of conscientious Christian disobedience).[31] By contrast, less abstract thinkers' activities could be explained by bringing to the reader's attention relationships between concepts and patterns of speech now lost which the subject of the study had assumed rather than made explicit. The major success here was the recovery of Harrington who was rescued from virtual oblivion and turned into a figure of crucial importance in a range of discourses concerning the application of republican ideas to England, and eighteenth century understandings of the constitutional implications of the socio-historical changes of the sixteenth and seventeenth century.

Pocock claimed that the identity of the appropriate local languages and the appropriate level of abstraction for dealing with a text were historically verifiable questions, not open ended or a matter of choice for the investigator. Interpretation was constrained (although not determined) by objectively identifiable characteristics of the text. To Stanley Fish's sceptical 'is there a text in the class?' Pocock's robust answer was that whatever other practitioners find, or fail to find, in theirs 'there certainly was a text in the historian's class'.[32]

Despite Pocock's commitment to 'present the text as it bore meaning in the mind of the author or his contemporary reader'[33] it has been a criticism that his narratives have sometimes operated at a level of abstraction 'far exceeding that attained by the writers he studied.'[34] However his identification of languages as the appropriate trans-historical units of study provides him with some justification for doing this. Inasmuch as a language may be said to comprise a set of relationships – logical and associative – and potentials, these might be unrealised by its users, who nevertheless rearticulated and transmitted them and so rendered them available

---

30. There were such thinkers as Sheldon Wolin's 'Epic Theorists': the 'fully self-conscious linguistic performer', Hobbes was one such, but their identification was a matter of empirical historical research. Pocock, *Virtue, Commerce and History*, 'Introduction: The state of the art', pp. 16–17.

31. *See* Hobbes, *Leviathan*, R. Tuck (ed.), (Cambridge, Cambridge University Press, 1991), pp. 395–396 (protection and obedience); Chapter 42 *passim*, esp. p. 271 ('profession with the tongue is but an externall thing'; p. 285 ('internall faith is in its own nature invisible, and consequently exempted from all humane jurisdiction') page numbers cited from original.

32. 'State of the Art', p. 21; the reference is to S. Fish, 'Is There a Text in This Class?', *The Authority of Interpretive Communities* (Cambridge, Mass., Harvard University Press, 1980).

33. 'Languages and their Implications', *Politics, Language and Time*, p. 6.

34. A. Lockyer, 'Pocock's Harrington', *Political Studies*, XXVIII (3) (1980).

to subsequent users of it.[35] A language can never be reduced to the propositions actually advanced in it at any one time.

Fertile, powerful, and suggestive as Pocock's methodological reflections are, they seem essentially subordinate to, or at least arising out of and developing through, periodic reflections on his practice.[36] Indeed it is tempting – looking back at *The Ancient Constitution and the Feudal Law* – to see Pocock's method as immanent in one of his earliest and recurrent subject matters: the common law mind and the customary character of even the most theoretical performances.

Quentin Skinner and speech acts

Quentin Skinner's earliest works, by contrast, were already self-consciously declaring a very precise methodological programme resting on the analysis given by John Austin and John Searle of speech acts.[37] Skinner's strategic focus was synchronic: on the performance of individual speech acts, rather than Pocock's diachronic concern with language. History was to be constructed from an analysis of successive significant innovatory (or conservative) speech acts performed by individuals in a given language or, as he sometimes called it ideology.

What did the idea of the speech act, bring to this programme? According to speech act analysis, speaking or writing is not adequately characterised as the production of audible sounds or graphic shapes, nor yet as words, nor even (usually) as referring (to some state of the world), or predicating (some property of some thing or person in the world): Language is not (usually, or at least not interestingly) used to describe some state of affairs in the world. Certainly political uses of language are rarely so one-dimensional. Rather, in politics, speech is used to *affect* the world. Political speech is paradigmatically speech *action*.

The idea of the speech act draws attention to the fact that in speaking or writing we commonly perform actions, and in the most simple cases the descriptions of these actions are cases cognate with the verbs the actor might him or herself use in performing the act. These were, in Austin's terms 'performative utterances', utterances which at the same time perform the action referred to.

---

35. See 'Languages and their Implications', *Politics, Language and Time*, pp. 23–4. 'It is true that (a user of language) could not have meant to convey any message which the resources of language in his lifetime did not render it possible for him to have meant; ... but within these limits there is room for it to have happened to him (as it happens to all of us) to mean more than he said or to say more than he meant.' Also 'State of the Art', pp. 20–1. Pocock's emphasis seems to have shifted here. The early works, and the flirtation with the 'paradigm', suggest logic or grammar as the primary quality of the 'language', the later offers a less formalistic characterisation as 'idiom' or rhetoric. 'It is a history of rhetoric rather than grammar, of the affective and effective content of speech rather than its structure.' 'The Concept of a Language', p. 22.

36. For example: 'The Concept of a Language and the *Métier d'Historien*' where he proposes 'to let them (meta-theory, a general theory of language) arise, if they arise at all, out of the implications of what I shall be saying we as historians do. The *Métier d'Historien* ... is primarily his craft or practice', p. 19.

37. J. L. Austin, *How to Do Things with Words*, J. O. Urmson (ed.), (Oxford, Oxford University Press, 1962) (delivered as the William James Lectures, Harvard, 1955); John R. Searle, *Speech Acts: An essay in the philosophy of language* (Cambridge, Cambridge University Press, 1969).

Thus if I say 'I warn you that I might go on like this for another half an hour' I have, in that very statement itself performed the act of warning. In saying, 'I warn', I do in fact warn you, I have performed an action in speech, or a speech act.[38] In saying, 'I promise not to stop even if the audience falls asleep' I perform the act of promising. Such verbs were 'illocutionary'. The fact of using them was sufficient (under certain definable rules) to successfully perform the action they described.[39]

Yet a further class of words described actions, the successful completion of which required some extrinsic effect to result. I can legitimately claim that in publishing this paper, I am trying to persuade my readers that all this has something to do with the study of the history of political ideas, without fear of refutation, for such is indeed my intention. What I could not claim, without independent corroboration, was that I was convincing you that it did. Your being convinced is not accomplished by my trying to persuade you, but only, in fact, by your being persuaded. *Illocutionary* acts characterise the deployment of authorial intentions in some linguistic performance, warning, advising, exhorting, denouncing, ridiculing, exposing etc. *Perlocutionary* acts describe intentions which intend to produce and do indeed bring about some change in the listener's understanding of the situation. Persuading, convincing, revolutionising, de-legitimating (on at least most counts of what it is to legitimate), include both intention and its successful completion. Of course not all would-be perlocutionary acts achieve their intended effect. The distinction, although only formalised by Austin, was used to good effect by Shakespeare. In the following exchange he depicts Harry Hotspur exploiting it to ridicule Owen Glendower's boorish attempt to impress his fellow conspirators by claiming supernatural powers:

Glendower: I can call spirits from the vasty deep.
Hotspur: Why, so can I, or so can any man;
But will they come when you do call for them?[40]

Skinner's claim then was that theorists and writers, no less than actors, do not simply write or say things, but that *in* writing or saying something they perform some illocutionary action and often a perlocutionary one as well. To understand any given linguistic performance one had to grasp its illocutionary force, and to do this one had to familiarise oneself with the linguistic conventions available to the author. That is to say, one had to understand *what* Machiavelli was doing

---

38. British Rail once took to issuing 'pre-warnings'. Thus if the buffet on the train was going to close down – characteristically just before supper time on long journeys – the passengers would be warned, but before being warned, there would be a pre-warning – that there was going to be a warning. But a pre-warning, as I pointed out in what I believe to be the only letter the Guardian has ever published on the subject of speech acts, is a logical impossibility. By uttering the word 'warning', you do in fact and irresistibly warn and no pre-warning can soften the blow.
39. Austin, *How to Do Things with Words*, p. 98. For the formal elaboration of the rules *see* J.Searle, *Speech Acts*, Chapter 3, 'The Structure of Illocutionary Acts'.
40. William Shakespeare, *Henry IV*, Part One, Act III, 1, 11.53–5.

in writing *The Prince,* or Hobbes in writing *Leviathan.* What was crucial here was the notion of intention, and its possible relationship to convention.[41] I can promise because I can formulate the intention to promise, and that intention is available to me because of the existence of the institution of promising in my language and amongst those to whom I promise. Promising without intention – least controversially in the case of someone who does not know the language and simply utters the sound – fails to perform the appropriate speech act. Knowingly promising (other things being equal), commits the promiser to their course of action – she cannot evade the obligation by claiming that 'I promise' is only a sound, or 'promising' only a convention.[42]

Against both textualists (who insisted that we simply read the text) and contextualists (who insisted that we use the (social) context to explain its meaning), Skinner urged, not that we could dispense with either activity, but that recovering the repertoire of socially given meanings and conventions available to the actor was a logical prerequisite of two activities.

The first one is locating their linguistic performance within the author's contemporary world of meaning, and so being able to show minimally, what an author might legitimately be taken to have meant when they wrote what they wrote. This suggested a non-trivial principle of interpretive exclusion: where certain linguistic meanings or conventions are not available to a writer or speaker, they could not possibly be construed as performing them and their work could not be so understood. Since all meaning is social in the sense that the meanings of a word are to be recovered from its possible uses in a given society of language users,[43] the recovery of meanings available to the author was an essential (but by no means exclusive or sufficient) criterion of scholars' interpretations of the author's own meaning, since, at least on this account of meaning, authors could not have framed an intention to convey a meaning which their existing linguistic resources did not allow, and any historical actor whose conception of prevailing linguistic conventions departed *too* far from that of his audience, would fail disastrously to bring off his linguistic performance.[44] Interpretations which presupposed such intentions could [therefore] successfully be rejected. Thus, Machiavelli's *Prince* could not be a satire, Chapter V of Locke's *Second Treatise* could not be an apology for capitalism, and Rousseau's *Du Contrat Social* could not be a justification for totalitarianism, since none of these categories were

---

41. Here Skinner drew on another topic from contemporary philosophy of action, the relationship between action, intention and convention. G. E. M. Anscombe, *Intention* (Oxford, Blackwell, 1957); A. Meldon, *Free Action* (London, Routledge and Kegan Paul, 1961); P. Geach, *Mental Acts* (London, Routledge and Kegan Paul, 1960).

42. See the classic article by J. Searle 'How to derive "ought" from "is"', *The Philosophical Review*, 73, 1 (1964) pp. 43–58.

43. 'Meaning and Understanding', in Tully (ed.), *Meaning and Context*, p. 55.

44. As may have happened during the attainder of Strafford in 1641 when Edmund Waller asked in the English Parliament – as if for a specific list of statutes – what the fundamental laws of the Kingdom were, and was told by speaker Maynard, that if he did not know he had no business sitting in the House!

available to those authors, and could not have entered into their intentions in writing them.

But the second and crucial task which an understanding of existing conventions permitted us to perform was that of identifying innovation, conflict and subversion when it was taking place. As Skinner pointed out to those who accused him of being unable to account for innovation – knowledge of the prevailing meanings and genres was actually a condition of even recognising innovations in usage when it was achieved, let alone of giving a successful account of it.[45] The claim was that an understanding of speech acts – the accomplishment of some social or political performance through linguistic utterance – rested not only on the identification of conventional meaning, genre and practice, but also and perhaps more importantly, on the identification of departures from these.[46] Thus we could only understand the *Prince* properly by understanding the conventional performances thitherto conducted in that genre (handbooks for princes) and the way in which Machiavelli disconcerts, subverts, and in various ways departs from the expectations normal to that genre.[47] This analysis involved exploiting the margin which, in any linguistic world, divides, or one should rather insist, connects, the sayable and the unsayable.

It was precisely in this innovative, or at least a typical, deployment of linguistic conventions that we could understand what an author was doing in writing the way he or she did. Such accounts are particularly salient it might be added, to the recovery of *political* meaning since the act of polical persuasion most commonly involves the rhetorically innovative extension or restriction of conventional meanings or repertoires as the author seeks to capture or deny the commendatory force of the term or to extend or restrict the particular application of it under discussion.[48]

Although the speech act was best introduced and understood by reference to its deployment in the standard, uncontroversial exemplars – such as promising – with which Skinner lucidly illustrated his accounts, its deployment in understanding the history of political ideas was primarily in assisting analysis of the ways in

---

45. 'Meaning and Understanding', in Tully (ed.), *Meaning and Context*, pp. 63–64.
46. The theory of speech acts may be approached most easily in J. L. Austin's *How to Do Things With Words*. A more developed account is J. R. Searle's *Speech Acts*; Skinner's major statement was 'Meaning and understanding in the history of ideas', *History and Theory*, 8 (1969), reprinted with other essays by him, criticisms of his position and his 'Reply to My Critics'. [Skinner's revised and collected methodological papers have since been published in *Visions of Politics*, 3 vols. (Cambridge, Cambridge University Press, 2002); vol. I: *Regarding Method*].
47. Especially: 'Meaning and Understanding', in Tully (ed.), *Meaning and Context*, p. 48, 55, 64; 'Motives, Intentions and Interpretation', in *ibid*. pp. 76–7. On *The Prince* as subversive *see* Skinner, *Foundations of Modern Political Thought*, vol.1, p. 128 f., and less extensively in the 'Introduction' to *The Prince*, Q. Skinner and R. Price (eds), (Cambridge, Cambridge University Press, 1988).
48. For example in 'Some Problems in the Analysis of Political Thought and Action', 114 ff. Pocock broadly endorses this account, 'The Concept of a Language', p. 34. [*See also* in this volume, Chapter Three: 'Classical and Empirical Theories of Democracy'.]

which (innovatory) speech acts departed from these conventions.[49] There are thus two levels at which speech action can be identified – the conventional, and the subversive, which latter is parasitic on the existence of the conventional, and which is of course itself liable to become conventional.

One classic example of such a political speech act seeking to subvert conventional meanings for political purposes occurred in the ratification debate for the American Constitution. The period of the American Founding is one which offered great possibilities for all three forms of analysis discussed in this chapter.[50] One particular strand in that debate concerned the contested meaning of that open-textured term 'republic'. During the course of the War of Independence 'republic' had gained increasingly commendatory overtones.[51] But what exactly – apart from the absence of a monarch – was a republic? Americans were concerned that conventional political wisdom of the time – epitomised in Montesquieu – stressed that republics had to be small. The anti-federalist opponents of the new Constitution, and indeed Thomas Jefferson himself, increasingly tended to identify a 'republic' with either a direct democracy or at least a majoritarian and possibly mandated representative democracy. John Adams, whilst arguing that equality before the law defined a republic, nevertheless conceded that 'democracy' was one species of republic. The drift towards identifying the buzzword 'republic' with direct and or small-scale democracy was seized on by the anti-federalists, and posed a problem for Madison seeking to enamour his readers with the new constitution – which, it could be objected – consolidated rule at the federal rather than the state level, and which did so through relatively remote representative bodies. As anti-federalists occasionally protested, such an elected ruling class of the better sort was conventionally understood as a form of aristocracy. Madison's 'linguistic move' was to exploit the still negative connotations of 'disorderly democracy' by claiming that this was what his opponents wanted. Conceding in this way the relevance of the Aristotelian classification might have allowed the damaging conclusion that what Madison and the 'Federalist' supported was indeed an aristocracy. But in a complex yet unified linguistic move, Madison, in persuading his readers that direct 'democracy' was not a kind of republic (which must be elective) at all but an alternative to it, not only denied his opponents' claims to be republicans, but evaded the otherwise almost irresistible implication that what he was defending must be the alternative – a kind of aristocracy – an elective

---

49. That illocutionary verbs are vulnerable to this kind of subversion follows logically from the fact that they are definable in terms of rules, the criterion for the application of which cannot be exhaustively specified. This is hinted at by Searle, *Speech Acts*, p. 71.

50. For examples of Pocock's approach and Anglophone conceptual history applied here *see* J. G. A. Pocock, 'The Americanization of Virtue', ch. 5 of *The Machiavellian Moment*, and Ball and Pocock (ed.), *Conceptual Change and the Constitution*.

51. Paul Adams, 'Republicanism in political rhetoric before 1776', in *Political Science Quarterly*, LXXXV (1970).

one. The term 'aristocracy' he now reserved for what had been but one species of it – hereditary aristocracy – the commendatory overtones of 'republic' were captured for what had hitherto been designated elective aristocracy.

Skinner's insistence that speech act analysis directs our attention not only at the conventional level of speech action but to what someone is doing in claiming or arguing what they do, here pays dividends. For we can recognise that the complexity, innovation and elegance of Madison's rhetorical move is that *in* the (conventional speech act of) persuasively defining a republic as essentially representative government he, in that very same move, both saddles his opponents with the much more equivocal identity of democrats, and precludes his own party's vulnerability to the charge of aiming to establish an aristocracy.[52]

Thus Skinner could – and did – argue that not only did his method restore the priority of the true *historical* meaning of any political theory or argument, and was uniquely capable of characterising innovation and by implication historical change and process, but a general theoretical understanding was being given of what it was that made them *political*, in the sense of seeking to change, for the purposes of recommending action, some conventionally established meaning or application, and that this understanding could only be gained by situating the speech act in its synchronous context.

Comparisons and reflections

Some commentators make a virtue of sharply distinguishing between the methodological foundations of Skinner and Pocock, and indeed at one time they seemed concerned to do so themselves.[53] However, their two positions can be seen – and I think are now recognised by themselves – to merely place emphasis on different moments of an essentially unified account of political language use.[54] Pocock places the emphasis on identifying the *language* of political discourse which he has helpfully described as 'a complex structure comprising a vocabulary; a grammar, a rhetoric, a set of usages, assumptions and implications, existing together in time and employable by a semi-specific community of

---

52. For a fuller account *see* T. Ball, 'A Republic – if you can keep it' in: Ball and Pocock (eds), *Conceptual Change*, and Hampsher-Monk, 'Publius, The Federalist?', in *A History of Modern Political Thought* (Oxford, Blackwell, 1992), pp. 227–231.

53. Dario Castiglione, *Political Theory Newsletter*, 512 (1993) 89–109, esp. pp. 92–4. Pocock considers the interplay between language and speech act in 'The State of the Art' in *Virtue, Commerce and History*, esp. pp. 4–7 and ff; Skinner indicates the inadequacy of 'language' itself as the unit of analysis in 'Some Problems in the Analysis of Political Thought and Action' in Tully (ed.), *Meaning and Context*, p. 106.

54. Skinner advances the view that 'One way of describing my original [methodological] essays would be to say that I merely tried to identify and restate in more abstract terms the assumptions on which Pocock's and especially Laslett's scholarship seemed to me to be based.' 'Reply to my Critics' in Tully, *Meaning and Context*, p. 233.

language-users for *purposes* political.'[55] This, as we saw, comprises both the identity of what is being historically investigated – language is the historical subject – and a means of explaining the writings or speech of an individual actor. Skinner's focus is on the single performance of a linguistic actor, and his criticism of the explanatory power of 'language' was that mere identification of the language did not tell the historian what [speech] actions were being performed in it.[56] Nevertheless, his claims about the embeddedness of use, and hence the importance of context, genre and convention show that an understanding of the individual speech act is logically dependent on (although not guaranteed by) an understanding of the language in which it is performed. For example, to understand an English speaker's deployment of the term 'virtue' in the eighteenth century we need to know to what extent they understood themselves to be invoking (and so intended to invoke in their hearers) civic or puritan language or associations. Conversely Pocock's detailed charting of linguistic change proceeds by identifying what he has only recently started to label, but what is clearly indistinguishable from Skinner's account of the innovatory or, defensive speech acts performed by linguistic actors.[57] Consequently, despite their different philosophical starting points and emphases, Skinner and Pocock have each had to concern themselves *both* with the diachronic question of the identity of the language and its conventions over time *and* with the synchronic question of the individual locutions performed within it at any one moment. As a result Skinner – who famously once delivered an iconoclastic paper to the [UK] Political Studies Association entitled 'The Unimportance of the Great Texts' – like Pocock, is concerned with empirically identifying and according significance to the less abstract works of political theory as well as – indeed as a way of identifying – the more singular and innovative theorists, so as to create a history of political ideas of a genuinely historical character.[58] Each see the same historical commitment as grounding scepticism about the possibility of identifying for investigation purposes anything more abstract than the actual linguistic patterns and arguments which can be found *in use*. In characteristic Anglophone empiricist fashion they would reject the notion that anything as abstract as a 'concept' could be a possible subject of primary historical investigation.[59]

---

55. 'Concepts and Discourses: A difference in culture?' conference paper, in *The Meaning of Historical Terms and Concepts – New studies on Begriffsgeschichte*, H. Lehmann and M. Richter (eds), German Historical Institute Occasional Papers no. 15 (Washington DC., German Historical Institute, 1992), p. 48.

56. 'Problems in the Analysis of Political Thought and Action', *Meaning and Context*, p. 106.

57. Pocock, 'The Concept of a Language' in Pagden (ed.) *Languages of Political Theory*, p. 29 ff.

58. Skinner, *Foundations of Modern Political Thought*, p. xi.

59. Early works of Skinner are quite unequivocal about this, but later works have become less so. *See* for example 'Liberty before Liberalism', (Cambridge, Cambridge University Press, 1997), and 'The State' in T. Ball, J. Farr and R. Hanson (eds), *Political Innovation and Conceptual Change* (Cambridge, Cambridge University Press, 1989).

Comparative remarks

Neither Skinner, nor, until recently, and then only briefly and tentatively, Pocock, have addressed the *Begriffsgeschichte* enterprise directly.[60] This is particularly remarkable since each of them have addressed problems central to it.[61] However, Skinner has been outspoken (and unrepentant), in his denial that a history of concepts was a possible enterprise.[62] Although a number of writers have devoted occasional essays to a consideration of the genre, or of comparisons between it and the work of Skinner and Pocock, only Melvin Richter has engaged in the sustained championship of *Begriffsgeschichte* in the Anglophone world.[63]

I stressed at the start of this chapter that the possibility that *Begriffsgeschichte* and linguistic approaches might have ultimately different objects.[64] One way of bringing this out is to note the different routes taken in arriving at the approaches. In Germany, *Begriffsgeschichte* was conceived of as an approach to *social* history. Keith Tribe writes: '*Begriffsgeschichte* is not intended as an end in itself but rather as a means of emphasising the importance of linguistic and semantic analysis as a contribution to the practice of social and economic history.'[65] It nevertheless shares with the Anglophone theorists two concerns:

1. The 'critique of a careless transfer to the past of modern context-determined expressions ... (and) the practice of treating ideas as constants'.[66]
2. Establishing instead the 'minimal claim that the social and political conflicts of the past must be interpreted ... in terms of the mutually understood, past linguistic usages of the participating agents'.[67]

---

60. Pocock responds to Melvin Richter's characterisation of *Begriffsgeschichte* in the German Historical Institute of Washington's Occasional Paper, 15 'The Meaning of Historical Terms and concepts, new studies on *Begriffsgeschichte*', H. Lehmann and M. Richter (eds), (Washington DC., German Historical Institute, 1996).
61. Skinner, for example in an extended discussion of Raymond Williams' *Keywords* which might be described as essays in conceptual or at least lexical history, 'Language and Social Change', in *Meaning and Context*. The concerns of Pocock's 'Modes of Political and Historical Time' in *Virtue, Commerce and History*, bear a striking resemblance to those of Koselleck's essays (especially 'Modernity and the Planes of Historicity' and 'History, Histories and Formal Structures of Time') in *Futures Past*.
62. 'Reply to my critics', p. 283. [But *see* fn 59 above].
63. His *The History of Political and Social Concepts: A critical introduction* (Oxford, Oxford University Press, 1995), includes material from a number of previously published essays. One should also mention Keith Tribe's path-breaking and prescient effort in translating *Futures Past* as long ago as 1979, (Cambridge, Mass., MIT Press, 1979).
64. In a critical response to one of Richter's earlier articles, Jeremy Rayner claims that Richter is wrong to present it as an end in itself, and so a direct alternative to the 'Cambridge School', when Koselleck *et al.* themselves present it as an aid to the understanding of history more broadly understood. Rayner, 'On *Begriffsgeschichte*', *Political Theory*, 16 (3) (1988). [Now *see also Why Concepts Matter: Translating social and political thought*, M. J. Burke and M. Richter (eds), (Leiden and Boston, Brill, 2012)].
65. Translator's introduction, to Koselleck *Futures Past*, xiii.
66. Koselleck, '*Begriffsgeschichte* and Social History', *Futures Past*, p. 80.
67. *Ibid.*, p. 79.

Koselleck makes clear that whilst *Begriffsgeschichte* can offer insights into a history, the subject of which is purely theoretical, this is only a preliminary and that he is concerned with the relationship between two distinct domains, the linguistic/conceptual and the social/material: '*Begriffsgeschichte* lays claim to an autonomous sphere which exists in a relation of mutually engendered tension with social history'.[68] And he cautions us that, 'once this history of concepts is laid bare the autonomy of the discipline must not be allowed to lead to a diminution of the actual historical materiality simply because the latter is excluded for a specific section of the investigation.' His objection is that this would lead to the view that nothing could be said to have happened historically that was not conceptualised as such. Koselleck wants to use conceptual history to register 'a tension between concept and materiality'.[69] The relationship between these two spheres is elusive, but they are presented as possessing distinctive epistemological, if not ontological identities. For him extra linguistic conditions for historical occurrences include not only 'natural and material givens', but 'institutions and modes of conduct'.[70] Historiography for him involves essentially two levels – the recovery of the past as it bore meaning for the actors involved, and the application of ex-post categories (for example those of modern economics) onto historical material. *Begriffsgeschichte* not only exposes this dichotomy, but forces us to confront the resolution of it, and so write an adequate history. It is not, however, itself that adequate history.

By contrast the object of Anglophone history of political thought tends to understand conflicts in the development of political discourse and vocabulary either as an object of historical investigation in its own right or as *constitutive of political reality,* and not a factor in or relative to a reality existing independently of it.[71] Even Anglophone writers who write the history of concepts insist: 'there is a general temptation ... to understand conceptual change as a *reflection* of political change ... this temptation must be avoided at all costs'.[72] The reason for this is that they see political institutions, practices and conflict as constituted in and through the languages used by, and constructing and restricting the self-perceptions of, those who hold office, perform or compete politically; moreover political action is and can only be understood as linguistic action: commanding, negotiating, conceding, exhorting, mobilising, compromising, agreeing and all the other verbs comprising

---

68. *Ibid.,* p. 80.
69. '*Begriffsgeschichte* & social history', *Futures Past,* p. 85, 88.
70. '*Neuzeit*', *Futures Past,* p. 231.
71. Whilst Pocock tends to the former ('it is not my business to say that language is the only ultimate reality' – 'Concepts and Discourses', p. 9): Skinner tends to the latter (*see* his approving summative quotation of Charles Taylor's stress on the 'artificiality of the distinction between social reality and the language of description of that social reality'. 'Language and Social Change' in Tully (ed.), *Meaning and Context,* p. 132. However, *see also* Pocock, 'Political Ideas as Historical Events: Political philosophers as historical actors', in M. Richter (ed.), *Political Theory and Political Education* (Princeton NJ., Princeton University Press, 1980).
72. J. Farr, 'Understanding Conceptual Change Politically', in T. Ball, J. Farr and R. Hanson (eds), *Political Innovation and Conceptual Change* (Cambridge, Cambridge University Press, 1989), p. 31.

the vocabulary of political action are verbal performances. Declaring independence, no less than founding a constitution are actions not only inconceivable without language, but without, at least to me, any evident residual non-linguistic content.[73]

Some of the most exciting reinterpretive work on the French Revolution associated with the names of François Furet, Lynn Hunt and Keith Baker has insisted not only on a kind of intimate relationship between social reality and language, but on the constitutive character of the language of revolution. Inasmuch as 'social and political arrangements are linguistically constituted ... efforts to change them (or to preserve them) can never occur outside of language ... social and political changes *are* linguistic'.[74] The revolution was first and foremost a linguistic act, it was by inventing and deploying the language of revolution that the revolutionaries effected one. To understand it in this way is 'to emphasise its character as a cultural construction – a symbolic ordering of human experience – rather than as a predetermined (or, one might add, even a non-predetermined) social process'.[75] Indeed one might argue that the failure of the British radicals to effect a similar revolution is to be explained by their failure to perform the appropriate linguistic actions. They for the most part became bogged down in the interpretive question of whether they *had,* already performed the act in question in 1688, rather than devoting themselves to the business of declaring or performing it in the 1790s.[76] It is only if we can conceive of moving beyond politics to the realms of naked power, that we can move beyond the linguistic world. Yet all social power is exercised linguistically. We can indeed kill kings with swords or axes, but it is only with words that we can abolish monarchies. In this sense is the pen truly mightier than the sword, and to this extent too, linguistic reality and action cannot be seen as conceptually distinct from an independently existing political or social reality: political reality cannot be other than linguistically constituted.

A second point, concerns the different relationship which a language-focus sees between its internal parts and its own existence over time, from that suggested by Koselleck for *Begriffsgeschichte*. *Begriffsgeschichte*, he claims, seeks to establish the diachronic dimension, along and within the changes observable in particular distinct concepts, by extracting these from their synchronic contexts and then only subsequently reassembles these discrete strands in order to recreate a totality.[77]

---

73. For example, on the linguistic problem of founding as a speech act *see* Bonnie Honig, 'Declarations of Independence: Arendt and Derrida on the problem of founding a republic', *American Political Science Review*, 85 (1) (1991).

74. K. Baker, *Inventing the French Revolution* (Cambridge, Cambridge University Press, 1990), p. 9.

75. *Ibid.* p. 204.

76. Iain Hampsher-Monk, 'On Not Performing the British Revolution', paper presented to the Anglo American Conference, Historical Institute, London, 1990. [Now published 'On Not Inventing the English Revolution: The radical failure of the 1790s as linguistic non-performance' chapter 6 in Burgess and Festenstein (eds) *English Radicalism, 1550–1850* (Cambridge, Cambridge University Press, 2007).

77. '*Begriffsgeschichte* and Social History', *ibid.,* p. 82.

He claims that it is only by doing so that the tension between a social or political concept 'and its corresponding structure' or its 'extra linguistic content' can be recovered.[78] This is revealing both of the assumption that concepts in some kind of way represent or correspond to an independent social reality and that concepts not only are but must be traceable independently of the linguistic contexts in which they are deployed.[79]

Anglophones, by contrast, not only stress the linguistic constitution of political reality; they see concepts as necessarily taking their meaning from the specific patterns of discourse, or more grandly, theories within which they are deployed. Diachronic change occurs within and can only be recognised in the context of, larger units – languages, discourses. Even those Anglophone writers who have become involved in the analysis of individual concepts have characteristically insisted that 'concepts are never held or used in isolation, but in constellations which make up entire schemes or belief systems. These schemes or belief systems are theories…'.[80] Diachronic analysis on this view *must* operate primarily at the language/discourse level, and not at that of the concept, since it is only within the language that use-change can be observed.[81]

One further point relates back to the connection between the history of thought or speech and social history. The programmatic statements about *Begriffsgeschichte*, share with social history the tendency to see history as a field of impersonal processes, in which humans are almost passive vehicles. Conceptual change is a process, the locutions characteristically used to describe its dynamic are natural metaphors: 'flow, processes, phenomenon, structure',[82] rather than being driven by identifiable agents.[83]

By contrast the two Anglophone writers I have discussed – Skinner perhaps more than Pocock – see linguistic change as the actions – sometimes admittedly, incompletely comprehended – of agents, and both the questions they tend to ask, as well as the way they seek to answer them, seem to presume that explaining linguistic change involves catching a language user red-handed – in the (speech) act, as it were. To what extent history is a history of agents' acts, as opposed to

---

78. *Ibid.*, p. 82.
79. *Ibid.*, p. 80.
80. J. Farr, 'Understanding Conceptual Change Politically', in Ball, Farr and Hanson (eds), *Political Innovation and Conceptual Change*.
81. The essays in *Political Innovation and Conceptual Change* come as close to contradicting this assertion as any, but notice how the most successful of them – that by Quentin Skinner on the State, is actually an exploration of the different ways in which the word 'state' and its vernacular cognates changed meaning within a number of different renaissance and early modern political languages, it is thus more the story of a range of languages than the story of a single concept. The least successful, in my view – that of Hanson on Democracy – is so because it fails to locate the discussion of the word within any identifiable discrete language(s).
82. *Futures Past:* '*Begriffsgeschichte* and Social History, pp. 90, 86, 79; 'Representation, Event, Structure', *passim* esp. p. 115.
83. Cf. Richter, *History of Political and Social Concepts*, p. 10.

processes is a matter for dispute; and it might be a political as well as an historical issue. Skinner at least sees the recovery of agency as incompatible with the history of an idea, for what:

> ...we cannot learn from any such history is in the first place, what part, the given idea may have played in the thought of any individual thinker ... what questions the use of the expression was thought to answer, what status the idea may have had. What point ... or range of uses it may have sustained ... there is no history of the idea to be written but only a history necessarily focussed on the various agents who used the idea and their varying situations and intentions in using it.[84]

Now – particularly in recent French thought – seeing particular languages, their concepts and configuration as constitutive of the human world and history can seem to entail the denial of human agency, and to present speakers, authors and actors as determined by the language and texts which they appear to perform. This is to reproduce within the linguistic construction of reality, the determinism which pervades some kinds of material history. The stress on linguistic agency, however, makes the opposite claim, and rightly so it seems to me: for whilst men (and, as is increasingly recognised, women) do not make their history in the linguistic circumstances which they have chosen, they do nevertheless make their history. Making history involves deploying the available language(s) in innovative, creative, and agent-full ways. To wish that they could do so without language – which must always be a specific language – is to believe, with Kant's dove, that their creative flight would be less constrained without the only medium which in fact makes it possible at all.

---

84. 'Meaning and Understanding', *Meaning and Context*, pp. 55–6.

PART TWO

Chapter Three

Classical and Empirical Theories of Democracy: The Missing Historical Dimension[1]

To call a state a democracy was not always to praise it; the argument here is that an understanding of how this came about can clarify some of the issues involved in considering whether or not states are to be called democracies in the truest sense of the word. Although the methods used derive from linguistic philosophy, the purpose is to direct attention towards the values and aspirations of historical agents using the term, rather than to a purely conceptual analysis of it.

The major thrust of empirical theorists has been to demonstrate that the empirical characteristics of modern liberal-democratic states contravene the values and ideals of classical democratic theories. Berelson and others demonstrated in a series of voting studies that citizens were largely uninterested and uninvolved in politics, ill-informed on issues and irrational in their choices. It was further argued that where citizens were not apathetic, the existence of highly partisan attitudes threatened the stability of the whole democratic system. The assertion that political power, far from being in the possession of the people was competed for between elites, further undermined one of the more literal characteristics imputed to democratic polities. Instead of concluding, as they might, that modern democracies needed to embark on a major campaign of political education, or alternatively concluding that they were not, in some important sense, democracies at all, these investigators proceeded to redefine the term in accordance with the empirical evidence: 'what we call "democracy" ... does seem to operate with a relatively low level of citizen participation. Hence it is inaccurate to say that one of the necessary conditions for "democracy" is extensive citizen participation'.[2] Empirical theorists incorporated the oligarchical structures of modern society, no less than the 'functional apathy' of the individual citizen, into their revised theories of democracy. Since such features, no matter how incongruous, were found in actual democracies, it followed that such features must form a part of the meaning of 'democracy'.

Defenders of classical theories, on the other hand, argued that the presence of these incongruous features was precisely what prevented these states from being

---

1. This article is a contribution to the debate between 'empirical' and 'classical' theories of democracy. It draws attention to a hitherto neglected aspect of that debate, namely the historical process by which a word like 'democracy' gains its commendatory overtones. A short bibliography of the protagonists can be found at the end of Q. Skinner's article: 'Empirical theorists of democracy and their critics', *Political Theory*, 1 (1973), pp. 304–6.
2. R. Dahl in H. Eulau *et al.*, *Political Behaviour* (Glencoe, Free Press, 1956), p. 87.

justifiably called democracies. The empiricists were 'abandoning a whole tradition of political thinking';[3] their argument was variously presented as misleading, false, or ideological. Some analysts even claimed to expose the mechanism of the empiricists' conceptual legerdemain. Although all accept that 'rule by the people' is in some sense the core meaning of democracy, there is less agreement as to what this means in institutional terms. Empiricists, it was claimed, had used this lack of consensus to extend the denotation in order to include modern Western societies. Since to call a regime democratic is implicitly to praise, even to legitimise it, the result of this strategy was to achieve 'a conservative and apologetic effect'.[4]

However, it is not yet clear that there is anything necessarily underhand or ideological about such a move. Each side premises its argument on an assumption about the proper content of the notion of 'democracy', but since it is precisely this which is at issue the argument makes little progress. What is lacking specifically is any demonstration that there *is* a limited and legitimate way of recognising what is to count as 'rule by the people' which *has* been eroded. The problem is not that the empirical theorists have illicitly distorted the criteria for deciding when the people are ruling, but that traditional theories and usages (whatever is meant by this) have not been shown to have agreed or determinate criteria in the first place. Unfortunately, to expect classical theorists to have provided some trans-historical institutional criteria, applicable equally to their own and to modern societies is at the least unlikely, and according to some accounts of the nature of the history of ideas, impossible.[5] It seems, then, that any concentration on the purely empirical criteria that characterise democracies will be incapable of resolving the issue. There is no agreement on such criteria, and in addition such criteria as there are, must, *ex hypothesi*, relate to the specific historical conditions experienced by a past society, which may be quite foreign to ours.[6]

But there is another criterion we can invoke here. As already suggested, to use the word 'democracy' not only indicates certain, evidently rather imprecise, institutional arrangements, but also commends the political system concerned. Now, a crucial gap in the analysis offered so far is any attempt to demonstrate a link between these two functions of the word, between its 'propositional' and 'illocutionary' functions. As J. L. Austin and others have pointed out, words do more than describe; they can at the same time express a variety of judgements

---

3. G. Duncan and S. Lukes, 'The new democracy', *Political Studies*, XI (1963), pp. 156–77.
4. The most extensive claim is made by Skinner, 'Empirical theorists of democracy ...'.
5. I have in mind the more extreme versions of Skinner's own methodological claims as to the importance of intentionality as a criterion of interpretation, although he has considerably revised his position. *See* 'Meaning and understanding in the history of ideas', *History and Theory*, VIII (1969), pp. 3–53, which represents a position from which much has been conceded.
6. In classical and renaissance political thought election was considered an aristocratic device. In true democracies public positions were to be filled by lot. (Aristotle, *The Politics*, 1300b and J. G. A. Pocock, *The Machiavellian Movement* (Princeton, N. J., Princeton University Press, 1975), Ch. V and VII).

about what is described, as well as performing more complex operations.⁷ As the heat generated by the debate over democracy makes clear, the act of using the word involves both descriptive and evaluative elements. The charge made by critics of empirical theorists amounts to one of theft: they have, it is suggested, stolen the evaluative connotations of 'democracy' for a system which is not entitled to them. Such a charge requires the complainant to demonstrate a sound title to the values, on which the accusation is logically dependent. Only such a demonstration could render any move which attempts to relocate the criteria identifying 'rule by the people' vulnerable to the charge of unjustifiably and therefore ideologically appropriating the commendatory force of the word. But this in turn presupposes a demonstration that some kind of necessary link between the two speech acts performed by using the word has been violated. The nature and strength of the objection to the violation will depend on the kind of link that can be established. It is only by examining in more detail the relationship between the two points made about any political system by calling it democratic – its popular nature and the fact that one praises it – that the existence and nature of the link can be established.⁸

By way of introduction some observations must be made on that general category of 'evaluative-descriptive' words which form so much of our social vocabulary and of which 'democracy' is one. Such words are used to commend or condemn, and to that extent the criteria for their use are subjective. On the other hand there are sometimes quite rigid conditions attached to their use. How this can be so is clearly demonstrated in the account given by scholars of the emergence of the capacity for individual judgement in pre-classical Greece:

> The society reflected in the Homeric poems is one in which the most important judgements that can be made on a man concern the way in which he fulfils his allotted social function. It is because certain qualities are necessary to discharge the functions of a King or Warrior, a judge or a shepherd, that there is a use for such expressions as authoritative, courageous, just ...

> It has often been held to be an essential feature of such moral predicates that any judgements in which one is ascribed to a subject cannot follow logically as a conclusion from premises which are merely factual. But in the Homeric poems, that a man has behaved in a certain way is sufficient to entitle him to be called αρετή; When this hierarchy collapses, the question can be opened up in a more general way, of what the qualities are which we should wish to see in a man ...⁹

The new criteria for the application of moral terms does not, of course, always disintegrate to the extent that they have in the case of words such as αρετή;

---
7. J. L. Austin, *How to Do Things With Words* (Oxford, Oxford University Press, 1962), and J. R. Searle, *Speech Acts* (Cambridge, Cambridge University Press, 1969).
8. Skinner, 'Empirical theorists ...', p. 298.
9. A. C. MacIntyre, *A Short History of Ethics* (London, Routledge and Kegan Paul, 1967), p. 5.

which becomes equivalent to our 'good'. Although it is important to indicate the qualities in virtue of which we praise something, it is also important in an open society to be able to choose which judgements to make. For this purpose language commonly contains pairs of evaluative-descriptive words which enable us to evaluate differently actions which have a similar descriptive content. Thus 'brave-foolhardy', 'generous-prodigal', and 'obstinate-persevering' are pairs which evaluate similar actions according, it might be argued, to a 'chivalric' or a 'protestant' ethic.

If we accept this account of the generation of moral terminology and of the relationship between their descriptive and evaluative potential, then the relationship between the two is clearly not contingent. By calling someone a gentleman we do not simply praise him, and also indicate an arbitrarily connected style of behaviour; rather we indicate a distinctive mode of life and praise him for just that, because we endorse the social approval of the kind of behaviour embodied in the illocutionary force of the word. We can do all this at once because such behaviour used to be characteristic of certain dominant and respected groups in society whose values are, or at least were, considered worthy of emulation even by those excluded from such groups. The nobility effected a similar contribution to our moral language: 'noble' individuals no longer have to exhibit a pedigree to qualify as such but they do have to exhibit behaviour regarded as typical of thoroughbreds.

The non-contingency of the two speech acts that such words perform can be demonstrated by considering the case of the male sympathiser with the women's movement who might decide not to pick up handkerchiefs, open doors or give up seats to women on the grounds that in doing so he would insidiously reinforce their social subjection. Such action might well be praiseworthy but could hardly be called gentlemanly: it involves a rejection of the whole set of assumptions and values on which being 'gentlemanly' rests. Of course it is highly unlikely that anyone practising such actions would want to employ that term to commend them. What is important to notice is that anyone who did so would be performing an identifiably ideological redefinition of the word 'gentleman' and its cognates. Such a move would be illegitimate at least to the linguistic (and, perhaps, the social) conservative, because it attempts to use the generally commendatory force of the word as the hinge on which to swing the meaning away from one identifiable set of acts and values towards a totally different set of acts and values. Both sets of actions arguably count as 'socially praiseworthy attitudes towards women', and this makes the move conceivable. However, because there is still considerable consensus over what counts as 'gentlemanly' behaviour (even on the part of those who disagree with the values implied by it), the revision is patently objectionable. If the relationship between the descriptive and evaluative functions of the word became so tenuous that the act of praising was unspecific as to the particular values approved of, then such objection would be difficult to substantiate.

There is clearly a point in the life of such words when the presumption that they refer to specific values rather than to generalised praise or blame is lost. As in the case of αρετή they can then be applied according to completely subjective criteria of evaluation. This is not a deliberate or even a self-conscious tactic; it is a shift which may occur unnoticed and unintended, but for all that it is as irrevocable as any other change in intellectual climate. As the would-be believer, George Moore II, puts it in *Jumpers*, despondently reflecting on another equally imperceptible and irreversible shift:

> Well the tide is running his (the atheist's) way, and it is a tide which has turned only once in human history ... There is presumably a calendar date – a moment – when the onus of proof passed from the atheist to the believer, when, quite suddenly, secretly, the noes had it.[10]

We also find another phenomenon. Rather than being completely evaluative and devoid of empirical reference, where the criteria for correct application have become sufficiently vague, words may become detached from their original referent and attached to a new one.

It is interesting to reflect on the two linguistic strategies available to moral and social innovators. They might introduce a new idea explicitly by denying old and conflicting values; alternatively they might attempt to appropriate a suitably fuzzy but commended concept for the purpose. Popper finds Plato doing the latter with 'justice' and our critics find the empiricists doing the same with 'democracy'.[11]

As suggested in the previous section the word 'gentleman' does not simply praise, it praises in respect of certain specific qualities; its evaluative potential is not adequately characterised as 'performing the speech act of commending'.[12] This specificity with respect to the values invoked in praising is true of all but the most general of our evaluative vocabulary. Thus, the failure to specify the values invoked in the use of 'democracy' and their supposed relationship to the empirical criteria governing its use renders the analysis of the supposed 'ideological move' committed by empirical theorists incomplete. As already pointed out, traditional theorists cannot be expected to give trans-historical institutional criteria by which to determine correct usages of 'democracy'. However, they did give reasons for thinking that rule by the people was a good thing, and the acceptance of such reasons must be related to the change in the speech act performed by using the word 'democracy' from one of condemnation to one of commendation.

One possible way of making a charge of ideological redefinition stick would be to show that the empirical conditions now presented as embodying 'rule by the people', are incompatible with the original values which democracy was supposed to realise, especially if it could be shown that empirical theorists still claimed democracy was desirable for those same reasons. In the first case we might be entitled to consider such usage at least an extension, and possibly a perversion of historically established meaning; in the second case the usage would be incoherent

---

10. T. Stoppard, *Jumpers* (London, Faber, 1974), p. 25 [with hindsight the tide seems less irreversible].
11. K. Popper, *The Open Society and its Enemies* (London, Routledge and Keagan Paul, revised 1966), pp. 91–9.
12. Skinner, 'Empirical theorists ...', p. 298.

in that the referring and commending components of the meaning would be incompatible.

It is important to stress that democracy has only recently come to be seen as a good thing. Filmer wondered: 'Why all our modern politicians, who pretend themselves Aristotelians, should forsake their great master, and account democracy a right or perfect form of government when Aristotle brands it for a transgression, or a depraved or corrupted manner of government'.[13] Filmer's judgement of his contemporaries was ahead of his time, for not even the Levellers claimed to be democrats, although some of their opponents tried to brand them as such. Even in the next century, the best states were like the best hives:

> They were not slaves to tyranny
> Nor rul'd by wild Democracy;
> But Kings, that could not wrong, because
> Their power was circumscribed by laws.[14]

Assertors of democracy in late eighteenth-century England had to contend with polemical and eventually physical opposition.[15] This opposition was understandable in an oligarchical society but it provoked a number of justifications of democracy which appealed to the values which the implementation of 'rule by the people' in the form of manhood suffrage would supposedly realise. How otherwise, argued Cartwright,

> ... can we give the poor man such an attachment to the constitution, such a respect for the land, and such a love of his country; such a desire for public peace, and such a satisfaction of his own personal condition, as by leaving him the proud and pleasing consciousness that even he has a voice in electing the rulers of the land.[16]

John Thelwall put it more brusquely: 'If you wish people to be humanised you must restore to them the privileges of humanity'.[17] The illocutionary force of 'democracy' as a term of commendation in our language was generated by such early radicals' justifications for the implementation of what *they* understood as 'rule by the people'. Now whether such systems are in fact capable of realising the values they supposed is ultimately an empirical question. Our early democratic

---

13. Sir Robert Filmer, *Patriarcha and Other Political Works*, Peter Laslett (ed.) (Oxford, Basil Blackwell, 1949), p. 197.
14. Bernard Mandeville, *The Fable of the Bees*, F. B. Kaye (ed.), (Oxford, Oxford University Press, 1949), vol. I, p. 17.
15. The infamous 'Two Acts' (36 Geo. II c 7 and 8) extended the definition of treason and prohibited the act of associating for political discussion in an attempt to suppress the agitation of the reform societies. For an evergreen history *see* G. Stead Veitch, *The Genesis of Parliamentary Reform* (London, Constable, 1913).
16. Major J. Cartwright, *The Commonwealth in Danger* (London, 1795), p. 90.
17. J. Thelwall, *The Natural and Constitutional Rights of Britons* (London, 1795), p. 47.

theorists may have simply been wrong in thinking such a dramatic moral rebirth possible as a result of instituting universal suffrage, or their prescriptions may have been at the least incomplete. But to say that calling a political system democratic is a speech act, involves characterising that locution as an intention, and the intention of early advocates of democracy was not simply to praise systems of popular rule, but to praise them as the embodiment of certain values. If contemporary 'democratic' systems do not realise these ideals it may be that the early theorists were simply wrong in asserting a relationship between a certain institutional arrangement and certain values. We would be stuck with an historically acquired linguistic connection between the form and values of democracy which historical experience has denied. Alternatively it may be that the institutional arrangements that constitute popular rule are today so attenuated as to make the realisation of such values impossible. If this is the case there seems some justification for criticising those theorists who still claim the classical ideals for models derived empirically from contemporary states.

One example of a value which has been neglected in most accounts of contemporary democracy is participation, a characteristic widely attributed to classical models. Clearly if empirical theorists claim a high degree of apathy is compatible with, or even essential to democracy, there is something incongruous in their claiming for such systems values which are related to a high degree of citizen participation. Of course the belief that one can legislate for usage is an illusion, and whilst we might want to claim that correct usages of 'democracy' had to demonstrate entitlement to at least some of the values or qualities for which 'democracy' originally became a term of praise, the best that can be hoped for is that such analysis will at least shift the argument away from the more sterile areas of linguistic propriety and onto more substantive issues.

One of the more telling points to be made against critics of empirical and classical theories alike is that they seldom refer their criticisms to identifiable theories. Clearly the case outlined in this article depends on identifying the characteristics and claims of individual theories. This is a detailed task for which there is not scope here. A good example is the attempt made by Ryan to compare the values and institutions advocated by James Mill as against his son John Stuart Mill. However, Ryan uses the contrasted theories merely, as he puts it, 'to illustrate a wide thesis concerning two contrasting images of the nature of politics.'[18] What is suggested here is that these political paradigms can be presented as historical phenomena influencing the development and connotations of such words as 'democracy'.

Two particularly revealing and historically prominent models of political life within which the term democracy was much deployed are the economic or market model, and the developmental conception, which sees it as an intrinsically valuable human activity. The former model sees politics as essentially instrumental, a means for achieving some other non-political end. The latter sees it as an activity

---

18. A. Ryan, 'Two Concepts of Politics and Democracy' in M. Fleisher (ed.), *Machiavelli and the Nature of Politics* (New York, Atheneum, 1972), p. 76.

that is in some sense constitutive of human social life, and certainly a prerequisite of the full development of individuals' personalities.

Both these modes of political thinking have played a part in the historical development of the idea of democracy. William Godwin argued a case for democracy on these essentially developmental grounds in the last decade of the eighteenth century, when 'democracy' was no longer confined to scholars' tomes on the mixed constitution. Godwin's developmental ideal of political life rested on the unlikely foundation of the sensationalist psychology of the eighteenth century. In common with writers of that school he argued that 'everything within (man) that has a tendency to voluntary action, is an affair of external or internal sense, and has relation to pleasure or pain'. Godwin also held the more extreme Hobbesian position that, at least in origin, all our actions are determined by our desire to avoid our own pain, and maximise our own pleasure. Godwin avoids the extreme egotism that would seem to follow from this by arguing that the intellect's ability to abstract from the particular to the general affects not only the thinking but the sensing mind, and this enables the cultivated individual to be moved by utilitarian considerations of the *total* pleasures and pains resulting from his action, rather than only by his own: 'That which gives the last zest to our enjoyments, is the approbation of our own minds, the consciousness that the exertion we have made, was such as was called for by impartial justice and reason.'[19]

For Godwin the intellectual pleasures that result from knowing that our act increases the sum of pleasures in the world becomes the motive force of the developed human being, and the generalising capacity of the mind is what enables it to escape the determining force of our own particular physical experiences. Godwin thus attempts a highly rationalist explanation of the move from individual hedonism to utilitarianism as a principle of action. But it is only when the individual has arrived at his convictions through the exercise of his own understanding that they are effective and reliable guides to his behaviour. This is where Godwin perceives the effect of a class divided society. Deference prevents the exercise of individual judgement, and class (and indeed national and cultural) divisions prevent us from allowing full rein to our capacity to abstract from our own particular situation and consider the needs of others as equal to our own. The evil of monarchical and aristocratic societies is essentially that in them 'The basis of all morality, the recollection that other men are beings of the same order as himself is extirpated.' The argument that men are imperfect and imperfectible beings is itself the product of a radically deformed society: 'In the estimate that is usually made of democracy one of the sources of our erroneous judgement, lies in our taking mankind such as monarchy and aristocracy have made them ... (These) ... would be no evils, if their tendency were not to undermine the virtues and understanding of their subjects.'[20]

---

19. W. Godwin, *Enquiry Concerning Political Justice*, F. E. L. Priestley (ed.), (Toronto, Toronto University Press, 1946), vol. I, pp. 75–6.

20. Godwin, *Enquiry*, II, p. 16; p. 119.

The progressive improvement of mankind can take place only through individual criticism and reflection resulting in the dispersal of ignorance, deference and unthinking adherence to traditional patterns of behaviour. Theories of human nature which place emphasis on the historically acquired 'prejudices' so beloved by Burke, or on any purely causal account of behaviour, are themselves a part of the evil apparatus that prevents men from realising their true natures. Nothing can be done until we 'consider the human mind as an intelligent agent, guided by motives and precepts presented to the understanding, and not by causes which have no proper cognisance and can form no calculation.' Democracy is for Godwin both a precondition for the full flowering of these conditions as well as a political system which embodies them.

> Democracy restores to man a consciousness of his values, teaches him, by the removal of authority and oppression, to listen only to the suggestions of reason, gives him confidence to treat all other men with frankness and simplicity, and induces him to regard them no longer as enemies against whom to be on his guard, but as brethren whom it behoves him to assist.[21]

Such a picture of the relationship between a human agent and his social environment is obviously behind what a lot of writers want to claim as essentially 'democratic' values, such as Benn and Peters' claim that the effect of democracy is to 'moralise politics'.[22] It lies behind criticisms that empirical theories 'have fundamentally changed the normative significance of democracy', that classical theories were 'concerned above all else with human development, the opportunities which existed in political activity to realise the untapped potentials of men and to create the foundations of a genuinely human community'.[23] Clearly such theories as those put forward by Godwin appeal to such values; furthermore, although this is a matter for historical demonstration, views such as Godwin's were influential in the change that occurred in the connotations of the word 'democracy'.[24]

However, even if it can be demonstrated that such a 'developmental' conception of man and politics attached itself at an early stage to connotations of 'democracy' and rendered them commendatory, there are still two arguments open to empirical theorists. One is that they are not claiming these particular values for

---

21. Godwin, *Enquiry*, I, p. 5; III, p. 140; I, p. 44; II, p. 119.
22. S. Benn and R. S. Peters, *Social Principles and the Democratic State* (London, Allen and Unwin, 1959), p. 352.
23. J. L. Walker, 'A critique of the elitist theory of democracy' *American Political Science Review*, LX (1966), 28, p. 288.
24. Such a demonstration is of course beyond the scope of this paper but it is important to recognise the scope of Godwin's influence at the time. 'Tom Paine was considered for the time as a Tom Fool to him, Paley an old woman, Edmund Burke a flashy sophist.' (William Hazlitt, *The Spirit of the Age* (London, Dent, 1969), p. 36.) The high price of Political Justice, did not, as Pitt had confidently predicted, render its influence on the lower classes negligible (he had denied it was possible for a book costing as much as three guineas to be seditious!) Working men's clubs subscribed to buy the expensive volumes and organised readings were held.

the systems they describe and praise. As noted above it is not always clear exactly what values are being claimed for systems praised as democratic, a point made by Dahl in the course of his exchange with Walker: 'I do not share Professor Walker's confidence that he can divine the implicit or explicit normative assumptions of the writers he has tried to summarise'.[25] Yet implicit in most of Dahl's own work, and occasionally explicit, is a strong revisionist ethic which seems to justify the fears of the fundamentalists whilst recognising that some fundamental value shift is taking place: 'Attractive as such ideals as equality are, to continue to demand that they be fulfilled in the conditions of modern society only leads to cynicism about democracy itself'.[26] Yet perhaps Dahl himself, in making the revision explicit, is conceding too much. For there is another democratic tradition, almost as old, but with an equal claim to historical influence and which shows much more congruence with empirical theories of democracy: that of radical utilitarianism. Here politics is valued not for itself, but as an instrument in the pursuit of other goods, mainly economic, which it can safeguard. James Mill's *Essay on Government* is the clearest exposition of the extreme version of this view which sees popular rule, not as valuable in itself, but as the only way to evaluate the demand for and ensure the production of such goods. The value of democracy is not intrinsic to the activity of politics itself, but only as a means; indeed political activity is itself a cost incurred in the course of such efforts.

Mill's view in the *Essay* is that the desirable goods of life are produced by the undesirable expenditure of labour. Men are assumed to be selfish, and the political order exists to ensure that rewards are distributed equitably. The assumption of egoism extends also to governors, and consequently the only form of government that can guard against exploitation is democracy. Since time spent on politics is considered a cost, a distraction from intrinsically valuable activity, some method must be found of minimising the amount of political activity in a community. Representative government provides a general answer to this difficulty, the problem being to find the optimum point beyond which increased political activity imposes greater costs than it prevents by checking the exploitation by rulers. Notoriously, Mill finds this point where the franchise excludes children, women, and men under forty.[27]

As emphasised, the justification for democracy here is essentially instrumental. If other political arrangements produce the same ends, it becomes at least plausible to suggest that they realise democratic values and can count as 'democracies'.

Clearly the implications of this view of politics are the cessation of all political activity when no-one feels they can marginally improve their position for any given expenditure of effort. Indeed the absence of significant political action

---

25. R. Dahl, 'Further reflections on ... *The Elitist Theory of Democracy*' *American Political Science Review*, LX (1966), pp. 296–305.
26. R. Dahl, 'Power, Pluralism and Democracy' address to the American Political Science Association, Chicago, 1964.
27. James Mill, *Essay on Government* (Indianapolis, Ind., Bobbs-Merrill, 1955), *passim*.

by minority groups has been claimed as evidence of political satisfaction. The utilitarian model is in broad outline, and in some cases in detail, similar to the economic, empirical and elite theories of democracy spawned by American and British political scientists since the war.[28] Relative judgements that we might care to make between the developmental and the instrumental models are beside the point. Both possess good *prima facie* claims to historical importance in endowing 'democracy' with its potential for commendatory illocutionary performances.

Just as there is no democratic theory, but only democratic theories, so there are democratic values rather than a single value to democracy. Particular theories generate and are congruent with particular sets of values. The champions of that snarklike creature, the Classical Theory of Democracy, which turned out to be more hydra than snark, were perhaps over-hasty in accusing the empirical theorists of 'abandoning a whole tradition of political thinking'. One major classical tradition of democratic thought has in them its true contemporary heirs. The values attached to such theories are not those that are most often claimed for 'democracy', but they are values deeply embedded in liberal society.

It is tempting to go further, and suggest that the developmental values could be shown to be more intimately connected with protagonists of democracy, whilst the more instrumental, utilitarian paradigm belonged strictly to nineteenth-century liberalism.[29] But that argument would take up another article. My point here is a fairly limited one: ultimately whether or not we endorse the values of a political system depends not on our usage of words but on our moral and political standpoint; but this should not dismay us for we surely do not want our language to do our evaluating for us.

---

28. B. Barry draws attention to this in his *Sociologists, Economists and Democracy* (London, Collier-Macmillan, 1970), pp. 9–11 and throughout.

29. As urged by C.B. Macpherson. I am grateful to an anonymous reviewer of the *British Journal of Political Science* for pointing out this aspect of my argument.

Chapter Four

Is There an English Form of Toleration?

The principle of toleration might seem at first sight to be a close relative of the principle of liberal neutrality.[1] A principle of toleration would require of rules or policies that they be neutral with respect to the different groups on which they might impinge. A tolerant state, according to this view, would not only not persecute, but would not, either by design or inadvertently,[2] disadvantage any minority within its legal purview; unless of course, that minority was itself defined as a lawbreaking one. Such a qualification signals trouble ahead of a fairly obvious kind. Whilst a limited (but still desirable) dimension of toleration would be the neutral *application* of the laws with respect to different communities or identities within the state, the wider dimensions of toleration (or arguably even fairness) cannot be satisfied by mere procedural regularity in the application of rules or laws; for, if there is a law against heresy, dissenters are definitionally lawbreakers. This hardly sounds like toleration, and raises what is the more primary question of what it is that ought properly – according to an ideal of toleration – to come within the field of legislation at all.

This is a well hoed row, but I want, at least initially, to approach the toleration/neutrality question by a slightly different route. An argument for toleration gives reasons for not interfering with a person's beliefs and practices (and, implicitly, a tradition of practising toleration embodies particular degrees or ways of non-interference). Different arguments for toleration can of course be given, and it matters what the arguments are, for without arguing for the causal priority of the one over the other, arguments and practices are related to one another. Different arguments, and, by implication, different practices produce different types and degrees of commitment to toleration. For example, it seems important to distinguish between what might be called committed toleration as the enactment of an intrinsically valued principle of neutral respect (even where limited in scope), and instrumental toleration as the (perhaps grudging and provisional) putting-up with (even a wide variety of) actions regarded as wrong or even evil in themselves.[3] These two conceptions of toleration mark out very different

---

1. The relationship is explored by A. Weale in his 'Toleration, Individual Differences and Respect for Persons' in J. Horton and S. Mendus (eds) *Aspects of Toleration* (London, Methuen, 1985), and some of the works cited there.
2. These two conditions are logically separate and entail different policies, *see* the discussion in Weale '... Respect for Persons', p. 26–8.
3. Roughly in line, B. Crick, 'Toleration and tolerance in theory and practice' in *Government and Opposition 6* (1971). Reprinted in his *Political Theory and Practice* (Harmondsworth, Penguin Press, 1969). *See also* Tom Paine's famous observation, fn 16, in following section.

practices and different forms of political society. The prevalence within a society (and, by extension, within a society's history) of particular kinds of justifications for toleration characteristically reveal toleration not as a neutrality principle abstracted from culture, but as peculiar to and integral to a culture. My argument is in two parts.

The first is historical and seeks to specify the practice and kinds of arguments advanced for toleration in early modern England when the question was very much a lively and contested one. Such arguments, it needs to be emphasised, were elaborated virtually exclusively to deal with those individuals within the national Christian community (or who had lapsed from it). Those who were clearly outside the national community were not subject to the same discipline, or even laws. Separate churches were licensed to foreign resident (Protestant) Christian communities without any of the concern shown about separatist domestic congregations, although there was some nervousness about naturalised English-speaking immigrant descendants continuing to worship separately. With the exception of the occasional flurry of millenarian interest in converting the Jews, there was, once they were officially re-admitted under Cromwell, no question of interfering in Jewish religious practices (although there was, from time to time, considerable concern about their commercial ones).[4] 'Mohammedans' were an essentially academic issue in the early modern period.

The second part of the argument looks at the structure of contemporary, and supposedly secularised 'toleration issues' in the light of this, suggesting parallels between them and the structure of the historical arguments which suggests continuity in English ideas and experiences of toleration. Finally I shall emphasise that this is not a surprising finding, and that, whilst toleration has clear logical limits, rather than pursue ideals such as universal neutrality, societies would be well advised to seek forms of toleration which offer accommodation to the actual range of cultural demands being voiced within them.

Comprehension and toleration

Returned from his Dutch exile to England in the aftermath of the Glorious Revolution of 1688, John Locke wrote back to his friend van Limborch describing the moves towards a religious settlement:

> The question of toleration has now been taken up in parliament under a twofold title, namely Comprehension and Indulgence. The former signifies extension of the boundaries of the Church with a view to including greater numbers by the removal of part of the ceremonies. The latter signifies toleration of those who

---

4. *See* D. S. Katz, 'The Jews of England and 1688', in O. P. Grell, J. Israel and N. Tyacke (ed.) *From Persecution to Toleration: The Glorious Revolution and religion in England* (Oxford, Clarendon Press, 1991) and the works cited there.

are either unwilling or unable to unite themselves to the Church of England on the terms offered to them.[5]

The distinction is an important one in English Church history. The establishment of Anglicanism had involved a long-term if intermittent search for a form of worship and a creed which would comprehend as many believers as possible under one Church, so that (as virtually all dissenters and orthodox alike agreed was desirable) the nation might worship together in an orderly and Godly fashion. The formula under which this solution was thought likely to be found was that of a distinction between the 'things' (i.e. forms of creed, church furniture, priestly dress, and church organisation) necessary for salvation and the *adiaphora,* or 'things indifferent': the attempted identification, on the one hand of a definitional core of Christian belief, and their distinction from, on the other, those outward forms of ceremony and worship which, although they might be matters of aesthetic or communal preference, were not in themselves of vital theological significance.

Perhaps strangely to the modern reader, the hope behind the identification of 'matters indifferent' was not that of providing grounds for tolerating religious diversity, but for overcoming it.[6] For against a shared, background assumption that for a national community to share a single form of worship was pleasing to God, the sphere of indifferency marked out an area where the ruler (God's vice regent) might legitimately impose his arbitration about chosen forms of worship without offending the undoubted claims of individual conscience.[7] The hope had been that by identifying and eliciting agreement on what was 'necessary for salvation', and what was a matter of indifferency, unity could be re-imposed.

Of course, locating the border of indifferency turned out to be what we would now call an essentially contestable issue; and as a result, the single project of unification became the dual one of comprehension supplemented by toleration to which Locke refers in his letter to Limborch. Toleration was required as a result of the failure of comprehension. The question of whether there is an English form of toleration is relevant to this origin, for it determined both the kind of arguments put forward for toleration and how much was granted.

---

5. *The Correspondence of John Locke*, 8 vols., E. S. de Beer (ed.); vol. III, letter 1120, pp. 583–4. and in *John Locke: Selected correspondence,* M. Goldie (ed.), (Oxford, Oxford University Press, 2002), p. 136. The occasion of the letter is discussed in Goldie, 'Locke, Proast and Religious Toleration' in J. Walsh, C. Haydon and S. Taylor (ed.), *The Church of England, c.1689–c.1833* (Cambridge, Cambridge University Press, 1993) p. 160, and the issues in Goldie, 'The Theory of Religious Intolerance in Restoration England' in O. P. Grell, *et al. From Persecution to Toleration*; and J. Waldron, 'Locke: Toleration and the rationality of persecution' in S. Mendus (ed.), *Justifying Toleration: Conceptual and historical perspectives* (Cambridge, Cambridge University Press, 1988).

6. As ironically argued by John Locke himself. *See* J. Locke, P. Abrams (ed.) *Two Tracts on Government* (1660), (Cambridge, Cambridge University Press, 1967), *passim,* esp. pp. 124–7, 175, 239.

7. P. Lake, *Anglicans and Puritans* (London, Unwin Hyman, 1988), pp. 197 ff; R. Hooker, *Of The Lawes of Ecclesiastical Polity* (1593–97), Bk III, (London, Everyman, 1907), esp. pp 298 ff, 326 ff.

Locke's most distinctive argument for toleration, and one which drew on a large contemporary literature of polemical debate, was not – as was Mill's later argument in the *Essay on Liberty* – an argument from moral agnosticism. Rather it was an argument about the character of religious – and by extension any other – belief.[8] Locke's central argument amounts to the observation that only true belief saves, and belief (true or otherwise) is not a matter of will. Since political coercion operates only on the will, persecution can never achieve the end it seeks:

> ... although the magistrate's opinion in religion be sound, and the way that he appoints be truly evangelical, yet if I be not thoroughly persuaded thereof in my own mind, there will be no safety for me in following it.

It is, claims Locke, a peculiarity of religious allegiance that it is only efficacious when utterly sincere:

> I may be cured of some disease by remedies that I have not faith in: but I cannot be saved by a religion that I distrust. ... Faith only and inward sincerity, are the things that procure acceptance with God.[9]

Locke's wider strategy in this argument was to substitute 'the sanctity of individual conviction' for the 'objective core of shared belief needed for salvation' as the principle determining the state's possible policy towards religious community. It was the impossibility of persecution achieving its declared end that grounded the argument for toleration.[10]

Now it has been suggested, that this is an argument which we can be invited to consider 'abstracted from the antiquity of its context and deployed in a modern

---

8. Jeremy Waldron brings out well the distinction between Locke's and Mill's arguments. *See* Waldron, 'Toleration and Rationality ...'. Locke's drew on very well-rehearsed arguments about the freedom of religious worship conducted during the restoration. On this *see* R. Ashcraft, *Revolutionary Politics and Locke's 'Two Treatises of Government'* (Princeton, Princeton University Press, 1986).

9. J. Locke, *A Letter Concerning Toleration* (1689), J. Horton and S. Mendus (eds), (London, Routledge, 1991), p. 32.

10. Cf. Albert Weale who has argued that it only makes sense to characterise a policy as one of toleration if it involves 'acceptance of differences that really matter' and where 'those who are tolerant could get their way if they chose (Weale, '...Respect for Persons', p. 18). These criteria must be modified to note that tolerance or intolerance depends on the beliefs of the potential tolerators about what is possible. In Weale's view, the intolerant policies pursued by the supporters of prohibition believed (incorrectly) that they could affect the consumption of alcohol through legislation. But even this does not seem quite right. Inasmuch as it was recognition that this belief was false, or entailed unacceptable other consequences, that led to repeal, the resulting policy was not, on Weale's account more tolerant. Since Locke's case too, ultimately rests on the inefficacy of religious coercion, the result would not either, on this view, be toleration. [I discuss further the relationship between the concept of toleration and the empirical capacities of the tolerator in 'Toleration, the Moral Will and the Justification of Liberalism' pp. 17–37 in S. Mendus and J. Horton (eds) *Toleration Identity and Difference* (Routledge, 1998).

debate about liberal theories of justice and political morality.'[11] But to accept this invitation is to avert our attention from the fact that in making the quality of individual belief central to his account of religious affiliation, Locke reveals that he has a very particular conception of religion in mind. It was a conception which the Romans, for example, found quite inexplicable, preventing as it did, its adherents from performing the normal, polite, and purely ritual acts of homage due to the gods of Rome. Arguably Locke had in mind not only to a particular religion but a particular – and quite radically Protestant – branch of that religion.[12] Religions can, and do claim all sorts of grounds for membership – including birth and formal participation in rites. 'Faith and inward sincerity' is – to many – a familiar, but for all that no less parochial and local ground.

Moreover, even accepting the ultimate importance of sincere faith has (notoriously) not always led Christian theologians or statesmen to read off from it a policy of toleration. The relationship between coercion and faith could still be construed as a question to be settled on the basis of competing empirical evidence about human psychology. Viewing the human body as 'a vessel containing an intellect' allowed, if it did not invite the strategy of coercing the vessel into a physical location where the right influences could be brought to bear on the intellect. St. Augustine, after all, had early come to the view that '*compellare entrare*' ('force them to come in') was a reasonable policy for schismatics, since although coercion could not indeed of itself create faith, subjection to the right theological discipline could *subsequently* lead to the requisite conviction, and so: 'Let constraint be found outside: the will is born within'.[13]

Locke's major argument, then, rested on highly contestable and culturally localised premises, both about the character of religious affiliation and about the conditions giving rise to sincere conviction: it presumed the centrality and ineluctable role of individual's autonomous wills in establishing the grounds of their faith, and in consequence, their salvation.

Even so, the claims of conscience were not capable of infinite extension. For Locke and those of his generation who shared his arguments, following one's conscience was the undoubted – and exclusive – *means* to achieving redemptive

---

11. Waldron, 'Toleration and Rationality ...' p. 98.
12. Cf. Waldron, who claims that Locke's central argument is emancipated from a particular religious background and 'devoted to considerations which proceed on a more general front and which purport to show the irrationality of intolerance and not just its uncongeniality to a particular religious point of view.' *Ibid.*, p. 63.
13. *Serrno*, 112.8, cited in R. Markus, *Saeculum, History and Society in the Theology of St Augustine* (Cambridge, Cambridge University Press, 1989) 2nd edn, p. 143. On the widespread use of Augustinian arguments to justify religious compulsion in the Restoration period *see* M. Goldie, '... theory of religious intolerence', in Grell *et al.* especially pp. 335–50. Waldron is aware that Locke's opponents used this argument (Waldron, 'Toleration and Rationality', p. 118), yet he ascribes the peculiarity and narrowness of Locke's argument to the fact that, tactically, it addresses the rationality (and by implication the interests) of persecutors, rather than the moral interests of victims.

religious faith, but although inseparable as a means to that end it was not identifiable with it, and had no intrinsic claims of its own, as individuality was to have for Mill. There was always an area – the boundaries of which shifted – outside of which claims to conscience were likely to be disbelieved, and disallowed. Antinomians – who claimed to break the sexual, moral or civil laws on grounds of conscience – got short shrift. Early moderns knew that subjective conviction was no guarantee of moral or theological truth, although they had a much greater degree of certainty – if only slightly less disagreement than us – about the existence and content of such a code.

The second point to be made, which is implicit in Locke's report to Limborch, is that what *toleration* was going to mean when it was established in England, *was not neutrality at all, but the absence of persecution,* and even that only for a limited group. Non-conformist Trinitarian Protestants (that is, broadly, those who dissented on grounds of liturgy or church organisation) were to be allowed to worship under fairly restrictive conditions. Catholics and non-Trinitarians were not strictly 'within the toleration', and denying the Trinity remained technically an offence throughout the century – that is, arians, socinians and unitarians (who denied the divinity, eternal pre-existence, or distinct identity of Christ) could be – and were – persecuted under the law.[14]

Moreover toleration was a matter of degree. At least in matters of religion we now tend to think of a state as either being tolerant or not. But it is important to recognise the range of possibilities available to and practised in early modern states. Political rulers might or might not require – under threat of punishment – a suspected dissenter to give a satisfactory statement of their personal religious belief, or it might ignore privately held beliefs and render punishable only the public expression of unorthodox belief; it might or might not grant to dissenters the privilege of public or collective worship; again, whilst not criminalising unorthodox beliefs or practices, the state might nevertheless impose certain legal or political disqualifications on those exercising them. Catholics in Ireland for example were not legally entitled to practise in the professions or to inherit land (the latter not invariably enforced), non-communicants of the state church in Britain were debarred from holding elective office. All these positions formed a spectrum which ranged from well within what we would today call persecution to not quite reaching what we would today call toleration. Even in our modern 'tolerant' England there are still two offices constitutionally denied to Catholics – the Monarchy and the monarch's consort.[15]

---

14. The old Canon Law offences lapsed with the abolition of the lay jurisdiction of church courts in 1640. An Act of William III made denial of the tenets of Christianity a crime and a common law offence of blasphemy was recognised in a seminal judgement by Sir Mathew Hale in Taylor's case of 1676, which emphasised the secular and consequential grounds of the crime: 'to say religion is a cheat is to dissolve all those obligations whereby civil societies are preserved ...', Cited by Edwards in Horton and Mendus, *Aspects of Toleration*, p. 76.

15. The Succession to the Crown Act, 2013 (c. 20), has removed the latter exclusion, but not that pertaining to the Monarch – who is also head of the Church of England.

The general point is that those who could not accept the 'comprehension' were, although 'tolerated', distinctly 'outsiders'. England was a confessional state, its religion was Anglicanism.[16] Non-Anglicans could not expect the same civil rights as full members of the national church community. They were indeed to be *tolerated* – in the sense that they were not to be subject to persecution, but not being persecuted was regarded as quite consistent with their suffering disabilities. In short, in post-revolutionary England, toleration *meant* a sufferance: a differential and disadvantageous but not (except in Ireland) a systematically vindictive or suppressive treatment of those who differed.

What follows from this position fits well with the concessive status accorded to Britons' other political rights and liberties (such as they are) and with the deferential character often ascribed to English political culture. Non-conformists were expected to be grateful for the 'indulgence' they received, they were not expected to make demands, cause a fuss, set themselves up as equals of the orthodox. Their being tolerated was *not* a [secure] right, it was an indulgence, and as such might be withdrawn. Joseph Priestley and Richard Price were quite correct in insisting – very much with disfranchised non-conformists in mind – that civil liberty was not worthy of the name without the political rights which enabled citizens to safeguard it. Tom Paine with his usual astute directness was also right in pointing out that English toleration (in this sense of 'sufferance') was 'not the *opposite* of intolerance but was the *counterfeit* of it ... The one assumes to itself the right of withholding Liberty of Conscience, the other of granting it'.[17]

Whilst the claims of conscience inherent in the Protestant Reformation were increasingly acknowledged from the seventeenth century on, they were by no means universally accepted. Casual agnostics could recant or equivocate: but that extraordinary phenomenon, the conscientious unbeliever (especially less well-connected ones) could find themselves at the stake or (in Scotland) on the end of a rope right up to the end of the century, and in prison well into the next.[18] Even today, in circles where it seems readily accepted that an individual's religious beliefs should be respected, it is far less common for convictions of religious *unbelief* to be accorded the same respect. Why should not an atheist find the intrusion of religious homilies into, say the 'Today' programme, as offensive as believers might claim to find a short daily encomium on the benefits of secular

---

16. J. C. D. Clark, *English Society 1688–1832* (Oxford, Oxford University Press, 1985).
17. T. Paine, *Rights of Man* (Harmondsworth, Penguin Press, 1984) p. 107.
18. The very existence of full atheism in early modern Britain is problematic. *See* D. Berman, *History of Atheism in Britain: From Hobbes to Russell* (London, Routledge, 1988); M. Hunter, and D. Wootton, *Atheism from the Reformation to the Enlightenment* (Oxford, Clarendon Press, 1992). However, standards were stricter than now. Rejection of the Trinity or the incarnation, or criticism of the Scriptures if open and persistent could result in prosecution. The last execution for such offences – in which Locke seems to have taken close interest – was that of Thomas Akenhead in 1697 (*see* Hunter, *Atheism*). As late as 1762, the seventy year old Peter Annet was set twice in the pillory and sentenced to a year's hard labour for asserting that the Pentateuch was an invention.

emancipation?[19] There is more than a residue in our culture of the Protestant notion that beliefs should be respected because they are a) religious and b) held as a result of positive personal conviction. Beliefs – such as those of atheists or religious traditionalists – which fulfill only one of these criteria are not accorded the same respect.

However, whilst the argument that religious affiliation was essentially a matter of belief, and as such could not be coerced, had its limitations as an argument for toleration, it – if widely held – had useful properties too. *Prescribing* that religion was a matter of inward conviction not only provided what turned out to be an (admittedly inadequate) basis for the search for comprehension within the church, it also formed the basis of an argument separating the role of the (voluntary) church from that of the state. Such an argument eventually allowed, as Locke had pointed out it would, all churches which accepted this definition of religious membership to operate freely and without interference in the realm of persuasion and preaching, whilst preventing them from doing anything which the state properly prohibited on secular grounds. Thus churches might impose spiritual penances on, or ultimately excommunicate their members, but not take away their civil goods (without their will) or impose corporal punishments (even with their consent). There were two realms for humans, the civil and the religious. Since the religious dealt with the realm of belief and personal conviction, it could not be affected by political power, which operated only on outward things; however the converse was also true: that religious pretexts could not, either, be used unilaterally to abrogate the civil protections established by the secular power. Thus no church could, under pretext of practising its religion, sacrifice infants, or engage in 'promiscuous uncleanliness' (supposing that to be the proper concern of the secular sphere). On the other hand the religious sacrifice of animals was within the law, since if a person 'may lawfully kill his calf at home, and burn any part of it that he thinks fit ... he may kill also his calf at a religious meeting'. Whether the doing so be well-pleasing to God or no *is their part to consider that do it.*[20] Churches, like other forms of association, had to obey the civil law. With the decline of the church courts this eventually became true even of the state church.

The vocabulary of toleration, one might say, grew up in the space provided by the distinction between the religious and the political, and it was largely dependent on the tolerated groups sharing [with the political powers] a conception of whereabouts in the conduct of life, that space was, for it was this which allowed agreement that the coercive order of the state could and should stay its hand with respect to religious practice in a way that granted the freedoms required. Such a policy was plausible where religious identity, defined in terms of belief and religious affiliation rested on voluntary subscription to a creed. However where religious identity required other acts, such as child sacrifice or mutilation, toleration on the grounds we have been talking about is problematic.

---

19. There is indeed some evidence that they do. *See* the letter in *The Guardian*, 10–12 January 1994.
20. Locke, *A Letter Concerning Toleration*, p. 36, (my emphasis).

Moreover it was not only some practices which transgressed the boundary of this species of toleration. Some beliefs did too. Notoriously, atheism was not defined as a belief, but as a lack of it, moreover a lack of that without which no-one could be deemed morally reliable. Since there could be no moral community with atheists, they were, literally, intolerable. Catholics too were held to subscribe to beliefs incompatible with political society. Firstly they owed allegiance to a foreign power, namely the Pope, secondly they were absolved by that power in its spiritual form, from keeping faith with Protestants, specifically including Protestant rulers, and so could never be reliable subjects. Despite the emphasis on the integrity of individual belief and the claims that toleration could be established on the basis of a distinction between it and action, it could not be denied that action was shaped by belief. Even Hobbes, who went further in this direction than most, recognised the threat that mental reservation posed to political stability. Whilst the claims of the individual conscience had a presumption in its favour for the reasons given earlier, there was another, secular consideration, namely that when the claims of religion – in belief or practice – threatened the integrity of society then the magistrate was bound to intervene. And although Locke thought it unlikely that any 'sect can easily arrive to such a degree of madness, as that it should think fit to teach, for doctrines of religion, such things as manifestly undermine the foundations of society' he knew some that did, and they were rightly not to be tolerated.[21]

Contemporary echoes

If there is a specifically 'English' tradition of toleration surely this is it. English 'toleration' was firstly based on a reluctant acceptance of the claims of the individual's conscience, and secondly it occupied the space between outright persecution and the shared equality of religious insiders. It was quite compatible with the imposition of 'disabilities'. It was not a notion of neutrality, or true equality for those of different viewpoints, but one which whilst it condescendingly allowed space for dissenters from the mainstream, maintained, by that very condescension, the distinction between the 'orthodox' and the 'heterodox' to whom it gave shelter. It was – certainly initially – an assimilationist view, in the sense, firstly that there was no real acceptance of the moral authority of the minority view, and secondly there was an assumption – as there was by earlier Christian advocates of toleration such as Erasmus – that over time dissent would disappear and be re-incorporated into the orthodox.

Such a history of toleration at the very least provides a repertoire of experience on which contemporary theory and practice – and maybe prejudice too – can draw. John Rawls – speaking from a culture which inherited an intensified version of the Protestant ideas set out above – not only takes religious liberty to be 'settled ...

---

21. Locke, *A Letter Concerning Toleration*, p. 45.

one of the fixed points in our considered judgements of justice' but characterised his whole enterprise in *A Theory of Justice* as being to 'generalise the principle of religious toleration to a social form'.[22] Although, for Rawls, this was a programme for his theoretical exploration, it could be read as descriptive of that historical evolution which has most structured our present and which is highly suggestive of cultural continuities between the formative period of the modern state and current practices and attitudes. For example, the peculiar combination of social conformity and personal eccentricity so remarked on as an English characteristic seems to be a secular echo of the Anglican insistence on outward conformity in things which it nevertheless recognised were essentially a matter of indifference. If sport has replaced religion as the opiate of the people, is it too fanciful to perceive, in Norman Tebbit's infamous 'cricket test' an echo of the fear of Catholics 'allegiance to foreign princes'?[23]

The vastness of America allowed separate religious communities the space for independent existence. Thus toleration in America allowed a wider variation *of* religious communities, whilst sheltering more intolerance *within* them, resulting in Tocqueville's [observation of the] well known paradox of greater cultural diversity with more personal conformity. Whilst England, without the luxury of space, permitted a narrower range of toleration, it did so within less heterogeneous communities, whilst allowing greater tolerance of nonconformity between proximate individuals.

Is there any structural similarity in the relationship between the modern realms of 'the personal' and 'the public' and that which obtained between the church and the state? Just as the state came to see that it could not coerce belief, but could, 'for order's sake' impose in the area of indifferency forms of religious worship which many would not have chosen, so in the modem secular world, public authority operates with an assumption that citizen's dearest private beliefs and practices cannot, or may not be coerced, nevertheless for the sake of secular order certain (putatively neutral) rules may be imposed in an area where they cannot possibly cause offence. Yet it may be that the search for secular 'matters indifferent' may prove as elusive as did the search for their religious analogue.

Any workable [religious] toleration depends on all groups sharing roughly the same boundary between political and religious community;[24] the workability

---

22. J. Rawls, *A Theory of Justice* (Oxford, Oxford University Press, 1971), p. 206.

23. In 1990, the conservative cabinet minister, Norman, now Lord, Tebbit, had proposed, as a test of civic identity amongst English citizens of immigrant background, the 'cricket test' – i.e. which team would they support in a test match between England and the side representing their country of origin? He subsequently claimed that failure to support England rendered people 'dangerous', and the application of it could have pre-empted terrorist attacks of 2007.

24. As Jeremy Waldron put it at the time: 'To appeal to another for toleration is to invoke some value we both share. But we cannot make that plea if we have no interests in common, or if all our interests are coloured differently by our rival faiths and outlooks. If someone is convinced that life is not worth living, truth not worth seeking, or freedom not worth exercising in the company of the infidel, there is no foothold for arguing.' (J. Waldron, 'Rushdie and Religion', in his *Liberal Rights* (Cambridge, Cambridge University Press, 1993), p. 137.

of the English tradition depended, roughly, on that boundary being defined in terms of a distinction between inner belief and outward actions. Where religious affiliation involves, especially in infancy, an act constituting the invasion of the individuals' physical integrity – ritual scarring or male or female circumcision – or requires at any time of life, acts which are reckless of (other) individuals' health – refusal to allow life-saving medical treatment for example – the state's capacity to protect the natural individual is called into question, and an important boundary is breached. Where religious affiliation is claimed (as it is by some religions) to be involuntary – based on heredity say – or voluntary but irrevocable – as was claimed for Islam by some supporters of Khomeini's incitement to murder Salman Rushdie [25] – or where the church claims a right to exercise sanctions going beyond mere exclusion, the operation of such a principle of toleration is [logically] impossible.

Nor is it only respect for the personal integrity and freedom of religious identity of the individual that is sought. Other personal choices must be guaranteed too, so no parental coercion for marriage or other major life decisions. Moreover this is seen to entail also guaranteeing individuals access to the approved means of acquiring proper exercise of that personal freedom. This includes physical and psychological nurturing during upbringing (the state will take away children who are abused or severely deprived in the 'private' realm), and it includes state, or state-approved education (so no differentially 'domestic' education for women). More generally, with the precarious and now only sometime exception of the Church of England, religion itself is now acquiring the position previously occupied by 'dissent'. No religious or other 'private' claims are to be allowed which contravene what the state deems necessary for 'secular salvation' – and this is essentially conformity to a certain ideal of individual autonomy.[26]

The area which has been defined as indifferent is the area of the personal (family, religious affiliation – with the above exceptions) and the area of free exchanges known as the economy. Certain exchanges – especially those which might be regarded as encroaching on individual autonomy – relating to the supply and consumption of (some) mind-altering drugs, membership of personality-changing cults or associations, contracts relating to others' [and even one's own] use of one's body – prostitution, surrogacy, organ donorship, etc. cause nervousness and are liable to regulation by the state. Certain practices which

---

25. [A claim which, as I revise this, is being vigorously reasserted, and put into practice by 'Islamic State' in its treatment even of coerced converts to Islam in Syria and Northern Iraq.]

26. Between the time of starting this piece and finally revising it, John Major initiated his 'Back to basics' campaign which impugns some of the claims made here. I am, however, writing in a long time scale, against which I am confident, Major's theme is a minor eddy, rather than portending a major change in historical evolution. Indeed the confusion and embarrassment already caused by it suggests this. [The massive re-emergence of 'religious' education in the private (but still state-funded) academies proliferating amidst the dismantling of state education system shows how misplaced was my optimism at the time of composition. However the recurrent difficulties in ensuring such schools respect secular educational standards confirms the wider point].

might be – as were certain sects – regarded as harmless in small numbers, yet become harmful, and subject to regulation once they become widespread. Certain groups – whilst regarded as temporary 'resident aliens' – might – like the Jews and foreign churches of later seventeenth and eighteenth-century England – have their practices initially ignored; yet, once it becomes clear that they are naturalised and resident British citizens, attract more unwelcome official (and unofficial) attention. Certain clearly challenging principles or beliefs which might safely be ignored whilst their full implications are not drawn on in public debate, might nevertheless invoke political repression when deployed in particular ways. These latter observations reveal a pragmatic attitude towards discipline and doctrine that is very English, yet in structure also recognisably Anglican.

The range of parallels are insistent, yet, two major ones stick out. One is that a particular prescriptive conception of the individual is being used to mark the limits of what may be claimed by the personal and the private against the guarantees of the state, and indeed of what may be imposed by the state on the private. This conception of the individual bears, in a secular dimension, a striking similarity to the individual believer of the earlier debate: it is an individual whose supposed autonomy is her most striking feature. Moreover this autonomy is not only descriptive but *prescriptive*. Just as the individual of Protestant theology was an individual whose personal convictions could only come from within, he was also an individual whose convictions *ought* only to come from within. (There is a logical problem here – but it is in the history of theological argument, not in my own – the argument that the use of religious tests as a condition of admission to corporations and public office provided individuals with an incentive to allow their mundane interests to sway the claims of their conscience paradoxically came from the same non-conformist stable as Locke's argument that coercive, or 'external' forces could not affect religious belief.) Just as preserving the integrity of religious conviction required the abjuration of certain means of influencing it, so preserving an approximation of autonomy in modern individuals not only requires the state not to coerce in certain areas, but requires it to use coercion to prevent the forces of civil society – families, religious groups, cultures – from using means or devices which affect the individual's autonomy. It is a particular view of the individual which informs such prescriptions. The idea of an individual born into and embedded irrevocably in a particular sub-culture (sub – that is, in relation to the national culture), the idea of an individual whose gender prescribed certain limited life-roles, the idea of an individual with overriding obligations of obedience to parents, foreign *or* domestic clerics, to the prescriptions of particular sacred texts and so forth are increasingly antithetical to this ideal of autonomy.

In this sense one important – and implicitly generalisable – contemporary argument in favour of toleration as a general presumption is indeed a parochially secular echo of Locke's religiously parochial argument for religious toleration; but the secularised version, far from becoming universalised, repeats, at the secular level, those particularising characteristics of it.

In a characteristically elegantly-argued essay for toleration Albert Weale points to the equivocation in a conception of toleration as neutrality which he urges can only be overcome by an ideal of equal respect for individuals. His argument is that neither contractarian nor utilitarian/consequentialist arguments provide sufficient justification for toleration, but that an ideal of neutrality might, if it were itself grounded in a principle of equal respect for persons. Whilst the principle of neutrality is, he urges, an attractive one on which to rest a case for toleration, it is, in itself, systematically ambiguous in at least two senses. The first is whether the neutrality of the principle resides in the intention, or the effect, of a rule or law. The law requiring motor cyclists to wear crash helmets was not intended to discriminate against turban-wearing Sikhs, but that was its effect. The second ambiguity is as to whether neutrality requires governmental intervention or non-intervention. Does neutrality between a minority and a dominant language, for example, require governmental inactivity, or government intervention?[27] (I leave aside the deeper question of whether the existence of road signs, official forms, radio and television services *at all,* in the dominant language is not itself already intervention!). Weale's argument is that seeing neutrality itself as underpinned by a principle of equal respect for persons at least assists us in resolving such issues, even if it is not always decisive. How far it can help is not the concern here, rather what is, is the invocation of the concept of the person presumed by the principle of equal respect, which turns out to be a secularisation of our old friend the individual who determines, through their free choice, the means of their personal salvation:

> ... persons have goals and purposes in their lives that are meaningful for them ... persons are capable of reflecting upon their circumstance and act on reasons that derive from these reflections ... the goals that give meaning to people's lives are the product of their reflection, so that their goals are in part self-chosen.

In sum:

> Respect for persons ... involves the claim that persons should be allowed to act on their own conception of what is good and valuable for them, and that in so far as they are doing this they are expressing their natures as rational and reflective beings.[28]

Such a principle is surely on that would exclude certain empirical persons – who wish to accept traditional role ascriptions, or who wish to derive their conception of the good from an authoritative other – from being accorded respect.

The second parallel between the earlier and modern conception of toleration is – paradoxically – the concern with the preservation of a particular community – or a particular self-image of it. The preservation of the secular state requires both a belief in the value of secular autonomy as an ideal and the preservation of a

---

27. Weale, *Respect for Persons* ... pp. 26–7.
28. Weale, *ibid,* p. 28.

community providing the conditions which foster that ideal. Included amongst those conditions is the self-referential belief in the value of the ideal. The rise, or resurgence of beliefs and communities which threaten that value, threaten the identity of the community itself. Interestingly it is not only support for foreign clerics which provokes the threatened response. When Margaret Thatcher infamously denied the very existence of society, she was rejecting the claim that 'autonomy' (and primarily, for her purposes therefore, moral culpability) was affected by impersonal factors which might collectively be called 'society'. Early modern Britain too, even though proud of its 'toleration', subordinated that principle to the maintenance of the identity of the community. In some obvious cases – Catholics and Atheists – the reasons for the exclusion from full membership were obvious. But in times of public anxiety – the radicalism of the later eighteenth century being a good example – the threat was seen to be a good deal wider. Paradoxically, for a society which now insists on it, the threat was then seen to come from precisely the disastrous insistence of the radicals on 'extending those Ideas, which were true only in what concerns Religion, to Matters of a mere Civil Nature, and even to the Civil Government itself'.[29]

The conjunction of these two considerations – individual autonomy and the preservation of the community's identity – are perhaps not as paradoxical as they appear at first sight. Each can be seen as a response to both the depersonalising social and economic forces and the impersonal philosophical arguments which threaten the distinctive claims made for secular personality in the modern world. Each involves the maintenance of difference (and so the protection of autonomy) through the hardening of boundaries, in one case around the individual, in the other around the community which shelters the individual. As Michael Mosher has put it in reviewing the relationship between the major participants in the debate on these issues:

> ... attentive to the loss of a distinctive point of view in the demands of Rawls's theory, Nozick and Sandel fail to see the potential losses in their own. Rawls's dystopian portrait of persons ever ready to abandon prior postures is precisely a virtue to inhabitants of a market society; yet Nozick thought that conformist price-seekers were sturdy defenders of individualism. Sandel seems unconcerned about either the potential for manipulation or conformity within communities, because he is so concerned to affirm the specific perspectives of small communities.[30]

And whilst it is true this is a debate conducted by Americans, the terms in which it is conducted have widespread circulation in Britain.

---

29. J. Tucker, *A Treatise Concerning Civil Government* London, (London, 1781, reprinted New York, A. M. Kelley, Reprints of Economic Classics, 1967), p. 30.

30. M. Mosher, 'The deconstruction of moral personality in Rawls, Nozick, Sandel and Parfit', *Political Studies* 39 (2) (1991), p. 301.

Toleration: Local and historical or universalisable value?

The argument so far has suggested particular features of the English historical experience which might have informed contemporary views of toleration. However, whilst I think it important and useful to recognise these for what they are, I do not want to suggest that all arguments about toleration must be reduced to the status of pursuing historical intimations. For inasmuch as all ideas, arguments and institutions are thought, advanced and conducted within history, they have an historical origin. If that fact *per se* were either to define the range of policy options or indeed to impugn their usefulness or importance we should have no viable arguments at all, justificatory or analytic, and if that were the case we should only be able to solve our differences by coercion. At various points in the above account allusion has been made to the conditions of toleration in more general terms. Toleration requires the acceptance of differences. Acceptance can come about through a positive evaluation of diversity (as some radical liberal theorists would argue), or (as originally in the English case) through a willingness to compromise uniformity over things that matter less. But it is simply a matter of logic, quite apart from history or culture, that the more extensive the claims a set of beliefs makes on the external world and the behaviour of others, and the fewer 'matters indifferent' there are, the more difficult the achievement of toleration is likely to be. For the group to whom everything matters, toleration will be impossible, for the group to whom nothing matters, toleration is an irrelevance. But it is also (logically) true that the more extensive a set of rights or susceptibilities any system of toleration seeks to accommodate, the fewer groups will be encompassed. To extend equal toleration to groups who claim a need to be protected from 'offence' by limiting the behaviour which others see as purely self-regarding exemplifies in the particular this general proposition.[31] Between these extremes plural societies work out their schemes of the tolerable. Different societies will work out different schemes according to their needs and the relative power of the communities involved, both of which will undoubtedly change over time. Each of these historically particular products will have different logical properties in terms of the range and diversity of groups and beliefs that can be accommodated by them.

So whilst we may seek to *understand* a form of toleration in terms of its historical or cultural provenance, or indeed gain insights into the character of a society in terms of its particular history of toleration, it would be a mistake to regard either as fixed. The needs generated by a society change over time. Societies which have become more diverse may need to operate with different and enlarged conceptions of toleration from those with which they have historically operated.

---

31. The idea that one group can be intolerably offended by what others do or consume in their own private space, or at least without intruding it on the offended, has been a persistent feature of the debate. The 'Rushdie' affair was reprised in major way – both the claims to have experienced unbearable offence, and the threat of violent reprisals as a response – by the publication in the Danish Newspaper *Jyllands-Posten*, of cartoons depicting the prophet Mohammed (30 September 2005).

We do not, it is true, make our history under conditions which we chose, and we must start with the political culture we have, but we can and do, nevertheless, and within these limits, make our own history. On the other hand, although we are not prisoners of our past, the abstract universal ideal of a workable, universal, neutral form of toleration seems logically implausible. In aspiring to universality it would undoubtedly offend or impose on many within any given society in order to make provision for merely hypothetical ways of life or belief which do not actually obtain or exist within it.

Chapter Five

Political Liberty and the Concept of Citizenship in Early Modern English Political Discourse[1]

This chapter[2] draws together two bodies of literature, one in the history of political ideas, specifically in the history of the recovery of republican discourse, and one in social and political history, exploring the structure, practice and extent of early modern office-holding. In doing so it not only gestures at the recently influential German genre of conceptual history (*Begriffsgeschichte*) but respects F. W. Maitland's injunction that in considering these matters the historian should 'neglect neither English life nor Italian thought.'[3]

A distinctive claim of conceptual history is that practices, as well as discourse, periphrasis and lexical markers can demarcate and bear the historical subject, i.e. the concept, under investigation. 'Political liberty' and 'citizenship' can each be construed as lexical markers and as social practices. But the reason for treating them together is not just that both therefore offer the opportunity to examine the discourse – practice relationship but also because of the intimate ways in which their practice, meanings and lexical markers have been mutually entangled in English history.

Whilst the practices we associate with citizenship were surprisingly widespread in early modern England, the use of the word 'citizen' was highly restricted. 'Citizen' was used in a largely specific and institutionally descriptive sense and even there the preferred English locution was often 'freeman'. What both 'citizens' and 'freemen' possessed were liberties, and they possessed those liberties in consequence of membership of some institutional body.[4] One was not *presumed* free unless one possessed some such membership. One particular early-modern locution is revealing of this. Men (it was usually, but not exclusively men) were said to be free of – meaning *by virtue of* – the corporations of which they were members. By contrast, in modern usage, the locution 'free of' is used

---

1. Thanks to Quentin Skinner and to Wyger Velema for organising the two conferences at which versions of this were originally presented, and to them and conference participants, Jonathan Scott, Terence Ball, [and the referees for the CUP volumes in which it was originally published,] for their comments.
2. *In Freedom and the Construction of Europe*, Skinner and Van Gelderen (eds), 2 vols., (Cambridge, Cambridge University Press, 2013), vol. II.
3. F. W. Maitland, *Township and Borough* (Cambridge, Cambridge University Press, 1898) p. vi.
4. This is true of town corporations, and of trades or craft guilds.

to designate not what *endows* one with freedom but what it is that might have *impeded* one's enjoyment of it. In modernity, freedom has become a universal, ascriptive property of individuals, and not a contingent possession that they might or might not enjoy; there is now accordingly, no point in rehearsing how one might have come to posses it. In the countryside too, liberty was a privilege, individuals, like cities, could be free in the sense of possessing privileged exempted from otherwise universal obligations, or possessing tenures that did not involve personal service, by contrast with 'base tenures' as they came to be called.[5] In England – and perhaps in Europe generally – we have moved from a conception of freedoms as specific, institutionally defined and derived, and so contingent, to a conception of freedom as inclusive – indeed universal and, ascriptive. The conceptual history of 'freedom' I suggest, tracks that of 'citizen', in moving from being a specific and institutionally linked description to playing a universal and ascriptive role.

I proceed by taking four snapshots, one around 1600, one during the English Civil War, [a brief overview of eighteenth-century developments] and a final one of the 1790s.

Around 1600

The earliest recorded uses of the term 'citizen' in England (1314 – citizenship is a much later coinage),[6] refer, as in many European vernaculars, to the inhabitants of a city, and more especially those possessing the rights, privileges, or freedoms of the corporation of that city. Whilst the distinction between cities and towns was ecclesiastical (cities possessed Cathedrals), on a purely secular level towns too characteristically possessed a charter granting liberties or freedoms from feudal obligations, such as the right to hold a market, rights of assembly, and to benefit from educational and other foundations associated with the town. Those rights were guarded and exercised by the aldermen or burgesses appointed or elected under the charter, and although only 'freemen' of cities were technically 'citizens', in both city and town such individuals might describe themselves as 'freemen'. In all but the most oligarchic charters, a wider group of 'freemen' also enjoyed franchises, rights, and privileges – freedoms, we might say – which might include the right to stand for election; or to elect or review the acts of those who could. Such 'freemen' commonly contested their 'freedoms' with the local oligarchy. Even those below such exalted positions enjoyed *some* freedoms; for by living in a town one largely escaped the web of feudal obligations characteristically incurred by living in the manorial countryside. The existence of wide, and narrow denotations of 'citizen' – to refer to office-holders in, as well as inhabitants of urban centres – thus had some reflection in real life, and there was sense in lumping the two categories together.

---

5. For the Mediaeval background to such 'freedoms' and the argument that political liberty of action (as opposed to merely free legal status) is derived essentially from such privilege *see* A. Harding 'Political liberty in the Middle Ages' *Speculum,* 55 (1980).
6. *O. E. D.* 'citizen'.

Indeed one longstanding conceptual opposition in English was between a 'citizen' (or townsman) and a 'countryman'. A curious feature (for moderns) of this tying of citizenship to cities was that those most likely to be fully active agents of the national political community (Lords, knights of the shire or county representatives and their 40/-electors – conceptually citizens in the modern sense) were most unlikely to be lexically designated 'citizens'.

However, as indicated above, there was competition as to how to designate those who enjoyed these corporate and urban privileges. A more English way of expressing their status was to call them a 'freeman' of London, or Exeter, or wherever; and 'freeman' too had this double meaning of being entitled to hold office but also of being 'free of' the feudal nexus. There were thus, at this point, two locutions in which to express what was one undoubted meaning of the concept of citizenship – the possession of the freedoms resulting from urban or corporate membership. Our two lexical markers here overlap in designating the activity we might conceptually identify as that of a citizen but it was the term freeman that was more commonly deployed. Part of our story must be to outline how the term 'citizen' came to map onto its concept.

Twenty years ago Patrick Collinson published the seminal article: 'The Monarchical Republic of Queen Elizabeth I'. The argument, and indeed its imagery recalled Montesquieu's famous claim that in England a 'republic was disguised as a monarchy'.[7] In England, claimed Collinson, 'citizens were concealed within subjects'. Collinson thereby not only developed his predecessor, Geoffry Elton's criticism of the idea of 'Tudor Despotism', but, more germane to our concerns, questioned for some, J. G. A. Pocock's assertion that the idea of 'civic society as a ... republic of equal citizens' was 'something not to be found in England and (as yet) scarce imagined there, prior to 1642'.[8] Pocock had been a champion of the recovery of a republican narrative in the English – and British – Civil Wars, and Collinson's argument seemed to some to open up the possibility of a 'republican' vision going back sixty years, and hinted at an answer to the puzzle as to why and how full blown republican aspirations could have emerged with such celerity in the 1640s.

Collinson's initial case rested on the interpretation of two social phenomena at different ends of the social scale. The 'republic' of Elizabeth's privy councillors and MPs comprised individuals who had benefited from enough of a civic, renaissance education to imagine themselves as virtuous citizens contributing not to a realm or a kingdom but to a commonwealth – the neologism although dating from the later fifteenth century, becoming famously widespread in the sixteenth century.[9] Not only did they so conceive of themselves; they acted accordingly. In the Bond

---

7. Charles Louis de Secondat, Baron Montesquieu, *The Spirit of the Laws*, Cohler, Miller and Stone (trs and eds) (Cambridge, Cambridge University Press, 1989), V, 19, p. 70.
8. J. F. McDiarmid, *The Monarchichal Republic of Early Modern England: Essays in response to Patrick Collinson* (Aldershot, Ashgate, 2007), p. 2.
9. O. E. D. 'Commonwealth'.

of Association of 1584, they pledged themselves – by the authority 'residing in the body politic' – to exclude from the throne anyone (including an otherwise legitimate successor) who might be the beneficiary of a violent act against the Queen. Even more strikingly, a Bill introduced by Lord Burghley provided for interim rule by the Privy Council and *their* choice of successor, in the event of Elizabeth's sudden death; a move that has provoked irresistible proleptic parallels with the events of 1688.[10] Clearly, major actors at the state level conceived of themselves in civic mode, as citizens – highly aristocratic citizens it is true but as citizens nonetheless – and ones with strikingly extensive freedom of political action.[11]

Collinson's second sketch was at the other end of the social spectrum. It provided a view of the village of Swallowfield, Wiltshire, a village, like many, without gentry, where the local administration devolved fully on the common people. In such villages, countless English subjects, with very modest incomes and no knowledge of Cicero, spoke in public meetings, voted on local issues, raised and disposed of local taxes, and believed themselves to have the standing and prerogatives to do so.[12] Collinson thus pointed us to practice at two levels in Tudor society where identifiably free and 'civic' activity was going on, activity which, at least in one case, was self-consciously identified as such.

A second seminal article took up this theme: Mark Goldie's 'The Unacknowledged Republic: Office-holding in Early Modern England'.[13] Goldie massively extended the evidential base of office-holding. State office-holders were few (the Court employed only 1,200 people) and confined to a narrow elite. Yet beyond Westminster, throughout early-modern England, Goldie demonstrated how widespread office-holding was, providing examples of brick-makers, tanners, bakers and soap-boilers (a proverbially lowly occupation). At the lowest, parish, level, he estimated there were 50,000 office-holders at any one time. This, with rotation, implied that over any fifteen year period, half the adult male population would have held office. This figure is more than confirmed by detailed local studies, one of which found that one in three householders in London's Cornhill ward held office in any one year.[14] Office-holding could be seriously burdensome – records of complaints and excuses abound – but it could clearly stimulate wider political

---

10. J. Guy, *Monarchy and Counsel in the Sixteenth Century*, P. Collinson (ed.), (Cambridge, Cambridge University Press, 2002).

11. For a discussion of the way the bond of association betokens a 'radical dimension' to Elizabethan political thought *see* S. Alford, 'A Politics of Emergency in the Reign of Elizabeth I' in G. Burgess and M. Festenstein, *English Radicalism 1550–1850* (Cambridge, Cambridge University Press, 2007), esp. p. 29 ff.

12. E. Shagan, 'Two Republics: Conflicting views of participatory local government in early Tudor England', in McDiarmid (ed.), *Monarchical Republic...*, p.19.

13. M. Goldie, 'The Unacknowledged Republic: Office-holding in early modern England' in *The Politics of the Excluded*, T. Harris (ed.), (Basingstoke, Palgrave, 2001).

14. I. Archer, *Social Relations in Elizabethan London* (Cambridge, Cambridge University Press, 1991), p. 163.

reflection and engagement: Nehemiah Wellington a London puritan carpenter and freeman of the city, juryman, and churchwarden left 2,600 pages of records and reflections on the relationship between his religious and political duties and loyalties.

These two works are complemented by others[15] which have thickened our sense of the texture of civic language and sensibilities in the period, and which sometimes appeal (as Collinson was careful not to) to continuities between the civic self-image of the court elite of the 1580s and the 'country' republicanism emerging in the later 1640s. These flesh out claims of a submerged and 'unacknowledged' republic in late sixteenth and seventeenth century English culture, where the 'concept' of citizenship was collectively held as a combination of practice and literary and discursive resources.

The emergence of claims to full blown republican liberty during the English Civil War and Interregnum has always been something of an historical puzzle. Where did they come from? And how could they make headway? The answer could now be argued to lie in the neo-classsical literary culture of the English renaissance where classical Roman literature reprised its oft-performed historical role of importing a civic content under the guise of formal and stylistic models. But congruent with such elite, discursive, or literary civic awareness were the practices of a huge body of middling, and even quite lowly sorts of people. Many elements of the concept of citizenship were in place here: the practice of the self-reliant decision-making community, at both national and local level, the idea of the responsible 'citizen', the idea, and practice of specific rights, privileges and liberties pertaining to the occupancy of a particular political status.

However three differences between the discourse and the practice of officeholders stand out. Firstly the latter were often much more lowly than the idealised classical citizen, for it was at the very local level that office-holding was most widespread. Secondly, and again contrary to the secular way in which early-modern citizenship has been recovered and theorised, that most local, and widespread level was an ecclesiastical, and only secondarily a civil, unit of administration – the Parish. The final point to make about the unacknowledged and monarchical republic was its *unacknowledgedness*. Lowly office-holders – unless members of the urban corporations of cities – did not describe themselves as citizens at all.

This disconnect between the vocabulary and practice of citizenship is exposed by the difficulty early modern commentators had in applying the classical vocabulary to the prevailing practice, revealing how uncomfortably language and practice, institution and their lexical markers related at the time.

Sir Thomas Smith was ideally equipped to bridge the worlds of classical discourse and vernacular practice: a classical scholar and first Regius Professor of Civil Law at Cambridge, he was also a JP, MP and Secretary of State to both

---

15. E.g. M. Peltonen, *Classical Humanism and Republicanism in English Political Thought 1570–1640* (Cambridge, Cambridge University Press, 1995); David Norbrook, *Writing the English Republic: Poetry, rhetoric and politics 1627–1660* (Cambridge, Cambridge University Press, 1988).

Edward VI and Elizabeth. His *De Republica Anglorum*, subtitled 'A discourse on the commonwealth of England', was written in English whilst Smith was ambassador in France between 1562–5, and circulated widely in manuscript. After Smith's death it was revised and published posthumously by an unknown editor in 1583.[16] Historians have divided over how much credence to give to Smith's account.[17] But further editions were published in 1584, 89, 94, 1601, 1609, and a Latin translation published in 1610 was republished three times by mid-century. There is thus considerable evidence as to its popularity, as well as its invocation as an authority.[18] My concern here is with the way it reveals the extraordinary tensions between classical terminology and vernacular practice, and the relationship between each of these and liberty.

Smith opens by rehearsing Aristotle's tripartite classification of the 'three most simple kindes, or fashions of government': monarchy, aristocracy and democracy, accepted by 'they that have written heretofore of Common wealthes', and of 'another division of each of the three into two: good and just ... evil and unjust', with a warning that in practice these are often to be found mixed.[19] However, despite this classical opening, in which Smith shows off his Greek, the bulk of the book is concerned with the hugely gothic issue of status, and his conception of the polity and of politics is highly juridical, since the whole of books two and three are concerned with judicial structures and processes.

In several passages Smith address the concept of citizenship and its relationship to freedom. At 1.16 he considers the 'parts and persons of the commonwealth' as households and families, villages and towns, and freemen 'as subjects and citizens[20] of the commonwealth'. (These are) opposed to 'bondmen who can beare no rule nor jurisdiction over freemen (and are) but instruments and the goods and possessions of others.' However he goes on to observe that this distinction is 'not enough' for the distinction he wants to highlight is between 'them that beare office', and those 'that beare none: the first are called magistrates, the second private men'. But then, reviewing the practice of the Romans, Greeks and French, he notes that 'we in England divide our men commonly into foure sortes, gentlemen, citizens, yeomen artificers, and labourers'.[21] In his discussion of the nobility, knights and squires – who 'have the greatest charge and doings in the

---

16. Sir T. Smith, *De Republica Anglorum* (1583) Mary Dewar (ed.), (Cambridge, Cambridge University Press, 1982, repr. 2009). Smith possessed a very substantial collection of 90 volumes of Latin and Greek texts (now in Queen's College Cambridge).

17. P. Withington, 'Two Renaissances: urban political culture in post-reformation England', *Historical Journal*, 44, (2001).

18. Smith, 1982, Appendix I, 'The Printed Editions'. For Smith being invoked as an authority, *Introduction*, p. 5 ff.

19. Smith, *De Republica Anglorum*, pp. 49, 50, 52.

20. The – to civic sensibilities somewhat oxymoronic – 'subject and citizen' – is quite conventional. See the pervasive early Stuart epithet 'freeborn subject' in R. Foxley, 'John Lilburne and the citizenship of "Free-Born Englishmen"', *Historical Journal* 47, (2004), p. 851.

21. Smith, *De Republica Anglorum*, pp. 64–5.

commonwealth' – Smith continually seeks to establish parallels within the Roman social order.²² Having briefly dealt with 'Citizens and Burgesses ... as officers within the cities (and burrowes)'²³ he then turns his attention to the Yeoman. Yeomen are 'freemen borne English, (who) may dispend of his owne free lande in yerely revenue to the summe of xl. s(hillings) sterling (the qualification for the franchise in the counties).' They 'confess themselves to be no gentlemen ... and yet they have a certaine preheminence and more estimation than labourers and artificers, and commonly live welthilie.' Such upwardly mobile people, by working and trading hard, 'come to such wealth that they are able to buy the lands of unthriftie gentlemen',²⁴ send their sons to university, and leave them enough to make them gentlemen. Yeoman was 'next to gentleman' and was to be distinguished from the 'husbandmen labourers' and the 'lowest and rascall sort of people'. Slipping briefly into classical mode, Smith recalls that these yeomen were what 'Cato called the Aratores, and the *optimos* (sic) *cives in Republica*', and that Aristotle too had good things to say about this quiescent middling sort who 'tende their own businesse, come not to meddle in publike matters and judgments but when they are called, and glad when they are delivered thereof'.²⁵ However, they are the backbone of the army: English archers, and footsoldiers generally being the most successful part against the French.

Smith now seems to have reached the limit of the politically active inhabitants. The next chapter is headed 'Of the fourth sort of men which doe not rule', who are immediately identified with the Roman *proletarii*. They are labourers and artificers – tailors, shoemakers, carpenters, brickmakers and layers – but also merchants and traders who had no freehold land. Such people 'have no voice or authoritie in our common wealth, and no account is made of them but onelie to be ruled not to rule others'.²⁶ However this claim to their exclusion from ruling and being ruled by turn, the classic Aristotelian characterisation of citizenship, is curiously almost immediately contravened. For Smith continues:

> Yet they be not altogether neglected. For in cities and corporate towns, for default of yeomen, enquests and juries are impaneled of such manner of people. And in villages theyme commonly made Churchwardens, alecunners, and ... constables which office toucheth more the common wealth and at the first was not implied upon such lowe and base persons.²⁷

Despite the distinct tone of regret with which Smith reports the need for recourse to these 'mean and rascall' persons, he is quite clear that they *do hold*

---

22. Smith, *De Republica Anglorum*, pp. 17, 18.
23. *Ibid*, p. 73.
24. *Ibid*, p. 74.
25. *Ibid*, pp. 75–6.
26. *Ibid*, p. 76.
27. *Ibid*, p. 77.

office, a fact that militates against his earlier clear division between those who do and do not 'beare office' on the basis of status. Might all of these people be said to share in some sense in citizenship?

One group clearly does not; that is treated in the chapter 'Of Bondage and Bondmen'.[28] Again a classical analysis *segues* into a feudal background to modernity. Justinian's code recognises two forms of bondmen; the classical slave, taken in war, bought or born into bondage, and the emerging serf of the late classical *latifundia*, who 'appeareth in *Justinians* time … bond not to the person but to the mannor or place'. English law actually recognises both categories, but of the first Smith 'never knewe any in the realme in my time'. The influence of Christianity led men 'to have conscience to hold in captivity and such extreme bondage him whom they must acknowledge to be his brother' and so they were all manumitted; and of the second there were so few 'that it is not almost worth the speaking'.[29]

As if anticipating an objection, Smith recognises that villein or servile tenure might be said to continue this status. But 'to consider more deeply' he points out that in fact no land in England is technically held freely (allodially), since 'all lande, even that which is called most free lande, hath a bondage annexed unto to it … (and) doth bring a certain kind of servitude to the possessor. For no man holdeth land simply free in Englande; (except the King), all others holde their land in fee, that is upon a faithe or trust, and some service to be done to another …'. If such a form of tenure rendered the tenant unfree, even the lords and knights of the shire would be servile, a position he is understandably loth to concede.[30]

Smith's account maps interestingly onto the arguments used by Collinson and Goldie. His admitted facts – which agree with theirs – about the lowly status of officeholders, continually tend to disconcert the classically influenced categorical distinctions he initially makes between rulers and ruled, bond and free. Similarly the pervasively feudal character of land tenure seems to threaten to preclude the independence required to identify the classical citizen with the early modern knight or esquire. More generally he struggles to apply his classical conceptual categories to his contemporary social and political world.[31] But nowhere does he assert the *language* of citizenship or identify citizens, except as officeholders in cities: 'citizens and burgesses (are) such as not onely be free and received as officers within the cities, but also be of some substance to beare the charges.' They serve only 'in their cities' and 'in the shires (countryside) they be of none accompt, save only in the common assembly of the realm to make lawes which is called the Parliament.'[32]

---

28. Smith, *De Republica Anglorum*, Bk. 3, ch. 8.
29. *Ibid*, pp. 136, 130.
30. *Ibid*, p. 138.
31. Cf. Peltonen, *Humanism and Republicanism*, 2002, p. 87: 'Smith had no difficulties in combining monarchy and citizenship …'.
32. Smith, *De Republica Anglorum*, p. 73.

The Levellers in the English Civil War

During the English Civil War the potentialities in the concepts and the terms 'citizen' and 'liberty' were exploited to the full by a flowering of classical republican thought, paradigmatically with James Harrington, whose republican experience included not only a careful reading of Machiavelli, but military service in The Netherlands and travel in the vestigially republican landscape of Italy. Despite the excitement Harrington and others generated amongst historians of political ideas, the failure of republicanism as a practical project suggests that the concept of citizenship on classical lines, as a category applicable at the level of the national state, struck no chord. Moreover, despite the regicide, it is not clear that a story about the gradual coincidence of those two explains the emergence of interregnum republicanism. In the view of several commentators there is no pervasive concept of republican liberty or attendant active citizenship which is performing any orchestrating role in the 1640s, or even (except very marginally) in the 1650s.[33] As late as 1643, Henry Marten MP had been sent to the tower (by the House of Commons itself!) for suggesting that kings were unnecessary. The regicides did not 'use the language of civic republicanism' nor 'execute the king in order to change the constitution'.[34] The rebels evaded the constitutional question until after the act, and even then did not introduce a republican constitution, but 'merely eliminated those aspects of the old constitution against which they had turned or which had got in their way',[35] a feature of the regime distinctly if embarrassingly signalled for a while by the existence of the Rump (parliament). Moreover *real* republicans, such as Harrington, inveighed against the 'kingless rule' by a parliamentary oligarchy who appeared ignorant, or wilfully heedless, of the principles under which alone liberty and freedom might flourish. Republican or not, the regimes of the interregnum – unsurprisingly given their increasing isolation – placed little emphasis on active citizenship as an essential feature of constitutional arrangements. But then neither did Harrington, who required – even of his commons – only that they vote, and not debate.[36]

One group that did stress political activism were the Levellers. Yet it has proved difficult to cast them as writers – or actors – of a classical republican script for the English Civil War. There is scant evidence in their writings (prior to their

---

33. B. Worden, 'Milton and Marchamont Nedham' in *Milton and Republicanism*, Armitage *et al.* (ed.), (Cambridge, Cambridge University Press, 1995); J. Scott, 'The English Republican Imagination' in J. S. Morill (ed.), *Revolution and Restoration in England in the 1650s* (London, Collins and Brown, 1992). Milton and Nedham are conceded to be exceptions by Scott in his *Commonwealth Principles* (Cambridge, Cambridge University Press, 2004), pp. 233–43.

34. B. Worden, 'Republicanism, Regicide and Republic: The English experience' in *Republicanism: A shared European heritage*, Van Gelderen and Skinner (ed.), 2 vols. (Cambridge, Cambridge University Press, 2002), vol. I, p. 315.

35. Worden, 'Republicanism …', p. 317.

36. J. Harrington, *The Political Works of James Harrington*, J. G. A. Pocock (ed.), (Cambridge, Cambridge University Press, 1977), pp. 274, 336. For this view of Harrington *see* the discussion by Scott in van Gelderen and Skinner, *Republicanism*, vol. 1, pp. 71 ff.

enforced withdrawal from politics in 1649) of any awareness of renaissance or even classical sources or of the political uses to which could be put, nor in their blunt or – as in the case of whispering William Walwyn – sometimes Bunyanesque prose, of the rhetorical skills so praised and exemplified by classical republican writers.[37] Yet the Levellers unswervingly championed an impeccably republican agenda over the fifteen years of their existence. In one of their last tracts, published in the dying days of the Commonwealth they summarised their position in four strikingly phrased fundamental principles:

1. 'The government of England ought to be by Laws and not by Men' and to this end judges should not hold office at the pleasure of political rulers.
2. They asserted the constituent and continuing legislative authority of the people, and the priority of the common good as an aim of legislation: 'all lawes, levies of Monies, War and Peace, ought to be made by the peoples deputies in parliament, to be chosen by them successively at certain periods of time, and that no Council table Orders or Ordinances or Court Proclamations …' and they denied the legality of any law, regulation or authority not issuing from the legislative assembly of the people.
3. Equality before the law: 'That every man of what Quallity or Condition Place or Office whatsoer ought to be equally subject to the Laws.'
4. Citizen militia, and no mercenaries: 'the People ought to be formed into such a constant Military posture, by and under the commands of their Parliament that by their own strength they may be able to compel every man to be subject to the Laws and to defend their Country from forrainers and inforce right and Justice', since 'no government can stand without the force of arms.'[38]

Moreover, the Levellers, unlike many commonly *cited* republicans, propounded an *activist* view of citizenship: getting 'the people' involved in petitioning, subscribing and agreeing, was a major, and at times the only, strategy available to them. The construction of a free, constitutionalist and self-governing republic (with or without a chief magistrate) was not, they insisted, 'our worke only, but every man's conscience must look to itselfe, and not dream out more seasons and opportunities.'[39] It was not only at the Republic's birth that activism was required, they made it clear that, although forfeitable through delinquency (royalism) or, for some, dependency (poverty), there was at least an initial presumption that all must participate in the choosing of the legislature.

Withholding the epithet republican from the Levellers is understandable given that, however republican the practices they sought to promote, they did not do so

---

37. But for the most sustained attempt *see* S. Glover, 'The Putney Debates: popular vs elitist republicanism, *Past and Present*, 164, (1999).

38. 'The principles and maxims … of those that are commonly called Levellers'. (1659), repr. in *The Levellers*, J. R. Otteson (ed.) 5 vols., (Bristol, Thoemmes Press, 2003), vol. 5, p. 426 ff.

39. 'Agreement of the Free People of England …' (1649) in *The English Levellers,* Andrew Sharpe (ed.), (Cambridge, Cambridge University Press, 1998), pp. 168–9.

in terms of the language of classical – or any other – self-identified republicanism. Indeed it is extraordinary how they manage to conduct long reflections on the importance of self-governance in communities, of the active defence of rights, the unreliability of mercenaries and the importance of an indigenous soldiery, exemplified not only in England but in Rome, in Turkey and The Netherlands, without once reaching for the vocabulary of citizenship which they reserved for the technical sense of members or electors of a city or town corporation. So for example, 'England's new chains discovered' (1649), which was described as being 'presented ... by Lt. John Lilburne and diverse other citizens of London and the Borough of Southwark'.

Careful readings of possible counter examples reveal them not to be as such. The 'Remonstrance of many thousand citizens' (1646) addressing as it does a national complaint to parliament might be thought to imply a national conception of citizenship. But the full title is 'The remonstrance of many thousand citizens *and other freeborn people of England* ...' revealing that citizens were, for them, a discrete group amongst the freeborn, and not co-extensive with them, and nor, therefore, with the possession of liberty. In contrast to many petitions which were from citizens, country-wide petitions and agreements are from 'the people': 'many thousands, ...', 'diverse well affected people in and about the City of London'..., 'many thousands of well affected people',[40] 'the freeborn people of England'; and addressed to 'countrymen and fellow commoners'; their *Agreements of the People* were 'agreements of the free people of England'.

So although the Levellers often equated 'citizen' with 'freeman' in the technical sense to refer to a member of, or elector in, a civic corporation, they never, as far as I can find, extended the use of citizen in the way they did 'freeman' – in a rhetorically innovative and ideologically redescriptive move – to argue that *all* Englishmen were citizens. Their extension of 'freeman' was a melding together of the universality of 'freeman', in the sense that all were now freed from feudal obligations, with the specific and institutional freedoms of 'freeman' in the narrow sense of the rights acquired though corporation membership. Through such rhetoric, as Rachel Foxley shows, Lilburne made the phrase 'free-born Englishman' into a shorthand for an emerging concept of citizenship.'[41] He did not, however, attach the *word* citizen to it.

At times, indeed, they seem scrupulous in avoiding the temptation to do so. Wildman's late 'London's liberties' (1650) asserted the rights of the citizens of London to elect their officers, aldermen, lord mayor etc. When arguing from within positive law or institutions Wildman uses the term 'citizen' interchangeably with 'free-man' – a legal status. When he argues – although ultimately conceding not to press his case on these grounds – in general terms, he uses the term 'people'. Thus the aim of the petition was 'to have the ancient right of the citizens of London restored to them'; again: 'I humbly propose no other end, but to inforce the petition

---

40. W. Walwyn, 'Gold tried in the fire' (1647) in *The Levellers,* vol. 2, pp. 222, 232, 234.
41. Foxley, '... Free-Born Englishmen', p. 251.

of the free-men of this city.' But he buttressed his claim to be recovering ancient right with a more general and abstract claim based on common and natural right which informs 'the very first principles of just Government'. And here he drops the term citizen, referring instead to 'the people' – whose 'just subjection under government, ought to proceed from consent. (Office-holders) 'are but trustees for the good of the people' and 'The original of all just power under God proceeds from the people.' Before again switching back to the specific case of London – the liberties of the citizens of which 'appear more ancient than any charter of the city that's visible to us.'[42]

The Levellers were, and saw themselves as, exponents of a continuous, if always threatened, autochthonous political tradition of liberty which owed more to common law, and the freeman-villein polarity – which, with the demise of villeinage, left all free.[43] These principles, they claimed, laid them open to no charges of novelty or inconsistency, 'the same fundamentals of Government having been claimed by our Ancestors as their right, for many hundred years.'[44]

It was a freedom that they presented as pervading the physical terrain of England – to the extent, Lilburne claimed (evidently with Harrison's case in mind) that even a slave, should he set foot on English soil, would cease to be a slave. Not to be a slave was admittedly, not yet in most discourses, to be a citizen, but the Levellers insisted that being *free* – all inhabitants had a right to the political privileges that undoubtedly protected specific freedoms where they had already existed – foremost amongst which was the vote. As Rainsborough, the soldiers' representative at the extraordinarily preserved debates held in Putney Church in 1647, famously put it when asked by the bullying Ireton why non-property owners should have a vote:

> For really I think that the poorest he that is in England hath a life to live as the greatest he, and therefore ... every man that is to live under a government ought first by his own consent to put himself under that government; and I do think that the poorest man in England is not at all bound in a strict sense to that government that he has not had a voice to put himself under.[45]

This right was not merely, for the Levellers, a right of individual self-protection (although it was that). It was informed by a sense of the common (collective) good. Where they give concessions on the extent of citizenship they are worried by the strength of the power relations that might force 'some men to give their voices (votes) to their friends, landords or the richest, weighing men's merits by

---

42. J. Wildman, *London's Liberties* (1650), (repr. Exeter, 1972), pp. 4, 7, 8.
43. The Levellers demanded the 'abolition of base (i.e. insecure or service-based) tenures' (e.g. *The Foundations of Freedom or An Agreement of the People* (1648) in *Levellers*, vol. 4), the latter being the original distinction between free and villein. This suggests that although villeinage may have been strictly an empty legal category, it was in practice still a preoccupation.
44. *The Leveller* (1659) in *Levellers*, vol. 5, p. 429.
45. Sharp, *The English Levellers,* pp. 199, 103.

the pound or the acre.' So Lilburne warns people to 'be careful in their elections, to have an eye apon the publick and chuse such as have appeared most eminent and active in the Establishment of Love and Freedom'.[46]

The Levellers used the ambiguity of 'freeman' to link the undoubted sense in which, with the passing of villeinage, all were freemen, to the much more exclusive sense in which being a freeman of a corporation endowed one with certain privileges – such as political participation. Yet the seamlessness of such liberty is continually fragmented by their claims and aspirations to specific and plural freedoms, rights, liberties, privileges and immunities, leading to the suspicion that however much 'Lilburne ... remodels freedoms into a more unified conception...' nevertheless 'freedom was seen by the Levellers as a composite'.[47]

The eighteenth century

In the first part of the eighteenth century, opportunities for urban office-holding increased dramatically. The expansion in the numbers of charity boards, hospital and poor-relief trusts, educational, mutual and friendly societies of one kind and another as well as canal, turnpike and highway, pavement and street-lighting, trusts, all emerged as voluntary associations, managed by unpaid local committee members. Whilst not yet technically part of the state apparatus, they were undoubtedly civic, in the sense of relating to the management of the needs and activities of the *civitas* or city. Jonathan Barry has coined the term 'bourgeois collectivism' as a way of challenging the notion of the archetypical bourgeois as individualist and self – rather than socially-focused.[48] This work can be seen as an extension of the Goldie thesis – that it is in the *practice* of office-holding that we should look for an understanding of the concept of citizenship. Philip Withington has made the case explicitly:

> England's towns and boroughs underwent two 'renaissances' over the course of the period: a 'civic renaissance' and the better-known 'urban renaissance'. The former was fashioned in the sixteenth century; however, its legacy continued to inform political thought and practice over 150 years later. Similarly, although the latter is generally associated with 'the long eighteenth century', its attributes can be traced to at least the Elizabethan era.[49]

---

46. J. Lilburne, *Lilburne's Ghost* (1659), p. 9, and *in extenso*: I. Hampsher-Monk, 'Putney, property and Professor Macpherson', *Political Studies*, 24 (1976).
47. Foxley, '... Free-Born Englishmen', p. 857, endorsing P. Wende, '"Liberty" und "Property" in der politischen Theorie der Levellers', *Zeitschrift für Historische Forschung*, 1 (1974).
48. J. Barry, 'Bourgeois collectivism? Urban association and the middling sort' in Barry and Brooks (eds) *The Middling Sort of People: Culture, society and politics in England, 1550–1800* (Basingstoke, Palgrave, 1994).
49. Withington, 'Two Renaissances...', p. 239.

Yet the very diversity of these new opportunities must surely provoke reconsideration of their relationship to citizenship. Citizenship is a status that overrides others, in the same way as, as Aristotle states, the political association overrides other associations.[50] Citizenship is what all the members of a polity have in common with each other, indeed what gives them a common to have. Whilst the practice of office-holding in these voluntary associations looks like the kind of thing citizens *do*, and when done in pursuit of the city's increasingly divergent needs, might indeed be called 'civic', their very diversity and particularity surely militates against the equality and uniformity presupposed by the bond of citizenship. The possession of 'citizenship *skills*' that is, does not entail the possession of a shared civic *identity*. The relationship of associational skills to political freedom and citizenship itself might be thought to depend on *where* and for what purpose those skills were deployed.

Another aspect of this second urban renaissance is its tenuously *political* character. It has been described as *urban* rather than civic. With corporations becoming more oligarchic, and many towns modelling the 'urban' on the new West End of London and on Bath, urban renewal (like the arts-led renewal programmes of the late twentieth century) was not linked to any specific political traditions, or citizenship roles. Although urban renaissance occurred *within* cities, it was largely dominated by landed elites, rentiers and mobile professionals whose uneasy relationship with local citizens begins to be chronicled in the social novels of the time. Jonathan Barry writes:

> To participate, townspeople had to cast off their old civic particularism and dissociate themselves from the culture of their fellow townsfolk. Although a whole new world of association for leisure and cultural purposes developed, the associations involved were restricted to those who could afford to aspire to the values and life-styles of a refined elite.[51]

The opening up of the eighteenth century public sphere promoted associational diversity, a leisure and luxury sector, commercial opportunities, and a multiplicity of communities of concern and interest. In England, the increasing toleration of different devotional communities cut across the old parishes; and the professionalisation of the army gradually replaced the local militias and *their* associational forms subverting two important organisational dimensions of citizenship. This diversity looked congruent with the kind of modern citizen appropriate for Constant's modern liberty: fragmented and in competition with the salience of traditional offices and militating against the dominance of the individual's civic identity, which was not only a part of the classical model and meaning of citizenship, but also of an indigenous tradition of freedom attached to widespread and institutional community – but nationally articulated – office-holding.

---

50. Aristotle, *Politics*, 1252a.
51. Barry, 'Bourgeois collectivism', p. 87.

This associational diversification – much remarked on by Scottish enlightenment thinkers – ushered in a new understanding of the tension between monarchy and liberty, recognising the possibility indeed the desirability, of the free, limited and commercial monarchy. How then was one to describe its inhabitants? Adam Smith normally reserves 'citizens' for his discussion of the politically active members of classical Greece and Rome.[52] When talking of his contemporary Britain he refers to 'the people' or sometimes – I think revealingly – the collective 'the public'. But his usage is very context sensitive, sensitive that is, to his argumentative, rather than the descriptive context, and he seems happy to use 'citizen' in quasi-judicial situations. For example in talking of gradations of social condition in Britain he refers to 'particular classes of citizens'.[53] In the *Lectures on Jurisprudence* his discussion of access to citizenship compares Athens, Rome, and modern republics with England and other modern European monarchies, and the term citizen seems comfortable to him in discussing this legal position. But he uses subject and citizen interchangeably. For example in discussing 'Whether the sovereign may be guilty of crimes against the subjects' he finds himself having to discuss 'who are the subjects?' Here he immediately substitutes 'citizen' for 'subject'. He points out that in smaller countries – where citizenship entitles one to particular privileges – 'being descended from one who is a citizen' tends to be the rule. In countries of large population (such as England) '(place of) Birth determines citizenship'. There are he concludes, 'two foundations of citizenship in all countries; in the larger ones birth, in the smaller ones having one's father a citizen.' But this conclusion is as true for subjects of monarchies as for members of republican regimes.[54] And in the report of the 1766 version he concludes the same discussion of being a citizen and how one acquires citizenship with the words 'Having thus considered who are properly the 'subjects of a state'.[55] 'Citizen' carries no distinctive animus and the distinction between it and 'subject' dissolves into a civically amorphous 'member' of a state.[56]

The late eighteenth century saw a number of campaigns for parliamentary reform invoking 'liberty'.[57] One strand of this took up the claim that the rights claimed by charter in the boroughs 'should rightfully have been the perquisite of

---

52. A. Smith, *The Wealth of Nations* (1776), Campbell and Skinner (eds), 2 vols. (Oxford, Oxford University Press, 1976) vol. 2, pp. 556, 774 ff.
53. Smith, *WON,* vol. 1, p. 21.
54. Smith, *Lectures on Jurisprudence*, Meek, Raphael and Stein (eds) (Oxford, Oxford University Press, 1978) p. 306 ff.
55. Smith, *Lectures on Jurisprudence,* p. 433.
56. Other views were possible: Richard Hurd claimed that whilst 'in the more absolute monarchies of Europe, all are courtiers. In our freer monarchy all should be citizens'. Richard Hurd, Bishop of Lichfield, *Dialogues on the uses of foreign travel; considered as a part of an English gentleman's education: between Lord Shaftesbury and Mr. Locke*, (Dublin, 1764 (London, 1754)), p. 100.
57. I. R. Christie, *Wilkes, Wyvill and Reform: The Parliamentary Reform Movement in British politics, 1760–1785* (London, Macmillan, 1962), E. Black, *The Association: British extra parliamentary political organisation* (Cambridge, Mass., Harvard University Press, 1963).

every freeborn Englishman'[58] Amongst some of these the invocation of the epithet 'citizen' began to acquire a truly political character. Amongst the first to do this was historian and radical pamphleteer, Catherine Macaulay. Moreover, she glosses 'citizen' in a way that exposes how the term has cut loose from its longstanding institutional attachment: 'Citizens (that is men who have a just regard for the rights of nature, for the general happiness of the human species, and for the happiness of their countrymen in particular) ...'.[59]

The 1790s

The 1790s saw a campaign for political liberty already foreshadowed by these movements and by the religious dissenters' campaign against their legal disabilities.[60] Joseph Priestley explicitly linked religious and political liberty. Given the disabilities imposed on dissenters for their religion he argued: 'it was hardly possible that we should be other than friends to the civil liberty of our fellow citizens'. Rights more generally, Paine argued, in what we now recognise as a classic neo-Roman statement, 'could only be preserved by giving each person an equal right in the exercise of power; for to deprive a man of the right to vote reduces him to the status of a slave, since slavery consists in being subject to the will of another, and he that has not a vote in the election of representatives is in this case.' The right to vote was 'the primary right by which all other rights are protected'.[61]

Such arguments play a role in the history of the discourse in which is embedded the history of the *concept* of citizenship and its complex relationship with liberty – still at this stage being conceived of as a discrete number of rights. I have tried to point to the distinctive histories enjoyed by of the word 'citizen', political liberty, and of the concept of citizenship as embodied in institutional practice. It is only in the 1790s on the street, as it were, where theory, social history, and the word citizen finally come together as never before. However infused with the concept, Paine's *Rights of Man* barely mentions the term 'citizen'. Yet, in the political conflict within which that work was situated it comes to assume an agency of its own.

The political reform associations active in the wake of French events constituted the most focused expression of political agency from the un-enfranchised since the English Civil War. The most famous of these was the London Corresponding Society. The LCS sought constitutional and franchise reform, reviving elements of

---

58. R. Sweet, 'Freemen and independence in English borough politics c. 1770–1830', *Past and Present*, 161 (1998), p. 96.

59. C. Macaulay, *An Address to the People of England, Scotland and Ireland* ... (Bath, 1775), pp. 13–14.

60. On the 1790s see A. Goodwin, *The Friends of Liberty: The English Democratic Movement in the age of the French Revolution* (London, Hutchinson, 1976).

61. T. Paine, *First Principles of Government* (1795), in P. S. Foner (ed.), *Complete Writings of Thomas Paine*, 2 vols., (New York, Citadel Press, 1969), vol. II, p. 579.

the Leveller programme: universal (male) suffrage and annual parliaments, and a decidedly active conception of citizenship, but unlike the Levellers they explicitly linked the term 'citizen' to this programme.

The Society published addresses and appeals, records of its minutes and correspondence with other societies within and beyond the kingdom.[62] In the absence of political rights themselves and with the decline in the number of offices of political self-government in the sprawling new urban spaces, the political association enabled ordinary men, and sometimes women too, to construct for themselves a forum in which they could be free in the civic sense of practising and exhibiting political activity – and hold office. The Society's internal minutes and correspondence were conducted and recorded with a self-conscious concern for appropriate procedures that endows them with the kind of portentous self-importance of a British Trades Union Congress ca. 1980. But such formality was important in evading charges of unruliness, in matching the *gravitas* of their political masters, and most of all of in *enacting* their political maturity and earnestness. Nor was it only a formal imitation of Parliamentary (or perhaps Conventional) procedures, it was a demonstration of their capacity to replace it by supplanting a corrupt Parliament through a national convention of corresponding societies.[63]

The invocation of the term 'citizen' was the epitome of such civic self-invention. It was not immediate: early publications were addressed to 'the inhabitants of Great Britain', to 'Friends and fellow Countrymen', 'Frenchmen!' (to the National Convention), 'Fellow Countrymen!', and 'The Nation at Large'. However, towards the end of 1792, the salutation 'Citizen!' starts to figure prominently in the forms of address prescribed for the conduct of meetings, admission of members, etc. It was clearly a self-conscious programme – and not without opposition. The minutes of the General Committee record the objection of some divisions to the introduction of the word 'citizen'. In other cases more radical divisions had struck out 'Mr' or 'Sir' and replaced them by 'fellow citizen'.[64] An active civic identity was, through such vocabulary, to be inscribed on the passive subject. The Society's public addresses appeal to a shared 'duty to preserve inviolate the liberty of his fellow citizens', reminding readers that it is 'no less the right than the duty of every citizen to keep a watchful eye on the Government of his country'; and that it 'not substitute Private Interest for Public Advantage'.[65]

---

62. *London Corresponding Society, 1792–1799*, M. T. Davis (ed.), 5 vols. (London, Pickering, 2002); *Selections from the Papers of the London Corresponding Society 1792–1799*, M. Thale (ed.), (Cambridge, Cambridge University Press, 1983).

63. J. Gerald, *A Convention the Only Means of Saving us from Ruin*, (London, 1793). On the invocation of such 'conventions' *see* T. M. Parssinen, 'Association, convention and anti-parliament in British radical politics 1771–1848', *English Historical Review*, 88 (1973).

64. *LCS General Committee minutes*, Thursday 1 August, in Thale, *Selections*, p. 77.

65. *The London Corresponding Society's Addresses and Resolutions*, April 1792, in *London Corresponding Society*, vol. 1, pp. 77–8.

In the repressive atmosphere of the mid-1790s – and with the increasingly republican example of France – 'citizen' became a loaded and subversive term. By 1794 and the first treason trials of reformers following the National Convention in Edinburgh, the LCS was insistently addressing their pamphlets simply to 'Citizens!' (at the head of each paragraph).[66] Authorities and radicals alike knew that uttering the very word was a speech act of clearly political import: a brazenly subversive consciousness-raising device, but one for which radicals could scarcely be prosecuted. *The Tribune* records how the court official sent to arrest Thelwall and others for examination before the Privy Council 'flew into a rage' when they referred to each other by the title 'citizen'.[67] In the 1790s the word 'citizen' did not merely re-emerge as a distinctive way of referring to active political agency, its very use was that agency.[68]

It is not merely the meeting, associating, and agitating that is important here, but the ostentatious publication of their having done so in records minutes, proceedings and so on, which constitute effectively a new political genre – albeit one with social roots as far back as the *Spectator* itself. Their communicating the fact of their associative activity was dramaturgical – seeking to embolden and elicit similar actions and associations elsewhere – and the proliferation of corresponding societies across the country shows their success in doing so. Corresponding Societies, as well as asserting a concept of citizenship, invented a space in which to rehearse it. They aspired to insert both within the state. Although they never succeeded, in their attempt they brought together, unequivocally, and for the first time in English history, the *concept* of active citizenship as a practice and condition of liberty – ascribed extensively to members of the state and not merely to those of a town or city – and the very word *citizen* itself.

Early modern freedoms, and modern freedom

The 'citizen', or 'freeman', was originally an office-holder within a civic or occupational corporation, in virtue of which he acquired certain freedoms. But the English citizen, unlike his Aristotelian or Ciceronian counterpart, was not conceived of as entering a *realm of freedom* by virtue of their office-holding; rather the freedoms they enjoyed were *specific freedoms*, privileges, (commonly described as such), exemptions from the presumptive and widespread constraints endured by non-freemen. Further, the freedoms they possessed were those required to discharge the duties of their office. Freedom was a [circumscribed] range of discretion related to office.

---

66. *See* e.g. J. Thelwall's lecture: 'On the Moral and Political Influence of the Prospective Principle of Virtue', in his *The Tribune* (1795), reprinted in *The Politics of English Jacobinism: Writings of John Thelwall*, G. Claeys (ed.), (Pennsylvania, University of Pennsylvania Press, 1995), pp. 88 ff. where almost every paragraph begins: 'Citizens!'.

67. Thelwall, *The Tribune*, 4 April 1795.

68. Correlatively, oligarchical councils such as Liverpool's denounced re-assertions of (longstanding) right by freemen citizens as 'Jacobinical'. Sweet, 'Freemen and independence...', p. 108.

If this is right, then any temptation – which a conceptual history approach suggests – to yoke the practice-base of early modern office-holding to the presence of a discursive conception of *classical* citizenship as a realm of freedom and a definitive quality of persons – needs reining in considerably. For what office brought to the office-holder was not freedom as a quality of his person, but particular freedoms as a consequence of his role.

This brief survey suggests that a similar trajectory was described by the history of the concepts of both citizenship and liberty. The universalisation of the concept of citizenship from denoting those possessing particular roles and responsibilities in corporate bodies, to anyone (or at least any male one) seems to be paralleled by the way liberty moves from connoting particular liberties entailed by the possession of office, to connoting an abstract and universal liberty connected with an abstract and universalised concept of the person. The treatment of the early-modern claim that freedoms were 'chartered' reflected this shift. The Brady controversy between Whigs and Tories over the collective and immemorial or royal origins of representative institutions was repeated at local level; as at the national level it gave rise to ideologically charged histories – here of local corporations.[69] Tom Paine's famous rejection of chartered freedoms as exemptions from a presumed structure of subordination, was a redeployment of the ancient constitutionalist presumption, pointing out as he did that they created the subordination of the unprivileged: 'it is a perversion of terms to say, that a charter gives rights. It operates by a contrary effect, that of taking rights away. Rights are inherently in all the inhabitants; but charters … leave the right by exclusion in the hands of a few'.[70] T. B. Oldfield's influential *History of the Boroughs* agreed: since the franchise had originally extended to all householders, the 'granting' of charters purporting to create that right were 'political injuries against the whole body of boroughs unchartered, that had an equal claim …'.[71]

This presumption of universal liberty is not, however an incremental change in the *concept* of liberty, it is a gestalt-like reversal. The move is not merely to universalise the class of (initially male) persons in possession of particular liberties, but to move from liberties as a *description* of *particular* positive, legally (or customarily) defined permissions to a specific range of actions, to liberty as an *ascription* of a presumptive right of action. Whilst the concept of liberty as a legal condition – in opposition to slavery or villeinage – became, as the latter conditions ceased to exist, something universally claimed; the liberties personally enjoyed by individuals were still commonly related to specific offices or roles.

The idea that early modern liberties were office-dependent is not a particularly new one.[72] But the extent to which this constrains and limits the *concept* of liberty

---

69. Sweet, 'Freemen and Independence…', p. 105, lists many such histories.
70. Paine, *Rights of Man*, p. 242.
71. T. B. Oldfield, *An Entire and Complete History … of the Boroughs of Great Britain*, vol. 1, (London, 1792), p. 111.
72. C. Condren, *Argument and Authority in Early Modern England: The presuppositions of oaths and offices* (Cambridge, Cambridge University Press, 2006), chapter 3, *passim*.

available is not always acknowledged. It can still seem possible to conceive of early modern actors with access to a *concept* of unconstrained personal liberty, of which liberty of office can be thought of as granting, as it were, small parcels or *quanta*. Accumulating enough of these, it might be thought, could create a *plenum* of liberty in the modern sense. Such, after all, was the process by which the Emperor had acquired his.

But that this is not, at least initially, the case, is clear from the evident and interminable casuistry as to how we should understand the 'freedom' of the one individual who, it might be thought, *had* accumulated all the available parcels of liberty – namely the absolute monarch. For the distinction between Monarchy and Tyranny – retained by all but one of even the most absolutist theorists of monarchy – is surely unsustainable without a conception that freedoms – even all of them put together – are there to discharge duties and not to evade constraints. The exception, of course, is Hobbes, and it is no accident that for Hobbes, liberty is not distinctively human (in either the classical or renaissance senses) at all, and certainly not conceptually tied to the *telos* of office. Rather it is the persistence of nature into the artificial world of politics; and significantly, Hobbes's sovereign is the one individual who retains this natural liberty. If this is right, the effrontery with which Hobbes entitles Chapter XXX of Leviathan: '*Of the Office of the Sovereign Representative*', is one of his more startling rhetorical coups, quite on a par with (and not unrelated to) his rhetorical re-description of Liberty as the absence of external impediment.[73]

If office-dependent liberties were not parcels of natural freedom, how are they to be conceived? One of those who has pressed most insistently their distinctiveness has been Conal Condren. He claims that although:

> ... liberties of office could be as strenuously defended as are liberties now, ... the very terms through which liberty of office was delineated and defended takes us to a world of semantic and conceptual relationships rather alien to our own patterns of political discourse.[74]

In such a world the antonym of subordination was not liberty but licence. Not, as Hobbes might have put it, that 'licence was merely liberty misliked', but because licence was dislocated from the structures of moral purpose within which human life and liberties were to be conducted. Crucial to that alien world was the perception that liberty was not merely a (partial and specific) exemption from a structure of authority, but that it was embedded in and held by authority of one (or a body) to whom one was properly subordinate. For early moderns – even though slavery and villeinage had gone – 'No man ... (was) without office, no aspect of

---

73. I am grateful to Tim Stanton for raising Hobbes' use of the term 'office' here as a problem.

74. C. Condren, 'Liberty of office and its defence in Seventeenth Century political argument', *History of Political Thought*, 18 (1997), p. 461.

life without rule'.[75] As a result, their concept of liberty, far from being incompatible with subordination and authority, presupposed it. For whilst the liberties one enjoyed in one's office did indeed offer a degree of discretion in performing the tasks incumbent on it, the possession and scope of those liberties was established and delineated by, and could only be vindicated by, a higher authority within which that office, its purpose, and necessary discretions was nested. The pursuit of liberty beyond such scope – what Condren calls the 'Luciferic case' – was seriously licentious and anarchic.

Now it is true that in early modern England ultimately – and in some cases proximately – that higher authority was God; and failing a church that could authoritatively claim to speak in His name, an appeal to vindicate liberty could only be made in prayer, or, as Locke finally acknowledged, through the contingencies of physical resistance, which, it was hoped, would be providentially superintended. It is at this point – at the end of Locke's second *Treatise* – that we reach, *de facto*, if not quite yet *de jure*, the modern concept of liberty as the presumption in favour of self-legitimating action.

---

75. Condren, *Argument and Authority*, p. 54; quoting Edmund de Bohun, *The Justice of the Peace, His Calling: A moral essay* (1684), A2r-v.

PART THREE

Chapter Six

The Individualist Premise and the Practice of Politics[1]

> To renounce or destroy politics is to destroy the very thing which gives order to the pluralism and variety of civilised society, the thing which enables us to enjoy variety without suffering either anarchy or the tyranny of single truths, which become the desperate salvation from anarchy ...
>
> For political rule must be preceded by public order just as love must be preceded by social acquaintance and contained by social conventions. Politics and love are the only forms of constraint possible between free people. Bernard Crick, *In Defence of Politics*

In Defence of Politics was in more ways than one a profound, courageous, and prescient work. Not only did it draw together strands from many of the classic works of politics, and in a now-unfashionable way focus them on the preoccupations of contemporary political science,[2] but it offered, and its author subsequently sustained, a liberal defence of politics by a socialist, at a time when most socialist politics was about to move sharply in another direction.[3] Finally, and impressively, it adumbrated what has since become a huge intellectual growth

---

1. Earlier versions of this paper were given to the Politics Department at the University of Exeter, and at the Fabian Society Socialist Philosophy Group. I am grateful to both sets of participants for their comments. [The controversial context that prompted the original composition of the piece was the first Thatcher government's attack on collectivism and the revival of neo-classical economics].
2. Crick's favourites were stated to be Machiavelli's *Discourses*, Montesquieu's *L'Esprit des Lois*, *The Federalist*, Mill's *Representative Government*, and Toqueville's *Democracy in America*. Against the comprehensiveness of these in their treatment of political rule, he thought, of modem works only Arendt's *Origins of Totalitarianism* and Kornhauser's *The Politics of Mass Society*, could compete. B. Crick, *In Defence of Politics* (revised ed., London, Harmondsworth, 1964), p. 174.
3. A personal footnote: I remember a demonstration in 1970 against the South African rugby tour. Demonstrators were moving up the street towards a phalanx of policemen. There were those determined to turn the demonstration into a brawl, urging the crowd on, there was Bernard urging everyone to sit down in the street. Bernard managed to make his political distinctions in the street as well as in the lecture theatre.

industry: the historical study of the moral economy of the republican tradition, and the debate about the implications of that for contemporary politics.[4]

However, the conduct of that debate has often stressed differences which Crick sought to minimise. In particular, recent American concerns to utilise that tradition, seeking to distinguish between whether the founding was liberal or republican (so reminiscent of the concern shown by ideologues of free renaissance Italian cities to trace their origins to Republican rather than Imperial Rome[5]), has sought to tease apart what Crick saw as a whole, and to run together what he sought to distinguish.[6] Thus for him both the central meaning of politics – as freedom, and what he takes to be the central problem of politics – the conditions under which *political* systems can flourish and be stable, drew elements from both of what have tended to be opposed as the republican and liberal traditions.[7] The republican tradition, as it has been reconstructed, has focused on the issue of the conditions of collective stability and survival, in ways which paradigmatically conflict with liberal, individualistic concerns, in some cases – particularly as we approach Rousseau – to the exclusion of politics itself.[8] The liberal tradition,

---

4. The major work here is of course J. G. A. Pocock's, *The Machiavellian Moment* (Princeton, Princeton University Press, 1975). Andrew Lockyer [Subsequently Professor of Citizenship and Social Theory at the University of Glasgow] was already researching these themes under Bernard's guidance when I arrived at Sheffield in 1969. There is of course a huge liberal versus republican debate in America. In the UK we have seen, recent revival of discussion about the notion of citizenship, both in academic and party political circles. Unfortunately, in the latter case, citizenship as in the case of the Citizen's Charter has been construed largely in terms of the private *consumption* of collective services, rather than in the sustenance of a structure of essentially political rights. [The pace of the revival of republicanism(s) has quickened since this piece was published, although not entirely in such a way as to highlight the divergence emphasised here between a rights-focused conception of individual freedom and freedom as a property of (political) collectivities.]

5. *See* for example Leonardo Bruni's *Laudatio Florentinae Urbis* (In Praise of the City of Florence) of 1403–4, tr. B. G. Kohl in B. G. Kohl, and R. G. Witt (eds), *The Earthly Republic: Italian humanists on government and society,* (Manchester, Manchester University Press, 1978) p. 151. The phenomenon is discussed in Hans Baron's classic *The Crisis of the Early Italian Renaissance* (Princeton, Princeton University Press, 1955).

6. For the republican interpretation *see* B. Bailyn, *The Ideological Origins of the American Revolution* (Cambridge, Mass., Harvard University Press, 1967), and a persistent critic from the liberal perspective, Joyce Appleby, 'Republicanism and ideology', *American Quarterly,* 37(4) (1985); for a review of the debate *see* Peter S. Onuf, 'Reflections on the founding: constitutional historiography in bicentennial perspective', *Wm. & Mary Quarterly,* XLVI, 2 (1989). A recent eirenic contribution is Lance Banning 'Some Second Thoughts on Virtue and the Course of Revolutionary Thinking' in *Conceptual Change and the Constitution,* T. Ball and J. G. A. Pocock (eds), (Lawrence Ka., Kansas University Press, 1988).

7. *Politics as Freedom, Freedom as Politics,* Inaugural Lecture delivered at the University of Sheffield, 12 January 1966, p. 1 and *passim*; *In Defence of Politics,* Ch. 1, *passim*, and the central problem, p. 173.

8. Both in, and increasingly since *The Machiavellian Moment* Pocock has charted the accommodation of a basically austere republicanism to the emergence of commercial and liberal political economy, despite analytically arguing their distinctive vocabularies in 'Virtue, Rights and Manners: A model for the political theorist', in Pocock, *Virtue Commerce and History* (Cambridge, Cambridge University Press, 1985).

by contrast, particularly in its more libertarian forms, has stressed the issues of economic liberty and political individualism, sometimes regardless of their implications for the stability and survival of the polity which might be needed to sustain them.[9] Yet the Crickean conception of politics was concerned, perhaps in a rather eighteenth-century way, both with the importance of an ultimately individual liberty, and with the creation *and* sustenance of the social conditions under which liberty – and politics itself – could thrive. For Crick, politics as freedom embraces both the republican and liberal conceptions of freedom, closely related to the positive and negative conceptions of liberty: Thus politics is both the 'public activity of free men' (and, no doubt, women), and it is also their 'privacy ... from public actions'.[10] Moreover, he stressed, the problem of stability can be solved in other ways than the political. The problem of *political* stability is one which is posed under very specific circumstances – those in which the method of rule is 'to listen to these groups so as to conciliate them as far as possible, and to give them a legal position, a sense of security, some clear and reasonably safe means of articulation, by which these groups can and will speak freely'.[11]

Now the defence of politics, like the practice of it, is an unending process. If some of the threats to politics identified in that now famous work (ideology, democracy, nationalism, technology and even the 'friends' of politics) may today seem less formidable, this may confidently be attributed to a foreshortened historical perspective; recognition of the value of politics itself though, as 'a great and civilising human activity' is, particularly in view of recent events in Eastern Europe, redoubled and beyond question.[12] But if, which must be doubted, the danger to politics from ideology has passed, the self-congratulatory complacency with which the eclipse of a variant of it has been greeted by many in the west, undoubtedly constitutes a new one, evoking Mill's warning about the ossification which besets uncontested truths. The focus of this chapter is on another danger to politics, one much nearer to home, and which has become increasingly pervasive

---

9. Notoriously Robert Nozick, *Anarchy, State and Utopia* (New York, Basic Books, 1974); but the articulation of a theoretical concept of freedom (or justice, or rights), irrespective of any concomitant concern for its viability within an actual political system has been a prominent feature of recent Anglo-American political philosophy. R. E. Goodin's, *Motivating Political Morality* (Oxford, Blackwell, 1992) is an exception.

10. Crick, *In Defence of Politics*, p. 18. In 'Freedom as Politics', Crick described politics and freedom as 'linked together, not merely in civil wedlock, but in a permanently progenitive embrace.' He amplifies this mildly scatological image by repeating the point made in the book: 'Freedom is relationships and activities; it cannot simply be regarded as ... freedom from – or the successful avoidance of – politics. Put in its most abstract way, the very possibility of privacy depends upon some public action; and conversely public life is just "telegrams and anger" if it does not accommodate private happiness.', p. 1.

11. *Ibid*, p. 18. By contrast 'The method of rule of the tyrant and the oligarch is, quite simply to clobber, coerce, or overawe all, or most ... other groups in the interest of their own.' Within the republican tradition Crick identifies Rousseau as an opponent of politics in his sense. *Ibid.*, p. 47.

12. [The date of composition – 1991 – is relevant here. The events referred to are the collapse of communism, and the re-emergence in Central and Eastern Europe of 'politics' in the Crickean sense.]

in the West over the last twenty-five years or so. Yet it is one which, because of its proximity to the ideal of liberty so closely connected with politics itself, is a danger difficult to analyse, and rhetorically, increasingly difficult to articulate. It is the individualist premise.

By targeting the individualist premise I do not wish to attack the broad epistemological conviction that societies comprise a variety of assemblages of natural individuals, nor to denigrate the importance of extensive areas of personal liberty. Indeed both such premises underpin the Crickean conception of politics which I wish to defend. Rather I refer to that particular and narrow conception of the individual as an essentially isolated actor, calculating economic means to ends which are individually identified, autonomously chosen and privately consumed. It is, I believe, a conception of the individual which is philosophically unsustainable in itself, and the conceptual incoherence of which gives rise to important and dangerous equivocations when applied to policy issues.[13] My focus here will, however, be on the relationship between it and politics in the now justly famous Crickean sense.

Unsurprisingly, given its date, *In Defence of Politics*, did not identify libertarian individualism as an enemy to politics.[14] The remarkable rise of the individualist premise in social science thinking, and indeed in public policy attitudes, took place largely since its publication.

Starting from a base in economic theory, the isolated rational egoist has first raided, then successfully annexed large areas of the territories of the surrounding disciplines of politics and international relations, sociology and economic and social history.[15] Even Marxism itself has succumbed: the capitulation of actual Marxist regimes in Eastern Europe and their adoption of market forces paralleled

---

13. For what I hope is a generalisable analysis and sustained account of one of these worries *see* my 'The market for toleration: a case study in an aspect of the ambiguity of "positive economics"', *British Journal of Political Science,* 21(1) (1991). [Chapter Ten in this collection. And see Chapter Seven]

14. It did however, draw attention both to the potential for liberalism (along with conservatism and socialism) to develop alarmingly doctrinaire variants when hard pressed, and he remarked how fertile a source liberalism has been in 'devices for putting politics at one side'. Prime amongst such devices is of course the market. *In Defence of Politics,* pp. 111, 126.

15. The classic works in politics are mostly by renegade economists: Anthony Downs' *An Economic Theory of Democracy* (New York, Harper, 1957), and Mancur Olsen's *The Logic of Collective Action* (Cambridge, Mass., Harvard University Press, 1965) which, in view of its predominant thesis might be better titled 'the illogicality of collective action'. A recent remarkably astute and synoptic account of the development of this literature as it relates to political science is to be found in Alessandro Pizzorno's 'On Rationality and Democratic Choice', in P. Birnbaum and J. Leca, *Individualism: Theories and Methods* (Oxford, Oxford University Press, 1990); for sociology P. M. Blau, *Exchange and Power in Social Life* (New York, Transaction Publishers, 1964) and G. Homans, *Social Behaviour: Its elementary forms* (New York, Harcourt, Brace and Janovich, 1961); on the 'new economic history', which at times seems ready to replace the need for doing any history at all with pure deduction, *see* Douglas C. North, *Structure and Change in Economic History* (London and New York, Norton, 1981) [For a critique of which see Chapter Nine in this collection], in social history there is the highly suggestive Abram de Swaan, *In Care of the State* (Cambridge, Polity Press, 1988).

the penetration of traditional Marxism as a distinctive theory by market-inspired rational-choice thinking.[16] If not exactly nature imitating art, then at least (and some would say, unusually) reality imitating theory. This success, in both academic and political terms, is all the more puzzling when one thinks of the widespread and apparently well-grounded rejection of the individual as an adequate premise in many other related, but less obviously policy oriented disciplines.

For example in philosophy, since Wittgenstein, the idea that meaning itself could be individually based has been widely rejected. All meaningfulness, from language itself through to complex forms of symbolic action is to be construed as a social form.[17] Indeed since action itself – as opposed to mere behaviour – is defined as meaningful, the very conduct of human life cannot ultimately be understood as the work of an individual agent but only as the deployment of resources which are irreducibly the product of social collectivities.[18] The persistence and deepening of this view within philosophy since the original publication of *In Defence of Politics* can be seen by considering two very influential works on personal identity, P. F. Strawson's *Individuals* (1959), and Derek Parfitt's *Reasons and Persons* (1983).

In the first work the self-attribution of personal identity is logically held to be possible only because of the existence of other persons to whom identity is likewise ascribed. The argument is roughly that it is impossible to see how, on the basis of only my external and empirical experience of others, I could come to attribute the property of consciousness to *them*, if my understanding of it were originally present only as a form of private self-awareness in *me*, as opposed to being constructed out of mutual interactions.[19] This is a modest enough epistemological embedding of the individual in a social context. It goes no further than Hegel's

---

16. A seminal article is that of Alan Carling, 'Rational choice Marxism', *New Left Review*, 125 (1981), perhaps the major work is that of John Roemer, *Free to Lose* (Cambridge, Mass., Harvard University Press, 1988).

17. '"So you are saying that human agreement decides what is true and what is false?" – It is what human beings *say* that is true and false; and they agree in the *language* they use. That is not agreement in opinions but in form of life ... could we ... imagine a language in which a person could write down or give vocal expression to his inner experiences – his feelings, moods, and the rest – for his private use? – Well, can't we do so in our ordinary language? – But that is not what I mean. The individual words of this language are to refer to what can only be known to the person speaking; to his immediate private sensations. So another person cannot understand the language.' L. Wittgenstein, *Philosophical Investigations,* tr. Anscombe (Oxford, Blackwell, 1963), I, §§241, 243.

18. As forcefully argued by the school of Wittgenstein, particularly through the exploration of the concept of intention. The social science implications of this were elaborated in such works as Peter Winch's *The Idea of a Social Science* (London, Routledge, 1958), and in a parallel development, by Charles Taylor, *The Explanation of Behaviour* (London, Routledge, 1964). The insight that meaning is inseparable from socially available intentions has been developed into an important methodological school within political theory by Quentin Skinner. For a recent anthology *see Meaning and Context: Quentin Skinner and his critics*, J. Tully (ed.), (Cambridge, Polity Press, 1988).

19. P. F. Strawson, *Individuals: An essay in descriptive metaphysics* (London, Methuen, 1959), pp. 102–3.

master-slave dialectic in the *Phenomenology*, even though it approaches the problem analytically and from the *fait accompli*, rather than dynamically and from the postulated absence of self-consciousness. In Parfitt's book, however, personal identity in the traditional sense, is pronounced an illusion and its loss is to be seen, not as something about which we might worry, but as a liberation. The relationship between experiences, and even sensations is not guaranteed by any integrity of the individual, it is more graded and open-textured than anything envisaged by traditional views of the subject. The very identity of a person merges imperceptibly into a social nexus provided by the thoughts and experiences of other persons. Hence, Parfitt on his death:

> Though there will later be many experiences, none of these experiences will be connected to my present experiences by chains of such direct connections as those involved in experience-memory, or in the carrying out of an earlier intention. Some of these future experiences may be related to my present experiences in less direct ways, there will later be some memories about my life. And there may later be thoughts that are influenced by mine, or things done as a result of my advice. My death will break the more direct relations between my present experiences and future experiences, but it will not break various other relations. This is all there is to the fact that there will be no-one living who will be me.[20]

In critical and literary circles too the individual has been largely written out of the script: deconstructed into her essentially social roles and context(s). Not only the literary character but the actual person is seen as an intersection and bearer of essentially socially constructed relationships, responses and emotions.[21] Even the author is no longer in charge of her text, but is, according to some, rather written, and constructed by and through it. The individual self is no longer a unique or continuous phenomenon, but a plurality derived from the range of contexts in, and by which they find and (momentarily) define themselves.

Despite 'the new economic history', which does indeed affect neo-classical forms of explanation, our understanding of historical development is again vastly different from that which prevailed when the foundations of economic thinking were being laid. Contrary to contractarian or quasi-contractarian views then widely canvassed, society was never established *from* individuals, rather, individuals were differentiated *out* of social wholes. The establishment of the legal

---

20. Derek Parfitt, *Reasons and Persons* (Oxford, Oxford University Press, 1986), p. 281. For a recent discussion of the political implications of the deconstruction of the individuality of personality in Parfitt and Sandel as responses to Rawls and Nozick, *see* M. Mosher, 'Boundary revisions: the deconstruction of moral personality in Rawls, Nozick, Sandel and Parfitt', *Political Studies* XXXIX (1991).

21. "'Haven't you ever been in love, then?", "When I was younger," she says, "I allowed myself to be constructed by the discourse of romantic love for a while, yes."' David Lodge, *Nice Work*, (London, Sacker and Warburg, 1988), p. 210.

and market social orders so characteristic of the modern state has, in all cases *supervened* on a pre-existing social whole or wholes, on which it has in many cases been hitherto reliant in establishing limits to the dangers otherwise inherent in unbounded individualism.[22]

This presents us with a paradox, for our policy-oriented social sciences are premised on a view of humanity which is widely contradicted by the findings of philosophical reflection. Now 'ought' does imply (perhaps (except for moral transcendentalists) more stringently, entails) 'can'. The prescriptions of a coherent moral culture should recognise the basic conditions of human existence, so far, at least, as it understands them at any one time. And on this view the individualist premise is a non-starter.

To this observation there are two defensive responses that can be made. The first is to remark that whatever the state of philosophy or literary theory, the evidence about what is politically practicable for human beings seems now to be heavily stacked in favour of individualism, both as social policy and perhaps therefore, also as a premise of theorising. The demise of communist regimes is widely urged as evidence against the practicality of the mildest and most limited forms of collectivist endeavour, even by some of those with a long record of dissent from individualist orthodoxies.[23]

The second response, to the confuting of which I wish to devote the rest of this chapter, is to claim, as is often done by apologists for economic individualist explanations, that the method does not purport in any way to model individual psychology, but rather to explain social phenomena by using the individualist premise as a way of generating testable hypotheses. The premises of the method, are, it is claimed, quite independent of the real motives of those whose behaviour is so modelled.[24]

I want first to consider whether the second claim can be sustained when individualist premises are used to generate policy initiatives, or, more widely, to structure the situation in which the individual makes choices. To put it plainly, can we really maintain agnosticism and indifference as to the realities of moral psychology, whilst operating policies which are both premised on, and incentive-geared to reward, individualistic reasoning? To hold such a view is

---

22. Edmund Burke draws attention to this and the attendant dangers of allowing economic motivations to overwhelm the 'manners' under which they grew up and have thriven. See J. G. A. Pocock's 'Burke's Analysis of the Political Economy of the French Revolution' in his *Virtue Commerce and History* (Cambridge, Cambridge University Press, 1985).

23. Recently rehearsing Hayekian arguments about the incompatibility of non-market orders and liberty, Frank Hahn invites the reader 'to consider what follows with a critical eye in the knowledge that the author would not be displeased to find that he has been mistaken.' Frank Hahn, 'On Some Economic Limits in Politics', in *The Economic Limits to Modern Politics,* John Dunn (ed.), (Cambridge, Polity Press, 1990), p. 142.

24. E.g. Ludwig von Mises, *Human Action: A treatise on economics* (New Haven, Yale University Press, 1949) p. 15; Milton Friedman, *Essays in Positive Economics* (Chicago, Chicago University Press, 1953) p. 15.

to believe one can create a situation where people will be rewarded for acting *as if* they were rational egoists without believing, indeed denying that they will actually respond by becoming one. Policy initiatives are framed in the *hope* that individuals will respond in the fashion predicted by the hypothesis of rational egoism. It is surely disingenuous to deny that one expects them to adopt such motives. How is the difference between acting *as if* one were a rational egoist, and actually being one to be sustained? Indeed, if the deconstructionist view of the individual as merely a kind of moment in a hermeneutic force-field is right, then the context provided by policy becomes more, not less of an issue. For, if the identity of individuals is exhausted by the co-ordinates of their context, the ability of agents to transcend their context-structured roles is seriously brought in question.[25]

Doctors and academics, to take a recent example, have been used to working in an environment where their actions are guided by professional ideals and norms internalised through long periods of training and socialisation. Policy initiatives in their fields which result from modelling the behaviour of economic agents wishing to economise on money, time and effort, commonly operate through imposing marginal costs on those who seek to maintain professional standards rather than obey the signals carried by pricing mechanisms. Professionals will often seek to maintain their standards, even at some considerable cost to themselves, at least in part, perhaps, because doing so is less a means to an end than it is expressive of their professional – and even personal – identity. However, eventually, if the costs are geared up enough, the professional ethic will succumb, and individuals will respond as the model had erroneously assumed they all originally did – egoistically and opportunistically.[26] John Hope-Mason's claim [27] that action constitutes the self, cuts here in a different way: by being nudged [28] toward acting as a calculating egoistic agent do we not, inevitably, constitute ourselves as one?

The [premise of the] story outlined above may be thought an idealised one. It is not meant to imply that there are no lazy or opportunistic professionals – it is merely meant to illustrate analytically the difference and mutual incompatibility

---

25. Yet there is, for the defender of politics, an upside, for that context is also seen as a product of human agency – we can, in suitable circumstances, decide to mutually construct or adjust our co-ordinates and so politics is ineluctably reborn.
26. Thus, incidentally, confirming the cynicism of the market-ideologue politician concerning the efficacy, or even existence of the professional ethic.
27. [John Hope-Mason's chapter in the original volume was 'Creativity in Action: The background to Machiavelli's "lion" and "fox"', pp. 1–21.]
28. [This reference to 'nudging' of course predated the emergence of 'nudge' as a policy implementation technique and term of art following the publication of *Nudge: Improving decisions about health, wealth, and happiness,* a book written by Richard H. Thaler and Cass R. Sunstein, (New Haven, Yale University Press, 2008), and the establishment of the Cameron Government's Behavioural Insights Team, often called the 'Nudge Unit', which is explicitly devoted to applying 'insights from academic research in behavioural economics and psychology to public policy and services'.]

between incentive – driven societies and those which run on the basis of ideals and the internalisation of norms.[29]

If what is suggested in this quote can be shown, namely that individual incentives are, in the long run, dominant over internalised, un- [or lightly-] policed, norms, it suggests that when the presuppositions of the rational egoist model are used to construct the social environment they will surely be transformed into the motives of agents. For rational-egoistic and ideal-following accounts are not merely competing social explanations, they are in the end, different possible forms of society, and different senses of the self.

Ironically, claims about the strategic dominance of egoism find theoretical support within the axioms of rational choice theory itself through the notion of moral hazard. If we imagine an insurance market supervening on a society in which individuals previously bore all their own risk, standards of self-care set through norms internalised in the high-risk environment would be high, and claims correspondingly low. However, high standards of care involve costs. Opportunist policy-holders will gain (time/opportunity/money) through relaxing their previous standards and relying on the insurance cover to remedy any loss. This, however, will result in more claims and consequently higher premiums over the next period. In the absence of any means of identifying high-risk contractors, these higher premiums will be born by all policy-holders and those who maintain the same high internalised standards of care will thus bear both their own monitoring costs *and* the premium rises resulting from the lower care of those claiming on their policies, eventually providing even them with an incentive to lower their care levels too. Obviously insurance companies seek to discriminate different risk categories within their potential market in order to avoid this, but such discrimination is invariably imperfect, and indeed not always possible.

Moral hazard is a particular problem where, as in modern mass society, strategic defaulters can achieve anonymity. Thus, at an even greater level of generality, one could observe that it is an instance of the universal vulnerability of unpoliced norms to free riding. Take, for example, the erosion of a norm of reciprocity such as that of allowing fellow drivers to pull into a busy stream of traffic from a side road. Following such a norm involves an immediate cost with no guarantee of reciprocity. The opportunist will accept invitations to enter streams of traffic himself, whilst not impeding his own progress to offer them to others. In large, impersonal societies, where the identification and sanctioning of defaulters from informal norms is impossible, it is reasonable to conclude that defaulting becomes a 'dominant strategem' – egoistic motivation drives out any generalised, or not

---

29. Once felicitously distinguished by Graham Ouchi as 'markets' and 'clans', 'hierarchies' referring to the possible internal organisation of the conventional firm. *See* G. Ouchi, 'Markets, bureaucracies and clans', *Administrative Science Quarterly,* 25 (1980), and in G. Thompson *et al.,* (ed.), *Markets, Hierarchies and Networks* (London, Sage, 1991).

immediately reciprocated, or sanctionable exchange.[30] That the essentially market behaviour of rational egoists might constitute a kind of moral 'Gresham law' is an interesting hypothesis, especially in view of the fact that Hayek has himself acknowledged the potentially generalisable power of this theorem, properly understood.[31] Such explanations are impeccably individualistic in form, but they do not justify or endorse substantive rational egoism as in any sense a superior or chosen form of self; rather they explain, or at best model, the logic of social forces that might encourage its dominance.

The basic idea that human personality is shaped by their social experience is, of course, not a new one. It may be present in Aristotle, is certainly to be found in late Roman political thought, for example in Tacitus *On Oratory*, and most notoriously present in Machiavelli's famous aetiology of the success and failure of republics, which is dominated by the issue of discriminating between those political and military experiences of citizens which are supportive and which destructive of virtuous (or *virtù-ous*) civic personalities. Against this view of political individuality and politics as mutually dependent for their survival, liberal individualists have, broadly speaking pitched a notion of the individual already accoutred with autonomy and rights, entering a pre-, and independently existing political arena.[32] As is now clear to us, one of the crucial problems faced by early defenders of a liberal market order was the issue of what effect such a society would have on the political personalities of those living under it, and whether an individualistic commercial order would produce persons capable of sustaining it.[33] But needless to say, the idea that the market structures and moulds individuals' dispositions rather than giving expression to them, although much older, has not recently commanded wide acceptance.[34] It comes as some surprise then, if not a

---

30. *See* the brilliant and emblematic story of the 'groomer' birds with the variant 'suckers', 'cheats' and 'grudgers' in Richard Dawkins, *The Selfish Gene* (Oxford, Oxford University Press, 1976) pp. 197, ff.

31. F. A. Hayek, 'The Uses of "Gresham's Law" as an Illustration of Historical Theory', p. 318, in F. A. Hayek, *Studies in Philosophy, Politics and Economics* (London, Routledge and Kegan Paul, 1967), reprinted from *History and Theory*, vol. 1 (1960).

32. For an excellent characterisation *see* Pocock, 'Virtue, Rights and Manners'.

33. The works of Donald Winch, *Adam Smith's Politics* (Cambridge, Cambridge University Press, 1978), and Duncan Forbes, *Hume's Philosophical Politics* (Cambridge, Cambridge University Press, 1975) explore these themes, (which had been provocatively exposed by Bernard Mandeville).

34. The earliest theorists of modern economics, who understood themselves to be talking, not about an abstraction, but about a particular historical social formation, not only acknowledged, but stressed the moral and epistemological consequences of the spread of commercial transactions in invigorating the mind, enlarging its powers and faculties, and refining tastes; indeed they were virtually required to do this, finding themselves in the midst of a debate about the social effects of commerce. E.g. D. Hume, *Essays, Moral, Political and Literary* (Oxford, Oxford University Press, 1963); 'Of Refinement in the Arts', p. 277, and 'Of Commerce' p. 270. The idea that 'the market' could be construed simply as a set of marginal rates of substitution between any desired goods was unknown to such thinkers and derives from the 'marginalist revolution' of the late nineteenth century associated with Edgeworth and Marshall.

nice irony, that the theory of social choice associated with rational egoism itself, and so often used to defend the market as a neutral social institution, also offers a particular explanation of the way that social circumstance feeds back and enters into the formation of individuals' personalities and choices.[35]

For on the liberal individualists' view, if markets are indeed perfect, they are transparent vectors of consumers' autonomous preferences. In a perfect market the signals carried by prices, the existence of alert entrepreneurs always seeking out, and striving to satisfy, unfulfilled desires, and the competitive context in which exchanges take place, in some way guarantees that the aggregate production schedule for a society is the embodiment of individual decisions as to how they value and how to allocate their resources. There is a sense in which the market justifies the social outcome which it generates, because, we are asked to accept, it simply *is* the innumerable expenditure decisions of individuals. For the libertarian individualist the objection to political decisions about allocative issues is that they *supervene* on allocative decisions the market has already made, the issue is thus at least redundant, the activity at best distorting (if you believe the market to be an efficient allocator), and at worst immoral (if you believe (with Nozick) that the rights acquired by free transactions between legitimate title-holders are absolute).

However, the market is acknowledgedly bad at supplying certain kinds of goods. The most notorious class of goods which the market supplies sub-optimally is of course public goods. If individuals act voluntarily, motivated only by their own individual benefit, in pursuit of goods to be privately consumed, how will goods which are intrinsically publicly available and/or can only be supplied collectively come about? The standard example of the lighthouse has it that in the absence of coercion, lighthouses will not be forthcoming because each individual will reason that their own contribution will not be crucial, since the lighthouse will be built or not depending on whether all the *other* potential contributors perform. Thus each individual, reasoning they may safely 'free ride' on the contribution of the others, will not contribute, and the lighthouse will indeed fail to be built.[36]

The goods normally discussed in the now massive literature range from such fairly tangible items as lighthouses through to more abstract notions such as public health, or even, in the case of the rationality of voting, to the good of the

---

35. The neutrality of the market, although a feature of idealised text-book models and political ideologues, is of course by no means uncritically accepted by academic theorists, even those disposed to work within the individualist premise. *See*, most recently, Robert E. Goodin and A. Reeve, (eds), *Liberal Neutrality* (London, Routledge, 1989). [And *see* Chapter Ten]

36. In a famous paper ('The lighthouse in economics', *Journal of Law and Economics*, 17 (2) (1974)). Ronald Coase argued that in defiance of the deductions of economic theory, privately funded lighthouses were nevertheless built by voluntary subscription. The subsequent debate has centred on the extent to which such efforts were made possible by government enforced tolls and/or port levies, and so not really a product of the free market. For an overview of the debate *see* Barnett and Block, 'Coase and van Zandt on lighthouses', *Public Finance Review*, 35 (6) (2007). The economic argument hinges on whether rational choosers would/did support lighthouse building. The unexplored dimension is what light this sheds on whether early modern individuals were rational egoistic choosers, or whether in a rather different culture, individuals were not (yet) entirely constituted by the 'individualist premise'.

persistence of democracy or democratic institutions themselves. There are, by now, a fairly standard range of solutions to public goods problems, each adapted to the particular properties of the good in question, and of course not unrelated to policy. One popular category of solution, particularly attractive to libertarians, consists in seeking ingenious ways of resolving the public goods into individual goods. Take for example the issue of public health. The prevalence of disease, if the mechanism of transmission is unknown and its incidence is therefore unpredictable, poses a public goods problem. Inasmuch as disease seems to be generated by the general squalor of impoverished city life, and inasmuch as there is no way in which even wealthy inhabitants of the city can avoid that squalor, protection for some becomes inseparably linked with relief for all. However, once the medium of transmission becomes known and individual means of protection become available – through inoculation for example – the safety of the individual becomes separable, from the health of the public.[37] If individuals can protect themselves by private initiative there is no particular reason (on the individualist premise) why they should be protected collectively.

Now this example neatly illustrates the fact that many public goods are public only because, and if, they are non-excludable (i.e. not privatisable), at the point of supply – as security from the 'miasma' of infection was thought to be. But this is often quite compatible with their being privately *consumed*. For example, unpolluted air is non-excludable but privately consumed, as is the information conveyed by a lighthouse beam to ships negotiating a hazardous reef. Other consumers cannot be excluded (given the technology); but it is not that there is anything in the enjoyment of the good that *needs* those others to be included. Their inclusion is, for the individual, a matter of indifference, and as far as the would-be entrepreneurs in the potential market for clean air or safety at sea is concerned, simply a regrettable aspect of the current technology, or prevailing normative assumptions. One might, for example, envisage [!] scrambled radio direction beacons, which could only be decoded by those paying a subscription for a suitable device; or the presumption of a right to breathe clean air being reversed to create a massive industry in the provision of personalised breathing apparatus. The analogous move is, in the case of drinkable tap water, already well under way. The enjoyment of personal security has been considered a public good because it was thought it could only be supplied jointly, but can clearly be supplied on a private basis, as, in a way, it was before Henry VII's abolition of private retainers,

---

37. Indeed, the most analytical treatment of the history of this episode suggests that public health developments in the nineteenth century were driven by an erroneous 'miasmic' theory of infection, which 'dictated a much more radical and effective programme of reform than the essentially individualist approach of contagionists ever could have.' A. de Swaan, *In Care of the State* (Oxford, Oxford University Press, 1988) p. 134. To the extent that this is right we may owe our sewage and water distribution networks to the historical accident that our understanding of the epidemiology of cholera lagged behind the massive growth of the cities by half a century. Third world cities largely manage on the individualist premise, by a combination of spatial separation and private protection.

and, increasingly again in parts of Europe and America, as security, in various forms is supplied through private contract, or geographical isolation.

However, such a solution is not available to one class of public good which is germane to our point here. As David Miller has pointed out, some goods are 'public' not because contingencies require their collective provision, but because their very goodness consists in their being jointly enjoyed.[38] He instances many goods connected with sociability, and ideal-regarding social goods such as equality. Games such as hockey or squash are irreducibly collective not only in the way they are supplied, but as they are consumed. Politics itself, in Crick's sense, is, I urge, such a good.

The difficulties posed by the more abstract collective goods issues are often presented in a way that suggests we are faced with a sharp dichotomy between an anomic libertarianism and a stifling communitarianism. This is premised on the not implausible view that political society must rest on moral consensus, that political conflict can only be kept within bounds if there is a moral consensus on a wide range of issue and that this can only be supplied by a shared moral tradition, and not by rational argument or analysis.[39] But if the adoption of a thick conception of community is a worryingly high (or unattainable) price to pay for the supply of social goods, surely a Crickean conception of politics can provide at least a coherent programme for exploring the problem?

The Crickean exhortation to pursue politics as a goal is not necessarily an appeal to altruism, civic virtue, or any such idealised conception of human nature. As suggested at the start, and as powerfully urged recently by Quentin Skinner, the bifurcation between rights-based liberalism and *virtù* based republicanism, and the related distinction between negative and positive liberty, may be both historically and theoretically procrustean.[40] Politics does involve a commitment to a kind of community, although it is a much more exiguous, and in the end procedural commitment, and allows the possibility of a much more diverse community than most communitarian critics of liberalism seem to have in mind. It is a commitment

---

38. D. Miller, 'Market neutrality and the failure of cooperatives', *British Journal of Political Science*, 11 (1981), pp. 326–7. Miller actually distinguishes 'group oriented desires' which require some degree of joint consumption short of social universality, from 'social desires' which require a certain condition of the whole society, such as a degree of equality, or the non-existence of slavery, say. *See also* chapter three, 'Market Neutrality' of his *Market, State and Community: The theoretical foundations of market socialism* (Oxford, Oxford University Press, 1989). *See also* J. Raz's related argument that living in a tolerant, cultured society is a good which is unlikely to be pursuable through a rights-based morality, 'Right-based Morality' in J. Waldron (ed.), *Theories of Rights* (Oxford, Oxford University Press, 1984), pp. 188–90.

39. As urged for example by A. MacIntyre, *Whose Justice, Which Rationality?* (Oxford, Duckworth, 1988).

40. Q. Skinner, 'The Republican Idea of Political Liberty' in *Machiavelli and the Nature of Republicanism*, G. Bock, Q. Skinner and M. Viroli (eds), (Cambridge, Cambridge University Press, 1990), shows how a defence of republican liberty, and a strong conception of politics is quite consistent with a negative, and even egoistic conception of liberty, and indeed that 'if we wish to maximise our own individual liberty, we must cease to put our trust in princes, and instead, take charge of the public arena ourselves', p. 308.

to 'at least some tolerance of differing truths (and we might add, conceptions of the good), some recognition that government is possible, indeed best conducted, amid the open canvassing of rival interests.'[41] For politics to be conducted in the absence of a homogeneous community it is moreover, necessary that there be rights; *precisely* which rights we cannot say, for it will be a matter for political argument – but they must include some notion of free speech and some notion of freedom of association. Conversely, for rights to sustain diverse communities they will need to have a commitment to Crickean politics itself as a good, indeed, at least strategically, the master good. But it is not analytically the case that politics is the master good – there are other possibilities.[42]

However, if the practice of politics itself is a social good then its capacity to exist in such a way as to overcome the sub-optimal supply of such goods resulting from effects in the social environment must be seriously brought in question. To overcome this we need firstly to recognise and assert the value of politics in sustaining freedom and in enabling us to achieve some things that could not otherwise be done. The often dispiriting logics of rational choice theory might as well be taken to show the absurdity of proceeding down the road of institutionalising such mentalities, rather than demonstrating the absurdity of political commitment. Secondly, once we recognise that the market order needs to be theorised as a pervasive social and psychological reality rather than as a logical construct, we need to enquire into the circumstances under which liberty – or politics – can be *practised*, as well as the logical question of what actually constitutes liberty, or politics, moreover one must integrate the two. Recent political theory has been dominated by the question of the identity of political ideals almost to the exclusion of questions about the practice of them.

As should now be clear, my argument is that one reason why social goods, and politics itself may be under-supplied in a market-oriented society is not necessarily that people do not value such things, but, as David Miller puts it, that 'a market economy converts preferences into behaviour in a certain sort of way: it gives people differentially strong incentives to act on their various preferences. (For example, it generally gives no incentive at all to act on preferences for public goods.)'

However it is not only that the market modifies our preferences, it also presents questions to us in ways, and it processes our preferences in ways, that produce very different outcomes than any of us might want, or indeed that we all might choose if we chose collectively. In pursuing my conception of the good in a market setting, I am constrained by other people's market-channelled behaviour, not by their underlying preference.'[43] Such constraints in turn alter our preferences;

---

41. Crick, *In Defence of Politics*, p. 18.
42. The answer to the question why there has to be 'some tolerance of differing truths', and the public conciliation of rival interests, 'is, of course, that they do not have to be. Other paths are always open. Politics is simply when they are conciliated.' *In Defence of Politics*, p. 30.
43. Miller, *Market, State and Community*, p. 94, n. 28.

preferences are notoriously adaptive to persistent thwarting.[44] These claims now require further elaboration.

One argument in support of such a claim is that it will rarely be the case that individuals would choose politically, that allocation of resources, which would result from their individual transactions. The effect of imperfect information is clearly one factor here: the assumption of perfect information being one of the most notoriously unrealistic axioms of market theory.

If most people were asked whether it was more important to provide more and better collective health, or indeed other welfare provisions, or a greater variety and choice of biscuits, the evidence suggests that people come down in favour of healthcare.[45] In fact, however, despite widespread concern about the health service there is no fall in the variety of available biscuits. Does this falsify the preferences expressed in the questionnaire responses? The fact is that when we buy a packet of biscuits we do not consider the nature of the 'signal' that our purchase may be conveying about the alternative uses to which social resources may be put, nor, even if we did, is it clear that we could buy a packet of biscuits at all and alter that supposed signal. By buying the biscuits I do, I undoubtedly express a personal preference from amongst those available, but nothing can be inferred from numerous such choices (without committing the fallacy of composition), about the preferences those choosers have concerning the desired range of choice of biscuits. It is just not valid to deduce from the fact that (collectively) shoppers choose from amongst the whole range, that the sum of their expenditure is a collective expression of the value they placed on having that range available. Thus there is no logical link between the individual choices of consumers, and the total social effort put into sustaining that *range of choice*. It is (usually) true, that when I go out to buy a packet of biscuits, I am choosing amongst biscuits, and not thinking about the health service, or the third world, or any other possible use of my small change. But even if I were, there is no way in which I could buy a packet of biscuits at all, without expressing a preference for a particular kind, and so contributing my mite to the apparent collective endorsement of the value of the current range of choice.

This suggests that the difference between individual choices expressed through the market and individual choices expressed through politics, should not be construed as expressions of some already existing essential public opinion (invariably to the detriment of politics); rather they should be construed as different activities, involving different practices and with different (not better or worse) outcomes. Choosing individually, privately, through the market, simply deprives each of us of both the knowledge and a context in which we might be able to make other choices. In this sense freedom has to involve the *public* action of

---

44. *See* Jon Elster, *Sour Grapes* (Cambridge, Cambridge University Press, 1983), esp. ch. 3.
45. Opinion poll data is silent on the precise issue but reveals consistent support for increased taxation for social services, and, in particular, for healthcare e.g. *The Independent,* 21 November 1991.

free citizens. Acting privately (through the market) restricts freedom by ruling out the possibility of expressing certain very important choices in the only way they can be made – through politics.

One way in which the practices of economic and political choice differ is, as already hinted, in terms of the moral psychology of choice; and one key consequence of a system of individualistic market choice seems to be to sever the link between action and moral responsibility. Now on a utilitarian, or even a consequentialist view, the question of the morality of an action only arises where a perceptible harmful consequence results from that action. Where no such consequence results, or cannot be assigned to an action or actor, moral issues do not arise. This is, for example, made the key to one of the distinctions between negative and positive liberty by Berlin.[46] If infringements on my liberty which are not assignable to any particular agent are not truly to be so construed and it follows that only impediments which can be assigned to specific individuals can be considered the proper subject of government or legislative action, then government interference in the cumulative effects of market actions are also excluded. We shall next question whether the exclusion justifies the precept, but the intuitive appeal of this argument derives, surely, from the fact that it does also seem to work at the level of moral psychology through emancipating the individual from considering (or in many cases even having to be aware of) the consequences of his or her acts. Thus morally dubious arms sales are justified on the grounds that others will only sell if we do not. (No morally different consequences follow from *our* selling arms as opposed to someone else – it merely happens to be us that is doing the selling.) Environmentally destructive market exchanges can be justified on the grounds that my unilateral withdrawal will make no difference. (I need a new hardwood front door, and the destruction of tropical forests will proceed irrespective of whether I buy it or not.) It is, of course one of the axioms of the perfect market that outcomes are unaffected by the decision of anyone actor within it.

These commonplaces of contemporary casuistry are nevertheless highly questionable. Consider the case of the morally squeamish torturers. Good utilitarians all, they construct an apparatus which enables each one of them to apply pain in increments below the level of perceptibility, yet which collectively delivers such agony as to produce the desired (and quite possibly beneficial) effect. Can we say that the imperceptibility of the consequences of each torturer's

---

46. 'I am normally said to be free to the degree to which no man or body of men interferes with my acting.' Whether the market could be construed as *a body* of men seems doubtful, although in the introduction to his 1969 edition Berlin is far more concessive to critics of *laissez faire* as a threat to *negative* liberty than has been acknowledged in the literature: 'the evils of unrestricted *laisser-faire* ... led to brutal violations of negative liberty' and he regretted his earlier failure to stress the failure of such systems to provide the 'minimum conditions in which alone any degree of significant negative liberty can be exercised by individuals *or groups.*' (my emphasis). Sir Isaiah Berlin, *Four Essays on Liberty* (Oxford, Oxford University Press, 1969), pp. 122 ('Two Concepts of Liberty'), xlvi (Introduction).

acts renders it blameless?[47] Does the imperceptibility of the consequences of each market actor's decisions then also put them beyond moral censure? The answer to this will depend, both on the facts of the case, and on how, precisely, we formulate the question. But this is not to say it is a semantic issue: it has enormous moral, and, if the argument here is correct, political consequences. It is not enough to ask, 'Will my act harm other people?'. I should ask 'Will my act be one of a set of acts that will together harm other people?' The answer may be 'yes'. And the harm to others may be great.[48] If this is the correct way to formulate the moral issue, the market does not emancipate us from moral responsibility, not even if the outcome of market transactions is Pareto-, or in some utilitarian sense, optimal (notice the squeamish torturers may also be working for a good outcome). If the cumulative consequences of our hitherto excusable (because infinitesimal) impacts on the market make a moral difference, what follows is not merely that we have responsibility for the *outcome*, but that we ought to construct institutional ways of ensuring that these outcomes do not eventuate. But since these outcomes may be the consequences only of *combinations* of spontaneous individual actions, and not the consequence (or often even the intention) of any one action, this perception requires that they be coordinated by something other than hidden hands, and the only other candidate for such a co-ordinator is politics.

So far the argument has been directed at the incapacity of the market to deliver certain kinds of goods, especially those of a moral or collective nature. But it might reasonably be objected that this 'moral dilution' argument could be applied to politics too. Both Burke and Madison made the point that because the moral responsibility for political action was proportionate to the number of actors 'a perfect democracy is therefore the most shameless thing in the world'.[49] But this becomes true, as Burke himself was stressing, only if and to the extent that politics is reduced to democracy. We do not need to subscribe to Burke's elitism to agree that politics needs defending from democracy.[50]

The dilution of moral responsibility is a phenomenon both of the market and of democracy. How can politics assist in resisting it? Firstly by stressing and valuing the distinctive character of political decisions.

Political decisions are different. Political decisions do indeed ask us to step back and to make hard choices about (amongst other things) the relative values of

---

47. The example is taken from Parfitt, *Reasons and Persons*, pp. 79–81; 'That Imperceptible effects cannot be morally significant' is the fifth of his 'Five Mistakes in Moral Mathematics', which constitutes Chapter 3.

48. *Ibid*, p. 86.

49. For 'the share of infamy that is likely to fall the lot of each individual in public acts, is small indeed; the operation of opinion being in the inverse ratio to the number of those who abuse power.' *Reflections on the Revolution in France*, C. C. O'Brien (ed.), (London, Harmondsworth, 1968), p. 191. For Madison fear of infamy 'has a less active influence when ... divided among a number of men', *The Federalist*, no. 15, para. 13.

50. *In Defence of Politics*, ch. 3, and *see* P. King's contribution [*Socialism and the Common Good* (London, Frank Cass, 1996)]

items we would normally regard as incommensurable. If taken seriously this not only engenders a kind of awareness not required of market actors, it holds out the possibility of ennobling, and efficacious action in fields where we are otherwise despairingly impotent.[51] When we make a political decision we are aware that we are in some way setting a framework within which individual acts and choices can subsequently be made, therefore, a different rationale to that open to the choosing individual consumer is both possible, and often forthcoming.

For example, given the decline of public transport I might decide as an individual that I need to use a car to get to work; but politically I may (and at the same time) actively support a policy of punitive taxation for motorists to subsidise public transport. As a parent, deploring the lack of resources put into public education I might decide to pay for my child's schooling (assuming that it is education, and not finishing or connections that I wanted) whilst politically supporting the abolition of private schools and massive re-resourcing of state education. I might politically champion a universal publicly funded healthcare, yet if I (or my aged parent, or my child) was unable to receive some life-saving treatment through an underfunded National Health Service, and I could afford to do so, might I not consistently choose to pay for it privately? Such cases are often read as evidence of hypocrisy: why should they not be read as idealism? If an individual puts time and effort into achieving a political ideal, does it follow that she or he is hypocritical because she does not sacrifice to it her child's education (if she believes that to be at issue), or her life, or that of her aged parent or child? Does the argument about moral dilution require these sacrifices?

I think these cases point to something else. They point to the social nature of the goods being sought, to the fact that such goods, as ideals, can only be realised at the political level, and that is therefore the level at which they must be addressed. Like the first performer in Hobbes's state of nature, he who does what is right alone 'does but betray himselfe (or his child, or his parent) to his enemy'; the rules of sociability, however clearly we may see them 'bind onely to a desire and an endeavour', and politics – not love or religion – is the only means by which that endeavour can be made real.[52] But market-based societies present to us choices between goods which are, by and large, consumed alone (or in the nuclear family), they tend always to conceal from us the social, or environmental externalities consequent on the aggregation of choices for such goods, and deny

---

51. The penetrating charity advertisement depicting some wretched, starving person, asks 'Do you really need £10 more than he does?'. The response is undeniable, but persistent awareness of the question renders normal living morally impossible, for it asks us to evaluate our trivial, everyday and mundane wants against human life itself. It is impossible to respond adequately as an isolated individual for I cannot equilibrate our needs without imposing relative destitution on myself and my family. Yet as a citizen and a political actor it is possible to respond in more adequate ways.

52. T. Hobbes, *Leviathan*, R. Tuck (ed.) (Cambridge, Cambridge University Press, 1991), p. 96, [original pagination, p. 68], p. 110 [p. 79]. Not love or religion, because even with the best *will* in the world many of the 'public goods' issues have a large element which is a co-ordination problem.

us the information, or ability to make the relevant discriminations in our choices. There are few profits to be made from the satisfaction of 'group oriented' desires.[53]

The second point to be made is that politics can resist the processes of individualism and moral dilution only inasmuch as it has the specific kind of properties Crick ascribes to it.

It has been remarked that the existence of diverse groups is one of the safeguards of liberty, and of this sense of politics. From Machiavelli's seemingly perverse attribution of Rome's liberty to the contestation between the plebeians and the patricians, through the tremendous eighteenth-century debate on party, of which Madison's reluctant championship of diversity is in some sense the flowering, and Burke's 'little platoon' as the nursery of public affections is the defence, diversity developed *pari passu* with the notion of a liberal and political regime. Since Rousseau, and the French Revolution, Tocqueville, taking his cue from Montesquieu's praise of 'intermediate powers', typified an essentially defensive position in which both (and each of) revolutionary and democratic politics were denounced for their tendency to destroy or erode social groupings, and to atomise the population, a vital element in what we have since come to recognise as mass society, and totalitarianism.[54] The existence of intermediate forms of association is vital to the practice of politics. Such associations educate, skill and empower actors, but some do so more than others. The more closely the ends and actions of the association mirror those of the polity the more they will provide a political education. 'All associations' writes Aristotle, 'aim at some good' but the nature of the good sought will largely determine the character of the association.

Are some forms of association threatened by the market or other manifestations of the individualist premise? It is difficult to deny that this is so. The market predictably intervenes to supply many of the selective benefits which, according to Olsonian logic, might help to support association aimed at collective non-excludable goods. For example, social and sports facilities, if truly being used to subsidise the provision of a non-excludable good, can surely be supplied cheaper

---

53. It is of course true that the Green movement has led to an increased *consumer* demand for environmentally friendly goods, and for demands for products to carry relevant information to consumers wishing to discriminate in their favour. But this is not evidence for the triumph of the market as such, it is the result of *political* argument about these issues, and *political* pressure to provide such information, on the part of green and consumer organisations. Sometimes practical considerations make discrimination impossible. Consider, for example, wanting to be supplied with electricity *not* produced by nuclear technology, or with food or pharmaceuticals which have at *no point* in their production involved genetically engineered organisms.

54. Tocqueville remarks on the 'democratic despotism' theorised by the economists of the eighteenth century, and in danger of being realised in the nineteenth century state: 'abolishing all hierarchies, all class distinction, all differences of rank, ... the nation was to be composed of individuals almost exactly alike and unconditionally equal. In this undiscriminated mass was to reside, theoretically, the sovereign power; yet it was to be carefully deprived of any means of controlling or even supervising the activities of its government ... the State was a law unto itself and nothing short of a revolution could break its tyranny. *De jure* it was a subordinate agent, *de facto*, a master.' *The Ancient Regime and the French Revolution,* tr. Gilbert, intr. H. Brogan, (London, Fontana, 1966) p. 183, and cited in Crick, *In Defence of Politics,* p. 63.

by an organisation devoted solely to the business of sports and social facilities. This would logically lead to the demise of collective action groups. Nor has this happened only through the action of the market. A government in the grip of rabidly individualist public policy initiatives has also had the effect of curbing – by a combination of fiat or studied neglect – many forms of association, notably, for good or ill, those associated with trade unionism, and with local government, but also many others connected with the provision of social goods – in the health service for example.[55] The last decade's privatisation policy, driven by at least a rhetoric of individualism has seen the private expropriation of a mass of wealth and capital accumulated by what were originally, in form, voluntary and local organisations savings banks, local water boards etc.

Moreover a part has been played by a perverse puritanism, which, since at least Mandeville has been the occasional compliment to the theorisation of egoism. For ironically, that same rational egoist premise which in theory argued the implausibility of all forms of association for collective action, led those holding it to mistrust the motives in those associations which they actually found in existence as mere promotional groups, the actions of which distorted the potential of the market to respond smoothly to individuals needs: all associations to influence politics, however altruistically motivated, were presented as a form of rent-seeking behaviour. Existing professional promotional and campaigning groups were therefore sidelined in the policy-making process. All this has been part of a quite explicit drive to replace politics by the market, and to substitute the process of collective, messy and negotiable solutions, with those arrived at impersonally by the individual calculations of isolated consumers.[56] Irrespective of the economic advantages (for whom?) of dismantling promotional groups' influence within the economy, their role in and the general case for a healthy *polity* is never considered. It is a measure of the dominance of the individualist premise that the argument is conducted in purely economic terms.

The demise of such groups, no less than that of an independent local government would involve not only the atomisation of what has ironically been praised so much for its tenuous survival in Eastern Europe civil society; it would involve the loss of all that goes with politics – the skills of negotiation and the disposition to accommodate, the diversity of political resources for the individual as well as for society as a whole, together with the political education they entail and require, a practical sense of the limits of what is possible, and the resulting commitment to working within those limits. What those espousing the individualist premise fail to

---

55. Even by 1986: 'The Centralization from Above and Decentralisation to Markets and Consumers Below has Weakened Local Government', D. Kavanagh, *Thatcherism and British Politics* (Oxford, Oxford University Press, 1987), p. 288. For a period of over ten years, from Margaret Thatcher first taking office until June 1991, there was not a single official meeting at Cabinet level with any representative of the trade unions.
56. For a brisk excursion over the terrain: Bill Jordan, *The Common Good* (Oxford, Blackwell, 1989), chapters two and three.

see, is that even the ability to indulge their individualism presumes the maintenance of vital yet intangible, moral, social and political 'collective goods'.[57] In 1963 Crick wrote: 'Political compromises are the price that has to be paid for liberty.' The startling claim of the new individualism is that liberty might also exact, as its price, the suppression of politics as compromise, and the means and practices by which it is accomplished. He also observed that politicians' aims should be limited 'if they are worthy of support by free men [and, no doubt, women], to things which can be done without destroying politics.' 'And', he went on 'one is not acting politically if one pursues as part of a policy, devices intended to ensure for certain that it can never be overthrown.'[58] The eighteenth century debate about liberty being dependent on party struggle, rather than threatened by faction is by no means dead when a prime minister persistently announces her intention of destroying the opposition.

But is not all this too alarmist? Surely there are always new groupings arising? Even a society devoted to the commercial supply of individually consumed goods will throw up forms of association. The drive of humans to associate, even for the bizarre purpose of private consumption, is a strong presumption in favour of our political nature. Nevertheless we need to discriminate. Machiavelli distinguished between parties based on disputes about liberty and those based on disputes about wealth. This is too crude for our purposes but it is a starting point. A politics which disqualified self-interest as a motive for association would be an exiguous category and an unusual activity. Nevertheless the question of what issues groups or parties take up politically is relevant. Fan clubs or associations of trainspotters are unlikely to generate or promote politics. But more contentiously single issue, want-regarding interest-groups may be, in an important (Crickean) sense less political than other forms of associations – there is one thing such groups want: inasmuch as their intervention into political activity is one-dimensional they cannot engage with others in politically creative, interactive, ways. A group defined in terms of a particular limited desire – to secure rights to a particular waterway for water-skiing for example – has (as a collectivity) little to offer other groups, and has no bargaining counters, for it has itself neither internal diversity, nor other goods to negotiate, it has no *grain* with or against which other political actors may work.[59] A group pursuing a complex, ideal-regarding end, however is not so politically amorphous. Groups seeking complex, principled ends – toleration,

---

57. Our very capacity to operate as 'individuals' is not something we are born with, it is the product of a certain kind of culture, a political culture, which arguably creates in those individuals wishing to avail themselves of the freedoms on offer, obligations to sustain it. *See* C. Taylor, 'Atomism' in *Powers Possessions and Freedom: Essays in honour of C. B. Macpherson*, A. Kontos (ed.), (Toronto, Toronto University Press, 1979), esp. pp. 55–61.

58. *In Defence of Politics*, pp. 145–6. Cf. Margaret Thatcher's oft-repeated aspiration to rid Britain forever of an alarmingly loosely construed 'socialism'.

59. At the extreme are 'sporadic interventionist' groups, which, it has been suggested, form a distinct category of interest group with characteristics of their own; *see* R. E. Dowse and J. A. Hughes, 'Sporadic interventionists', *Political Studies*, XXV (1) (1977).

cultural or ethnic survival, the alleviation of a complex bad, like poverty – are more political. They are more likely to be internally structured, providing points of common agreement and political contact for other groups. They are, or will need to be if successful, more politically educated, they will more likely be enduring.[60] A truly political society will therefore be rich in groups of the latter kind, whereas a 'market politics' envisages most groups being of the former kind. The prohibition of 'political' activity by charity organisations who wish to develop precisely these political aspects of their activity not only inhibits their own efficacy, but the depth and wealth of our own polity. In denying politics to such complex and ideal-regarding organisations, we deny those qualities to our politics. This is not a puritan argument for a politics composed exclusively of ideals (dangerous stuff, Bernard would no doubt say, and rightly so). It is an argument for a true diversity of political argument in a truly political arena and a warning about the narrowing effects of a politics, construed on the model of the economy, on the individualist premise.

---

60. J. Leca, 'Individualism and Citizenship' in P. Birnbaum and J. Leca (eds), *Individualism...* p. 154. Leca draws this distinction using the example of membership of Amnesty International, as against the movement against culling baby seals, hinting at a relationship also between public collective issues and private collective issues. Cf. Hegel's interesting distinction in the *Philosophy of Right*, sect. 236, 249, between truly public goods, and 'private goods that are common to all'.

Chapter Seven

Two Arguments Against Rawlsian Equality[1]

This chapter addresses a particular feature of Rawlsian justice, namely the claim that a concern with substantive equality is to be ruled out as a candidate principle involved in constructing the basic structure of society. It seeks to confute this prohibition by two very different routes. The first of these is to reconsider the eligibility of equality as an ideal which may be ascribed to individuals in the original position. The other, which is not altogether unrelated to the first, is to consider the impact of recent findings about the empirical properties of inegalitarian societies.

Section one lays out Rawls' reasons for rejecting substantive as opposed to background egalitarianism. Section two considers the case for readmitting egalitarianism as an eligible 'good' which individuals might wish to pursue in their construction of the principles of justice. Section three looks at the effect recent evidence about social inequality might have on Rawls' premise that original choosers might take into account those 'general facts about human society ... [that] affect the choice of the principles of justice.'[2] Section four considers the implication for Rawls' principles if the thrust of sections two or three were accepted.

Rawls' rejection of egalitarianism

To say that Rawls rejects egalitarianism is perhaps an overly strong claim to make – indeed Rawls himself claims his principles enshrine a tendency to equality.[3] Indeed his claim that the differentials in our natural endowments are 'undeserved' entitles us, he claims, to consider them a 'social asset to be used for the common advantage'. This has led to a line of criticism that this characterisation of the 'accidents of (differential) natural endowments' is such as to license control by others over our natural endowments (including bodily organs).[4] But of course, Rawls is not *this* much of a collectivist. Rejecting

---

1. As well as the audiences mentioned in the Acknowledgements, I am grateful to Andrew Hindmoor for comments on an earlier draft.
2. *A Theory of Justice*, John Rawls (Oxford, Oxford University Press, 1971; (hereafter cited as *T. J.*) p. 137.
3. *T. J.*, p. 100. And *Political Liberalism* p. 281: 'the obvious starting point is for [parties in the original position] to suppose that all social primary goods, including income and wealth, should be equal;' *Political Liberalism* (New York, Columbia University Press, 1991) hereafter cited as *P. L.*
4. For a review and refutation *see* Thomas Pogge, *Realising Rawls* (Ithaca and London, Cornell University Press, 1989) p. 63 ff.

the looming Nozickean criticism that social control over individual's natural qualities comprises forced labour, Rawls points out that 'natural talents are not a collective asset in the sense that society should compel those who have them to put them to work for the less favoured'.[5] There is almost, but not quite, a contradiction here. One way of saving it is to point out that, however undeserved our natural abilities, they are sufficiently intimately a part of *us* that such control cannot be given up, consistent with any reasonable degree of personal liberty.[6] To insulate it wholly from this line of argument, one also needs to make a distinction which will have importance for argument two, namely the distinction between natural primary goods ('health and vigour, intelligence and the imagination') and the *consequences that flow* from the interaction between those primary goods and social institutions. It is this distinction that enables Rawls to both deny that society has a right to control the deployment of individuals' natural assets, and yet to claim the distribution of advantages resulting from them that most benefits the least advantaged.

Certainly his starting point is that inequalities which derive from differential natural endowments, being 'arbitrary, from a moral point of view'[7] constitute an unfairness which is eligible to be redressed via principles of justice. According to his celebrated difference principle, redress is to be accomplished by selecting that institutional scheme which, in allowing inequalities to develop, most improves the social position of the worst off. The grounds for this is that original choosers, being ignorant of their eventual social position, whilst seeking to protect themselves in the event of their being at the bottom of the social order, could have no interest, once having secured that protection, in preventing the improvement in position of those above that base, since they might turn out to be such persons. Because Rawls is concerned to establish criteria at a meta-level, he is agnostic about what institutions or social policies will do this. Thus if redistributing educational resources to the less well endowed will achieve this end, that would seem to be sanctioned by the principle. But if giving the better endowed the full reward of their efforts will (through trickle-down or some such mechanism) improve the position of the worst off, then that (other considerations – such as the priority of liberty – being equal) is sanctioned.[8] In any event what begins as a presumption of equality becomes a side-constraint on the *growth of inequality*. For the difference principle notoriously licenses institutional schemes permitting *unlimited* differentials

---

5. Rawls, 'Some reasons for the maximin criterion', *American Economic Review*, 64 (May 1974) p. 145.

6. Pogge, *Realising Rawls*, p. 64.

7. *T.J.*, p. 312.

8. Note the role of claims about the empirical features of different social arrangements, a feature of Rawls' argument which is crucial to argument two.

between rich and poor, only so long as there is a minimal improvement in the position of the worst off.[9] Rawls thus adopts an initial principle of intrinsic desert with extremely egalitarian implications, but then relaxes it on utilitarian grounds.

One way of saving the egalitarianism would be to place some constraint on the degree of inequality allowed by the difference principle. For example, instead of the only criterion limiting the growth of inequality being an improvement in the position of the worst off, one could establish an arithmetical, geometrical, or even logarithmic scale of proportionality. The difference principle might require, not simply that the position of the worst off be bettered, but that the proportion of the difference between the best off, the worst off, and (say) subsistence, be maintained or (less stringently) constrained. Or that the ratio of the differences between the median, worst and best off, be sustained. Or that the proportionate improvement in the position of the best off be *matched* by the proportionate improvement in the position of the worst off. Any of these formulae permit inequalities. But what they also do is to limit the *proportion* of inequality permitted. Rawls' argument against any principles of this kind relies on his claim that it would be irrational for original choosers to select such a principle if it denied the worst off the chance of a better (absolute) position under some alternative institutional scheme – even if it allowed greater inequality through increasing differentials at the top end, because such a chooser might be that worst off person. This claim derives from Rawls assertion that the rational strategy for an original chooser to adopt is a maxi-min strategy, i.e. one which maximises the conditions of the minimal outcome. But this claim, in turn derives from the range of decision-making motives and knowledge with which Rawls *accoutres* the original chooser.

Limited egoism's extended reach

Part of his reasoning here is prescriptive. The psychological motivation ascribed to original choosers is one of 'limited egoism'. Egoism – even limited egoism – is an unpromising psychological foundation for generalised, *principled*, equality. But an even more insidious Rawlsian tactic against an egalitarian position is his apparent reduction of egalitarianism to envy. Behind the veil of ignorance, he holds, there could be no self- (or indeed other-) regarding reason for rejecting the difference principle and the consequent potentially unlimited wealth differentials. This is because any permissable growth in inequality could not benefit the successful

---

9. As Rawls himself concedes: 'in theory the difference principle permits indefinitely large inequalities in return for small gains to the less well favoured.' *T. J.*, p. 536. He softens the concession with the complaisant claim, that 'the spread of income and wealth should not be excessive in practice, given the requisite background institutions.' I say complaisant because even at the height of the postwar social welfare programmes, the inequalities generated by capitalist economies (as opposed to those persisting from pre-capitalist forms) showed no sign of diminishing. And of course, since the post 1970s retreat of social democracy, have vastly increased. See Thomas Picketty, *Capital in the Twenty-First Century* (Cambs. Mass., Harvard, Belknap Press, 2014) and J. Stiglitz, *The Price of Inequality* (London, Harmondsworth Press, 2012) p. 30 and passim.

improver without also benefitting the (representative) 'worst off' individual. Under this proviso, no individual accoutred as the OP implies, could have any rational, self-interested motive for objecting to such inequality since, even in the worst case scenario (where she turned out to be the worst-off individual), she would be (personally) better off under a rule that permitted such inequalities, than under one which did not. The veil of ignorance is of course the device that de-personalises the original choosers' motivations, preventing them from pursuing an identifiable personal interest, making self- and other-regarding choices indistinguishable. But this technical device is the avatar of a moralised principle. The only motive Rawls suggests, that could preclude original choosers from accepting such a rule would be a concern with the holdings of others (envious, or 'nosey' preferences), and envious motives (even altruistic ones) are to be excluded (*ex-hypothesi*).[10] It is this subsumption of a preference for substantive egalitarianism under the wider rubric of 'envious' preferences that precludes its role in establishing the basic structure of a just society. The question is: Is there a way of throwing out the envious bathwater whilst retaining the precious egalitarian baby?

Refuting the claim that departures from the difference principle in the direction of substantive egalitarianism involves sanctioning 'envious' preferences invites two possible tactics. One could argue that the assimilation of all motivation having regard to the holdings or treatment of others, whilst safeguarding one's own position to the category 'envy' is mistaken, and that clear distinctions can be made between envious and altruistic versions of such motives, or, more weakly, that, at the very least, maleficent other's-holdings-regarding motivations can be identified and ruled out. Sustaining this line might require a substantive conception of the good, or at least some more general notion of human (collective?) flourishing through which to make the distinction; and arguments that invoked or presumed such standards would, of course, be denied under the problem as Rawls stated. Indeed the avoidance of any such conceptions is a major feature of Rawls' arguments – which increases as he develops his work.[11] However, I do not want to pursue this for the moment.

I want to focus, perhaps more indirectly, on another argument, one which derives from an analysis of the way individualism is characterised.[12] In one of its forms there is no novelty in this strategy. Communitarian and collectivist critiques of Rawls, have spawned a whole counter-Rawlsian industry which rejects the possibility of the characterisation of the individual as distinct from their communally given aims and identities. From such positions, with their presumption

---

10. *T. J.*, p. 144.

11. Rawls describes this movement as one motivated by the attempt to address what he saw as a disconnect between the principles derived in *A Theory of Justice*, and the capacity of citizens in a morally diverse society to endorse them. (*P. L.* p. xvi). I have in mind the determined retreat signalled by 'Justice as fairness: political not metaphysical', *Philosophy and Public Affairs* 14 (summer 1985) pp. 223–251 and *Political Liberalism* itself.

12. And hence links to Chapter Six in this collection.

of the socially constructed character of identity, there would be little difficulty in generating support for greater degrees of equality than the Rawlsian project could countenance. However, such positions have the worrying implication of seeming to privilege collectivities and the self-understandings which they foster over the individual and his choices as such.

My argument, whilst directed at similar concerns, is, I hope, rather different. It seeks to retain the epistemic priority of the individual whilst rejecting the limitations imposed on her by Rawls' argument. One way of characterising the collectivist critique of Rawls in relation to this issue is to say that he ascribes to individuals a motivation which is simply too, and ungroundedly, egoistic.[13] Rawls was surely right to reject the easy if unrealistic ascription of altruistic motivations to original choosers. The social contract tradition in which he places himself found it not hard to derive generous theories of social justice from suitably generous psychologies. The place for altruism, one might say, is *this* side of the veil of ignorance, not the far side. Altruism, paradoxically, is best practised individually, using the liberty provided by the basic structure of society. However there is another dimension to the rational egoistic assumption, and this is the question of whether Rawls' argument is biased towards the assessment of returns not merely *to individuals*, but to *individually consumed* goods. Without abandoning the individual for the community as the locus of our understanding of and reasoning about justice, might it not be reasonable to consider preferences which involve goods which whilst enjoyed *by* individuals, can only be consumed and enjoyed collectively?

The major issues in the field of public goods and social choice have been on the problems of supply in cases of market breakdown. In almost all such cases the policy issues discussed relate to goods which, although public, are consumed individually. Transport, clean water, and even sunsets may be public goods but they are still consumed by individuals. But there are public goods, or perhaps the term collective goods is better here, where what needs to be collective is not merely the provision but the consumption, or those (such as playing team sports) where it is difficult to separate the two aspects. It is those kinds of goods that I focus on and my claim is that the good of living in an equal – or not grossly unequal – society is one such.

Rawls characterises any desire for equality, over and above the provisions of the Difference, and Equality of Opportunity principles, as an *envious* concern with the holdings of others. Granted Rawls' argument perhaps uses 'envy' in a technical rather than a moralistic sense, yet it is difficult not to see in this a (successful?)

---

13. There is a long digression, to be avoided here, about the relationship between Rawls' psychological ascriptions in the OP and those involved in the application of 'economic' models of reasoning to political phenomena. These exhibit an interesting equivocation on whether the 'egoism' in rational egoism, is taken to exclude returns to other agents. Briefly in his introduction to *Public Choice II*, Dennis Mueller says that 'the basic behavioural postulate of public choice, as for economics, is an egoistic, rational, utility maximiser' (p. 2), whereas for Iain McLean, *Public Choice* (p. 3) 'Rational does not mean self-interested'. *See* further on this: Chapters Eight and Ten in this volume.

attempt to trade rhetorically on the moral opprobrium that normally attaches to the term 'envy'.[14] The propriety of such a description privileges a certain feature of the social context derived from the possession and enjoyment by individuals of individually consumed goods. A's desire for more equality than the difference principle can deliver is, on this view, a desire that individual B should have less and individual A should have more of what A consumes or possesses. But why should *this* description of the situation be privileged? Might we not characterise a preference for equality as a preference – akin to the enjoyment of playing team sports – for a good which, whilst it is *enjoyed* by the individual, can only be consumed jointly with others? The preference for a more egalitarian society is, on any account different from an envious preference about others' holdings. Not least because the second could be satisfied by swapping the social positions of the two individuals. Whereas the former could only be satisfied by altering the social positions themselves. Another way of expressing this is to substitute a concern with individual *holdings* by a concern for the relationships which hold between individuals. Sincere egalitarians are concerned about the quality of social *relationships* obtaining where inequality prevails, rather than on the *quanta* of utility individually consumed by different individuals. To have a preference for living in a more, rather than a less, egalitarian society is then not normally to possess envious *motives*. Certainly it would be odd to so characterise the motives of those who enjoyed an income above the average and yet supported egalitarian policies, as opposed to merely lifting basic social provisions – as many do.

Whilst 'equality' clearly expresses a relational characteristic, Rawls' argument characterises that relational characteristic in terms of a comparison between the individual holdings of (say) citizen A and those of citizen B. But 'relation', 'relationship' and their cognates are systematically ambiguous. They can refer to the different quantities possessed by the two entities in the relationship in such a way that this comparison of differences is the most salient feature of it, but a relationship can also be a *quality of the connections* between two elements. This opens up a surely more plausible way of conceiving of the value of social equality, in that it refers to the properties or quality of the *ties between members* of a society, on the intrinsic properties of that relationship, properties which are

---

14. It is worth remarking that in public political debate, it is a common tactic of the economically libertarian right to ascribe envious motives to social democrats supporting egalitarian (or even mildly redistributive) policies. Thus for example: Winston Churchill; 'Socialism is a philosophy of failure, the creed of ignorance, and the gospel of envy.' (Online. Available http://www.nationalchurchillmuseum.org, last accessed 31/03/2015). Margaret Thatcher, in her inaugural (1950) candidacy claimed to be enlisting in: 'a battle between two ways of life, one which leads inevitably to slavery and the other to freedom. ... You cannot build a great nation or a brotherhood of man by spreading envy or hatred. Our policy is not built on envy or hatred, but on liberty for the individual man or woman.' (Online. Available http://www.margaretthatcher.org/document/102777, last accessed 31/03/2015). 'Envy is much older than any political system or any political ideology. Envy does not exist because socialism exists. Rather, socialism refers to and needs envy.' Robert Nef, 'Socialism, Envy and Redistribution.' (Online. Available http://www.libinst.ch/?i=socialism-envy-and-redistribution--en, last accessed 31/03/2015).

exhibited in the way that the *relationship between members is lived out*, rather than on a *comparison of the consumption opportunities separately available to each* of the individual members of it.

As Hegel pointed out, there is something perverse about characterising non-economic relationships – such as those of affective love, or political belonging, in terms of the relative inputs and benefits of the parties – an overly self-conscious or calculating approach to them effectively destroys them.[15] Rather, we claim in such cases that there is something intrinsic which *is the quality of the relationship itself* rather than the mere comparison between features of the two individuals comprising it, or even the description of what each of them does *in it*. Another way of characterising a valuing of equality, then, rather than say that it is an expression of concern about individual's comparative holdings, is surely to say that it expresses a concern for the intrinsic qualities of the relationships *between* citizens consequent on those holdings.

There is nothing particularly novel about this. When Rousseau (who thought *both* liberty and equality 'the greatest good of all') remarked that 'no citizen should be rich enough to have the power to buy another, nor so poor as to be reduced to selling himself'[16] – whatever he meant by that – he was expressing an important feature about equality as a relationship *between* citizens that had nothing to do with envy but much to do with power. (Although he did have another argument about the destructive psychological effects of inequality, which *does* refer to the emergence of envy and contempt.)[17]

Analytically, it is clearly difficult to find a way of characterising the relationship of equality which does not collapse into the kind of 'envious' comparison disqualified by Rawls. But a focus on the intrinsic qualities of the relationship is surely central to any such endeavor. But it is, it seems to me, difficult to be clear about what is meant by intrinsic. Justifications of the importance of the relationship for citizenship say, generate arguments which refer the benefits of equality to some other set of values or institutions, and so tend to undermine, in one sense, their claims to be intrinsic. If I want equality because it sustains relationships of mutual respect amongst citizens, and mutual respect is a prerequisite for the operation of the polity, is it the intrinsic qualities of the relationship that I am valuing, or is equality valued instrumentally in terms of what follows from it? Much hinges on the (empirical) question of whether equality is the only source of the kind of respect needed to sustain citizenship. Rawls himself addressed a version of this issue in part three of *A Theory of Justice*. But his claim there that his theory will

---

15. Hegel, *Philosophy of Right*, tr. T. M. Knox, (Oxford, OUP, 1952), 'the right which the individual enjoys ... takes on the *form* of right only when the family begins to dissolve.' §159; 'If the state is confused with civil society ... then the interests of the individuals as such becomes the ultimate end of their association, [and] ... membership of the state is something optional. But the state's relation to the individual is quite different.' §258.
16. Rousseau, *Social Contract* Bk II, Ch. 11.
17. Rousseau, *Discourse on the Origins of Inequality* (London, Everyman, 1992) pp. 92–6; Rousseau, *Emile* (London, Everyman, 1911) p. 95.

indeed be sustainable in its own terms, i.e. it would be affirmed by its own citizens, thus sustaining a sense of, and commitment to justice, is one that he subsequently recognises is vulnerable, and dominates his work in the papers preceding, and synthesised in, *Political Liberalism*.[18] But the aspect of the problem Rawls addresses is the cognitive and epistemic one of how to reformulate the status of the argument of *A Theory of Justice* in such a way that it can claim acceptability to a '*demos*' holding a diversity of reasonable, comprehensive doctrines. He sidesteps what has again become a salient issue, namely, of the degree of equality that might be needed to sustain a sense of justice.[19] Indeed, in Rawls' later works the salience of equality – and the operation of the difference principle – fades into insignificance. There are barely half a dozen references to the difference principle in PL, and no references at all to material equality – whereas 'constructivism', 'public reason' and 'reasonable' command whole columns of entries. But even if equality is valued and justified here consequentially (and most kinds of justification open up consequentialist perspectives on the value that is justified), the focus is still on the quality of the relationship, rather than on quantities of its elements. In this sense a distinction can be drawn between arguments for equality based on envious (disaggregative) considerations, and one based on the intrinsic (holistic) properties of the relationship (even where consequentialist considerations apply).

But my valuing of equality might be much more unequivocally intrinsic. It may be unrelated to any consequences that flow from it other than the mere enjoyment of relationships which are in fact egalitarian. I might simply relish the fellowship of equals (in a paradoxically quite selfish way?) – egalitarianism might simply be a social taste to which my life-plan turns out to accord a very high priority. It is, however, a taste which can only be jointly supplied. On what grounds does the Rawlsian enterprise establish bias against this kind of taste?

It might be objected that a preference for living in an egalitarian society looks much more like a preference for a particular way of life or even a (major component of a) conception of the 'good'. Thus, it might be claimed – as hinted at the beginning – that the argument in favour of equality was a way of smuggling in a conception of the good, about which the original choosers are supposed to remain agnostic. But calling it a taste may be to concede too much. Given the centrality of equality to a wide range of aspects of social, co-operative existence, a commitment to a degree of substantive equality looks surely much more like a reasonable comprehensive doctrine? But why should this preclude consideration of it. The Rawlsian objection cuts both ways. Rawls' conception

---

18. I paraphrase Rawls' own account of this intellectual trajectory in the introduction to *P. L.*, pp. xv–xvi.
19. *Vide* Rousseau, above, fns. 16, 17. And once again, Hegel: 'When the standard of living of a large mass of people falls below a certain subsistence level – a level regulated automatically as that necessary to be a member of society ... there is a consequent loss of the sense of right and wrong...'. *P of R*, §244; 'Against nature man can claim no right, but once society is established, poverty immediately takes the form of a wrong done to one class by another. The question [of abolishing poverty] ... is one of the most disturbing problems which agitate modern society.' *P of R*, Addition 149 to §244.

of justice is supposed to be neutral as between different (rational) comprehensive conceptions, and it is this that sustains the possibility of citizens' commitment to it. Characterising a degree of equality as an individually enjoyed, but necessarily jointly supplied good, is an attempt to meet the criterion of reasonableness. The egalitarian might, if Rawls' method proscribes his value, object that the Rawlsian is as guilty of smuggling *out* a reasonable conception of the good as the egalitarian is of seeking to smuggle one *in*.

Notice that the reach of these arguments, however brash, is intended to be a very modest one. It is not an argument for absolute equality (whatever that might mean). It is an argument against the outright *disqualification* of equality as a value. It is an argument for readmitting egalitarian considerations to the array of values and principles that might turn out to comprise a complex conception of justice. In the range of goods, preferences and possible lives we might turn out to value why should a preference for egalitarian relations be ruled out *a-priori*?

Argument two: Egalitarianism and empirical findings about inequality

This section pursues an entirely different tactic to the previous one. Instead of questioning the conceptual presuppositions on the basis which Rawls' principles are constructed, it proceeds by accepting the original position and the veil of ignorance as regulatory constraints on the generation of social principles. Its focus instead is on the way in which our increasing knowledge of the effects of inequality may affect the conclusions that original choosers may legitimately be thought to have drawn from them. I rely heavily on data provided in Richard G. Wilkinson's *Unhealthy Societies: The afflictions of inequality*, which synthesises a huge range of empirical work.[20] The thrust of it will, I hope, push in the same direction as the first, namely that of re-legitimising a concern with equality as a substantive principle, rather than only as concerned with the absolute holdings of the less well off.

The argument by which Rawls establishes his principles of justice relies heavily of course on the properties attributed to individuals, and conditions constraining their reasonings in the original position, conditions designed to guarantee the impartiality of any resulting principles. A major feature of those conditions is the original choosers' necessary *ignorance* of various aspects of their own existence once they emerge into the real world. By contrast, far less attention has been paid to the *knowledge* that the choosers *are* allowed and the difference this knowledge might make to the admission of egalitarian principles in structuring society. In deliberating about the informing principles of their political society, the original choosers know, Rawls claims: 'the general facts about human society ... understand political affairs and the principles of economic theory ... the basis of social organisation and the laws of human psychology. Indeed ... whatever general

---

20. Richard G. Wilkinson, *Unhealthy Societies* (London, Routledge, 1996); The argument is now restated with more evidence and applied beyond health to the wider field of social welfare in R. Wilkinson and Kate Pickett, *The Spirit Level: Why more equal societies almost always do better* (London, Allen Lane, Penguin Books, 2009).

facts affect the choice of the principles of justice.'[21] It is on this condition that the spotlight now falls.

Rawls' characterisation of 'general facts about society' has always seemed to me to be at best very naively expressed. He commonly implies that some of the more contestable claims in social theory, particularly economics, might enjoy a status, or at least be amenable to a more positivist appraisal, than many of us would wish to allow them. For example, although Rawls claims ultimately to be agnostic about, and seeks to insulate his theory from, the contingent features of how economies actually function, many of his discussions seem to assume the existence of a trickle-down effect in capitalist economies, just as they assume that a market system 'is consistent with equal liberties and fair equality of opportunity'.[22] That is to say, as far as the difference principle is concerned, Rawls is committed in principle to pursuing whatever economic arrangements (consistent with the prioritisation of the principle of equal liberty, and fair equality of opportunity) are necessary in order to realise it – even if – *per impossible* – this meant a socialised economy. But in fact, all his discussions seem to assume that it is an agreed social fact that some version of a free market with or without redistributive taxation is what will deliver this.[23]

This kind of 'social knowledge' is knowledge about social processes, mechanisms and institutions, which, even without advancing categorical skepticism about objective knowledge in such fields, such 'knowledge' is, I suggest, far more ideologically contestable than Rawls seems to allow. Which version of this 'knowledge' original choosers are provided with will clearly affect the kinds of institutional arrangements they formulate, and hence their formulation of the principles of justice. But I want to focus on the implications of relatively uncontroversial factual knowledge which original choosers might reasonably expect to have available to them.[24] Knowledge about the facts surrounding the 'indefinitely large inequalities' permitted by Rawls' difference principle has become increasingly salient recently. Factual claims about the economic consequences of inequality have been advanced by figures of some intellectual weight, and endorsed by commentators who can hardly be considered radical mavericks.

---

21. *T. J.*, p. 137.

22. *T. J.*, p. 272.

23. *T. J.*, p. 274. In the health sector a highly plausible such counter-claim, might be grounded in the 'social fact' that infant and maternal mortality rates in Cuba with its regime of socialised state-medicine, have for long considerably bettered those in the private-medicine regime of the USA.

24. As I revise this for publication, an Oxfam Report ahead of the World Economic Forum meeting in Davos predicts that on current trends, by the end of 2016, the richest 1% of people would own more than 50% of the world's wealth. One of the six co-chairs commented: 'The message is that rising inequality is dangerous. It's bad for growth and it's bad for governance. We see a concentration of wealth capturing power and leaving ordinary people voiceless and their interests uncared for.' *The Guardian*, 19 January 2015. When I say uncontroversial, I mean to say that the evidence for the facts is uncontroversial. The claims themselves, as opposed to their epistemic basis, remain of course, widely politically contested.

Nobel Economics Prizewinner Joe Stiglitz has argued at length that inequality in (particularly) the USA has reached the point where has a deleterious effect on economic growth, provides resources for the distortion of political representation and decision-making which feeds back into opportunistic rent-seeking that exacerbates inequality.[25] Some of these effects have clear implications for Rawls' principles. If inequality can reach a point where (as claimed) it affects both liberty and equality of opportunity, the difference principle cannot be allowed to generate the kind of unlimited inequalities Rawls described. This is because Rawls claims (i) priority for the liberty principle and (ii) that the difference principle is *subordinate* to the principle of equality of opportunity.[26] Yet if, as claimed by Stiglitz, and endorsed by the *Economist,* it is a fact that extremes of inequality threaten not only liberty through the political opportunities that discrepant economic power generates, but also the meaningfulness of equality of opportunity, and even growth itself, then there are surely serious problems which cut to the heart of Rawls' project. Individually, it might be argued that Rawls' principles can as it were, take these findings on the chin and process the empirical evidence accordingly. But the wider tenor of Rawls' discussion and the ordering of his principles suggests that they are more discrete and separable than the new facts warrant. Some of the 'social facts' identified by Stiglitz disconcert the very architecture of the Rawlsian project. In particular it makes it difficult to make sense of the claim to the absolute priority of equal liberty, and the priority of the principle of equality of opportunity over the difference principle, given the impact of possible outcomes of the latter on the operation of the former. But they also pose problems within the difference principle itself. Naively permissible increases in the position of the wealthy, sanctioned by concomitant increases in the position of the worst off, might nevertheless restrict growth, and hence the position of both. It is beyond the scope of this paper to tease out the full implications of these empirical findings, but if inequality beyond a certain level disrupts equality of opportunity, and even equal liberty, then the lexical ordering of the principles: satisfy equal liberty, then equality of opportunity, then the difference principle, cannot, in any simple sense, hold.

However complex these issues are, the argument I now want to advance concerns a much more clear-cut finding, one with, I urge, unequivocal consequences for Rawls' principles. It is of course a commonplace that wealth affects health and life expectancy. Poor countries have higher mortality rates than richer ones. Rawls acknowledges that during the process of economic development all aspects of life will improve, including, presumably, life expectancy.[27] Crucially, medical historians identify the 'epidemiological transition', the point in social and economic

---

25. Joseph E. Stiglitz, *The Price of Inequality* (London, Penguin Books, 2013). Amongst the mainstream commentators agreeing with Stiglitz that inequality seriously undermined equality of opportunity and had 'reached a stage where it can be inefficient and bad for growth' was *The Economist:* 'True Progressivism', 13 October 2012.

26. 'One applies the second principle by holding positions open, and then, subject to this constraint, arranges social and economic inequalities so that everyone benefits.' *T. J.*, p. 61.

27. 'The process of accumulation ... is to the good of all subsequent generations.' *T. J.*, p. 288, and ff.

development at which the predominant cause of death ceases to be infection related to living conditions. This transition is also marked by other features such as an increase in the social distribution of diseases of modernity and affluence – coronary heart disease, stroke, hypertension and suicide – and aesthetic shifts – once the poor cease to be thin and swarthy it becomes fashionable for the rich to diet and be tanned. A further feature of mortality after the epidemiological transition is the levelling off of the curve of rising life expectancy with increasing per capita GNP.[28]

However, time-series comparisons apart, within rich countries, wealthy people have healthier lives, and live longer than poorer people.[29] Strikingly, neither health nor mortality rates play a large part in Rawls' account of the primary goods which an individual might reasonably require in order to pursue whatever life-plan they adopt once situated in the real social world. One possible explanation is because he assumes health and longevity to be direct secondary effects of wealth.[30] There is a more detailed discussion of this by Rawls' champion, Thomas Pogge who acknowledges that Rawls is 'far too sanguine' in assuming healthcare to be 'of only marginal significance for the appraisal of a conception of justice.'[31] However his attempt to remedy this focuses on how justice impacts on issues of *access to medical treatment* and on the issue of socially produced illness 'due to the actions and interactions of participants in the social system' such as general pollution, or proximity to health-affecting plant or facilities.[32] This is in keeping with the spirit of Rawls, in the presumption that appraising justice is a matter of assessing returns to, and resources available to individuals. However, as in the first argument, what I want to focus on is not individual outcomes and their amelioration, but the health implications of the purely *relational* aspects of inequality. Specifically, the need for the rules of justice to be sensitive to the complexity of the relationship between the *distributional* aspects of wealth and longevity.

Let me first of all canvas the more ambitious claim that a roughly equal degree of healthy longevity should be considered as a weighty primary good, to be placed in the scales alongside (not subject to) even liberty in assessing the justness of a set of social arrangements. Focusing on health differentials as appropriate and independent objects of contemplation can hardly be considered beyond the Rawlsian pale. To an original chooser many of the considerations that establish the priority of liberty apply also to healthy longevity. For being alive and healthy is, like liberty, a condition of pursuing any of the more specific goods and life-plans that actual individuals may propose to themselves. Like liberty itself, a life is after all a condition for the pursuit of any *particular* life-plan. A longer, healthier life (just like a more extensive plan of liberty) will enable any individual to gain more

---

28. R.G. Wilkinson, 'Income distribution and life expectancy', *British Medical Journal* (1996); and *Unhealthy Societies*, (London, Routledge, 1996), Fig. 1.
29. *Unhealthy Societies* p. 73, Fig. 2. And many other studies.
30. *T. J.* p. 94.
31. Pogge, *Realising Rawls*, 16, p. 181 ff.
32. *Ibid.*, 16, 1–5.

of whatever particular goods they wish to achieve. Longevity and health, moreover, they might reflect, are arguably *more basic* goods than liberty itself. An important strand of criticism of Rawls derives from the claim that the prioritisation of a scheme of extensive liberties can conflict with some reasonable comprehensive doctrines. Unlike liberty, healthy longevity does not impose something on people whose life-plan, on emerging from the veil of ignorance, turns out not only not to value it, but to find positively burdensome. Life in a society with the most extensive plan of liberty may turn out to be anomic for those with communitarian dispositions. But having the social conditions for a potentially long and healthy life, we are always individually free, through devotion to fast food, cigarettes, alcohol, and serious drugs or just high risk sports, to shorten it. Denied that potential, it is not always (as we shall see) easily to be individually acquired. A long healthy life is a good which can, however quixotically, be abandoned in the way that the burden of freedom cannot. Rawls' arguments about the priority of liberty deriving from its strategic importance to other goods, could be applied *a fortiori* to health and longevity.

The core thought is that any rational, individual, original chooser would surely seek to maximise healthy life, as part of a more general principle of acting 'so that he need never blame himself no matter how things finally transpire ... any risks he assumes must be worthwhile, so that should the worst happen that he had any reason for foresee, he can still affirm that what he did was above criticism.'[33] The knowledge that they would need healthy longevity to maximise their life-plan would clearly be available to an individual behind the veil of ignorance, it should therefore properly enter into their calculations about the principles informing the basic structure of society. Healthy longevity may plausibly be considered not only a primary good, and as such a reasonable object of consideration to those behind the veil of ignorance, but even a principle to be incorporated within the lexical ordering of complex justice itself.

Up to now I have been exploring the implications of allowing healthy life expectations the kind of salience Rawls accords to liberty, and have argued that there would be a clear *prima facie* case for prioritising a concern with equality of life expectancy, just as he requires equality of liberty. I now relax such claims about that salience, and focus on healthy longevity merely as one possible object of an individual's effort and resources, in competition with other aims and projects (whatever they turn out to be). On this view, it might be thought, reflections on healthy longevity would not upset Rawls' conclusions regarding the irrelevance of substantive equality to the principles of justice. As original choosers do not know their eventual social positions, or priorities, they could not assume the salience *for them* of healthy longevity. They could still have an interest in living in a society which, in some *aggregative* sense, enjoyed more healthy longevity, but given the device of the original position there is no way in which they could, from behind the veil, express their interests in being the beneficiaries of health

---

33. *T. J.* p. 422.

or mortality *differentials*. Thus even allowing that healthy longevity was a good, and even acknowledging (which is undoubtedly true) that social and economic inequalities relate systematically to inequalities in health and longevity, and that original choosers can know this, it is not clear how such knowledge could inform their choices so as to reach different conclusions about the principle of justice from those who did not have access to these social facts. Nor does it seem that more detailed empirical knowledge about inequality could upset this conclusion. However, I want (1) to assert that this conclusion is not, in principle, inviolably insulated from such empirical evidence. And (2) to point to such empirical evidence as exists in respect of (1).

If we presume healthy longevity to be a consequence of individual decisions, whether about life-style or prudential investment in health insurance, the hard-nosed Rawlsian response might be to say that the existing difference principle deals with this in at least a rough and ready way already. Since it allows inequalities only on condition that the material condition of the worst off is improved, and since it is the worst off whose life expectancy is presumed to be most at risk, any increase in inequality will benefit those in the percentile experiencing the diminished life expectancy, and their average life expectancy will therefore be lifted through the operation of the difference principle. But this comforting (for Rawlsians) thought is vulnerable to two points, both of which rely on empirical findings about the relationship between inequality and mortality. The striking feature of these findings is that they appear to reveal healthy longevity to be sensitive to inequality *per se* and not merely *via* the paucity of the resources available to the worst off.

The first is the observation that it is not the case that mortality tracks poverty in the tight way that would enable the difference principle to cover concerns about the former through addressing the latter. In terms of mortality, some individuals are better off *without* the operation of the difference principle. Amongst comparable, modern societies, some slightly less well off societies which are more egalitarian turn out to have higher life expectancies not only on average but also amongst the worst off.[34]

The second discomfiting thought is as follows. Much of Rawls' argument – both his original argument and the 'Rawlsian defence' which I have constructed against my own position – presumes that the life-expectancy disadvantages of inequality attach specifically to those who are in the bottom percentiles. The presumption – already exposed – being that, at least on average, absolute material disadvantage tracks, and is a reliable proxy for, life expectancy. On this view distributional features affect average life expectancy in a society only through the contribution made to that average by those in low percentiles who possess less wealth or social goods. The presumption is that of two societies with the same GDP (sc. economic and social goods) the one with the more inegalitarian distribution will have a lower average life expectancy because the lower life expectancy of the more materially deprived, will not be offset by an equal increase in life expectancy amongst the

---

34. Wilkinson, p. 84, Fig. 3.

more wealthy. (Individuals in societies, like students in exams, find it marginally more difficult to extend their score as they pass seventy.)

However this will not help the hard-nosed Rawlsian, for the bad news is not only to be found at the bottom of society. The presumption that the lower average life-expectancy of inegalitarian societies is solely a function of the depressed expectations of the lower percentiles turns out not to be the case. The differential in life expectancy amongst the poor in inegalitarian societies is not arithmetically sufficient to explain the average difference in life expectancy between that and another, similarly, *or even less wealthy*, but more egalitarian society.[35] In other words (above a certain threshold, well exceeded by modern societies) there is an absolute distributional effect on life expectancy irrespective of the absolute levels of income involved, irrespective that is, either of the level of the worst off, or of the average. Individual expenditure cannot evade these distibutional effects. Strikingly – although clearly other variables such as social cohesion, themselves not unrelated to inequality might intervene here – *mortality rates in every social class* are higher in unequal England than they are in egalitarian Sweden.[36] Inequality, it turns out, kills, not only in poor societies, but even in very rich ones, and even in rich societies inequality kills not only the very poor but the very rich as well. Thus the original chooser would be able to maximise healthy living only by abandoning the difference principle for one that constrained the growth of inequality within such limits.

Implications for Rawls' principles

My first argument sought to admit a concern with equality as a reasonable principle of intrinsic worth, to be considered as a substantive ideal, worthy to be set against others in formulating the principles of justice. It did so by seeking to find a way of characterising inequality as a relational quality of social wholes, rather than an expression of the difference between individuals' holdings, and of re-inserting the legitimacy of such conceptions in arguments about social justice. The second argument was much more concessive. It granted the moral psychological and motivational ascriptions of Rawls' original choosers and considered the consequences of their assessing inequality only on the basis of the difference principle, in the light of contemporary evidence about the properties of unequal societies. Such knowledge, it is suggested, would lead the original choosers to give serious consideration to economic and social equality in its own right as a way of protecting their life expectancy, even where imposing such equality would entail a reduction in the absolute standard of living – not only for the rich but even for the worst off. In order to capture the impact of these inequalities on life expectancy I suggest the more puckish original choosers would come up with the following mildly subversive reformulation of the difference principle: 'Inequality should be restricted to the extent that it improves the life expectancy of the worst off.'

---

35. Wilkinson, p. 91.
36. Wilkinson, p. 88, Fig. 4.

Chapter Eight

Rational Choice and Interpretive Evidence: Caught Between a Rock and a Hard Place?

co-authored with Andrew Hindmoor

In a celebratory article published to mark the 25th anniversary of the journal *Public Choice*, Dennis Mueller predicted not only that public choice theory would 'dominate political science in a generation or less' but that 'alternative approaches to the study of politics would eventually wither away and die.'[1] Yet barely a year later Donald Green and Ian Shapiro's *Pathologies of Rational Choice Theory*[2] sparked a backlash against the use of rational choice theory within political science, culminating in the submission of a petition to the American Political Science Association in 2001 demanding greater methodological pluralism.[3]

Green and Shapiro did not object to the use of rational choice theory *per se*. Indeed they welcomed its attempt to study politics scientifically and, in a response to their critics, identified circumstances in which 'rational choice explanations should be expected, *prima facie*, to perform well'. What they objected to was rational choice's 'universalism'; to the misconceived attempt to 'construct a unified, deductively-based theory from which propositions about politics – or, indeed, all human behaviour – may be derived'.[4] Such an approach had, they suggested, encouraged the development of a 'method-' rather than 'problem-driven' approach to the study of politics and to what Shapiro subsequently termed a 'flight from reality'.[5] Finally, and more specifically, they argued that a commitment to using rational choice to explain everything had distracted its practitioners from seeking empirical evidence with which to support their accounts, had blinded them to the 'banal' character of many rational choice explanations and had encouraged them to select biased evidence, to ignore competing explanations and to engage in post-hoc theorising in order to reconcile their arguments with empirical anomalies or discordant facts.[6]

---

1. Dennis Mueller, 'The future of public choice', *Public Choice*, 77 (1993), 145–50, p. 147.
2. Donald Green and Ian Shapiro, *Pathologies of Rational Choice Theory* (New Haven CT, Yale University Press, 1994).
3. *See* A. Hindmoor, *Rational Choice* (Basingstoke, Palgrave Macmillan, 2006), pp. 15–19.
4. Green and Shapiro, *Pathologies...*, pp. 94–5; 54.
5. I. Shapiro, *The Flight from Reality in the Human Sciences* (Princeton NJ, Princeton University Press, 2005).
6. Green and Shapiro, *Pathologies...*, p. 6.

In examining rational choice's record, Green and Shapiro focused exclusively upon the extent to which theorists provided empirical evidence about the 'outside'[7] of an event: that is evidence, usually quantitative in form, about the behaviour and the effects of the behaviour of particular actors. They looked, for example, at the way in which rational choice theorists had sought to test their arguments using quantitative data on the spatial positioning of political parties, the formation of interest groups and legislative voting patterns. Evidence, on this view, consists in a 'fit' between the deductions of rational choice theory and observed institutional or behavioural outcomes in any particular case. In what follows we will refer to empirical evidence of this sort as being 'external'. However, we argue that rational choice is also compromised by its failure to provide another kind of empirical evidence, namely 'internal' or interpretive evidence about the beliefs of the agents whose actions comprise the phenomena to be explained. Our distinction between external and internal evidence maps on to the well-known distinction between a behavioural and ultimately positivist conception of political science and a hermeneutic or interpretive one. The former models external 'behaviour', seeking explanation by way of statistical or deductive fit without presuming any intimate relationship between belief and action (hence external). The latter presupposes that action instantiates belief, and thus that any explanation of action must incorporate statements about the beliefs of actors. Internalist explanations do not claim access to private mental states; they are 'internal' only in the sense of being internal to the world of meanings inhabited by the actor. External explanations, by contrast, which work via correlations or deductions on the basis of ascribed reasons, need not concern themselves with actors' understandings of the world.[8] In arguing this, we seek to discriminate among and clarify the roles rational choice might usefully play within political science.

---

7. R. G. Collingwood, *The Idea of History* (Oxford, Clarendon, 1946).
8. The distinction – widely discussed in a range of terminologies – is made and discussed in these terms by Bernard Williams, 'Internal and External Reasons', in R. Harrison (ed.), *Rational Action* (Cambridge, Cambridge University Press, 1979). Ian Shapiro, 'Realism in the study of the history of ideas', *History of Political Thought*, 3 (1982), pp. 568–69 has previously (and rather critically) discussed the status of interpretive evidence within political science in relation to Q. Skinner's work on the history of political thought. A small part of this argument is included in *The Flight from Reality* (2005), pp. 33–5. Papers by Schiemann (J. Schiemann, 'Meeting halfway between Rochester and Frankfurt: generative salience, focal points, and strategic interaction', *American Journal of Political Science*, 44 (2000), pp. 1–16; R. Bates, R. Figueiredo and B. Weingast, 'The politics of interpretation: rationality, culture and transition', *Politics and Society*, 26 (1998), pp. 156–221, and R. Bates, A. Greif, M. Levi, J. Rosenthal and B. Weingast, (eds), *Analytic Narratives* (Princeton NJ, Princeton University Press, 1999), H. Esser, 'The rationality of everyday behaviour: the rational choice reconstruction of the theory of action by Alfred Schulz', *Rationality and Society*, 5 (1993), pp. 7–31. J. Ferejohn, 'Rationality and Interpretation: Parliamentary elections in early Stuart England', in K. Monroe (ed.), *The Economic Approach to Politics: A critical reassessment of the theory of rational action* (New York, Harper Collins, 1991) pp. 279–305, and J. Dryzek, 'How far is it from Virginia and Rochester to Frankfurt? Public choice as critical theory', *British Journal of Political Science*, 22 (1992), pp. 397–413 have also, and to varying degrees, discussed the relationship between interpretive evidence and rational choice theory.

Our claim about the relevance of interpretive evidence will be more fully elaborated in the next section. However it may be useful at this point to outline the logic of explanation to which we subscribe here. We are not merely calling for more weight to be given to agents' self-descriptions or qualitative analysis in some eclectic explanatory mix. Our point is that even deductive explanations, if they purport to model agents' actions, must (logically) share premises with the agents, and that a failure to achieve this, while it might result in an explanatory conclusion that models the agents' actions, will only do so contingently. That is to say, while individuals may well economise in making choices, what they economise about is available to them via a cognitive repertoire through which they construe how the world is (and so what choices are available to them), what causal or other chains of efficacy operate there and how values are to be ranked. Evidence about such cognitive presuppositions can be derived from that person themselves whether directly through interviews or indirectly through speeches, memoirs, diaries or other records, or (more speculatively) can be ascribed on the basis of educational and cultural background, congruence with other evident belief features, etc.[9] The holding of such beliefs – even if they are false – thus constitutes demonstrable features of the actors, relevant because agents act on such beliefs.

It is our contention that any explanation that ignores this is radically dissociated from reality. On this account, any model of economic calculation is logically secondary to these cognitive features of the actors' world.[10] Hence we claim

---

9. There is not space here to develop how such 'circumstantial' evidence for beliefs can be constructed. Historians of thought such as J. G. A. Pocock in the USA (e.g. J. G. A. Pocock, 'Introduction: The state of the art', in Pocock (ed.), *Virtue Commerce and History* (Cambridge, Cambridge University Press, 1985); and 'The Concept of a Language and the *Metier d'Historien*: Some considerations on practice', in A. Pagden (ed.), *The Languages of Political Theory in Early Modern Europe* (Cambridge, Cambridge University Press, 1987); and R. Koselleck, *Futures Past: On the semantics of historical time*, with introduction by K. Tribe, (Cambridge Mass., Harvard University Press, 1985) in Germany have (in different ways) elaborated how 'languages' comprising key terms, their associations, oppositions and locutions might be identified as coherent wholes. This enables the identification of candidate subscribers to such a language or conceptual vocabulary on the basis of a speaker's or writer's deployment of certain key locutions. For discussions *see* M. Richter, 'Pocock, Skinner and *Begriffsgeschichte*', in M. Richter (ed.), *The History of Social and Political Concepts* (Oxford, Oxford University Press, 1995); and I. Hampsher-Monk, 'Speech Acts, Languages or *Begriffsgeschichte*?', in I. Hampsher-Monk, K. Tilmans and F. van Vree (eds), *History of Concepts, Comparative Perspectives* (Amsterdam, Amsterdam University Press, 1998) pp. 37–50.

10. The claim is that 'the base level of historical economic or sociological analysis must lie in an account of human action which is, in Weber's famous terms, meaningfully as well as causally adequate'. In consequence 'the moral sciences are interpretative'. For an acute analysis of this claim drawing on secession theory which reveals the important role of hermeneutic understanding in relation to rational choice theory, *see* J. Skorupski, 'Explanation and Understanding in Social Science', in D. Knowles (ed.), *Explanation and its Limits: Royal Institute of Philosophy Lectures: 27*, (Cambridge, Cambridge University Press, 1990). For a wider discussion by one of the authors drawing on a different literature in the philosophy of choice *see* Iain Hampsher-Monk, 'Prices as Descriptions: Reasons as explanations', in J. Melling and J. Barry (eds), *Culture in History: Production, consumption and values in historical perspective* (Exeter, Exeter University Press, 1992) [Reprinted in this volume, Chapter Nine].

that rational choice explanations overplay the calculative at the expense of the cognitive.

In the following section we show just how infrequently rational choice theorists employ such interpretive evidence within their work. Between 1984 and 2005 36 per cent of the articles published in the *American Political Science Review* and the *American Journal of Political Science* employed rational choice theory. Yet whereas around 60 per cent of these tested their arguments against some form of external empirical data, only 24 per cent provided any interpretive evidence; moreover, this proportion included instances in which as few as one quotation was provided in support of some argument. Only a small fraction of the articles we surveyed provided extensive interpretive evidence about how actors understood and reasoned about the world derived from, for example, questionnaires or interviews.

Does the neglect of interpretive evidence within rational choice theory matter? In castigating rational choice theory for its failure to provide interpretive evidence are we, as Dennis Chong[11] maintains more generally of Green and Shapiro's argument, holding rational choice to too high a standard? In the third section we argue that this can be seen to depend upon whether rational choice is understood instrumentally (as simply making falsifiable predictions about external behaviour or events), structurally (as providing accounts of the ways in which irreducible structural or relational social properties cause outcomes) or realistically (as making descriptive claims about how agents actually reasoned in acting as they did). Instrumental and structural approaches need not involve a commitment to any specific claims about the way in which actors understand, reason and make choices and can therefore reasonably plead agnosticism about providing interpretive evidence in support of their claims. Yet for reasons that we presently elaborate on, such understandings of rational choice theory risk encouraging the flight from reality.

If, however, rational choice is understood as an empirical modelling of the psychology of choice, the provision of interpretive evidence provides explanations with greater credibility by linking them more firmly to the reality they purport to explain.[12] So as to illustrate our argument about the explanatory value of interpretive evidence, the fourth section examines a paper on 'Coalition Policymaking and Legislative Review'.[13] This chapter, which in our view neatly

---

11. D. Chong, 'Rational Choice Theory's Mysterious Rivals', in J. Freidman (ed.), *The Rational Choice Controversy: Economic models of politics reconsidered* (New Haven CT., Yale University Press, 1994), pp. 37–57.

12. For a now classic exposition of this claim *see* Alasdair MacIntyre, 'A Mistake about Causality in Social Science', in P. Laslett and W. G. Runciman (eds), *Philosophy, Politics and Society*, 2nd series, (Oxford, Blackwell, 1969).

13. L. Martin and G. Vanberg, 'Coalition policymaking and legislative review', *American Political Science Review*, 99 (2005), pp. 93–106.

illustrates the strengths and the weaknesses of the rational choice approach, makes a series of quite specific claims about the goals politicians have and about the ways in which they attempt to achieve them. Yet no interpretive evidence is provided with which to substantiate these claims, which remain, therefore, mere ascriptions of motivations. An obvious implication of our critique would seem to be that rational choice theorists need to invest more time in the provision of interpretive evidence. There is, however, a problem here. The provision of such evidence risks making certain applications of rational choice explanation redundant. For if, as is the case in Martin and Vanberg's paper, rational choice explanation is directed toward showing that individuals can be expected to act in particular ways in order to achieve particular goals, interpretive evidence showing that actors did indeed behave in that way for just that reason calls into doubt the need for the rational choice explanation.

In the final section of the chapter we therefore seek to clarify the role rational choice theory might usefully play. Firstly, rational choice explanations may prove powerfully suggestive when actors are either unaware of the reasons why they acted in a particular way or cannot be trusted to provide an honest account of those reasons. Secondly, rational choice might be used to analyse and explain the unintended aggregate consequences of individual action. Finally, rational choice can be used to address comparative questions about the way in which institutions affect behaviour. In the first of these cases interpretive evidence is not needed because it cannot be relied upon. In the second and third cases, although it is relevant for the assessment of an explanation, it does not entirely subsume that which the explanation is intended to achieve. In these cases rational choice can also perform a programmatic role by suggesting how rational individuals might be expected to act, providing an agenda for empirical research as to whether such actions were indeed performed and, if so (and indeed if not), how the predicted behaviour was mediated by their beliefs.

Interpretive evidence and rational choice

The *American Political Science Review* and the *American Journal of Political Science* are routinely ranked as two of the leading journals in the discipline.[14] Between 1984 and 2005 they published 570 articles which we classified as using rational choice theory.[15] Figure 1 shows the number of such articles as a percentage of the total number of articles published in these journals. In total,

---

14. See, for example, the citation-based rankings used by Essential Science Indicators at http://www.in-cites.com/research/2006/february_27_2006-1.html where these are ranked as the top two journals (last accessed 1/4/2015).

15. While there is a general consensus upon the distinguishing features of rational choice theory (J. Elster, 'Introduction', in J. Elster (ed.), *Rational Choice* (Oxford, Blackwell, 1986), pp. 1–33; Hindmoor, *Rational Choice*, pp. 1–4; Mueller, 'The Future…', pp. 1–5), there is no simple way

and across both journals, over a third of the published articles employed rational choice theory.

Green and Shapiro claimed that 'a large proportion of the theoretical conjectures of rational choice theorists have not been tested empirically'.[16] Although it is not clear what ought to be counted as a large proportion, of the 570 articles we surveyed, 347, or just over 60 per cent, invoked some form of external empirical evidence in defence of their argument.[17] As a number of the remaining articles deal with normative or purely theoretical issues which it would not have been appropriate to test using evidence of this sort, this would seem to be quite a high total.[18] This does not, however, necessarily mean that Green and Shapiro mis-characterised the rational choice literature as, for example, is claimed by Shepsle,[19] for the publication of *Pathologies of Rational Choice Theory* may itself have encouraged journal editors and/or rational choice practitioners to be more scrupulous in invoking external empirical evidence. It is indicative that between 1984 and 1993 (prior to the publication of Green and Shapiro's work),

---

of drawing the boundaries between rational and non-rational choice approaches within individual papers. For this exercise, papers were classified as using rational choice theory on the basis of two criteria. (1) The assumptions they employed – including the commonly employed but not ubiquitous assumption of self-interested behaviour (Hindmoor, *ibid.*, p. 4), methodological individualism and the assumption of rationality, and more specifically the assumption that individuals respond in predictable ways to changes in the underlying incentive structure; and (2) the methods they select – including the use of formal models, spatial analysis, game theory, social choice theory and principal-agent analysis. Four hundred and nine articles were classified as satisfying these criteria. In a further 161 cases where one of the criteria was satisfied an article was then classified as using rational choice on the basis of a more detailed examination of the literature upon which the article drew. Those articles written as critiques of the rational choice approach were excluded. The identification of articles was undertaken by and is available from Hindmoor. We ought to emphasise that nothing in our argument about rational choice theory hinges upon the specific assumption of self-interest. The provision of interpretive evidence is of significance whether self- interested or altruistic motivations are ascribed to individuals.

16. Green and Shapiro, *Pathologies...*, p. 6.
17. Papers making use of computer simulations were *not* counted as making use of external empirical evidence. Papers making use of subject experiments *were* included. We have not attempted to identify the proportion of articles that, although tested against external empirical data, exhibit other methodological failings identified by Green and Shapiro such as the selection of easy cases or the failure to test competing theoretical explanations.
18. Examples of papers for which it would not be appropriate to provide empirical evidence would include K. Dowding and M. Hees, 'The construction of rights', *American Political Science Review*, 97 (2003) discussion of the 'construction of rights', Christian List's work on rationality and path dependence (C. List, 'A model of path-dependence in decisions over multiple propositions', *American Political Science Review*, 98 (2004), pp. 495–513) and Bendor and Meirowitz's demonstration that it is possible to derive existing insights about bureaucratic delegation from a smaller set of assumptions. (J. Bendor, and A. Meirowitz, 'Spatial models of delegation', *American Political Science Review*, 98 (2004), pp. 293–310.) To clarify, these papers were included in our initial list of rational choice work.
19. K. Shepsle, 'Statistical political philosophy and positive political theory', *Critical Review*, 9 (1995), pp. 213–22.

Figure 8.1: Percentage of articles using rational choice theory, 1984–2005

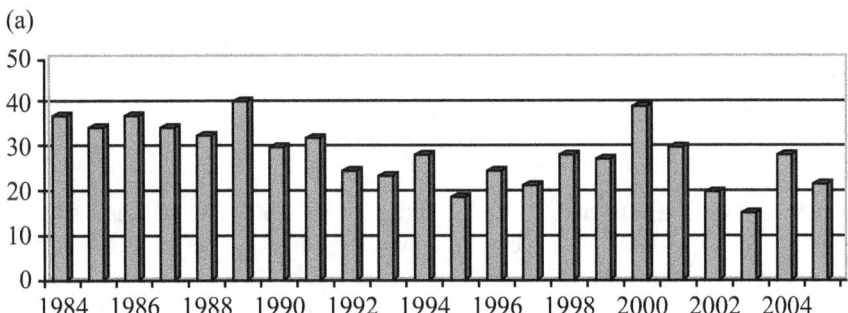

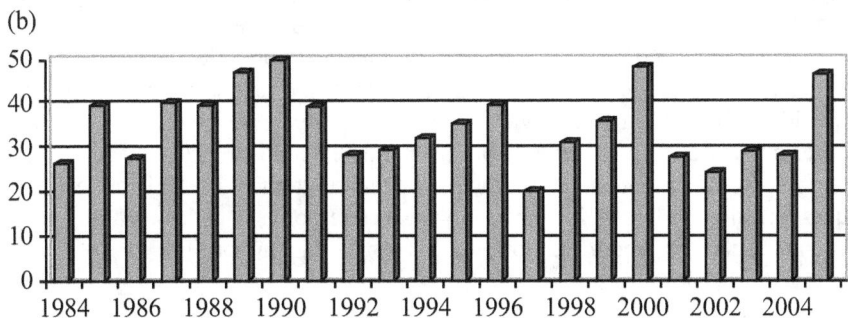

Notes: (a) Percentage of articles using rational choice in *American Journal of Political Science*, 1984–2005. (b) Percentage of articles using rational choice in *American Political Science Review*, 1984–2005.

the proportion providing this form of empirical evidence was 52 per cent. Between 1994 and 2005 this rose to 69 per cent.[20]

We also identified those articles providing some form of interpretive evidence about the way in which real-world actors actually perceive the situation they find themselves in or the reasons they gave for acting in a particular way. The standard we employed here was an extremely permissive one. We included in our total thirty-three articles that provided as few as a single quotation from a politician, bureaucrat or some other actor used to illustrate a general claim about motivation or belief. We also included forty-eight articles which, although they did not seek to test the veracity of their explanations against interpretive evidence, nevertheless used survey data on, for example, voting behaviour drawn from the

---

20. Our general argument in this article is that arguments ought to be tested against interpretive empirical as well as external empirical data. This particular argument ought, therefore, to be treated with considerable caution as we have not interviewed rational choice theorists and editors about whether, following the publication of *Pathologies of Rational Choice Theory*, they are conscious of having placed more emphasis upon the provision of empirical evidence.

Table 8.1: Articles providing interpretive and empirical evidence

	Provides interpretive evidence	Does not provide interpretive evidence
Provides empirical evidence	109 articles	238
Does not provide empirical evidence	30 articles	193 articles

American National Election Studies, as the basis of their argument. Yet even with this extremely permissive conception, only 139 articles, 24 per cent of the total, provided *any* interpretive evidence at all.

Table 1 indicates the way in which external empirical and interpretive evidence is combined within papers. Two hundred and thirty-eight articles (42 per cent of the total) provided external empirical but no interpretive evidence. One hundred and ninety-three articles (34 per cent of the total) provided neither external empirical nor interpretive evidence. One hundred and nine articles (19 per cent) provided external empirical evidence and interpretive evidence and only thirty articles (5 per cent) provided interpretive but no external empirical evidence. It is possible to point to a number of articles that make extensive use of interviews and questionnaires to test claims about how actors reason and understand the world and make choices. These are, however, very much in a minority.[21]

The status of rational choice

Does it matter that rational choice theorists make so little use of interpretive evidence? We want to argue that it does, although the way in which it matters depends upon the status accorded to rational choice explanations, and the purpose

---

21. As examples *see* L. Baldez, and J. Carey, 'Presidential agenda control and spending policy: lessons from General Pinochet's Constitution', *American Journal of Political Science*, 43 (1999), pp. 29–55; D. Carpenter, 'Adaptive signal processing, hierarchy and budgetary control in federal regulation', *American Political Science Review*, 90 (1996), pp. 283–302; P. Gurian, (1986) 'Resource allocation strategies in presidential nomination campaigns', *American Journal of Political Science*, 41(30) (1986), pp. 802–21; E. Muller, and K. Opp, 'Rational choice and rebellious collective action', *American Political Science Review*, 80 (1986), pp. 471–88; E. Muller, H. Dietz, and S. Finkel, 'Discontent and the expected utility of rebellion: the case of Peru', *American Political Science Review*, 85 (1991), pp. 1261–82; M. Potoski, and A. Prakash, A, 'Green clubs and voluntary governance: ISO 14001 and firms' regulatory compliance', *American Journal of Political Science*, 49 (2005), pp. 235–48; L. Rottenberg, 'Organizational maintenance and the retention decision in groups', *American Political Science Review*, 82 (1988), pp. 1129–52. One referee objected to this conclusion by arguing that journal editors impose strict word limits and that 'if you are going to do rational choice seriously and incorporate interpretive evidence, you need to write a book'. Developing this point it may be argued that journal articles are there to develop arguments and ideas that are subsequently provided with interpretive support during a book-length treatment. It is certainly possible to identify books that employ the rational choice method and make extensive use of interpretive evidence – key examples might include Dennis Chong's *Collective Action and the Civil Rights Movement* (Chicago IL., University of Chicago Press, 1991);

to which rational choice explanations are put. In relation to the first there are three broad possibilities.

(1) Rational choice is a realist theory that explains people's actions in terms of their conscious mental states.[22] A rational choice or action is one that an agent takes because they believe it to be the best action available to them given their beliefs and desires. Rational choice is, in this sense, a theory that seeks to describe, albeit in a much simplified manner, what is actually going on within someone's head when they decide to act in a particular way.

(2) Rational choice is an instrumental theory that can be used to generate predictions about behaviour. The crucial and defining assumption rational choice theory makes is that individuals are to be construed as being instrumentally rational in the sense of having reflexive, complete and transitive preferences that they seek to maximise. The status of rationality here is, following Ludwig Von Mises, that of an apodictic axiom that is ascribed to individuals and that generates testable claims about the world of behaviour. It is not meant to constitute a description of how people actually reason about the world and make decisions. All the assumption entails is that an agent's action can be interpreted as if they are maximising preferences in order to see what follows.[23]

(3) Rational choice is a structural rather than individualist theory.[24] Rational choice explanations are explanations about structural or relational properties of social wholes rather than individual actions. For this reason it does not matter what preferences are ascribed to individuals because it is structural forces that generate outcomes. For example, in the neoclassical theory of the firm, the argument that firms act to maximise their profits does not hold in virtue of the beliefs of any of the actors within the firm, but because in a competitive market only those firms

---

William Riker's *The Art of Political Manipulation* (New Haven CT., Yale University Press, 1986); Iain Mclean's *Rational Choice and British Politics: An analysis of rhetoric and manipulation from Peel to Blair* (Oxford, Oxford University Press, 2001); Diego Gambetta's *The Sicilian Mafia: The business of private protection* (Cambridge Mass., Harvard University Press, 1993). We have not attempted a general survey of published books using rational choice theory so cannot compare the use of interpretive evidence across books and articles. The referee who drew this argument to our attention is however clearly not arguing that all published books using rational choice theory make use of interpretive evidence so the critical argument developed here applies to at least a part of this wider body of rational choice scholarship. We do not however intend to concede too much ground here. We recognise the inescapable demands imposed by word limits but do not believe that these require authors to make an unpalatable choice between developing an interesting and original argument and providing interpretive evidence. Indeed, as we go on to argue, the real problem here is that the provision of interpretive evidence risks making the very *deployment* of a rational choice explanation redundant.

22. Frank Lovett, 'Rational choice theory and explanation', *Rationality and Society*, 18 (2006), 237–72, p. 268 describes such an understanding of rational choice as 'ubiquitous' while Debra Satz and John Ferejohn, 'Rational choice and social theory', *Journal of Philosophy*, 91 (1994), 71–87, p. 71) describe it as 'the received interpretation'.
23. Ludwig Von Mises, *Epistemological Problems of Economics* (Princeton, NJ., Von Nostrand, 1960), ch. I, section VI.
24. Satz and Ferejohn, 'Rational choice…'; and Lovett, '… theory and explanation'.

that maximise their profits survive. It thus holds whether entrepreneurs are actually motivated by the desire to maximise profit or by an other-worldly desire for eternal salvation.[25]

If rational choice is understood as a realist theory then it matters a great deal whether individuals do in fact understand and reason about the world in the way ascribed to them. If individuals are, in point of fact, salvation seekers when it has been assumed that they are profit seekers, then a rational choice explanation employing such an assumption will be factually incorrect, and likely to produce false predictions over at least part of the range of phenomena to which it is applied. As we argue in the final section of the article, there are situations in which it may be necessary to test the accuracy of assumptions indirectly against empirical evidence. But because a number of explanations, only one of which is correct, may nevertheless be consistent with the same set of empirical facts, the results of such tests ought to be treated with caution. Where it is possible to do so, the best way of determining whether actors understand, reason and make choices in the way ascribed to them is usually to ascertain as directly as possible whether they hold such beliefs. When it is construed in this way the paucity of interpretive evidence within rational choice theory is a cause for concern.

If, however, rational choice theory is understood in either instrumental or structural terms then it is not obvious that interpretive evidence ought to be accorded the same status. Understood instrumentally, all that counts in judging the value of some model is whether it can be used to make accurate predictions and, perhaps whether, on this basis, it can be used to inform policy decisions. Interpretive evidence about whether individuals really understand and reason about the world in the way ascribed to them does not matter since, it is claimed, nothing directly hinges upon the realism of such assumptions.[26] In a similar way, if rational choice is understood structurally then what counts is whether some argument provides an accurate account of the ways in which structural properties generate outcomes and not whether individuals have the preferences ascribed to them.

So can we therefore conclude that the paucity of interpretive evidence does not necessarily matter given that rational choice can be plausibly defended in instrumentalist or structuralist as well as realist terms? For two reasons, we want to argue that it does matter. Firstly, we concur with the views of those who argue that instrumental and structural approaches are problematic. We make a strong claim here: that as social scientists our primary goal ought to be to explain actions and the events constituted by them. Theories and arguments that ascribe to people reasons and understandings they do not possess cannot be considered to constitute satisfactory explanations even if they can occasion accurate predictions. If it is assumed that entrepreneurs are profit-maximisers when they are in fact seeking

---

25. Satz and Ferejohn, *Op. Cit.*, pp. 78–9.

26. P. MacDonald, 'Useful fiction or miracle maker: the competing epistemological foundations of rational choice theory', *American Political Science Review*, 97 (2003), pp. 51–65.

salvation then any argument using this assumption cannot constitute a satisfactory explanation of why entrepreneurs behave in particular ways, even if the aggregate outcome of salvation-seeking entrepreneurial activity is the same as that of profit seeking. As Daniel Hausman comments, 'there is no methodological magic wand that makes empirical complaints about the psychological constituents of rational-choice explanations disappear.'[27]

To suggest that it does not matter whether people reason and choose in the way ascribed to them is to license an explanatory flight from reality. Such a flight will have potentially harmful policy consequences if models that can be used to explain a population's behaviour in an instrumental sense but have not been grounded in positive claims about the actual motivation and beliefs of agents are used to predict how people will behave in new situations.[28] While the (rational) choices made by profit maximisers and salvation seekers will, for example, tend to be congruent in 'normal' times, they will diverge as the millennium arrives. For this reason the realist understanding of rational choice theory ought to be preferred to the instrumental or structural one precisely because it demands the provision of interpretive evidence that can be used to specify the range over which the explanation both actually explains, and hence can be used to provide, predictions.

Once it is recognised that the different explanatory statuses to be found under the 'rational choice' umbrella are methodologically quite distinct, it is our second argument that it is possible to observe clear equivocations between the methodological precepts rational choice theorists routinely commit themselves to and the claims that they sometimes make in their actual work. When called upon to defend the value of their work against charges that people are not 'really' rational or selfish, rational choice theorists routinely play the instrumentalist card and argue that the accuracy of the assumptions used in a particular model is of no importance. Yet while many of the articles we surveyed emphasised that their assumptions in general and their ascriptions of particular understandings and reasons to actors in particular were not meant to be realist, most nevertheless presented them as providing an account of actors' actual reasons and motivations.

We will shortly examine the claims made within one particular, and we think illustrative, article. But first consider more generally the kinds of claims made within other papers published in one randomly chosen year, 1996. They include the following: that the leaders of parties elected under multi-member districts will avoid adopting the same policy positions as their opponents and that parties elected in multi-member districts will therefore be more ideologically diverse than those elected in single-member districts;[29] that most of the increase in overall

---

27. D. Hausman, 'Rational choice and social theory: a comment', *The Journal of Philosophy*, 92 (1995), pp. 96–102.

28. D. Hausman, 'Why Look under the Hood?', in *Essays on Philosophy and Economic Methodology* (Cambridge, Cambridge University Press, 1992).

29. G. Adams, 'Legislative effects of single-member vs. multi-member districts', *American Journal of Political Science*, 40, 1 (1996), pp. 129–44.

incumbency advantage in America can be traced to increases in the experience of candidates;[30] that American politicians embark upon legislative reforms in order to gain partisan advantage;[31] that Congressmen seek reappointment to committees in order to increase their chances of re-election;[32] that prime ministers use confidence-vote procedures to exercise significant control over the nature of policy outcomes;[33] and that the decisions of judges to change their votes reflect strategic calculations rather than principled decisions.[34] These all appear to commit the authors to a realist rather than instrumental or structural understanding of their argument. This is, in one sense, to be welcomed; because, as we have just argued, instrumental and structural understandings are problematic. Yet given the realist status apparently claimed for them, the general paucity of interpretive evidence within these and other rational choice articles ought to be considered a cause for concern.

In the final part of this section we anticipate and respond to one possible objection to our argument so far. This is that explanations that invoke interpretive evidence are not really explanations at all but are simply 'thick descriptions'.[35] The claim here is that we can have rational choice explanations or we can have interpretive understandings but we cannot combine rational choice explanations with interpretive evidence. Phrased in this way, such a criticism only gains purchase through its stipulative claims about what explanation is. But it is rendered stronger by a widely endorsed view of the logic of explanation. This claims that true explanation involves a logical distinction between the *explanans* and the *explanandum* and that if what is to be explained cannot ultimately be distinguished from that which purports to explain it then there is something spurious about the claim.

Against this we wish to claim that any given action of an agent is framed by their perception of the situation, and their beliefs about the circumstances in which they find themselves and about how the world works. This is not a claim about the 'epistemic' authority of agents about their reasons for action; it is a realist claim about the ontology of action; about what action is. The claim that individuals' beliefs are a constitutive part of the act does not however, presuppose the completeness or adequacy of such 'thick description'. That is to say, it does

---

30. G. Cox, and J. Katz, 'Why did the incumbency advantage in US House elections grow', *American Journal of Political Science*, 40 (1996), pp. 478–97.

31. S. Binder, 'The partisan basis of procedural choice: allocating parliamentary rights in the House, 1789–1990', *American Political Science Review*, 90 (1996), pp. 8–20.

32. J. Katz, and B. Sala, 'Careerism, committee assignments and the electoral connection', *American Political Science Review*, 90 (1996), pp. 21–34.

33. J. Huber, 'The vote of confidence in parliamentary democracies', *American Political Science Review*, 90 (1996), pp. 269–82.

34. F. Maltzman, and P. Wahlbeck, 'Strategic policy considerations and voting fluidity on the Burger Court', *American Political Science Review*, 90 (1996), pp. 581–92.

35. C. Geertz, 'Thick Description: Towards an interpretive theory of culture', in Geertz (ed.), *The Interpretation of Cultures: Selected essays* (New York, Basic Books, 1973) pp. 3–30.

not exhaust the requirements of an explanation. It does not for example preclude the possibility that action might be maximising or strategic, or that there may be different possible aims; it is simply a claim that the elements of the maximising or strategic action imputed to the agent (the constituents of the world, the identity of what is to be maximised, the causal beliefs informing the relationship between action and intended outcome) must themselves be those which the agent would recognise as their own. For this reason we do not believe that rational choice explanations that invoke interpretive evidence thereby forfeit their explanatory credentials. Indeed quite the opposite is the case. For explanations that function without at some point engaging this feature of the act – without, as it were, hooking on to the understanding and intentionality of the actor who brings about what is to be explained – are essentially dislocated from the reality that they purport to explain.

The redundancy of rational choice?

So as to illustrate our general argument about the significance of interpretive evidence we now analyse in detail the claims made in an article by Lanny Martin and Georg Vanberg on 'Coalition Policymaking and Legislative Review'.[36] This article exemplifies the strengths of the rational choice approach in so far as it uses some very basic assumptions about politicians' motives to generate an original argument about political behaviour which is then tested against external data. It also provides us with a typical example of how rational choice theorists neglect interpretive evidence and, as we go on to suggest, a particularly stark example of how the inclusion of interpretive evidence risks rendering rational choice explanation redundant.

Martin and Vanberg start by arguing that coalition governments must grapple with an ongoing agency problem. On the one hand, parties within a coalition have good reason to cooperate with their partners in the pursuit of successful common policies. On the other, each party possesses continuing incentives to renege upon any prior agreements and use its control of particular ministries to pursue its own policy preferences.[37] Using a spatial model the authors then demonstrate that if monitoring and enforcing a coalition agreement is costly, coalition parties will find it in their interests to tolerate some level of agency costs. The central and original part of their argument lies in their claim that parties can lower the costs of monitoring and enforcing agreements (and thereby reduce agency costs) by relying upon members of their legislative faction, particularly those who are members of the committees reviewing legislation, to 'investigate the anticipated consequences of a proposed bill, to study the justifications offered by the drafting minister, to consider alternative policies, and to draft amendments to ministerial drafts.'[38]

---

36. Martin and Vanberg, 'Coalition Policymaking ...'.
37. *Ibid.*, p. 94.
38. *Ibid.*, p. 97.

This argument is then tested using external empirical data on amendments to drafts of government bills in Germany and Holland between 1983 and 1994. Controlling for a number of factors, the authors find that parties are more likely to amend those pieces of legislation over which they have different policy preferences from their coalition partner.[39] Yet they also find that this does not hold true for opposition parties. The degree to which opposition parties' policy preferences differ from those of the governing coalition makes no difference to the number of amendments they succeed in making. On this basis they suggest that legislative committees may be politically important not because, as is usually thought to be the case, they provide opposition parties with some degree of policy influence but because they provide a forum for parties *within* a governing coalition to scrutinise and so control each other's actions.

Martin and Vanberg's article makes a series of quite specific claims about how politicians understand the world, what they want and how they go about achieving it. The argument is, in other words, realist rather than instrumentalist or structuralist in spirit. Yet with the exception of one quotation from a textbook by a couple of German politics specialists to the effect that 'parliamentary groups of the coalition parties do not accept government proposals uncritically, particularly when such proposals derive from ministries held by another party to the coalition',[40] the only empirical evidence offered in support of the argument relates to the fate of particular pieces of legislation. Yet imagine that the authors had, with the same impressive attention to detail, asked senior German and Dutch politicians whether they believed that parties within governing coalitions of which they had been a part would, if given the opportunity, have pursued their own policy preferences and how they sought to prevent them from doing so. Furthermore, imagine that an overwhelming number had said that their coalition parties *would* have pursued their own policy preferences and that one way in which they sought to prevent them from doing so was to use members of their own party to investigate and, if appropriate, amend legislation emanating from ministries controlled by one of their coalition partners. When considered alongside the external empirical evidence, would this not constitute further and impressive evidence in favour of the purported explanation?

The provision of interpretive evidence can increase our confidence in the accuracy of explanations that make specific claims about how people understand, reason and choose. The potential benefits afforded by interpretive evidence do, however, come at a considerable cost to the claims made about the power and range of rational choice explanations. For in some cases the provision of interpretive evidence provides *such* strong evidence in favour of some rational choice explanations that it actually risks rendering them redundant. It is not at all obvious why you need a rational choice explanation that tells you that politicians placed in a certain situation will do Y for reason Z if you can simply ask politicians

---

39. *Ibid.*, pp. 101–3.
40. *Ibid.*, p. 97.

who have found themselves in that situation whether they did Y for reason Z. The danger of redundancy obviously applies to Martin and Vanberg's argument. But, to take a second example, it also applies to Ethan Bueno de Mesquita's argument about 'The Quality of Terror'.[41]

In this article the author develops a game-theoretic model of the 'interaction between a government, a terrorist organisation, and potential terrorist volunteers'. This shows how 'individuals with low ability or little education are most likely to volunteer to join the terrorist organisation' but that 'the terrorist organisation screens the volunteers for quality'. This means that actual terrorist operatives are not poor or lacking in education even though lack of economic opportunity and low levels of economic development are positively correlated with terrorism.[42] Yet having demonstrated how 'in a sub-game perfect equilibrium of the game the terrorist organisation always chooses the highest ability operatives available from the set of volunteers', the author then goes on to quote from an al Qa'eda training manual, captured by the British police and now available on the web, which encourages commanders to 'select ... trainees carefully' and recruit only those who display 'intelligence and insight, truthfulness, maturity, prudence, patience, and who possess the ability to act and to analyse and conceal information'.[43] Does the provision of this interpretive evidence give the argument greater credibility? At a first glance it certainly does. It is reassuring to find that a game-theoretic model can apparently tell us something about the behaviour of a little-understood terrorist organisation. Yet, upon reflection, it is not clear why we need game theory to tell us that terrorist organisations will screen volunteers for quality when this information can be downloaded from the web.[44]

---

41. E. Bueno de Mesquita, 'The quality of terror', *American Journal of Political Science*, 49 (2005), pp. 513–30.

42. Bueno de Mesquita, *ibid.*, p. 517. This argument – about the recruitment and screening of volunteers – is the central argument of the article and, as such, the one emphasised in the abstract. It is not, however, the only argument within the article. Indeed in many ways the article offers a useful illustration of the way in which rational choice theory can be used to account for the effects of comparative differences in costs and benefits in a comparative setting (*see* the final section).

43. *Ibid.* p. 523.

44. It has been suggested to us that rather than regard the provision of this kind of evidence as rendering rational choice redundant we ought, instead, to see it as establishing a test and confirmation of the explanation in much the same way that measuring temperature and pressure independently enables us to test the hypothesis embodied in Boyle's law. But such a comparison needs to discriminate carefully between what is being explained and the evidence for that explanation. The purpose of rational choice explanation is not (normally) taken to be to test the truth of the rational choice axiom but to provide a logically watertight explanation of the chosen event(s). The perfect gas law is an inductively arrived at descriptive generalisation, which itself is used as an explanation of individual phenomena (such as bursting balloons). Rational choice is an axiomatic formulation enabling deductive implications to be drawn which are themselves testable. Instances of gas behaviour confirm or disconfirm the law. The behaviours under discussion here are certainly subject to possible rational choice explanation but they neither confirm nor disconfirm the rational choice axioms since the latter are not assertions about the world, and they can hardly be 'proofs' of the existence of outcomes, or of beliefs or motives, since all of these are known independently to be the case.

The role of rational choice

This raises what is for us the following crucial question. If rational choice is best understood as a realist theory and if realist theories are best supported by interpretive evidence, of what value is rational choice theory if interpretive evidence also renders such explanations redundant? Is rational choice caught between the rock of providing explanations that lack a crucial kind of evidence and the hard place of offering redundant explanations? In the final part of this article we argue that rational choice *may* prove to be a useful technique for political scientists to employ in three particular circumstances.

Firstly, rational choice explanations may prove valuable when there is reason to believe that actors are either unaware of their reasons for acting in a particular way or have an incentive to provide a misleading account of their actions. In such cases there may be no alternative but to make assumptions about why people behave in particular ways and to test these indirectly against empirical data. As rational choice theory frequently assumes that people are self-interested and that in the political arena they will often have an incentive to dissemble about their motives, this is a significant qualification.

Consider, in this context, a paper by Torun Dewan and Keith Dowding on 'The Corrective Effect of Ministerial Resignations'.[45] Citing a paper by Ian McAllister[46] the authors suggest that ministerial resignations are usually seen as a cause of government unpopularity. Against this they hypothesise that it is likely to be the initial political problem or scandal leading to a resignation that causes the unpopularity and that a ministerial resignation is likely to 'provide a corrective device against falls in popularity' as a prime minister is rewarded for acting decisively in firing a problem minister or reshuffling a cabinet. Indeed the authors argue that ministerial resignations are 'designed' to produce just such an effect.[47] In testing this argument they analyse data on ministerial resignations in the United Kingdom between 1955 and 1988. They then claim to demonstrate, among other things, that 'when there is an issue deemed serious enough for there to be calls for a minister's resignation and where this issue has received substantial media attention, then a corresponding resignation will correct for the effect the problem has on government popularity'. Indeed they show that it will more than correct for it which suggests that 'Prime Ministers should welcome a certain number of resignation issues so that they can fire ministers, thereby enhancing government popularity'.[48]

---

45. T. Dewan and K. Dowding, 'The corrective effect of ministerial resignations on government popularity', *American Journal of Political Science*, 49 (2005), pp. 46–56.

46. Ian McAllister, 'Prime Ministers, Opposition Leaders and Government Popularity in Australia', Paper presented to the Australasian Political Studies Association Conference.

47. Dewan and Dowding, 'The corrective effect of ministerial resignations...', p. 47.

48. *Ibid.*, p. 54.

As is the case in most of the articles surveyed, no interpretive evidence is provided with which to support this claim. Does this matter? On the one hand, we would want to argue that it does. The impressive empirical evidence the authors provide shows that resignations do indeed correlate with an increase in government popularity. It does not, however, show that they are (as they claim) 'designed' to produce this effect. Candid extracts from memoirs, diaries or interviews showing that politicians who sacked ministers did so because they thought this would increase their popularity or at least prevent the haemorrhage of support would therefore constitute an alternative and powerful source of empirical evidence. Yet for the reasons already emphasised, evidence of this sort could be so overwhelming as to risk rendering the rational choice argument redundant as an explanation. In this case, however, we have good reason to doubt whether current or former prime ministers, even if they agreed to be interviewed, would confirm that they sacked ministers for this reason and we cannot therefore reasonably require that conclusive interpretive evidence be provided.[49]

Secondly, rational choice explanations may comprise part of an explanation where what is being explained concerns the unanticipated consequences of individual action. Explanations of this sort are usually grounded upon claims about how individuals understand, reason and act. Yet interpretive evidence used to substantiate such claims will not exhaust explanation in so far as that explanation also involves further claims about how individual actions generate unanticipated results.

Our survey of articles published between 1984 and 2005 included a number of articles that sought to explain the unintended consequences of individual action.[50] The classic demonstration of our point here is however Thomas Schelling's explanation of how racial segregation might arise within a city even though nobody wants this to happen.[51] Assume that a city is like a 'grid' composed of a

---

49. Since agents can (and in politics frequently have incentives to) misrepresent their motives, does this fatally undermine the claims of interpretive explanations? In our view it may complicate the explanation but it does not undermine the ontology on which it is based. While neither agents' motives nor their (public) accounts of their view of the world may be incorrigible, any strategic representation by them of their motives and beliefs is itself an action that must in turn be informed by those agents' most fundamental understandings of what there is out there. So while agents can seek strategically to misrepresent both their motives and their conceptions of the world to others, what they cannot do is to misrepresent these *to themselves*. Considered as conditions of action, agents could not be mistaken about the beliefs that inform their own actions. Although of course those beliefs themselves may be false.

50. J. Clinton, and A. Meirowitz, 'Testing explanations of strategic voting in legislatures: a re-examination of the compromise of 1790', *American Journal of Political Science*, 48 (2004), pp. 675–89; J. Freeman, and J. Hays, 'Democracy and markets: the case of exchange rates', *American Journal of Political Science*, 44 (2000), 449–68, p. 450; J. Snyder 'Committee power, structure-induced equilibria and roll call votes', *American Journal of Political Science*, 36 (1992), 1–30, p. 6.

51. T. Schelling, *Micromotives and Macrobehaviour* (New York, Norton, 1978), pp. 137–66. The description that follows is taken from Hindmoor, *Rational Choice*, pp. 216–8.

series of squares. Each square (with the exception of those on the borders) will be in contact with eight other neighbouring squares. Assume that there are two sets of inhabitants, noughts and crosses. Assume that these two groups are randomly allocated to spaces and, once this allocation has been completed, that there are still a number of empty squares. Assume nobody wants to live in a square in which their only neighbours are members of the same group. Assume finally that everyone wants to live in a square in which at least one-third of their neighbours do belong to the same group and that they will move to an empty square if this condition is not satisfied. Schelling then shows that for almost every possible initial distribution: (1) at least one person will want to move; (2) that each such move is likely to lead someone else to want to move; and (3) that the result of this process is likely to be segregation.

Could this constitute a good explanation of why segregation occurred in so many American cities?[52] By itself, it does not. But it does show that we cannot necessarily infer back from the fact of segregation that Americans must have wanted to live in racially homogeneous communities. But if we are to go beyond this negative point and actually explain why segregation *did* occur, we would need to show that the assumptions Schelling employs are tolerably accurate: that most residents in these cities *did not* want to live in a racially homogeneous community but that they decided to move when they felt that they were becoming a minority group. The most obvious way of finding out whether this was indeed the case would have been to ask residents of those cities about what kind of a community they wanted to live in and why they moved. The provision of such interpretive evidence would not however then make Schelling's explanation redundant. For the most interesting part of his argument is his counter-intuitive demonstration of how racial segregation occurs even if actors intend to live among racially varied neighbours and it is this, rather than the formal properties of rational choice reasoning ascribed to individuals, that drives the explanation.

Finally, it is possible to imagine how rational choice theory might help us to make sense of apparently conflicting interpretive evidence. In our earlier commentary on Martin and Vanberg's work we imagined that, when asked, an 'overwhelming' number of politicians said that they relied upon members of their own faction to control the opportunism of other parties. Yet what if a significant minority had said that they trusted their coalition parties or that they sought to control them in a different way? The provision of further interpretive evidence could not, by itself, explain such differences. Rational choice models might however suggest ways in which we could account for such differences. Such explanations could then be indirectly tested against empirical evidence.

---

52. Schelling describes the main concern of his work in this section of the book as being that of 'segregation by "color"' in the USA (*Micromotives...*, p. 138). He then goes on to suggest that 'the demographic map of almost any American metropolitan area suggests that it is easy to find residential areas that are all white or nearly so and areas that are all black or nearly so but hard to find localities in which neither whites nor non-whites are more than, say, three-quarters of the total'. It is this pattern that his argument is intended to explain.

Such explanations might open up interesting questions about the way in which institutional design structures actors' decision making – or interacts with political culture. In this way interpretive information, instead of providing evidence for an explanation, might constitute the problem to be explained.

But would any resulting explanation not then risk being rendered redundant by the provision of interpretive evidence bearing upon it? To see why we argue not, consider the following example. Vanberg and Martin suggest that German and Dutch politicians seek to control agency problems through the use of committees. Assume however that junior ministers in another country, let us say Italy for the sake of the argument, are quite powerful and given plenty of opportunities to scrutinise draft legislation before it is published. We might then expect Italian politicians to rely upon and to say that they rely upon junior ministers to control agency problems[53] and German and Dutch ones to rely upon and say that they rely upon legislative committees. But this interpretive evidence would not itself render redundant our comparative explanation, couched as it is in terms of the institutional differences between the countries. Because while Italian politicians may have opinions on why Dutch and German politicians do not rely upon junior ministers, these opinions would not actually constitute interpretive evidence in so far as it related to the behaviour of actors in other countries.

Conclusion

Green and Shapiro's *Pathologies of Rational Choice* provoked an often passionate debate about the value of rational choice theory within political science. There is little evidence that *Pathologies* has resulted in a significant reduction in the number of articles using rational choice theory published. In 1992 39 per cent of the articles published within the *American Political Science Review* used rational choice. By 2005 this had risen to nearly 50 per cent. Yet such has been the impact of Green and Shapiro's work that it is difficult to believe that anyone could now prophesy, as Dennis Mueller once did, the 'withering away' of alternative approaches to the study of politics.

One reason why Green and Shapiro's argument had such an impact was that it assessed rational choice on its own terms. It did not question, as others previously had, the plausibility of assuming self-interested behaviour or the attempt to derive complete explanations of events entirely on the basis of individual actions. It instead demonstrated that, contrary to the claims usually made by its proponents, 'a large proportion of the theoretical conjectures of rational choice theorists have not been tested empirically.'[54] Yet in developing this argument, Green and Shapiro focused, as had rational choice theorists themselves, upon the provision of what we have called 'external' evidence. So in assessing Downsian party competition,

---

53. M. Thies, 'Keeping tabs on partners: the logic of delegation in coalition governments', *American Journal of Political Science*, 45 (2001), pp. 580–98.

54. Green and Shapiro, *Pathologies...*, p. 6.

Green and Shapiro looked for evidence about the spatial positioning of political parties. In an attempt to broaden the debate stimulated by their work, we have argued that this has led to the neglect of a second but equally significant form of evidence. Where rational choice theorists seek to present a 'realist' account of the motives and considerations that led someone to behave in a particular way, the provision of interpretive evidence showing that the individual did indeed reason in the way ascribed to them is of potentially crucial significance.

The authors of this piece agree that rational choice theory needs to make more use of interpretive evidence. What we disagree about is the overall value of the rational choice project and this disagreement is reflected in the way in which we have developed our argument. Hampsher-Monk believes that rational choice is indeed caught, as the title of our article would have it, between a rock and a hard place: that rational choice is fundamentally compromised not only by the exclusion of interpretive evidence but also by its inclusion. The provision of interpretive evidence constitutes a logically necessary part of rational choice explanations yet its inclusion risks rendering redundant the use of rational choice. This is not to suggest that the provision of interpretive evidence by itself always provides a complete explanation of any specified behaviour or outcome, or that rational choice cannot suggest useful 'conjectures' for empirical investigation. But as we previously commented, it is not at all obvious why you need a rational choice explanation that tells you that politicians placed in a certain situation will do Y for reason Z if you can simply ask politicians who have found themselves in that situation whether they did Y for reason Z. Hindmoor recognises the existence of a trade-off between the provision of interpretive evidence and the explanatory 'lift' provided by rational choice theory. Nevertheless, rational choice can play a potentially invaluable explanatory role in those circumstances where there is reason to believe that actors are unaware of or have an incentive to dissemble about their motives; where explanations are concerned with the unanticipated consequences of individual action; or, finally, where there is apparently conflicting interpretive evidence. In often inhospitable circumstances rational choice provides an imperfect but still potentially valuable explanatory tool. Green and Shapiro object to the 'universalism' of rational choice theory: its attempt to construct all-encompassing propositions about all human behaviour. Yet the applicability of rational choice theory may be limited to those partial circumstances in which interpretive evidence is not available or not to be trusted.

Chapter Nine

Prices as Descriptions: Reasons as Explanations

The aim of this chapter is partly scene-setting: to provide an airing for patterns of explanation used in the study of history and the social sciences and in particular two modes of explanation intimately associated with the ideas of culture and economics which form the topic of this volume.[1] By economic explanation I refer to that family of explanatory devices spawned by the notion of man as a rational economic calculator, variously specified. Cultural explanation embraces many possibilities, but the focus will in particular be on those explanations that take as central to understanding an action, the reasons, beliefs, and intentions of the actors. To remind the reader of this, I shall refer to these as actor's reasons explanations.[2]

However, in the interests of debate a fairly extreme thesis will be pursued. This is that a logical analysis of economic-type explanations reveals them to be incapable of functioning as explanations in any strong sense at all, and the only way they can be made to do so is by feeding in other information about actor's reasons. Effective economic explanations are, I claim, logically parasitic on actor's reasons explanations. The relationship is parasitic and not symbiotic: actor's reasons explanations, I shall argue, are capable of forming a complete and self-sufficient mode of explanation in their own right. Clearly this is an easier case to argue with some than with other social phenomena. Explanation of the very long-term social processes discussed by Eric Jones and Stephen Mennell tests the limits of actor's reasons explanations – neither economic growth itself, nor the development of civility are the direct result of individuals' intentions.[3] Still, I shall argue, explanations even at this level of generality must be integrated at some point with agents' perceptions and beliefs, since it is these, after all, that produce the actions which individually or cumulatively constitute social and political phenomena. Whilst sketching the patterns of argument necessarily involves wide generalisation, arguing the thesis requires a detailed analysis of crucial parts of

---

1. [*Culture in History: Production, consumption and values in historical perspective*, J. Melling and J. Barry (eds), (Exeter, University of Exeter, 1992).]

2. I should like to express thanks for critical comment to the participants in the wonderful series of inter-disciplinary seminars for which this paper was written, but in particular to Eric Jones whose original paper initiated this riposte and to the two editors for their stimulating objections. Thanks are also due to Martin Hollis who commented with typical generosity and encouragement on an early draft and to Bill Jordan for years of discussions on these matters. The usual disclaimers apply.

3. A characteristically witty and accessible discussion of these issues is Martin Hollis, *The Cunning of Reason* (Cambridge, Cambridge University Press, 1987).

some versions of the explanations under discussion; as a result there will be some unevenness of treatment, for which apology is made in advance.

What makes a good explanation? In a rough and ready way, to explain something is to render the unfamiliar, or the unaccountable, familiar or lucid. There is a primitive sense in which a successful explanation is a matter of subjective experience: if the explanation satisfies you, it evidently explained. On these grounds, even a fuller description of an event counts as an explanation, and I would not at all want to underrate the importance of such enterprises. However, if we are interested in going beyond mere subjective satisfaction to some level of formality, we must have in mind two rather *minimal criteria as to what is to count as a satisfactory explanation.*

The first is that the explanation must be capable of being specified independently of the *explanandum* (or phenomenon to be explained). Why this must be so was indicated four hundred years ago by Thomas Hobbes in prose I could not hope to emulate. Speaking of the peddlers of bogus explanations then operating in the universities he wrote:

> ... if you desire to know why some kind of bodies sink naturally downwards toward the Earth, and others goe naturally from it; the Schools will tell you out of Aristotle, that the bodies that sink downwards, are Heavy; and that this Heaviness it is that causes them to descend. But if you ask what they mean by Heaviness, they will define it to bee an endeavour to goe to the center of the Earth: so that the cause why things sink downward, is an Endeavour to be below: which is as much as to say that bodies descend or ascend, because they do.[4]

The second criterion cannot, I fear, be so elegantly expressed. Most explanatory theories operate under *ceteris paribus* conditions. That is to say that the explanation will only hold under certain conditions. These conditions are not themselves strictly part of the theory. Galileo's theory about the behaviour of falling bodies specified the conditions under which it would be true: i.e. in a vacuum. There is no problem about specifying what we mean by a vacuum independently of the theory of falling bodies, nor any problem about knowing when we have one which might obscure the meaning or application of the terms used in the theory. In the social sciences, much economic explanation consists of purely mathematical formulations, in which, in order for the explanation to be applied, the terms of the formulae have to be specified as descriptions of the utility functions, incomes, outputs etc. of individual (or corporate) economic actors.[5]

A successful explanatory theory must be capable of discriminating between outcomes which are the property of the explanation, and outcomes which are

---

4. In the original collection (*Culture in History*) by Eric Jones and Steve Mennell contributed chapters that looked respectively at conditions of economic growth and the formation of manners.
5. Thomas Hobbes, *Leviathan,* (1651), part IV, ch. 46, pp. 374–5. The identification of a vacuum did historically involve severe difficulties. *See* Steven Shapin and Simon Schaffer, *Leviathan and the Air Pump* (Princeton, Princeton University Press, 1985).

merely [logically] entailed by a combination of the theory and the specifying conditions for its application. Failure, in principle, to meet this criterion will mean that the theory is unfalsifiable over the range of phenomena specified by the conditions for its application, and the explanations it is capable of generating will therefore be fundamentally equivocal. This is necessarily a little abstract at the moment but will be made clearer when we see the theory applied.

Economic explanation

The kind of economic explanation I have in mind comes in a number of forms, price theory, rational or social choice theory, social exchange theory.[6] One problem about trying to mount a generalised attack on it is precisely the variety of forms it takes. Let me take the plunge and try to characterise it generally before looking at some of its more closely specified variants.

One general way of characterising the economic theory of human behaviour supposedly underpinning such explanations is that human beings simply buy cheap and sell dear. This has the virtues of conformity both to observation and (for most of us) introspection. The intuition that human beings are, in the broadest sense, economisers, is the driving notion behind all of the attempts to make this kind of explanation stick, and it clearly has a lot going for it.

However, 'buying cheap and selling dear' simply will not do as a way of characterising economic explanation. The reason being that whilst in money markets we know what 'cheap and dear' mean (because we have a public medium to measure them by), in the case of other forms of activity or choice we do not. It is precisely when economic modes of explanation are extended to areas outside a normal money market that they start to get interesting for social theorists, and it is precisely at that point that the notion of 'cost' loses the generalisability that gives the explanations their clout. For the problem is – and it is a problem even within market forms of exchange, as economic theorists themselves acknowledge – that we must not make the mistake of assuming that only those objects traded, and their money values, enter into the equation. People set a value on all sorts of things – which come broadly under the category of the cultural – which may be affected by, although not formally part of, a financial transaction: friendship, rest and leisure, pride, patriotism, religious observances – all of which can affect whether an object is traded at a particular price, or at all. People may not trade because it infringes some cultural taboo, or simply because it is too much bother (the transaction costs are too high), as well as because the price is not right. It is in the attempt to model and explain these very kinds of choices that economic modes of explanation are extended beyond the marketplace in which they originated. And to do so we need some way of expressing the non-monetary value which actors place on these things too.

---

6. M. Hollis and E. Nell, *Rational Economic Man* (Cambridge and New York, Cambridge University Press, 1975), pp. 25–6.

The classic way of getting round all this, and including search costs, leisure, pride, religious commitment and whatever else might lead us to trade or not to trade, do or not to do an action, is to postulate some psychological equivalent of money, some universal and standardised unit of satisfaction as the object of consideration whenever action is contemplated. There are various ways of trying to formulate what this 'utility' might be. Martin Hollis recently mischievously characterised it as a 'micro watt of inner glow'.[7] This catches some of the problem. Utility starts its life as pleasure and pain (which Bentham insisted 'are real things'), but even if utility can be regarded as, in some kind of sense, a real psychic unit, it is one which is directly accessible only to the person who experiences it.

However, stated like this the theory is in danger of running foul of the considerations advanced [previous section] concerning explanation: since we do not know in advance what it is people find utility in, utility is revealed – or presumed to be revealed – only in the choices people actually make, and can only be inferred back from their choices. But then the notion that people are economisers because they are economising on their *utils* becomes a truism. Economising on your utils is doing what you do: if your actions (definitionally) reveal your preferences, and your preferences (definitionally) express your utilities, it could never be true that you failed to maximise your utilities, as long as you acted from choice.

This, it seems to me, remains the general difficulty for economic explanations. However, it cannot be dismissed by such a simplistic presentation of the objection as that stated above, and we shall have to pursue more disciplined formulations of the problem.

The next step in the move to prolong the life of economic man (it interestingly always is *man*) is to reject the latent psychologism in the notion of utility. The great philosophers of economics almost consistently pursue this line. Von Mises, Hayek and Friedman all, in slightly different ways it is true, nevertheless agree that the idea that the axioms of the economic model in some sense offer putative descriptions of individuals' psychological processes is a mistake. As Friedman puts it:

> To suppose that hypotheses have not only 'implications' but also 'assumptions' and that the conformity of these assumptions to 'reality' is a test of the validity of the hypothesis ... is fundamentally wrong and productive of much mischief ... the relation is almost the opposite of that suggested ... in general the more significant the theory the more unrealistic the assumptions.

In support of this Friedman draws attention to his own critique of empirical studies designed to find out whether, as a matter of fact, businessmen were motivated by the concerns suggested by marginalist theories of the firm: studying

---

7. For a good introduction *see* the relevant sections of Brian Barry, *Economists, Sociologists and Democracy* (Chicago, Chicago University Press, 1970) or Michael Laver, *The Politics of Private Desires* (Harmondsworth and New York, Penguin Books and Penguin Viking, 1981) or (more critically) Anthony Heath, *Rational Choice and Social Exchange* (Cambridge, Cambridge University Press, 1976). The literature has become extraordinarily sophisticated, for an accessible presentation see Russell Hardin, *Collective Action* (Baltimore, Johns Hopkins University Press, 1982).

(or at least seeking information on) the shape of the demand curve facing them, for example. Such studies he insisted were a waste of time. Economic hypotheses, properly understood, do not purport to be descriptions of individuals' behaviour. Indeed, he goes further:

> To be important, a hypothesis must be descriptively false in its assumptions ... the relevant question to ask about the assumptions of a theory is not whether they are descriptively realistic for they never are, but whether they are sufficiently good approximations [to what, one wonders?] for the purpose in hand. And this question can only be answered by seeing whether the theory works, which mean whether it yields sufficiently accurate predictions.[8]

And most major theorists agree. The interesting exception to this position is Samuelson, who argues that as a matter of logic, hypotheses whose consequences are fully specified, realistic and confirmed must rest on assumptions which are realistic. Of course not all, in fact very few, hypotheses' consequences can all be specified, and even fewer are all confirmed, so the force of the logical point is somewhat blunted. Nevertheless he falls back on a remarkably chauvinistic gut feeling that realism in hypotheses *is* important, which underscores why the models are always models of 'rational economic man'. In what must be a classic footnote he writes: 'All economic regularities that have no commonsense core that you can explain to your wife will soon fail.'[9] Despite the male chauvinism there is, it seems to me, a grain of truth in this. For the methodological postulates of Friedman, Hayek and Von Mises cut us adrift completely from commonsense perceptions of reality, and would have us trying out hypotheses in a random way (since there is no sense in which they are supposed to model psychology) until we get one that chances to produce accurate deductions. We seem to be in a world of meaningless events looking for a conceptually random 'fit' for our hypothesis, like the covering law model of explanation in the natural sciences, which makes a brief appearance elsewhere in this volume[10] and to which I shall come later.

Nevertheless, one might say, with Friedman *et al.*, the proof of the pudding is in the eating: if the method works, if 'fits' are indeed found between theories and data, if predictions are correctly made, the theory is confirmed. In that case then, surely retrospective explanations of a similar kind can be correctly asserted, explanation being, in some sense an analogue of confirmation?[11] I am not at all sure that this follows, for I believe there is a price to be paid for the desertion of realism, and of the theory's lowly psychological origins, and I shall next try to exact it by offering a critique of economic theory.

---

8. Hollis, *Cunning of Reason*, p. 17.
9. M. Friedman, *Essays in Positive Economics* (Chicago, University of Chicago Press, 1953), pp. 14–15.
10. P. Samuelson, 'Comment on E. Nagel's "Assumptions in Economic Theory"', in *The Collected Scientific Papers of Paul A. Samuelson* (Cambridge, Mass., MIT Press, 1966), vol. II, p. 1175.
11. P. Oppenheim, *Essays in Honour of Carl G. Hempel* (Dordrecht, D. Reidel, 1969), p. 3.

The rejection of realism in exchange for successful predictability throws the spotlight on the circumstances under which successful predictions are made. Those words liberally inscribed in the accounts of school science 'within the limits of experimental error' need closer specification. The positive economists' version of this is 'other things being equal'. The crucial role of this condition has worrying implications for economic theory even when it is applied on its home ground, although as I shall later show, these are of even greater concern when economic explanations play, as it were, away from home.

As Hollis and Nell, to whom this critique is indebted, put it, prediction is never of 'what would happen', but of, 'what would happen if ...'. Economic theory is never refuted by the failure of its predictions, for the predictions always predict what will happen under certain rather idealised circumstances, standardly perfect knowledge, cost-less entry to the market, no transactions costs, no collusion, etc.[12] The cumulative effect of these *ceteris paribus* conditions, is to turn what often sounds like an empirical prediction, e.g.: 'If Jaguar UK produce where marginal costs equal marginal revenue, they will maximise their profits', into an analytic statement. For given the definitions of marginal costs, marginal revenue and profits, if the market is perfect and the cost curves conventionally shaped near the relevant areas of production, and *ceteris* are *paribus,* the statement is a tautology. How could one falsify marginal analysis? For believers in the theory, negative results simply reveal the imperfections of the market; but even for those willing to suspend their faith it is impossible to distinguish the failure of theory from the failure of the circumstances in which it is applied to conform to the requisite conditions.

Or (to descend from the heights of marginal theory to the application of economic theory to individuals), if the axioms of rational egoism are not viewed as the psychological properties of individuals but tautologies, then once again, almost anything can be fitted into the account – altruism, sack-cloth and ashes, self-mortification, you name it. As Von Mises acknowledged, the theory:

> ... is indifferent to the ultimate goals of action ... It applies the term happiness in a purely formal sense ... The proposition: man's unique aim is to attain happiness, is tautological. It does not imply any statement about the state of affairs from which a man expects happiness.[13]

What does this reveal about the wider application of economic theories? Well, to parallel our example about the firm, predictions about individuals' or groups' actions will be purely analytical [formal] until we can fit the individual up with some *ceteris paribus* clauses, like wishing to maximise money holdings,

---

12. [I do not of course deny that interesting explorations are made by economists who selectively 'relax' one or other of these assumptions. But it is, invariably, still a question of seeing how the deductions pan out under these different conditions.]

13. L. Von Mises, *Human Action: A treatise on economics* (New Haven, Yale University Press, 1949), p. 15.

or wishing to maximise security, or leisure, or equality or sociability, or any number of other aims, ideals or values individuals might have. These can be filled in on an *ad hoc* basis or on the basis of some cultural knowledge, discovered independently of the theory, about what it is that agents believe, value or take pleasure in, until the theory produces the right predictions. In a society in which economic considerations *narrowly construed* form a cultural norm, such as modern commercial societies, the assumption of a pervasive economic rationality may operate inexplicitly to provide the theory with content, and thus predictive, and explanatory power. The presence of such motivation may, however, be a logical prerequisite for the adequate deployment of such explanations. Even so, we may note that such 'explanations', although not technically falsified, can be brought into question by historians drawing attention to different aspects of the situation which render different facts important, or even, as in the examples below, suggest that it is something different that needs explaining.

The implications of these assumptions are just as serious, if less obvious, for retrospective, explanatory uses of the theory in history, as they are for predictive uses of them in contemporary economics. If 'economic' predictions are formal and indeterminate without the specification of the desires and beliefs of actors, similarly structured retrospective explanations must also be formal and indeterminate. The failure of the theory is more likely to be *revealed* where it is applied predictively, for it can, and often in fact does, fail to predict, although it is invariably rescued by pointing to the absence of appropriate *ceteris paribus* conditions. In the case of its retrospective use as explanation, no obvious 'failure' occurs because the outcomes, being historical facts, are known, and are already fitted into the explanation. But convincing though the explanation may on the surface appear, if I have correctly characterised its logical structure, its claim to have explained will be logically dependent on our retrospective knowledge of the aims and beliefs of the actors, whether or not these are actually specified or merely imputed from the observed actions of actors. Let us now turn to an example of economic explanation in history.

A much praised and influential book, representative of the 'new economic history' exemplified in our collection by Professor Jones, is *Structure and Change in Economic History* by Douglas C. North. In it he constructs an economic model of the first socio-economic revolution, the transition from a hunter-gatherer to a predominantly agrarian economy.[14] The purpose of the model is, he writes, 'to derive the conditions under which the scarce labour resource of the band would shift from its traditional occupation of hunting/gathering to agriculture'. He assumes that reallocation of resources will be determined by 'the maximisation of the labour resource and, therefore, the economic welfare of the group'. Although there is no formal market for game or agricultural produce he assumes 'the band's preferences will establish these relative valuations', and

---

14. Douglas C. North, *Structure and Change in Economic History* (New York and London, Norton Press, 1981), pp. 74 ff.

he assumes those preferences will be stable over time. The conclusion he derives is that those stable preferences determined by the maximisation of welfare will lead to the substitution of agriculture for hunting as either population growth, or competition, or exogenous decline in game takes place. Not only that, he predicts, from a 'tragedy of the commons' type argument, that the same processes will lead to a substitution of exclusive for common property rights. Now he is on fairly safe ground in deriving these conclusions, for we know, more or less, that this is what in fact happened. But the 'group welfare maximisation' model itself only *entails* that result if certain assumptions are made. These are assumptions which, to archaeologists and anthropologists, are unjustifiable.

The model assumes population growth. Yet we know that many so-called primitive peoples have limited their populations, either through marriage practices, contraception or infanticide. So, in the absence of knowledge about cultural practices the *assumption* of population pressure, an assumption made generally explicit in Professor Jones' paper, cannot be sustained.[15] North's model assumes, and I quote, an incentive to exploit the resource 'to the point where the value of the last animal killed is equal to the (search) costs of killing it'. But we know, (and so, he reveals, does North) that hunting peoples have highly respectful, even reverential attitudes towards their quarry, and elaborate, ecologically conservative taboos about depleting that resource. However, we are assured, these taboos will be overcome by competition between culturally distinct bands, since 'in a competitive situation no band has any incentive to conserve the resource, since the animals left to reproduce would be taken by its rivals.'[16] The explanation is elegant, and more complex than this sketch can convey. But we need to notice several things about it.

Firstly, notice that in the overcoming of ecologically conservative taboos, North assigns a crucial role to *cultural* differentiation. Secondly, the assumption of rational egoistic calculation is now operating as a psychological motive ('an incentive', 'would have no incentive to') rather than as a way of generating testable conclusions. Earlier North had adopted the Hayekian line by denying 'that the assumption that prehistoric man, when confronted with two alternatives would choose the one that made him better off' accurately *described* their behaviour. Rather he pursued a Darwinian, survival of the fittest line: 'the bands that select the correct alternative, whether consciously or by chance will be favoured by a process of natural selection.'[17] But why is it in any case 'correct' for bands competitively to hunt game to extinction rather than co-operate in exploiting it at a sustainable level? If decisions are being arrived at randomly, there would seem to be as much likelihood of the one as the other. Indeed there is considerable rational choice literature which argues that, even assuming psychologically egoistic

---

15. As North admits, *ibid.*, p. 85.
16. *Ibid.*, p. 81.
17. *Ibid.*, pp. 80–1, 79.

motives, anarchic solutions to fish stocks and tragic commons are possible.[18] Indeed the existence of intra-band limitations on over-exploitation seem to confirm the plausibility of this story. Why does the rational actor hypothesis lead us to assume that individuals accept band level limitations on over-exploitation, but lead at the above band level to disastrous competition? What is it *within the theory* that decides which way the evolution pans out, apart from our knowledge of how in fact it did?

There is a final curiosity to note. Hunting peoples, as Marshall Sahlins has noted, are amongst the most leisured in the world.[19] The high nutritional quality of their food and the relative ease with which each calorie is acquired leave them with plenty of time on their hands. Why should they not have employed their leisure by cultivating their gardens? Indeed, in the New World there is plenty of evidence that they did, the cultivation of squashes and peppers there seemingly dating back as far as archaeological evidence for that kind of thing could reasonably go. But such polyculture would be dependent on the chance existence of suitable wild plants, which were not available in Eurasia. (Just as the chance lack of existence of a suitable draught animal in [North] America seems to have had important implications for their social and economic development). In the absence of such established alternative food sources, and given cultural conservatism, once the path to decline had been taken by a hunting band, one could imagine more and more time being spent, and greater and greater areas having to be covered to supply food needs from hunting. This would surely make it more and more difficult to find the time to effect the transition to agriculture or its substitution for hunting, as the factors which North suggests push the band in that direction become more salient.

It is true that North's story can be tied in to reality by filling in the specifications of the assumptions of the model with known facts about prehistory, or where these are unknown, plausible dummy variables. Once these are fully specified the particular explanation is complete and the model of explanation supposedly vindicated. But notice what this means. *A full specification of the circumstances turns out to include knowledge of the actual choices people made,* their 'revealed preferences', or, where formal markets exist, the prices at which goods are actually exchanged. The economic explanation thus relies crucially on a knowledge of the outcomes which enables us to work back to suppositiously derived statements about the rates or fact of substitutability of game and agricultural produce, or, in other circumstances, prices which it might be thought it was the task of the theory to explain. What is the status of substitution rates or prices in this account? Are they explanations or descriptions (or indeed *ascriptions* of behaviour or choices)? If they are explanations, what are they explanations *of?* For on one view, the 'price story' about the agricultural revolution is simply a *redescription* of one aspect of

---

18. Most influentially Robert Axelrod, *The Evolution of Cooperation* (New York, Basic Books, 1984); M. Taylor, *Anarchy and Cooperation* (New York and London, John Wiley and Sons, 1976) and *The Possibility of Cooperation* (Cambridge, Cambridge University Press, 1987).

19. Marshall Sahlins, *Stone Age Economics* (London, Tavistock Press, 1974), ch. I ('The Original Affluent Society').

it. We *know* that neolithic peoples had substituted agriculture for hunting. Does saying that this was because marginal returns to hunting decreased relative to those from agriculture tell us anything more? (Absent all the *reasons* why it might have decreased – reasons which might, and indeed have been elicited by researchers asking the answer to the original question without recasting it in terms of price theory.) The explanation is radically under-determined, and quite consistent with other histories.[20] Notice what it means if prices and marginal rates of substitution are not specifiable separately from the circumstances they purport to explain: they fail to fulfill the first of our very modest criteria for explanation, and, if not quite falling into Hobbes' category of 'insignificant speech', can at best claim to be (admittedly sometimes elegant) redescriptions.

One answer to the question of what it is that rates of substitution and prices are an explanation *of,* was, as we have seen, that they are explanations of the preferences of the peoples who do the substituting, buying, and selling. Yet surprisingly this turns out to be an extremely tendentious claim, one which the gurus of economic theory have, as we have seen, almost universally rejected, although with troubling consequences for the grip of their theories on reality. But *if,* nevertheless, the description of individuals as something like rational utility maximisers is correct, and *if* outcomes can be fitted into a story leading to the correct conclusions, we might indeed seem to be explaining or at least modelling the social consequences of individuals' preferences and motivations. But there are two unknowns in the above story, not one: the rational utility maximising hypothesis on the one hand and the preferences and motivations of individuals on the other. And we are only justified in presuming to have explained the second on the assumption that the truth of the first can be independently sustained, otherwise the 'truth' of the explanation may in fact be a property of the falsity of the hypothesis. If A+B=C, and A+B is the case, then C must be the case. But if we mistakenly *believe* A to be the case when it is not, then the fact that B is the case and that C is the case actually seriously undermines the A+B=C proposition. It is thus crucial that the truth of the rational utility maximiser hypothesis be demonstrable in isolation from its application to particular choices made by individuals. I shall now argue that it cannot.

Perhaps the most hard-nosed way of tightening up formulation of the rationality hypothesis is decision theory. Ironically this seems to demonstrate the impossibility of deciding the conceptual status of social choice theory. In decision theory an attempt is made to formalise the notion of rationality. There are two steps: the first specifies under what conditions an individual order of preferences could be said to be rational. A set of preferences are said to be rational if they are transitive (i.e. if A is preferred to B and B to C, A must be preferred to C), asymmetric (i.e. there is a rank discernible amongst preferences), connected (there are no gaps in the pairings over the range), independent (the independence of irrelevant

---

20. On under-determination in inductively based explanations *see* W. V. Quine, 'On empirically equivalent systems of the world', *Erkenntnis,* vol. 9, 3 (1975), pp. 313–28. I am not aware that this has been argued to be also a property of economic explanations.

alternatives) and if the preferences involving risk correlate coherently with the subjective values of the outcomes. The second part of the theory relates actions to preferences by asserting that a person with a rational pattern of preferences will choose from amongst those available the (or a) preference with the highest value.

This formulation may seem overly demanding, but it is really no more than an attempt to render precise the notion of consistent and unambiguous ordering, and this is surely about the minimum content that could be given to the notion of rationality. It may also appear to be one that is highly unlikely to be fulfilled, but that is, in a way, beside the point I want to make, which has to do with the way it reveals in general the difficulty of separating *any* formal criterion of rationality from the particular set of preferences of the individuals to whom the theory is applied.

Can the above account, or *anything like it,* be shown, to be true about human choice-making? Empirical investigations have invariably seemed to suggest not, and on the face of it this seems to imply that individuals are not rational. However, reflection on the results by theorists in this field has revealed to them the deeper problem of the indeterminacy of any such test.

The standard experiment in this field required individuals to make pairwise choices within a small range of alternatives. The same alternatives were offered in subsequent sessions, but suitably masked in order to conceal the fact. There were no payoffs to individuals, and so no normal conditioning. Choice sets were then examined for inconsistencies. Individuals had become steadily more consistent over time. But how was this to be interpreted? As learning? As changes in preference? As falsification of the rationality hypothesis? Investigators acknowledge that it was *experimentally* impossible to distinguish between these alternatives. The problem does not seem to derive from the particular way in which rationality is formulated, although I am not sure how this could be proved. Rather it seems to derive from the fact that any conceivable experiment necessarily tests simultaneously the hypothetical properties of the agent's preferences and their reasoning processes, and as a result it is not possible unequivocally to attribute wayward results to one or the other.

However, another experimental example may suggest at least one irreducible element of this indeterminacy. In a classic experiment Amos Tversky asked a series of subjects to choose between:

A: a 50/50 chance of winning $1,000 or nothing, and
B: a 100 per cent chance of winning $400
and
C: a 1/10 chance of winning $1,000, and
D: a 1/5 chance of winning $400.

Almost all subjects, naive or educated, chose B over A and C over D. This seems inconsistent with formal decision theory since the expected value of A is $1,000 x 1/2 = $500, whilst the expected value of B is only $400, thus indicating a negative preference schedule for dollars, whilst preferring C over D is preferring an expected outcome of $100 over $80, indicating a positive preference schedule for dollars. Formally C and D each represent gambles with a 1/5 chance of the same outcomes as A and B, yet the opposite cell is chosen in each pair, violating the principle that equal value outcomes should be substitutable in the preference schedule. But, as Tversky pointed out, the lack of *any* risk in choice B may in itself have had a value, so the results demonstrated risk aversion. However 'risk propensity' as another imputed psychological factor at work, only compounds the range of imputed unknowns we are trying to isolate and identify experimentally.

Moreover, it is worse than this, for Tversky then presented his subjects with the same choices, only with negative values:

A: a 50/50 chance of losing $1,000 or nothing, and
B: a 100 per cent chance of losing $400, and
C: a 1/10 chance of losing $1,000, and
D: a 1/5 chance of losing $400.

This time A was preferred to B and D to C, once again demonstrating both negative and positive preference schedules for dollars, and violating the substitution constraint, but this time demonstrating risk-seeking. When negative outcomes were involved subjects violated their other preferences to seek a gamble for the same integer outcomes for which they had violated their other preferences to seek certainty when faced with positive outcomes.

To claim that this falsifies decision theory as a descriptive psychological theory seems to depend crucially on whether the subjects of the experiment shared the experimenter's characterisation of the choices before them. The researcher wanted the individual to restrict their consideration to the relevant monetary values of the cells. But the negative outcome in A in the first table could be construed, *in the context of the other choices,* as 'missing out on getting $400', rather than an actuarial '$500'. Is this irrational? Only, it seems, by stipulation. Whether utility theory holds or not depends on how we allow individuals to construe the choices facing them. Tversky, Davidson, Hansson and others in the field conclude that there is 'no non-arbitrary way of deciding this within utility theory'.[21]

But if even the most rigorous attempts to specify what a rational economic actor is, turn out to produce indeterminate outcomes which *can only be rationalised by understanding how individuals construe the world facing them,* then surely, and as we have seen, any less rigorous formulations of the model must do so too. Rendering economic explanations determinate is then logically parasitic on an understanding of agents' knowledge. Accounts which offer explanations of past

---

21. A. Tversky, 'A critique of expected utility theory: descriptive and normative considerations', *Erkenntnis* 9 (1975), pp. 163–73. *See also* B. Hansson, 'The appropriateness of the expected utility model', *ibid.*, pp. 175–93 and D. Davidson, P. Suppes and P. Seigel, *Decision-Making: An experimental approach,* (Stanford, Stanford University Press, 1957). Davidson gave up his career as an experimental psychologist as a result of this work and became a philosopher: the resulting work is in *Essays on Actions and Events* (Oxford, OUP, 1980).

events without specifying agents' knowledge may appear successful, but they will always be under-determined without it.

Let me isolate the bones of the argument so far. Good explanation theories distinguish between what is to be explained and the terms used in the explanation. They also allow us to identify the conditions for the application of the theory independently from the formal part of the theory itself. Certain formulations of economic explanations, especially those of neo-classical economics as applied contemporarily, have serious trouble meeting the second criterion. They seem to meet the first criterion well enough since predicted prices seem distinct from the preferences they are supposed to model, indeed, distinct enough that their predictions sometimes fail.

When deployed retrospectively however, both of these problems are masked, for the historical data usually enables the circumstances in which the theory is being applied to be filled out, thus converting what might have been exposed as *ceteris paribus* assumptions into mere historical background fact. Secondly, the results of people's choices whether substitutions of one activity for another, or price changes, are in fact known, and the imputation that these reveal preferences or values seems innocuous enough. However a rigorous analysis of the presuppositions behind the economic model of explanations seems to demonstrate that one or other of the criteria for a good explanation is breached. For if prices or actions are simply *identified* with revealed preferences then the one is not specifiable independently of the other (breaching the first condition), and it is furthermore then unclear what else it is they explain; and on the other hand if the attempt *is* made to articulate the relationship between preferences and action, the conditions for the application of the theory do not seem to be specifiable independently of the theory itself.

Actor's reasons explanations

So far the argument has proceeded by looking at attempts to generate explanatory relationships between actors and their behaviour through a reconstruction of the agent's desires, beliefs and [reasoning] procedures. However there is another way of gaining access to this information, and that is by the devastatingly simple expedient of listening to or reading what actors aver in speech or writing about these matters. If this seems a commonsensical, even banal approach, it is not without its pitfalls. I hope to show that it is superior to the one we have been considering.

On this view the explanation of the action is the reason the agent gives or would give for his or her doing it. It may be objected that I have shifted the ground by specifying my interests in 'actions' rather than events, processes etc. But I take it that in historical and social research events and processes comprise the (sometimes numerous) actions of individuals, and that there is no conceptual discontinuity between the two. There are some events such as natural ones, e.g. the Lisbon earthquake, which of course do impinge on history (and they way they do so may well be seriously mediated by human action) but the event itself is not an action. Wars, famines, persecutions, enlightenments, revolutions (economic and otherwise) however are accumulations of, or constituted by, human actions. I take it we would rightly feel unhappy about the assertion of a social phenomenon that could not be unpacked in terms of individuals' actions, which is not of course to claim that the collective social result is always congruent with those acts or intentions. It is often claimed that genuine sociological explanations of the kinds essayed here in Bob Witkin's and Steven Mennell's essays[22] must operate at a level of generality, and relate to social and structural phenomena which are simply not available at the individual level. To take the most famous example of this – Durkheim's explanations of suicide rates – it is clear that neither suicide *rates,* nor the social *anomie* which forms his explanation for one form of suicide, are properties of an individual. But a suicide is the *act* of an individual, and *anomie* is shorthand for a range of phenomena which are experienced by individuals in an every day kind of way, frequent, or unexpected geographical relocation, absence of close relatives or supportive friends, uncertainty about how to evaluate social experiences and so on. To require that these explanations can always be *unpacked* in terms of actors' perceptions, is not to insist that they must always or continually be so, merely that we should be extremely sceptical about a social phenomenon which could not be.

The claim that reasons are explanations of actions may either seem uncontroversial to the point of banality, or so trivial as not to count as an explanation at all. Let us therefore, explore it further in the hope of anticipating each of these objections. One way of bringing out the distinctive nature of this explanation is to contrast it with a third kind of explanation commonly claimed to typify those found in the natural sciences, often referred to as the covering-law model of explanation. On this view instances are explained by showing that they fall under a suitable pre-established generalisation. Thus the bursting of my daughter's balloon when placed near the fire can be explained as an instance of Boyle's Law, which is a generalisation concerning the expansion of gasses exposed to heat, together with the finite elasticity of balloon rubber.

There are strong reasons for rejecting the applicability of this model to social phenomena, reasons well canvassed by J. S. Mill in his *A System of Logic*. In Chapter Seven of Book VI of that work Mill refers the reader back to his discussion of the 'Chemical Method' in Book III, Chapter Ten, where he had pointed out that deducing causes from observed effects can only operate where, as in the case of chemical phenomena, we can be reasonably sure that constant and simple causal relations obtain. This enables the 'method of difference' to be deployed. By looking at the different behaviour of compounds with and without, say, potassium, we can infer back from that behaviour certain properties of potassium without ever having to isolate it and analyse it individually. But where effects are the result

---

22. Robert Witkin, 'Bourgeois Production and Realist Styles of Art', and Stephen Mennell, 'Momentum and History', chapters 2 and 10 in *Culture in History: Production, consumption and values in historical perspective*, Joseph Melling and Jonathan Barry (eds), (Exeter, University of Exeter, 1992).

of complex causes, and capable of being brought about by different causes, this 'method of difference' cannot be deployed. As an example Mill takes the issue, central to our concerns, of economic growth. We might expect that:

> If two nations can be found which are alike in all natural advantages and disadvantages; whose people resemble each other in every quality, physical and moral, spontaneous and acquired; whose habits, usages, opinions, laws and institutions are all the same in all respects, except that one of them has a more protective tariff, or in other respects interferes more with freedom of industry; if one of these nations is found to be rich and the other poor, or one richer than the other, this will be found to be an *experimentum crucis* – a real proof by experience which of the two systems is most favourable to national riches.[23]

We might expect this to be the acid test, but it would not, and could not be. Firstly, the possibility of two countries being alike in all these respects is extremely remote. But even if we were to find such a case, says Mill, the existence of these similarities at an institutional and societal level 'are the effects of pre-existing causes' which may be many and interrelated in a variety of different ways, and quite incapable of being isolated by ticking off the similarities and leaving the differences:

> Why must the prosperous nation have prospered from one cause exclusively? National prosperity is always the collective result of a number of favourable circumstances, and of these the restrictive nation may unite a greater number than either of the others, although it may have all of those circumstances in common with either one or the other of them.[24]

The objections to this method apply whether we are trying to explain growth, assuming stagnation to be the norm, or, as Eric Jones does, explain non-growth, having assumed growth to be the norm. Several of the arguments reviewed in his paper seem to deploy this 'method of difference'.

However there is a further objection to this natural science model which, as promised, highlights the difference between explanations in terms of natural science generalisations and explanations in terms of cultural meaning or 'actor's reasons'. The classic exposition of this is Alasdair Macintyre's discussion of Weber's attempt to establish an explanatory link between Protestantism and capitalism. Weber's method is Mill's method of difference.

He shows that in China and in India all the preconditions of capitalism evident in Europe were present, except for Protestantism. But capitalism did not arise. Hence we have good reason to suppose that Protestantism is the cause of capitalism.[25]

---

23. J. S. Mill, *A System of Logic* (London, Longman, 1967), Book VI, vii, p. 575.
24. *Ibid.*, p. 576.
25. Alasdair MacIntyre, 'A Mistake about Causality in Social Science', in Peter Laslett and W. G. Runciman (eds), *Politics, Philosophy and Society*, vol. II (Oxford, OUP, 1962), p. 49.

Now MacIntyre is sympathetic to the idea that there is a link between Protestantism and capitalism. What he resists, and what I suggest he is right in resisting, is that the link can be established either through the measure of residues, or indeed through *any* assumption that the relationships between belief and action can be characterised in terms of scientific generalisations. Because the links claimed to be established by scientific generalisations are contingent, they *could* link any belief and any action. But if we reflect for a moment, this is not usually the import of explanations in terms of beliefs. If I claim to be concerned about my garden, and believe that drought will ruin it, and yet in the absence of water restrictions and with opportunity to do so, fail to water it, this must cast doubt on the belief. But it does not do so because it discomfits the generalisation that 'concern about gardens is highly correlated with watering activity in droughts'. Indeed there need be no such generalisation, indeed, no other gardens or gardeners but this one. The expectation that the gardener will water is established by the intentionality implicit in his statement of his concerns and the actions necessary to attend to them. In other words it is not by trying to construct generalisations in which capitalism and Protestantism figure (or fail to figure) that the link is established, but by looking at what a Protestant believer claims to believe and what actions such beliefs seem likely to result in. In fact, Weber does articulate such a connection between belief and action, and this, in both MacIntyre's view, and my own, renders at the least unnecessary, and at worst quite misleading the use of scientific type, generalisations:

> Weber in fact presents us with capitalist actions as the conclusion of a practical syllogism which has Protestant premises. To discern this logical relationship between belief and action was an enormous achievement. And because the achievement was this, the use of Mill's methods is entirely out of place; we do not need to juggle with causal alternatives. India and China did not strengthen and could not weaken his case about Europe. For it is not a question of whether there is a purely contingent relationship between isolable phenomena. And so constant conjunction is neither here nor there.[26]

Explanations based on actor's reasons (or beliefs) are then quite distinct from explanations of the covering law kind. For actor's reasons *are,* as we have seen, tied to their actions by more than constant conjunction. The relationship between intention and act is in fact far more intimate than that. So intimate that even though the intentions are present, and realised in practice, if the action does not instantiate the intention then the action is not sufficiently explained by it. Consider an admittedly extreme case:

> Oedipus hating his father, and bent on killing him, finds his way blocked by an old man.
> Enraged at being impeded, Oedipus killed the old man in his rage to get past.
> Unknown to Oedipus, the old man was his father.

---

26. *Ibid.* p. 55.

Although Oedipus intended to kill his father, indeed, although he *did* kill his father, and even although it was his desire to kill his father that caused him to kill the old man that was his father, we cannot quite fully explain his killing his father in terms of his intention to do so. And the reason is that his desire and intentions were not effectively linked to the act in the right way. That is to say his act did not instantiate his intention in such a way as to render the intention a (sufficient) explanation of the act. The recourse to such nice philosophical distinctions as these is often ridiculed by social scientists, and held up as an example of the banality of theory. Yet in explanation, no less than in assessing guilt, blame and responsibility, the identification of intention and the kind of link that exists between intentions and their outcomes is clearly crucial.

If actor's perceptions and intentions *are* intimately related, are they, perhaps *too* closely related? It is sometimes said in explaining why intentions do not relate to actions in the way that causes and effects relate to each other under the covering law model, that they relate to each other 'logically'. This, I think, is misleading, for the relationship is certainly not an analytic one – it makes *sense* to assert the existence of intention and deny the existence of action, indeed, in the Oedipus case both are present, but not properly connected. The sad fate of poor Oedipus' father illustrates a perhaps surprising feature of actor's reasons explanations. That is that in them intention and action are logically independent, thus fulfilling the first criterion of all good explanations. For although intentions *do* explain actions, intentions can be present without the action (although not vice versa). There is a sense in which the meaningfulness of the action is intimately related to the meaningfulness of the intention, and in such a way, as we have seen, that any failure to sustain that symmetry breaks the explanatory link. This notion is generally true but it begins to bear a lot of weight as we move away from particular individual actions to classes of actions which bear a lot of conventional content. Thus my action in running into no-man's land carrying a white flag, *can* be explained by my desire to surrender, because of the conventional meaning attached not only to 'showing a white flag', but also to the action of 'surrendering'. My reasons for surrendering, must, of course, also be exposed.

Actor's reasons seems to provide what the economic model lacked: a way into the specific values, aims, repertoire of tasks, conceptions of action and agency which might specify what an actor might have in mind in making choices. They are therefore capable of providing the economic model with what, if I am right, it cannot do without in order to provide an explanation, namely an understanding of the specific perceptions and values which inform agents' decision-making processes.

However, there is, or seems to be, a serious objection. Although actors reasons are logically specifiable independently of their actions and so stand in the right relationship to each other, it might still be asked: how do we empirically identify intentions? For if we cannot specify how an intention can be empirically identified independently of the actions they purport to explain then we are going to fail the second test of a good explanation, that of being able to specify the conditions for its application.

It is true of course that 'intentions' construed as the private mental antecedents of action are not directly recoverable, indeed, according to some philosophers, it is not even clear that it makes sense to talk of such events or actions. It is worth, nevertheless, making the not entirely polemical point that even this view of intentions makes them no more and no less mysterious and metaphysical than utilities or preference schedules proved to be in the economic story. But, despite what might appear from the discussion of the explanation of individual actions, this is not in any case what is meant by 'intention' or 'reason' by anyone who asserts this method. The construal of intention is an attempt to explicate an irreducibly public and not an inscrutably private meaning.

On one strong view, deriving from Wittgenstein, the irreducibly public character of intention and belief are entailed by two propositions. Firstly the impossibility of a private language, and secondly by the meaning-bearing content of action as opposed to mere behaviour. If actions are essentially meaningful, and if action, as I would argue, constitutes most of what social scientists and historians are interested in, those meanings must be publicly available. For only language, or language analogues, can bear meaning, and to do so they must be public. Meaningfulness is public.

The injunction to discover the intentions of agents, is therefore based on the belief that the possible kinds of activity, aims, and beliefs available to human agents in any historical circumstance must be drawn from a kind of public repertoire which is presented to them in their culture (not necessarily of course, 'high' culture either). Consequently what it could occur to someone to want to do at any particular time and place must be shaped and limited by that individual's cultural forms. To play a game of football, the game must exist. To be able to surrender, the conception and conventions of surrender must exist. To write a satire, the genre must exist. How genres are invented and repertoires extended is an interesting, but not insuperable problem which [may involve – *inter alia*] demonstrating the unintended emergent properties of cultural performances, the kind of demonstration at which social thinkers, following Mandeville, became increasingly adept in the eighteenth century. Thus 'intentions' are not private, but short for 'the socially available repertoire of meaningful actions'.

Agents' beliefs about what is the case, beliefs about the possible consequences of their actions, are, then, in principle recoverable.[27] In any given case the amount of information needed to establish this may or may not be available, but this is an empirical question. Such information must be gathered where it can. The Reverend Ian Paisley provided a most revealing insight into the nature of Protestant fundamentalism, and therefore into the whole Northern Ireland imbroglio when, on *Desert Island Discs,* he nominated as his one book to go with the Bible and Shakespeare, Foxe's *Book of Martyrs.* Unless we can reconstruct the pattern of beliefs that go with such choices, (and the accompanying conviction that the Pope is Antichrist) we will fail to understand an important part of the situation there.

---

27. [Although not, of course, by definition, in the case of prehistoric cultures.]

Such understanding is not entering actors' minds, or rethinking their thoughts or any one of a number of such fanciful, but impossible, enterprises often attributed to those espousing this kind of cultural explanation; nor has it anything to do with the project of intuitive empathy which caused so much trouble in the recent debate about history teaching in schools.[28] Recovering agents' intentions involves hard and painstaking work, reading what they read, seeking out the connections they might have made between apparently isolated or contradictory beliefs.

An example that catches what I am talking about is given in Stephen Mennell's recounting of the story of the French General, his troops and the eclipse.[29] The explanation of their different responses to the eclipse cannot even be articulated without reference to the intentions and meanings of the actors – by which I refer not to anything irrecoverably private, but to their shared and socially given sense of reality and their relationship to it.

It is important to be clear about what is being included and what is being excluded in the notion of 'actor's reasons'. I am including in 'actor's reasons explanations' an identification of their intentions in terms of their beliefs, their aims and ideals, and their conceptions of reality and available actions. I am dubious about the status of motives, and I am excluding roles or anything to do with them. Roles can be reasons for (a rather inauthentic kind of) action, but they cannot be reasons for belief. Or more specifically, the occupation of a role cannot be the actor's *own* reason for belief. Although people *say* things like 'having gas shares, I believe privatisation is good for the country', they never mean by that to justify the proposition supposedly believed: they never mean 'Because of the fact that I have gas shares, privatisation is good for the country.'[30]

It is of course possible that actors may have economic reasons for acting and that these can then constitute explanations for such action. But these would still be actor's reasons explanations, rather than the kind of economic explanations criticised in the earlier part of this paper. This is potentially confusing, and an example may help.[31]

In a major work, Robinson and Gallagher set out to challenge economic interpretations of imperialism in the particular case of the British occupation

---

28. [Introduced in 1980s from the Schools History Project's concern with child-centred learning, but denounced by traditionalists such as Margaret Thatcher, 'New History, with its emphasis on concepts rather than chronology and empathy rather than facts, as at the root of much that was going wrong.' Cited in Stuart Foster '…Some final thoughts' in O. A. Davis, E. A. Yeager and S. J. Foster (eds), *Historical Empathy and Perspective Taking in the Social Studies*, (Lanham and Oxford, Rowman and Littlefield, 2001), p. 168. A similar controversy emerged in the USA at the time over the UCLA National History Standards Project.]

29. The story, recounted by Norbert Elias, is how the French General's African troops refused to advance, fearing an eclipse was a bad omen sent by the Prophet. The General explained the astronomy involved, which the troops claimed to accept - but still refused to advance because the eclipse was *still* a bad omen sent by the Prophet. Mennell, *Culture in History*, p. 39.

30. G. A. Cohen, 'Beliefs and roles', *Proceedings of the Aristotelian Society*, 41 (1966–7), pp. 17–34 and Jonathan Glover (ed.), *Philosophy of Mind* (Oxford, Oxford University Press, 1976).

31. I am most grateful to Michael Havinden who originally introduced this example into the discussion.

of Egypt in 1882.[32] Studying the justifications provided by the political actors involved, they concluded that the reasons explaining the occupation were (as given) mainly political. In a celebrated and critical discussion of the Gallagher and Robinson thesis, Hopkins has reasserted a kind of 'economic' explanation. But his clinching evidence is not the circumstantial one of the scale of British economic involvement in Egypt, but the discovery that other actors involved, businessmen and officials in Egypt, convinced of the danger to their economic assets, deliberately lobbied Dilke at the Foreign Office and Lord Hartington the India Secretary, with exaggerated reports of the *political* danger. He concludes:

> ... the evidence collated in this essay has indicated that intervention did not spring from any danger to the Canal, from the spread of anarchy, or from French ambitions, but from the conscious and sustained defence of Britain's expanding economic interests in Egypt.[33]

This is emphatically *not* the triumph of 'economic explanation' over 'actor's reasons' explanations', rather it is the substitution of one set of actor's reasons for another, which we have reason to believe, in this particular case, to be those that operated. Being committed to actor's reasons explanations does not commit us to anything quite so naive as always believing what actors *tell* us are their reasons: people do of course, dissemble.[34] But even when they do it is not invariably the case that the concealed reasons are 'economic'.

Explanation can often only render the unfamiliar familiar, once it has succeeded in first refamiliarising us with a sometimes very strange background. Stephen Mennell suggests, following Elias, that belief in animism and witchcraft can be explained through a supportive interaction between individuals' 'extreme insecurity and hazard to life' and their concentration on emotional responses needed to deal with that. As a result 'their knowledge remains innocently egocentric and emotionally involved.' This may fit the supposedly credulous peasant but it does not explain why obviously sophisticated and intelligent writers like Bodin believed there were witches in league with the devil – with, needless to say, important consequences for many old and lonely women. To do this it is vital to understand the status of the Bible in Bodin's world in order to create the context within which witchcraft belief can be rendered explicable as part of a whole, and highly developed, culture. Once we do this, paradoxically it is the (for us) perfectly comprehensible rejection of witchcraft by Thomas Hobbes that needs

---

32. R. Robinson and G. Gallagher, *Africa and the Victorians: The official mind of imperialism*, 2nd edn., (London, Macmillan, 1981).

33. A. G. Hopkins, 'The Victorians and Africa: A reconsideration of the occupation of Egypt, 1882', *Journal of African History*, 27 (1986), p. 385.

34. It is quite possible to sophisticate the account so as to deal with deception. *See*, e.g. Quentin Skinner, 'The Principles and Practice of Opposition: The case of Bolingbroke versus Walpole', in N. McKendrick (ed.), *Historical Perspectives on English Thought and Society: Essays in honour of J. H. Plumb* (London, Europa Press, 1974).

explaining, not Bodin's 'credulity'.[35] Focusing on actors' reasons is necessary even to re-establish correctly the agenda of what it is that requires explaining.

The ambivalence of economic explanation insidiously undermines the possibility of realising this. For inasmuch as economic explanations function as *covert ascriptions* of motives to historical actors, they block off attempts to discover actors' true perceptions and intentions. In doing this they render the unfamiliar, familiar, by making other and earlier cultures *appear* to be motivated in the same way as our own. But this, however comforting it may be, is to falsify and impoverish history (or indeed other perceptions of contemporary reality) as well as to blind us to the culturally specific nature of our own motivational self-description, which, as Dario Castiglione's essay[36] reminds us, is itself a cultural product, and a highly ambiguous one at that.

Conclusion

Actor's reasons explanations, unlike economic explanations, I hold, fulfill the minimal 'good explanation' criteria laid down at the start of the paper. The explanation (actors' beliefs, intentions, conceptions of action etc.) are logically distinct from what is to be explained: what they did. Secondly the conditions for the application of the explanation: the particular circumstances of the agent and their particular interpretation of the theory's categories are independently specifiable – it is possible to frame an account of Oedipus intending to commit patricide (and even actually killing his father in the process), yet distinguish the intention from the act. Actor's reasons explanations explain by locating a unique act within a potentially ever-increasing network of beliefs and perceptions on the part of the actor which are mutually supportive and validating. The more we learn of these, the more we understand the action, the more we can explain it.

---

35. The example is discussed by Quentin Skinner, 'A Reply to my Critics', in James Tully (ed.), *Meaning and Context: Quentin Skinner and his critics* (Oxford, Polity Press, 1988), pp. 236–8.
36. D. Castiglione, 'Excess, Frugality and the Spirit of Capitalism: Readings of Mandeville on commercial society', in *Culture in History* ... .

Chapter Ten

The Market for Toleration: A Case Study in an Aspect of the Ambiguity of 'Positive Economics'*

Introduction

This chapter concerns an aspect of the supposed neutrality of the market – in particular, to counter the claim, widely advanced by free market apologists, that the operation of the freemarket promotes toleration, or to put it another way, erodes discriminatory practices amongst market actors. Although market actors clearly discriminate, in the sense of making judgements about what, how much and with whom to trade, the import of the claim is that a free market environment will necessarily undermine the exclusion of, or partiality towards, particular groups identified by apparently non-economic criteria such as kinship, ethnic, cultural or religious backgrounds. This claim is logically related to wider claims concerning market neutrality, which, it turns out, are incompatible with claims about the erosion of tolerance. Such critiques are difficult to mount. The argument of the apologist hovers elusively between impregnable logical tautology and falsifiable, but parochial, empirical assertion. There are well-canvassed technical reasons for this. They relate to the difficulty, in neo-classically inspired economic models, of distinguishing between the falsification of the theory and the falsification of the *ceteris paribus* conditions which must invariably be specified for any application of it. Friedman's simple criterion that the test of an economic theory lies in the accuracy of its predictions cannot be operationalised unequivocally, because, as two of his major critics put it, 'we cannot distinguish the failure of a model to agree with the true values of observed variables from the failure of "other things" to be "equal"'.[1]

---

* I should like to record my thanks to Edward Goodman and the Acton Society for stimulating my interest in this area and financing a sabbatical term. Earlier versions of this article were given at the Morrell Trust Conference on Toleration, at the University of York in 1985 and at the Graduate Political Philosophy Seminar at the London School of Economics in 1989. I am grateful to both audiences and to the *British Journal of Political Science's* referees and editors, and in particular to David Miller, for critical help in developing the argument.

1. Martin Hollis and Edward Nell, *Rational Economic Man: A philosophical critique of neo-classical economics* (Cambridge, Cambridge University Press, 1975), p. 34. Ch. 1, 'Relevance and Falsification', contains a more extended discussion of the issue. Further discussion of the precise nature of Friedman's claims can be found in the last section of the article. See also Chapter Nine.

This equivocation has important policy implications. Ensconced in power, the market ideologue is apt to respond to apparent instances of the free market's failure to realise its predicted virtues with the observation that the world must be falling short of the demanding characteristics of the ideal market and should be rearranged forthwith. Indeed, it often seems that the benefits supposed to follow from the market are themselves forgotten in a series of attempts to reduce the configuration of society to the characteristics of the economic model, fragmenting and atomising labour, and forcing increasingly incongruous goods through market mechanisms in order to ensure that they are supplied at supposedly optimal amounts and prices. Since defences of the free market equivocate between the retreat to the defence of an ideal type (if the operations of actual markets are criticised) and the repudiation of the ideal type as a mere simplification if the attack is then switched to the model, I shall seek to impale the defender of the market on one or other horn of a dilemma, using a two-pronged attack which both marshals empirical evidence and claims to expose methodological confusion.[2]

The libertarian argument

Among the virtues claimed for the market as a social mechanism are its supposed impersonality and tolerance of variety in individual's tastes and life-styles. Indeed one might, with others, hazard that the rise both of the market and of market theory was signally preceded by the demise of shared and putatively objective moral and aesthetic standards. Despite J. S. Mill's utilitarian reservations about the market[3] and the caution of some more reflective theorists, latter day libertarians have exhibited an enthusiasm for it which has appeared unbounded by empirical or critical caution.[4] Nozick's flights of theoretical fancy in celebration of the diversity guaranteed by a completely contract-based society have proved the harbinger of many far more cumbersome and earthbound policy vehicles. But his position is not a new one. Consider the venerable economic Nobel prize-winner F. A. Hayek:

---

2. Clearly within the scope of an article there is not room for an extensive treatment of the different positions of individual libertarians. I simply seek to characterise a claim commonly made by them and to consider the theoretical grounds which underpin it. The choice of Friedman, Hayek and von Mises was inspired not only by the desire to avoid the charge of ducking the issue by picking straw men. Their relevance is heightened by my claim that underlying methodological assumptions play a crucial part in the issue. The figures discussed were chosen because their treatment of such meta-theoretical issues is commonly regarded as also grounding the work of others who deploy, but do not analyse, the same arguments.

3. See particularly the first and last chapters of Book V of *The Principles of Political Economy*.

4. These words are carefully chosen. It is true that Hayek and von Mises acknowledge the empirical limitations in applying the model of the perfect market, although it is notable that others such as Nozick and Friedman, especially in his policy-oriented writing, do so hardly at all. However qualified by some of the more sophisticated 'new right' theorists, the perfect market model is an immensely powerful and simplistic paradigm, and it is this version which 'has lodged in the crania of politicians' as Nick Bosanquet puts it (*After the New Right* (London, Heinemann, 1983), p. 44). To suggest that anyone taking it seriously should be dismissed as jejune (as have several commentators on earlier versions of this article) would seem to be a rather chilling way of marginalising criticism of a position which has gained immense political and rhetorical power.

It seems to me one of the great merits of a free society that material reward is not dependent on whether the majority of our fellows like or esteem us personally. This means that as long as we keep within the accepted rules, moral pressure can be brought on us only through the esteem of those whom we ourselves respect and not through the allocation of material reward ... we are free because the success of our daily efforts does not depend on whether particular people like us, or our principles, or our religion or our manners...[5]

A more precisely formulated and defended version of the claim is advanced by Milton Friedman in his *Capitalism and Freedom*. Since the issue is not simply an empirical one, but hinges at least partly on the properties of the argument justifying the claim, such properties must, consequently be clearly articulated. I have focused on Friedman's argument as a classic statement of the reasoning behind the assertion that free markets erode discrimination.

Friedman's argument is that the market guarantees non-discrimination in economic relations (and by implication fosters toleration more generally) by imposing costs on those who would exclude certain classes or groups from the range of potential customers for the goods or services they are providing. The same argument holds for those seeking employees or suppliers. Discrimination on any basis other than price, it is held, narrows the range of the choices available to market actors, placing them in a disadvantageous position *vis-a-vis* actors who make no such discriminations.[6] In addition, Friedman makes an empirical argument. The growth of capitalism, he claims, has historically been accompanied by a reduction of the extent to which discrimination occurs, thus validating the theoretical explanation. Maintenance of the general rules of private property and the market (and little else) have acted in the interests of black and other minority

---

5. F. A. Hayek, 'The Moral Element in Free Enterprise', in *Studies in Philosophy, Politics and Economics* (London, Routledge and Kegan Paul, 1967), pp. 233–4. Hayek almost universally appears as a libertarian, as he does here and, for example, in the *Constitution of Liberty*, where he criticises cultural and national conservatism for providing a 'bridge ... to collectivism' (*The Constitution of Liberty* (London, Routledge and Kegan Paul, 1960), p. 405). But it is interesting to note that his policy interventions can reveal a preoccupation with the very maintenance of cultural hegemony to which his libertarian defence of the market would seem opposed. *See* his letter on immigration to *The Times*, 1 March 1968, cited in part in Ruth Levitas, (ed.), *The Ideology of the New Right* (Cambridge, Polity Press, 1986), p. 71: 'the ordinary man only slowly reconciles himself to a large increase in foreigners amongst his neighbours, even if they differ only in language and manners,... the wise statesman ... ought to aim at keeping the rate of influx low'.

6. A similar case is made by von Mises in *Human Action: A treatise on economics* (London, William Hodge, 1949), p. 280: 'it is true that the employer has the right to fire the employee. But if he makes use of this right to indulge in his whims, he hurts his own interests. It is to his own disadvantage if he discharges a better man in order to hire a less efficient one. The market does not directly prevent anybody from arbitrarily inflicting harm on his fellow citizens; it only puts a penalty upon such conduct.' However, von Mises is rightly more cautious about the ultimate power of the market to overcome the individual's ideal (or prejudice) regarding economic behaviour: 'Dependence upon the supremacy of the consumers is not unlimited. If a man has a weighty reason for defying the sovereignty of the consumers he can try it ... he may have to pay a price for his conviction ... but it is left to a man's own decision to choose between a material advantage and the call of what he believes to be his duty' (pp. 283–4).

groups. The free market separates out irrelevant characteristics, by rewarding those who, in their dealings, separate economic from other considerations. Thus, the arguments runs, other things being equal – although government intervention and misguided welfare liberalism being what it is, they very rarely will be – the profit motive, given free reign, as well as providing commodities at optimal prices, will erode the exclusiveness of various groups on which other forms of intolerance is based. Interference in the freedom of contract, designed to produce the same effects by legislation, infringes liberty, harms entrepreneurs, distorts prices and fails even to produce the desired result of ending discriminatory practices.[7]

Detailed empirical investigation of the role and persistence of discrimination in markets can be found in both economic and anthropological literature. Important studies of the long-term historical evidence can be cited both supporting and contesting Friedman's claim.[8] But the liberal claim, as formulated by Friedman, Hayek and their epigones, is that (*ceteris paribus* of course) there is something like a necessary connection between the operation of a free market and the erosion of discrimination. This is too strong a claim to be validated by any limited set of empirical observations. It is so strong, on the other hand, that it is vulnerable to quite limited evidence to the contrary, evidence which can be evaded only by the move of denying the truly 'perfect' nature of the markets discussed. Such evidence will be presented, for it not only exists, but is a phenomenon well known to empirical students of the market such as economic historians and anthropologists. Then, against the 'But no truly perfect market ...' move, it will be demonstrated that according to the liberals own methodological assumptions, their claim is too strong on purely logical grounds. The argument advanced in the article is not that free markets *never* erode intolerance, only (against the claim that they *invariably*

---

7. See also T. Sowell, *Race and Economics* (New York, McKay and Co., 1975), ch. 6. Sowell argues that the higher discrimination found in state and regulated industries can be explained by their not having to bear the full costs of job discrimination. His explanation of this cost is substantially the same as Friedman's (*Race and Economics*, pp. 168–9). A further *resumé* of the libertarian case is to be found in G. Gilder, *Wealth and Poverty* (New York, Basic Books, 1981), ch. 12 ('The Myths of Discrimination').

8. For example, Sowell's previously cited work and his *Markets and Minorities* (Oxford, Blackwell, 1980); Richard Freeman, 'Black economic progress since 1964', *The Public Interest*, 52 (1978), pp. 52–68; and Edward Banfield, *The Unheavenly City Revisited* (Boston, Mass., Little, Brown and Co., 1974). The opposing case is discussed in the next section, but *see also* I. Garfinkel and R. Haveman, *Earnings Capacity, Poverty, and Inequality* (New York, Institute for Research on Poverty, 1977). Since the historical context of black emancipation can hardly be claimed to approximate to free market conditions, the relevance of such studies must raise problems and always begs the *ceteris paribus* condition outlined above. Indeed, in some cases the failure of the data to fit the thesis is brazenly blamed on counterfactuals whose relevance is directly contingent on the truth of the very thesis in question. Thus Gilder, trying to explain a 20 per cent discrepancy between white and black earnings, when other identifiable indices are held constant, avers quite speculatively that 'the remaining gap, the evidence increasingly suggests, relates not chiefly to discrimination against blacks but to earlier discrimination against their parents and to government-induced dependency and female-headed families'. No evidence is offered for the first statement, while the second hinges on the blithe assumption that 'welfare can be shown to intensify and perpetuate the causes of poverty'. *See* Gilder, *Wealth and Poverty*, pp. 132–133.

do) that they *can* sustain it. To show this we shall firstly, in the next section, cite empirical evidence that they have and secondly show why the theoretical or deductive aspect of the market guarantees toleration claim is faulty, to which the final two sections will be devoted.

Empirical evidence concerning the claim of markets to promote toleration

In a perfect market, contracts are uncoerced, there are numerous buyers and sellers, exit and entry are relatively unimpeded, products are relatively homogeneous and divisible, externalities are minimal and there is an adequate flow of information necessary for actors' decision-making. Under such situations contracts will be discrete, enabling actors to change their trading partners in response to price fluctuations. Such a situation is of course an economists' dream, yet they insist, there are actual markets which come close to it. Street vegetable markets, at one end of the scale, and the financial market in stocks and futures, at the other, are both commonly cited as approximations to these ideals in economic textbooks. In particular, economic anthropologists have remarked that Third World peasant markets in general exhibit many of the objective characteristics demanded by the perfect market model: 'Peasant markets facilitate trading in small lots... Buyers and sellers are innumerable, leading to conditions which as closely approximate pure competition as any institution other than markets of the sophisticated financial world'.[9]

Field workers too, frequently comment on the 'perfect' conditions of such markets:

> Now that so much of the world is filled with corporate directors and advertising men, the bazaar is the nearest thing to be found in reality to the purely competitive market of neoclassical economics, the one place in the world where isolated, interest-rivalrous, profit-maximising sellers still confront isolated, non-propagandised, utility-maximising consumers on equal ground, deterministic actors in the cosmic drama of supply and demand.[10]

Despite revealing many of the empirical properties of perfect markets however, anthropological studies commonly also discover the emergence of discriminatory conventions designed to favour known trading partners in long-term dyadic relationships which survive the temptation of extraordinary profits to be made in one-off contracts. Although not explicit or enforcible contracts, they are highly formalised and specifically named practices: *pratik* in Haiti, *suki* in the Philippines,

---

9. C. S. Belshaw, *Traditional Exchange and Modern Markets* (Englewood Cliffs, NJ., Prentice Hall, 1965, p. 77).
10. C. Geertz, 'Suq: The bazaar economy in Sefrou', in C. Geertz, H. Geertz and L. Rosen, (eds), *Meaning and Order in Moroccan Society* (Cambridge, Cambridge University Press, 1979), p. 198.

onibara in Nigeria. In general, these conventions involve unilaterally offering a market advantage to one's trading partner which is not immediately reciprocated but which establishes an unspoken obligation of loyalty. In Sahlins' typology of exchanges it falls midway between the generalised reciprocity characterised by gift exchange and hospitality and the balanced reciprocity of immediate and direct exchange.[11]

In the Haitian study it was found that in a *pratik* relationship the purchaser will buy from a producer at a slightly higher price than transactions which are undertaken in the spot market. Moreover, she (the intermediary traders are all women) will buy all that she needs from that producer, rather than shopping around, on the understanding that she is assured a regular supply of the goods traded. The exceptions are highly perishable goods which are sold to the first comers at market rates in order to clear supplies before they spoil. But here again *pratik* buyers will lend money in anticipation of the harvest of perishables and will be repaid in kind at prices below the going rate, with the earliest crop. There is no collateral for such loans (although a conventional market in capital exists alongside the *pratik* market). The loan forms a part of the long-term bi-lateral trust relationship. At the other end of the distribution system retailers too practise *pratik*, seeking regular customers, mostly in this case by quantity concessions to avoid giving the impression that market prices allow too high a profit margin.

Market prices are set by the textbook operation of competition very soon after the opening of the market, but *pratik* concessions are not advertised or known in advance. Only at the end of the transaction will the retailer drop in the extra amount of goods, or the small luxury item which sustains the relationship. Characteristically, the selling *pratik* will refuse to sell to others even at inflated prices until the buying *pratik*'s needs have been met.

Mintz, who carried out the Haitian study, emphasised the non-contractual nature of the relationship: 'except in instances of granting credit and lending money, and often even then, the guarantees that a *pratik* relationship will persist are personal and customary, not legal and contractual ... dishonesty ends the tie'.[12]

In the Philippines a similar practice is known locally as *suki*. A *suki* is a customer whose status, although special, is not established by any explicit contract, but simply by the seller's casual indication that cash need not be paid on this particular occasion. *suki* sellers are expected to offer price concessions, or – for perishables – increased quantities, to ensure good quality, to provide services such as bagging and to hold back stock for their *suki* buyers when supplies are short. The buyer, on the other hand, is supposed to patronise the *suki* supplier exclusively, to advertise his virtues and to pay, not necessarily immediately, but regularly.[13]

---

11. Marshall Sahlins, *Stone Age Economics* (London, Tavistock Press, 1974), pp. 191 ff.

12. S. Mintz, 'Pratik: Haitian personal economic relationships', *Proceedings of the American Ethnographic Association* (Seattle, Washington University Press, 1961), pp. 54–63.

13. W. G. Davies, *Social Relations in a Philippine Market: Self-interest and subjectivity* (Berkeley, University of California Press, 1973), p. 216.

These practices cannot be dismissed as the nostalgic residue of generalised exchange or social solidarity, made possible only by the absence of a competitive market and doomed to collapse under its increasing penetration. For modern markets, similarly free, exhibit the development of similar practices. Under study, the New England fish market 'appeared to operate under a set of conditions which reasonably approximate the textbook picture of a perfectly competitive market: there are many buyers and sellers; exit and entry are easily accomplished, there appear to be relatively homogeneous products and adequate flow of information'.[14] Nevertheless, it revealed the emergence of long-term, informal, bilateral understandings between boat owners and wholesalers. These involved commitments to sell or buy the whole of the catch, even if it was unwanted, at a price which would not be known until disposed of by the wholesaler! Breakdowns in such relationships were accepted without impugning the trustworthiness of the parties, who would subsequently be courted by other actors. However, repeated failure to maintain such agreements apparently led to the widespread shunning of that particular party and their relegation to the much more precarious spot market.

A smaller scale study of Soulard, the St Louis fruit and vegetable marketplace 'similar to the purely competitive market of classical economic theory', found that 'when confronted with the maximal freedom of market choice, many actors nevertheless established confining relationships'. Both with their retail customers, when acting as sellers, and with their suppliers in the big wholesale market, regular but informal relationships are preferred and cultivated in order to minimise the variations in takings – which can be large – even if it means foregoing 'quick' profits on one-off spot contracts.[15]

If such practices are not explicable in terms of a historical progression from less to more perfect markets, how are they to be explained? The answer is that they are increasingly seen as responses to aspects of uncertainty and irregularity in the market.[16] *Pratik*-type relationships provide a degree of security and control over the otherwise irregular supply and demand for goods which are vital to small traders with little capital to sustain them over periods of dearth or glut. They economise on search time and transaction costs which increase with the size of the market.[17] In a Nigerian study, the practice of *onibara*, as it was

---

14. J. A. Wilson, 'Adaptation to uncertainty and small numbers exchange: the New England fresh fish market', *Bell Journal of Economics*, 11 (1980), 491–504, p. 491.
15. Stuart Plattner, 'Economic custom in a competitive marketplace', *American Anthropologist*, 85 (1983), 848–58, pp. 852, 856.
16. An economic historian noting the phenomenon in the emergent commodity markets of England's commercial revolution, comments: 'buyers and sellers often attempted to reduce the risks of short-run fluctuations in supply and demand by attempting to nurture special trading relations with an opposite number' (B. L. Anderson, 'Entrepreneurship, Market Process, and the Industrial Revolution in England', in B. L. Anderson and A. J. H. Latham (eds), *The Market in History* (London, Croom Helm, 1986), p. 16).
17. One might (charitably) suggest that the social exclusivity of the pre-Big Bang London Stock Market was another way of minimising risk in a market where trust was at a premium and surveillance difficult and costly.

locally known, was confined to two commodities which involve a high level of risk; other commodities were traded on a conventional market.[18] There is, in an important sense, more than one good being traded. In *pratik*-type relationships not only the material commodity, that, as it were, crosses the counter, but certainty, credit, insurance and various other intangibles are being packaged together in the deal.[19] Such goods, like Hobbes' covenants of future performance, can only be transacted with the aid of trust, a fragile and vulnerable commodity, if evidently not quite as elusive or dependent on coercive sanctions as he would have had us believe.

If this explanation is correct, it is noteworthy that it is the very perfection of these markets, in terms of the large numbers of powerless agents operating in them, which generates amongst their actors the need (or at least desire) for these relationships that so impede the persistence of the idealised, impersonal spot-contract, theoretically required for the market to respond perfectly to supply and demand.

What are we to conclude from this evidence? One conclusion might be that these relationships reflect excessive risk-aversion by contractors. But who is to say what is excessive? The language of 'revealed preferences', which will be further discussed in the next section (see 'Conceptual criticisms of the hypothesis that markets guarantee toleration'), counsels caution or agnosticism about the motives behind the preferences. Whether these decisions are beneficial or 'rational', or whether there is any way of deciding, is strictly beside the present point, which is that the libertarian argument concerning market neutrality would seem to require that freely expressed preferences must, irrespective, be regarded as sovereign. What freely expressed preferences in some free market circumstances undoubtedly produce is stable preferential relationships rather than market-price led spot contracting.

It is now time to relate these observations to the issue of toleration and discrimination. Empirically, the conditions which sustain such trusting relationships are habit, tradition, kinship, shared culture, religion or ethnicity; precisely the dimensions along which toleration is required and often fails to materialise. The kinds of market practices described above often require and sustain ethnic separateness, indeed they can be used to exclude 'out' groups. In the Philippines, '*suki* relations tend to be influenced by ethnicity and when

---

18. L. Trager, 'Customer and creditors: variations in economic personalism in Nigeria', *Ethnology*, 20 (1981), pp. 133–46.

19. Davis, *Social Relations in a Philippine Market*, p. 216 (for *suki*); Trager, 'Customer and creditors', p. 137 (for *onibara*); Plattner, 'Economic custom in a competitive marketplace', p. 852; all these emphasise the risk-minimising function of the practice. Risk-aversion in peasant economies is well documented: Allen Johnson, 'Security and Risk-taking among Poor Peasants', in G. Dalton, (ed.), *Studies in Economic Anthropology*, American Anthropological Association Monograph, 7 (Washington, American Anthropological Association, 1977); Michael Lipton, 'The theory of the optimising peasant', *Journal of Development Studies*, 4 (1968), 327–51, esp. pp. 334–5; C. J. Bliss and N. H. Stern, *Palanpur: Economics in an Indian market* (Oxford, Oxford University Press, 1982), pp. 300 ff.

ethnic boundaries are crossed ... *suki* becomes more difficult to establish', 'Such relationships ... are vastly more common among lowlanders than among other categories, binding together lowland Filipino buyers and sellers with loyalties not easily obtainable by competition from members of other ethnic categories'. Davis' informants 'debated whether Chinese could appropriately be considered *suki* at all for they were generally held to be untrustworthy' (i.e. one suspects, 'textbook' rational, spot-contracting, market actors!).[20]

Sometimes the dyadic link is reinforced by actual kinship ties rather than mere ethnicity. In the Soulard market study, not only were 168 out of 180 market personnel interrelated (51 per cent had more than ten relatives involved), but 'most of the merchants ... are southern Italian (as opposed to the local farmers of German descent who sell their own produce) and have extensive kinship relations with the wholesalers they depend on for their supplies'.[21]

Pioneering anthropological studies of market relations, such as Arensburg's in Ireland have long emphasised the importance of kinship in trading relations.[22] Even where real kinship ties do not exist, 'ritual' kinship is sometimes established in order to cement the link, as in Mexico where such relationships are called '*compadrazgo*'.[23]

Thus, trust-based, dyadic ties, which appear to be endogenous products of free multi-participant markets, far from eroding intolerance, generate and perpetuate if not intolerance itself, then at least the kind of discrimination which supports intolerance. There would therefore seem to be no grounds for sustaining the claim that free markets invariably promote toleration. Furthermore, discrimination is clearly an externality imposed on those groups which, because of their 'difference', cannot be sufficiently trusted to be admitted to the practice and are thus excluded from the market or are admitted to it only on less favourable terms. How costly this externality is to bear will depend on various empirical factors, to be discussed in the next section.

Conceptual criticisms of the hypothesis that markets guarantee toleration

It might well be argued that it is economically naive to see these developments as contradicting the free market hypothesis. Post-marginalist economics claims to make no presuppositions about the nature of the commodities, goods or values exchanged on the market. Indeed it is the basis of a related defence of the free market that it is unbiased in its responsiveness to the choices made by the actors constituting it. This is itself a more general, and perhaps more sophisticated,

---

20. Davis, '*Social Relations in a Philippine Market*', pp. 229, 256.
21. Plattner, 'Economic custom in a competitive marketplace', p. 851.
22. C. Arensberg, *The Irish Countryman* (London, Macmillan, 1937), pp. 154, 161.
23. *Compadrazgo* involves the ritual 'adoption' of a trading partner. The practice is cited in Davis, *Social Relations in a Philippine Market*, p. 229. *See* further: S. Mintz and E. Woolf, 'An analysis of ritual co-parenthood (*Compadrazgo*)', *South West Journal of Anthropology*, 6 (1950), pp. 341–68.

version of the claim that the free market is a guarantor of toleration. Ideally, a market should be capable of revealing a price for anything for which there is a demand that could be satisfied by exchange and, in some sense (which is admittedly difficult to operationalise for reasons mentioned in the introduction), it should act as a transparent medium, not contaminating the goods passed through it. If all goods were offered for sale voluntarily in a perfect market, the price paid for them would represent their true (i.e. intersubjective) values *vis-a-vis* other goods.[24]

The limits to this are of course those cases of market failure where voluntary individual contracts would fail to secure a desired good because of its public nature and the destructive effects of anticipated free-riding.[25] But such exceptions, it may be argued, are fewer than we suspect and unduly dependent on practical considerations, such as available technology, and our determination to provide goods *via* a market mechanism. Could not lighthouses be substituted by transmitters of electro-magnetic directional information, scrambled in such a way that only lessees of expensive decoding receivers could make use of the warning information, thus at a stroke depriving marine traffic of free safety and textbooks on public choice and the theory of externalities of their prime example?[26]

Anything that can be privately supplied can be sold through the market. However, that this in turn guarantees access through a suitable concentration of market purchasing power is an empty claim. Moreover, it is so for reasons which hinge on the very lack of bias which is the basis of the libertarians' celebrations of the market. For to take seriously the market's neutrality with regard to agents' choices is to acknowledge the possibility, indeed the likelihood, that one of the things people will wish to purchase through the market is discrimination itself. It is or may be true, as Friedman claims, that employers who refuse to hire blacks or Catholics, or shoppers who chose to avoid being served by them, will pay a cost.[27] But it is a cost they may

---

24. Market neutrality is a complex concept. A good recent discussion of the various possible connotations is to be found in A. T. O'Donnell, 'The Neutrality of the Market', in R. E. Goodin and A. Reeve (eds), *Liberal Neutrality* (London, Routledge, 1989). Most importantly, for the discussion here, O'Donnell distinguishes between issue of neutrality between transactors and neutrality between preferences (p. 42).

25. Another rather different problem relates not to public goods, as normally conceived, but to jointly-supplied, ideal-regarding goods – what D. Miller has called 'group-oriented desires', such as the desire to produce in a co-operative rather than a hierarchical environment. Here, too, as Miller shows, the market fails to deliver without political intervention. *See* D. Miller, 'Market neutrality and the failure of co-operatives', *British Journal of Political Science*, 11 (1981), 309–29; and *see also* his more recent *Market, State and Community* (Oxford, Oxford University Press, 1989), pp. 83–93.

26. Radio-direction beacons already exist at sea of course, but any suitably tuned radio-receiver can pick them up without charge. In the present political climate one hesitates to put forward what might appear as a *reductio ad absurdum*. (On the 'Lighthouse example', see further Chapter Six; fn. 36.)

27. In this sense discrimination may be 'inefficient', but not sub-optimal, given the inclusion of discrimination in the preference-schedules of employers. Even so, affirmative action legislation may be a necessary device to bring home to an employer the financial cost of his prejudice, by coercing at least some in-group market actors to break ranks and thereby realise the market advantage available to them. *See* O'Donnell, 'Market neutrality…', p. 55.

well, and quite consciously, be prepared to pay. Only if we assume that the only commodities involved in the exchange are what passes across the counter and that buyer's aims are solely to acquire that good whilst maximising their money holdings, could they be said, as Friedman claims, to be suffering a market disadvantage for something they could buy as cheaply elsewhere. They might simply prefer to pay for their prejudice by paying a premium for hiring or shopping where they can indulge it. Just as economic actors in the 'perfect' markets of Haiti, the Philippines and Missouri decided to pay a little extra and buy some security along with their yams or mangoes, and tended to choose their known and understood ethnic fellows as the best bet for providing it; so in other markets, such as for labour or housing, individuals may choose to spend a little more for indulging their prejudices as well.

Are the two cases sufficiently similar to sustain this extension of the argument? Does the fact that there may appear to be an economic reason for the former case but only what we call 'prejudice' in the latter case make a difference? It is not at all clear that it should. As we have suggested several times, whether costs attach to such discrimination depends on how we define a normal cost. Once the idea of a cost ceases to refer directly to money prices and simply, as it should, to the marginal preference of consumers for one kind of good over another, the argument about the relative sustainability of prejudice against the desire to maximise money holdings is much less clear cut. These are simply two preferences for which individuals establish a ratio of exchange. There seems to be no reason, moral considerations aside, why shoppers should not prefer carrots at 20p a pound served by whites, to carrots at 15p a pound served by blacks. Server and carrots come as a package deal. Whilst the would-be discriminator might well be incurring an 'uneconomical' cost in money terms, it may be a perfectly acceptable ratio of exchange for the degree of exclusion the buyer wishes to maintain. A revealed preference reveals only the preference. The attribution of 'rationality' – or even reasons – to that preference is invariably tendentious, and on some influential views, unverifiable.[28]

---

28. Decision theory runs into difficulties in deciding whether observed 'inconsistencies' in preferences 'disprove' the axioms of decision theory or reveal changes in *ceteris paribus* conditions, for example by displaying 'learning', or require the attribution to subjects of differential risk aversion, or of perverse characterisations of the choices facing them. It appears to be impossible to devise satisfactory tests for discriminating amongst these various possibilities. A classic article is A. Tversky, 'A critique of expected utility theory: descriptive and normative considerations', *Erkenntnis*, 9 (1975), pp. 163–74. For a brief discussion, *see* Donald Davidson, 'The Philosophy of Psychology' in Donald Davidson, *Essays on Actions and Events* (Oxford, Oxford University Press, 1980), pp. 269 ff. A related issue is the difficulty traditional economic theory has in accommodating the notion of commitment. On this point, *see* the seminal article by Amartya K. Sen, 'Rational fools: a critique of the behavioural foundations of economic theory' in (*inter alia*) *Philosophy and Public Affairs*, 6 (1976–7), pp. 317–44; and in F. Hahn and M. Hollis (eds), *Philosophy and Economic Theory* (Oxford, Oxford University Press, 1979): 'The characteristic of commitment with which I am most concerned here is the fact that it drives a wedge between personal choice and personal welfare, and much of traditional economic theory relies on the identity between the two' (Sen, in Hollis and Hahn, (eds), *Philosophy and Economic Theory,* p. 97). Intolerance, or the prejudicial behaviour resulting from it, may be regarded analytically as a form of commitment.

To press the objection further, it might be argued that conceding that the discriminator pays a money cost (rather than possibly making a money gain, as risk-averse trading could be construed) makes a difference to the likelihood of the discrimination being sustained in a money-market context. Empirically this is not borne out. Ideal-regarding discrimination, say against South African fruit (logically, of course, indistinguishable from other forms of discrimination), far from being eroded, has emerged and grown at some (money) cost and inconvenience to supporters of the boycott. But furthermore, as we shall argue below, this assertion simply prejudged the issue of *other* agents' relative preference for ideal-satisfaction as against economising in money terms.

A further objection might be to point out that different economic agents are exposed in different ways to market pressures. Although the ultimate consumer may simply be made to trade off a preference for prejudice against money, other economic actors may not. Once again, how true this is seems to be an empirical question. Even if it were conceded that money economising does, at least for a *firm* (as opposed to an individual) in a competitive situation, at some point exert an irresistible imperative, that point need not be reached. If in-group cohesion is strong, no formal cartel will be necessary to exclude say, blacks or Catholics from the job market, and so long as no one (or not a sufficient number) breaks ranks, no discriminating employer will suffer sufficient comparative disadvantage to lead to pressures to follow suit.[29] Moreover, to pursue the case of the labour market, if the cumulative effect of the out-group's social and economic disadvantages were such as to render them less attractive as potential employees, it is easy to see the emergence of a vicious circle in which prejudice gives rise to discrimination which creates deprivation which in turn reinforces 'groundless' prejudice with well-grounded discrimination, because say, lack of experience in the labour market has lowered their productivity.

Whether Friedman's inverse Gresham's law operates or not, then, would seem to rest on contingencies. This confirms our position, which is only to challenge the claim that free markets guarantee its operation. Two particularly relevant factors might be emphasised from the above discussion. Foremost among these is the relative size of the groups involved. Ethnic groups which are subject to discrimination might simply be too small or economically powerless to be able to offer any deserters from the majority group the compensatory advantages of scale on which Friedman's argument largely rests. Much would then seem to depend on the particular notional rate of exchange obtaining between cash advantages and in-group membership.

A second relevant consideration is informational. It rests on the visibility of the criteria on which discrimination is based. Much of the discussion of these issues centres around the retail industry, where the criteria on which consumers might wish to base discrimination are highly visible. Labour markets more

---

29. Indeed, if in-group cohesion extends to other workers and customers, as well as to the employing group, boycott responses could actually impose costs on defecting employers.

generally and housing are also susceptible to discriminatory practices. However, where a product is inherently mixed in origin, or the result of long and complex processes, often undertaken overseas or by a variety of different firms, an intended discrimination may be difficult to sustain. The purchaser wishing to discriminate against all products with components originating from, say, South Africa faces difficulties only slightly worse than those of the consumer not wishing to consume nuclear-generated electricity.[30] Government legislation on the kind of information that must be made available to consumers or suppliers can also influence these possibilities. The general point is that, once again, as in the case of the size of the excluded group, contingent factors seem crucial.[31]

It is the interaction of such factors as group size, relative preference for exclusivity, the information available and the technological nature of the production process which seems to determine whether or not particular market processes support or erode discrimination. *No abstract argument can determine what these will be: it is purely an empirical question.*

Methodological basis of the mistake

The fallacy of Friedman's argument results from an attempt to deduce guaranteed positive conclusions from purely analytical premises (a danger to which he himself drew attention in his own methodological writings). The plausibility of Friedman's case about the effect of the market on discrimination rests on an equivocation in the notion of cost between a money price realised in an objective market and the subjectively perceived marginal substitutability between two goods or outcomes supplied through a market mechanism. For most modern economists, the postulate that individuals are maximisers precludes us from predicting in what precisely an individual will find their utility – profit or prejudice.[32] If individuals were profit maximisers, or maximisers of money holdings, Friedman's argument might hold. For if the final consumers always preferred to swallow their prejudices in order to buy cheap, discriminating employers would incur serious costs. But as an empirical assertion this seems clearly false; and as an analytical claim it can discount the possibility of markets sustaining discrimination only by attempting to define away discriminatory

---

30. The latter example was suggested to me by Jeremy Shearmur, who was present on the original occasion when the paper on which this article is based was delivered.
31. Sowell, one of the more judicious apologists for free market policies in these areas, does concede that 'under special conditions, discrimination can be made profitable' (*Race and Economics*, p. 169). But these 'special conditions' turn out to be not at all unusual: significant imbalance of numbers between the groups, easy identification, a high desire to exclude and a low cost of exclusion. 'Cost' to Sowell is clearly a money-price cost and therefore begs the whole question (pp. 169–72).
32. For example: 'Praxeology is indifferent to the ultimate goals of action ... It applies the term happiness in a purely formal sense. In the praxeological terminology the proposition: man's unique aim is to attain happiness, is tautological. It does not imply any statement about the state of affairs from which man expects happiness' (von Mises, *Human Action*, p. 15).

behaviour in this crucial economic group. Making it true that individuals always prefer to maximise their financial position would seem to require not only some impressive Orwellian techniques of indoctrination; but also, by requiring individuals to narrow the range of preferences expressed through the market, involves violating the primary value the libertarian perceives in the market: that it is neutral with regard to individual's values and tastes.

Being agnostic about the relationship between psychology and the empirical properties of the market, we could put the point the other way round. If it turned out to be empirically demonstrable that paradigmatically free markets did, as a matter of fact, erode discriminatory (or ideal-regarding) preferences while sustaining narrowly 'economic' ones, this would, ironically, *disprove* the claim that the market mediated neutrally between participants' preference schedules. It would show that some preference schedules – those which place a high value on maximising money holdings and physical goods – were dominant over others.[33] In other words it would show that markets systematically changed people's values and tastes.

Markets cannot be ascribed both virtues. Market neutrality can only be claimed if it is as transparent with regard to intolerant or discriminatory preferences as it is to desires for commodities. Disallowing preferences other than the maximisation of money holdings, or the commodities they purchase not only renders false one of the key assumptions of the market model but, far more seriously, destroys – both in practice and in theory – the libertarian aura claimed for the market by its defenders. Conversely, if the market does discriminate in this way, and we wish some preferences – such as ideal regarding or 'group-oriented' ones – to survive, we must limit the role or scope of the market accordingly.

The nature of Friedman's illicit move can be shown by considering the philosophical underpinnings of the market model. For the major methodological theorists of modern liberal economics, although differing in detail on these issues, agree in their insistence that assumptions of rational egoism, however formulated, are not putative psychological data about humans which might, if true, predict the kind of profit-maximising and prejudice-eroding behaviour predicted by Friedman. They are axioms, capable of generating testable predictions about behaviour, and it is these, in turn, which are falsifiable by looking at the behaviour revealed in

---

33. Some discussion of the difficulties involved in defining neutrality in political procedures can be found in J. Raz, *The Morality of Freedom* (Oxford, Oxford University Press, 1986), ch. 5, and in David Gauthier, *Morals by Agreement* (Oxford, Oxford University Press, 1986), ch. iv: 'The Market: Freedom from morality'. However, whilst both celebrate the formally liberating effect of the market from moral and other-regarding considerations, neither author seriously considers the issue of the scope thereby allowed for those who wish to sustain such elements in their choices. David Miller, in *Market, State and Community* (ch. 3), acknowledges the importance of the issue but elects to 'forgo any criticism of the market on the grounds that it induces people to adopt (e.g.) commodity-based conceptions of the good' (note 7, p. 75).

markets. But the axioms do not themselves have the character of such verifiable hypotheses.[34] Thus Ludwig von Mises:

> The theorems of economics are derived not from the observation of facts (which rather serve to indicate areas of concern) but through deductions from the fundamental category of action, which has been expressed sometimes as the economic principle (i.e. the necessity to economise); sometimes as the value principle or as the cost principle. They are of aprioristic derivation and therefore lay claim to apodictic certainty that belongs to basic principles so derived.[35]

Friedman accords a different conceptual status to the principles from which his hypotheses are derived but is nevertheless just as concerned as von Mises to deny that they are empirical (and therefore falsifiable) descriptions:

> To suppose that hypotheses have not only 'implications' but also 'assumptions' and that the conformity of these assumptions to 'reality' is a test of the validity of the hypothesis ... is fundamentally wrong and productive of much mischief ... the relation is almost the opposite of that suggested ... in general the more significant the theory the more unrealistic the assumptions.

---

34. The interesting exception to this position is Samuelson, who argues that as a matter of logic, hypotheses whose consequences are fully specified, realistic and confirmed must rest on assumptions which are realistic. This is strictly entailed only if all the consequences are specified and confirmed and no other assumptions will generate equivalent hypotheses. Of course, not all – in fact very few – hypotheses are such that their consequences can all be specified, and even fewer are all confirmed, so the force of the logical point is considerably blunted. He falls back on a chauvinistic gut feeling that realism in assumptions is indeed important: 'All economic regularities that have no commonsense core that you can explain to your wife will soon fail' (*see* P. Samuelson, 'Comment on E. Nagel's "Assumptions in Economic Theory"', in *The Collected Scientific Papers of Paul A. Samuelson*, 3 vols. (Cambridge, Mass., MIT Press, 1966), vol. II, p. 1175.

35. L. von Mises, *Epistemological Problems of Modern Economics* (Princeton, NJ., von Nostrand, 1960), excerpted in Hahn and Hollis, (eds), *Philosophy and Economic Theory*, p. 64. Von Mises sees what he calls the basic principles of human action as akin, in the practical world, to Kant's synthetic *a prioris*. 'They are the necessary mental tool to arrange sense data in a systematic way, to transform them into facts of experience, then these facts into bricks to build theories, and finally the theories into technics to attend ends aimed at'. See Ludwig von Mises, *The Ultimate Foundation of Economic Science* (Princeton, N. J., von Nostrand, 1962), p. 16; *see also* pp. 19–21. Unlike Friedman, who is a fairly unreconstructed logical positivist, and Hayek, who endorses positivistic science but sees it as a basis for deductive forays into untestable territory, von Mises rejects the application of positivism to the human sciences. This is because he sees positivism as an historical reaction of the natural sciences to the subversion of their paradigm, Euclidean geometry, by non-Euclidean geometries. But destruction of synthetic *a prioris* in natural science has, he claims, no implications for the study of human action, where they can therefore continue to be applied (*see* Hayek, 'Degrees of Explanation' in *Studies* (which is dedicated to Popper), pp. 5–7; and von Mises, *The Ultimate Foundation*, p. 5). Thus, although each of the three thinkers occupies a different position on the epistemological status of hypotheses or axioms, they are united in denying that they are descriptions of reality.

In support of this argument Friedman draws attention to his own critique of those empirical studies designed to find out whether, as a matter of fact, businessmen were motivated by the concerns that marginalist theories of the firm suggested they should be: studying the shape of the demand curve facing them, for example. These studies, he insisted, were a waste of time. Such theories, properly understood, do not even purport to be descriptions of individual's behaviour:

> To be important, a hypothesis must be descriptively false in its assumptions ... the relevant question to ask about the assumptions of a theory is not whether they are descriptively realistic for they never are, but whether they are sufficiently good approximations for the purpose in hand. And this question can only be answered by seeing whether the theory works, which means whether it yields sufficiently accurate predictions.[36]

The upshot of these methodological prescriptions must be to insist, firstly, that the assumption of utility maximisation merely postulates some relationship between desires and the effort or holdings expended to achieve those desires: but that we can assume nothing about the nature, eligibility, or ratios of exchange between those desires, or between the desires and efforts or holdings. Secondly, to emphasise that the hypotheses used to construct theories (including *ceteris paribus* clauses) are of a completely different conceptual status from the prediction (an aspirant empirical description) which they generate. But once the libertarian accepts this (and to retain preference neutrality it must be accepted), we can see the truly wish-fulfilling nature of the market apologist's equivocation between the ideally free market and the actual world. For the claim that reality would have the predicted properties of the perfect market if only this, that or the other aspect of reality were rearranged to conform to it, is a claim that is, on the account of their own leading methodologists, impossible, for it mixes conceptual modes. Axioms inhabit different conceptual worlds from descriptions of reality. It is quite nonsensical to claim that the workings of reality would conform to the implications of a set of axioms defining a free market if only the empirical characteristics which (necessarily, on their own account) lead reality to deviate from those axioms could (*per impossible*) be rearranged or reformulated to fit them.

---

36. M. Friedman, *Essays in Positive Economics* (Chicago, University of Chicago Press, 1953), pp. 14–15.

Bibliography

Adams, G. 'Legislative effects of single-member vs. multi-member districts', *American Journal of Political Science*, 40 (1) (1996).
An Agreement of the People (*The Foundations of Freedom or*) [1648] in J. R. Otteson (ed.) *The Levellers*, vol. 4. Bristol, Thoemmes Press, 2003.
Alford, S. 'A Politics of Emergency in the Reign of Elizabeth I' in G. Burgess and M. Festenstein (eds, *passim*), *English Radicalism 1550–1850*, Cambridge, Cambridge University Press, 2007.
Anderson, B. L. 'Entrepreneurship, Market Process, and the Industrial Revolution in England', in B. L. Anderson and A. J. H. Latham (eds), *The Market in History*, London, Croom Helm, 1986.
Appleby, J. 'Republicanism and ideology', *American Quarterly*, 37(4) (1985).
Archer, I. *Social Relations in Elizabethan London*, Cambridge, Cambridge University Press, 1991.
Arensberg, C. *The Irish Countryman*, London, Macmillan, 1937.
Aristotle, *Rhetoric*, London, Penguin Classics, 2005.
Armitage, D., Himy, A. and Skinner, Q. (eds) *Milton and Republicanism*, Cambridge, Cambridge University Press, 1995.
Ashcraft, R. *Revolutionary Politics and Locke's 'Two Treatises of Government'*, Princeton, Princeton University Press, 1986.
Axelrod, R. *The Evolution of Cooperation*, New York, Basic Books, 1984.
Ayer, A. J. *Language Truth and Logic*, 2nd edn, London, Dover, 1946.
Bailyn, B. *The Ideological Origins of the American Revolution*, Cambridge, Mass., Harvard University Press, 1967.
Baldez, L. and Carey, J. 'Presidential agenda control and spending policy: lessons from General Pinochet's Constitution', *American Journal of Political Science*, 43 (1999).
Ball, T., and Pocock, J. G. A. (eds) *Conceptual Change and the Constitution*, Lawrence, KS., University Press of Kansas, 1988.
Banfield, E. *The Unheavenly City Revisited*, Boston, Mass., Little, Brown, 1974.
Banning, L. 'Some Second Thoughts on Virtue and the Course of Revolutionary Thinking' in T. Ball and J. G. A. Pocock (eds) *Conceptual Change and the Constitution*, Lawrence, KS., University Press of Kansas, 1988.
Barnett, W. and Block, W. 'Coase and van Zandt on Lighthouses', *Public Finance Review*, 35 (6) (2007).
Baron, H. *The Crisis of the Early Italian Renaissance*, Princeton, Princeton University Press, 1955.
Barry, B. *Sociologists, Economists and Democracy*, London, Collier-Macmillan, 1970.

Barry, J. 'Bourgeois collectivism? Urban Association and the Middling Sort' in J. Barry and C. Brooks (eds), *The Middling Sort of People: Culture, society and politics in England, 1550–1800*, Basingstoke, Palgrave, 1994.

Barry J. and Brooks, C. (eds) *The Middling Sort of People: Culture, society and politics in England, 1550–1800*, Basingstoke, Palgrave, 1994.

Bates, R. Figueiredo, R. and Weingast, B. 'The Politics of interpretation: rationality, culture and transition', *Politics and Society*, 26 (1998).

Bates, R., Greif, A., Levi, M., Rosenthal, J. and Weingast, B. (eds), *Analytic Narratives*, Princeton NJ, Princeton University Press, 1999.

Belshaw, C. S., *Traditional Exchange and Modern Markets*, Englewood Cliffs, NJ., Prentice Hall, 1965.

Bendor, J. and Meirowitz, A. 'Spatial models of delegation', *American Political Science Review*, 98 (2004).

Benn S. and Peters, R. S. *Social Principles and the Democratic State*, London, Allen and Unwin, 1959.

Berlin, I. 'Does Political Theory Still Exist?' in P. Laslett and W. G. Runciman (eds) *Philosophy, Politics and Society*, Oxford, Blackwell, 1962.

— *Four Essays on Liberty*, Oxford, Oxford University Press, 1969.

Berman, D. *A History of Atheism in Britain from Hobbes to Russell*, London, Routledge, 1988.

Binder, S. 'The partisan basis of procedural choice: allocating parliamentary rights in the House, 1789–1990', *American Political Science Review*, 90 (1996).

Birnbaum, P. and Leca, J. *Individualism: Theories and Methods*, Oxford, Oxford University Press, 1990.

Black, E. *The Association: British extra parliamentary political organisation*, Cambridge, Mass., Harvard University Press, 1963.

Blau, P. M. *Exchange and Power in Social Life*, New York, Transaction Publishers, 1964.

Bliss C. J. and Stern, N. H. *Palanpur: Economics in an Indian market*, Oxford, Oxford University Press, 1982.

Bock, G., Skinner, Q. and Viroli, M. (eds), *Machiavelli and the Nature of Republicanism*, Cambridge, Cambridge University Press, 1990.

Bohun, E. de *The Justice of the Peace, His Calling: A moral essay*, 1684.

Bruni, L. *Laudatio Florentinae Urbis (In Praise of the City of Florence)* [1403–4], tr. B. G. Kohl, in B. G. Kohl and R. G. Witt (eds), *The Earthly Republic: Italian Humanists on government and society*, Manchester, Manchester University Press, 1978.

Brunner, O., Conze, W. and Koseleck, R. (eds), *Geschichtliche Grundbegriffe*, Stuttgart, Klett-Cotta, 1972–90.

Burgess G. and Festenstein, M. *English Radicalism 1550–1850*, Cambridge, Cambridge University Press, 2007.

Burke, E. *Reflections on the Revolution in France*, C. C. O'Brien (ed.), London, Harmondsworth, 1968.

Burns, J. H. (ed.), *The Cambridge History of Medieval Political Thought*, Cambridge, Cambridge University Press, 1988.

Carling, A. 'Rational choice marxism', *New Left Review*, 125 (1981).
Carpenter, D. 'Adaptive signal processing, hierarchy and budgetary control in federal regulation', *American Political Science Review*, 90 (1996).
Cartledge, P. *Ancient Greek Political Thought in Practice*, Cambridge, Cambridge University Press, 2009.
Cartwright, Major J., *The Commonwealth in Danger*, London, 1795.
Cassirer, E. *The Philosophy of the Enlightenment*, Princeton, Princeton University Press, 1955.
Castiglione, D. 'Historical arguments in political theory', *Political Theory Newsletter*, 5 (1993).
Catlin, G. *The Story of the Political Philosophers*, New York and London, McGraw Hill, 1939.
Chong, D. *Action and the Civil Rights Movement*, Chicago IL., University of Chicago Press, 1991.
— 'Rational Choice Theory's Mysterious Rivals', in J. Freidman (ed.), *The Rational Choice Controversy: Economic models of politics reconsidered*, New Haven CT., Yale University Press, 1995.
Christie, I. R. *Wilkes, Wyvill and Reform: The Parliamentary Reform Movement in British politics, 1760–1785*, London, Macmillan, 1962.
Churchill, Winston, http://www.nationalchurchillmuseum.org
Clark, J. C. D. *English Society 1688–1832*, Oxford, Oxford University Press, 1985.
Clinton, J. and Meirowitz, A. 'Testing explanations of strategic voting in legislatures: a re-examination of the Compromise of 1790', *American Journal of Political Science*, 48 (2004).
Coase, R. 'The lighthouse in economics', *Journal of Law and Economics*, 17 (2) (1974).
Cohen, G. A. 'Beliefs and roles', *Proceedings of the Aristotelian Society*, 41 (1966–7).
Coleman J. (ed.) *The Individual in Political Theory and Practice*, vol. 6 of W. Blockmans and J.-P. Genet (eds) *The Origins of the Modern State in Europe 13th–18th Centuries*, 7 vols., Oxford, Clarendon Press and the European Science Foundation, 1993–4, and in French, Paris, Maison des Sciences de L'Homme, 1996.
Collingwood, R. G. *The Idea of History*, Oxford, Oxford University Press, 1946.
— *Autobiography*, Oxford, Oxford University Press, 1970.
Collini, S. 'Afterword', in D. Castiglione and I. Hampsher-Monk (eds), *The History of Political Thought in National Context*, Cambridge, Cambridge University Press, 2001.
Collinson, P. (ed.) *The Sixteenth Century*, Cambridge, Cambridge University Press, 2002.
Condren, C. *Argument and Authority in Early Modern England: The presuppositions of oaths and offices*, Cambridge, Cambridge University Press, 2006.
— 'Liberty of office and its defence in seventeenth century political argument', *History of Political Thought*, 18 (1997).

Cox, G. and Katz, J. 'Why did the incumbency advantage in US House elections grow?', *American Journal of Political Science*, 40 (1996).
Crick, B. *The American Science of Politics: Its origins and conditions*, Berkeley and LA, University of California Press, 1964.
— *In Defence of Politics*, (rev.ed.), London, Harmondsworth, Penguin Press, 1964.
— *Political Theory and Practice*, Harmondsworth, Penguin Press, 1969.
— *Politics as Freedom, Freedom as Politics*, Inaugural Lecture delivered at the University of Sheffield, 12 January 1966.
— 'Toleration and tolerance in theory and practice', in *Government and Opposition* 6 (1971).
Dahl, R. 'Further reflections on ... The Elitist Theory of Democracy', *American Political Science Review*, LX (1966), pp. 296–305.
— 'Power, Pluralism and Democracy', *Address to the American Political Science Association*, Chicago, 1964.
Dalton, G. (ed.), *Studies in Economic Anthropology*, American Anthropological Association Monograph, 7, Washington, American Anthropological Association, 1977.
Davidson, D. *Essays on Actions and Events*, Oxford, Oxford University Press, 1980.
— 'The Philosophy of Psychology' in D. Davidson, *Essays on Actions and Events*, Oxford, Oxford University Press, 1980.
Davidson, D., with Suppes, P. and Seigel, P. *Decision-Making: An experimental approach*, Stanford, Stanford University Press, 1957.
Davies, W. G. *Social Relations in a Philippine Market, Self-interest and Subjectivity*, Berkeley, University of California Press, 1973.
Davis, O. L., Yeager, E. A. and Foster, S. J. (eds), *History Empathy and Perspective Taking in the Social Studies*, Lanham and Oxford, Rowman and Littlefield, 2001.
Dawkins, R. *The Selfish Gene*, Oxford, Oxford University Press, 1976.
Deleuze, G. *Nietzsche et la philosophie*, trans. H. Tomlinson, London, Athlone, 1983 [Paris, Presses Universitaires de France, 1962].
— *Kant's Critical Philosophy*, trans. H. Tomlinson and B. Habberjam, London, Athlone, 1984.
Dewald, C. and Marincola, J. (eds) *The Cambridge Companion to Herodotus*, Cambridge, Cambridge University Press, 2006.
Dewan T. and Dowding, K. 'The corrective effect of ministerial resignations on government popularity', *American Journal of Political Science*, 49 (2005).
Dowding K. and Hees, M. 'The construction of rights', *American Political Science Review*, 97 (2003).
Downs, A. *An Economic Theory of Democracy*, New York, Harper, 1957.
Dowse R. E. and Hughes, J. A. 'Sporadic interventionists', *Political Studies*, XXV (1) (1977).

Dryzek, J. S. 'How far is it from Virginia and Rochester to Frankfurt? Public choice as critical theory', *British Journal of Political Science*, 22 (1992).
Dunn, J. (ed.) *The Economic Limits to Modern Politics*, Cambridge, Polity Press, 1990.
— 'The identity of the history of ideas', *Philosophy*, XLIII (April 1968), and in, *Philosophy, Politics and Society*, (VI series.)
— *The Political Thought of John Locke: An historical account of the argument of the 'Two Treatises of Government'*, Cambridge, Cambridge University Press, 1982.
Dworkin, R. 'Review of Michael Walzer, *Spheres of Justice*', *New York Review of Books*, 14 April 1983.
The Economist, 'True Progressivism', 13 October 2012.
Elster, J. (ed.), *Rational Choice*, Oxford, Blackwell, 1986.
— *Sour Grapes*, Cambridge, Cambridge University Press, 1983.
Esser, H. 'The rationality of everyday behaviour: the rational choice reconstruction of the theory of action by Alfred Schulz', *Rationality and Society*, 5 (1993).
Ferejohn, J. 'Rationality and Interpretation: Parliamentary elections in early Stuart England', in K. Monroe (ed.), *The Economic Approach to Politics: A critical reassessment of the theory of rational action*, New York: Harper Collins, 1991.
Filmer, Sir R. *Patriarcha and other Political Works*, P. Laslett (ed.) Oxford, Basil Blackwell, 1949.
Fisher, R. 'How to do things with books: Quentin Skinner and the dissemination of ideas', *History of European Ideas*, 35 (2) (2009).
Floyd J. and Stears, M. (eds) *Political Philosophy versus History?*, Cambridge, Cambridge University Press, 2011.
Forbes, D. *Hume's Philosophical Politics*, Cambridge, Cambridge University Press, 1975.
Foster, S. 'Some final thoughts', in O. L. Davis, E. A. Yeager and S. J. Foster (eds), *History Empathy and Perspective Taking in the Social Studies*, Lanham and Oxford, Rowman and Littlefield, 2001.
Foxley, R. 'John Lilburne and the citizenship of "free-born Englishmen"', *The Historical Journal* 47, (2004).
Franklin, J. H. *Jean Bodin and the Sixteenth Century Revolution in the Methodology of Law and History*, New York, Columbia University Press, 1963.
Freeden, M. 'Editorial', *Journal of Political Ideologies* 2 (1) (1997).
Freeman, J. and Hays, J. 'Democracy and markets: the case of exchange rates', *American Journal of Political Science*, 44 (2000).
Freeman, R. 'Black economic progress since 1964', *The Public Interest*, 52 (1978).
Freidman, J. (ed.), *The Rational Choice Controversy: Economic models of politics reconsidered*, New Haven CT., Yale University Press, 1995.
Friedman, M. *Essays in Positive Economics*, Chicago, Chicago University Press, 1953.

Gadamer, H. G. *Truth and Method*, trans. W. Glen-Doepel, London, Sheed & Ward, 1989.

Gallie, W. B. 'Essentially contested concepts', *Proceedings of the Aristotelian Society*, vol. 56 (1956).

Gambetta, D. *The Sicilian Mafia: The business of private protection*, Cambridge Mass., Harvard University Press, 1993.

Garfinkel, I. and Haveman, R. *Earnings Capacity, Poverty, and Inequality*, New York, Institute for Research on Poverty, 1977.

Gauthier, D. *Morals by Agreement*, Oxford, Oxford University Press, 1986.

Geertz, C. (ed.) *The Interpretation of Cultures: Selected essays*, New York, Basic Books, 1973.

— 'Thick Description: Towards an interpretive theory of culture', in C. Geertz, *Interpretation of Culture: Selected essays*, New York, Basic Books, 1973.

— 'Suq: The Bazaar Economy in Sefrou', in C. Geertz, H. Geertz and L. Rosen, *Meaning and Order Order in Moroccan Society*, Cambridge, Cambridge University Press, 1979.

Geertz, C., Geertz, H. and Rosen, L. (eds), *Meaning and Order in Moroccan Society*, Cambridge, Cambridge University Press, 1979.

Gerald, J. *A Convention the Only Means of Saving Us from Ruin*, London, 1793.

Gewirth, A. (ed.) 'Introduction', *Marsilius of Padua – the Defender of the Peace*, 2 vols, London and New York, Columbia University Press, 1961.

Gilder, G. *Wealth and Poverty*, New York, Basic Books, 1981.

Glover, J. (ed.), *Philosophy of Mind*, Oxford, Oxford University Press, 1976.

Glover, S. 'The Putney Debates: popular vs elitist republicanism, *Past and Present*, 164, (1999).

Godwin, W. *Enquiry Concerning Political Justice*, F. E. L. Priestley (ed.), Toronto, Toronto University Press, 1946.

Goldie, M. 'Locke, Proast and Religious Toleration' in J. Walsh, C. Haydon and S. Taylor (eds), *The Church of England, c.1689–c.1833*, Cambridge, Cambridge University Press, 1993.

— 'The Theory of Religious Intolerance in Restoration England' in O. P. Grell, J. Israel and N. Tyacke (eds) *From Persecution to Toleration: The Glorious Revolution and religion in England*, Oxford: Clarendon Press, 1991.

— 'The Unacknowledged Republic: Office-holding in early modern England' in T. Harris (ed.), *Politics of the Excluded*, Basingstoke, Palgrave, 2001.

Goodin, R. E. *Motivating Political Morality*, Oxford, Blackwell, 1992.

Goodin, R. E. and Reeve, A. (eds) *Liberal Neutrality*, London, Routledge, 1989.

Goodwin, A. *The Friends of Liberty: The English Democratic Movement in the age of the French Revolution*, London, Hutchinson, 1976.

Gough, J. W. *John Locke's Political Philosophy*, Oxford, Clarendon, 1950.

Gray, J. 'On liberty, liberalism and essential contestability', *British Journal of Political Science*, 8 (4) (1978).
Green, D. and Shapiro, I. *Pathologies of Rational Choice Theory*, New Haven CT, Yale University Press, 1994.
Grell, O. P., Israel, J. and Tyacke, N. (eds) *From Persecution to Toleration: The Glorious Revolution and religion in England*, Oxford, Clarendon Press, 1991.
Gurian, P. 'Resource allocation strategies in presidential nomination campaigns', *American Journal of Political Science*, 41(30) (1986).
Guy, J. 'Monarchy and Counsel' in P. Collinson (ed.), *The Sixteenth Century*, Cambridge, Cambridge University Press, 2002.
Hacker, A. *Political Theory: Philosophy ideology, science*, New York, Macmillan, 1961.
Hahn, F. 'On some economic limits in politics', in J. Dunn, (ed.) *Economic Limits to Modern Politics*, Cambridge, Polity Press, 1990.
Hahn, F. and Hollis, M. (eds), *Philosophy and Economic Theory*, Oxford, Oxford University Press, 1979.
Hampsher-Monk, I. W. 'Classical and empirical theories of democracy: the missing historical dimension?', *British Journal of Political Science*, X (1) (1980).
— 'The Conceptual Formation of 'Democracy', in M. Lenci and C. Calabro (eds) *Viaggio nella democrazia: il cammino dell'idea democratica nella storia del pensiero politico*, Edizioni ETS, Pisa, 2010.
— *Defending Politics: Essays on politics and pluralism in honour of Bernard Crick*, British Academic Press, London, 1993.
— 'The Historical Study of Democracy', in G. Duncan (ed.), *Democratic Theory*, Cambridge, Cambridge University Press, 1984.
— *A History of Modern Political Thought*, Oxford, Blackwell, 1994.
— 'The Individualist Premise and the Practice of Politics' in I. Hampsher-Monk (ed.) *Defending Politics...*, British Academic Press, London, 1993 and in P. King (ed.), *Socialism and the Common Good*, London, Frank Cass, 1996.
— 'Is there an English form of toleration?', *New Community: European Journal on Migration and Ethnic Relations*, 21 (2)(April, 1995).
— 'The market for toleration: a case study in an aspect of the ambiguity of "positive economics"', *The British Journal of Political Science* 10 (1) (1991).
— 'Political languages in time: the work of J. G. A. Pocock', *British Journal of Political Science*, XIV (1) (1984).
— 'Political Liberty and the Concept of Citizenship in Early Modern English Political Discourse', in Q. Skinner and M. van Gelderen (eds) *Freedom and the Construction of Europe*, Vol. 2, Cambridge, CUP, 2013, chap. 6.
— 'Politics, Political Theory and its History' in J. Floyd and M. Stears (eds) *Political Philosophy Versus History?*, Cambridge, Cambridge University Press, 2011.

— 'Prices as Description: Reasons as explanations' in J. Melling and J. Barry (eds) *Culture in History: Production, consumption and values in historical perspective*, Exeter, University of Exeter Press, 1992.
— 'Putney, property and Professor Macpherson', *Political Studies*, 24 (1976).
— 'Rousseau and Totalitarianism - with hindsight?' in R. Wokler (ed.), *Rousseau and Liberty*, Manchester, Manchester University Press, 1995.
— 'Salman Rushdie, the Ayatollah and the limits of toleration', in A. Ehteshami (ed.), *The Islamic Revolution and the West*, London, Routledge, 1991.
— 'Speech Acts, Languages or Conceptual History?' in I. Hampsher-Monk, K. Tilmans and F. van Vree (eds), *History of Concepts, Comparative Perspectives*, Amsterdam, Amsterdam and Michigan University Presses, 1998.
— 'The State and the Individual, Seventeenth–Eighteenth Centuries: Theorising the challenge of subjective individualism in Britain', in J. Coleman (ed.), *The Individual in Political Theory and Practice* vol. 6 of W. Blockmans and J.-P. Genet (eds) *The Origins of the Modern State in Europe 13th–18th Centuries*, 7 vols., Oxford, Clarendon Press and the European Science Foundation, 1993–4, and in French, Paris, Maison des Sciences de L'Homme, 1996.
— 'Toleration, the Moral Will and the Justification of Liberalism' in S. Mendus and J. Horton (eds), *Toleration, Identity and Difference*, London, Routledge, 1998.

Hampsher-Monk, I. W. and Castiglione, D. (eds) *The History of Political Thought in National Context*, Cambridge, Cambridge University Press, 2001.

Hampsher-Monk, I. W. and Hindmoor, A. 'Rational choice and interpretive evidence: caught between a rock and a hard place', *Political Studies*, 58 (1) (2010).

Hampsher-Monk, I. W. with Phillips, T. and Abramson, P. 'The excavation and reconstruction of the recumbent stone circle at Strichen, Aberdeenshire, 1979–82', *Proceedings of the Society of Antiquaries of Scotland*, 136 (2006).

Hampsher-Monk, I. W. and Tilmans, K. and van Vree, F. (eds) *History of Concepts: Comparative Perspectives*, Amsterdam, Amsterdam and Michigan University Presses, 1998.

Hardin, R. *Collective Action*, Baltimore, Johns Hopkins University Press, 1982.

Harding, A. 'Political liberty in the Middle Ages', *Speculum*, 55 (1980).

Harrington, J. *The Political Works of James Harrington*, in J.G.A. Pocock (ed.) Cambridge, Cambridge University Press, 1977.

Harris, T. (ed.) *The Politics of the Excluded*, Basingstoke, Palgrave, 2001.

Harrison R. (ed.) *Rational Action*, Cambridge, Cambridge University Press, 1979.

Hausman, D. *Essays on Philosophy and Economic Methodology*, Cambridge, Cambridge University Press, 1992.

— 'Rational choice and social theory: a comment', *The Journal of Philosophy*, 92 (1995).
— 'Why Look under the Hood?', in D. Hausman, *Essays on Philosophy and Economic Methodology*, Cambridge, Cambridge University Press, 1992.
Hayek, F. A. *The Constitution of Liberty*, London, Routledge and Kegan Paul, 1960.
— *Human Action: A treatise on economics*, London, William Hodge, 1949.
— 'The Moral Element in Free Enterprise', in F. A. Hayek, *Studies in Philosophy, Politics and Economics*, London, Routledge and Kegan Paul, 1967.
— *Studies in Philosophy, Politics and Economics*, London, Routledge and Kegan Paul, 1967.
— 'The uses of "Gresham's Law" as an illustration of historical theory', in *History and Theory*, 1 (1960); and in *Studies in Philosophy, Politics and Economics*, London, Routledge and Kegan Paul, 1967.
Hazlitt, W. *The Spirit of the Age*, London, Dent, 1969.
Heath, A. *Rational Choice and Social Exchange*, Cambridge, Cambridge University Press, 1976.
Hegel, G.W.F. *The Philosophy of Right*, tr. T. M. Knox, Oxford, Oxford University Press, 1952.
Herodotus, *The Histories*, London, Penguin Classics, 1996.
Hindmoor, A. *Rational Choice*, Basingstoke, Palgrave Macmillan, 2006.
Hobbes, T. *Leviathan*, R. Tuck (ed.), Cambridge, Cambridge University Press, 1991.
Hollis, M. *The Cunning of Reason*, Cambridge, Cambridge University Press, 1987.
Hollis, M. and Nell, E. *Rational Economic Man*, Cambridge, Cambridge University Press, 1975.
Homans, G. *Social Behaviour: Its elementary forms*, New York, Harcourt, Brace and Janovich, 1961.
Hooker, R. *Of The Lawes of Ecclesiastical Polity*, London, Everyman, 1907 [1593–97].
Hope Mason, J. 'Creativity in Action: The background to Machiavelli's "lion" and "fox"', in I. Hampsher-Monk (ed.) *Defending Politics: Essays on politics and pluralism in honour of Bernard Crick*, British Academic Press, London, 1993.
Hopkins, A. G. 'The Victorians and Africa: a reconsideration of the occupation of Egypt, 1882', *Journal of African History*, 27 (1986).
Horton J. and Mendus, S. (eds) *Aspects of Toleration*, London, Methuen, 1985.
Huber, J. 'The vote of confidence in parliamentary democracies', *American Political Science Review*, 90 (1996).
Hume, D. *Essays, Moral, Political and Literary*, Oxford, Oxford University Press, 1963.
Hunter, M. and Wootton, D. *Atheism from the Reformation to the Enlightenment*, Oxford, Clarendon Press, 1992.

Hurd, R., Bishop of Lichfield, *Dialogues on the Uses of Foreign Travel; Considered as a part of an English gentleman's education: between Lord Shaftesbury and Mr. Locke*, Dublin, 1764 [London, 1754].

Innes, J. and Philp, M. (eds), *Re-Imagining Democracy in the Age of Revolutions: America, France, Britain, Ireland, 1750–1850*, Oxford, Oxford University Press, 2013.

Jackson, B. 'At the origins of neo-liberalism: 1930–1947', *Historical Journal*, 53 (1) (2010).

Johnson, A. 'Security and Risk-taking among Poor Peasants', in G. Dalton (ed.), *Studies in Economic Anthropology*, American Anthropological Association Monograph, 7, Washington, American Anthropological Association, 1977.

Jordan, B. *The Common Good: Citizenship, morality and self-interest*, Oxford, Blackwell, 1989.

Jyllands-Posten, 30 September, 2005.

Katz, D. S. 'The Jews of England and 1688', in O. P. Grell, J. Israel and N. Tyacke (eds) *From Persecution to Toleration: The Glorious Revolution and religion in England*, Oxford, Clarendon Press, 1991.

Katz, J. and Sala, B. 'Careerism, committee assignments and the electoral connection', *American Political Science Review*, 90 (1996).

Kavanagh, D. *Thatcherism and British Politics*, Oxford, Oxford University Press, 1987.

Kelley, D. R. *Foundations of Modern Historical Scholarship, Language, Law and History in the French Renaissance*, New York, Columbia University Press, 1970.

Knowles, D. (ed.) *Explanation and its Limits: Royal Institute of Philosophy Lectures: 27*, Cambridge, Cambridge University Press, 1990.

Kohl, B. G. and Witt, R. G. (eds), *The Earthly Republic: Italian humanists on government and society*, Manchester, Manchester University Press, 1978.

Kontos, A. (ed.), *Powers Possessions and Freedom: Essays in honour of C. B. Macpherson*, Toronto, Toronto University Press, 1979.

Koselleck, R. *Futures Past: On the semantics of historical time*, trans. K. Tribe, Cambridge, Mass. MIT Press, 1985.

— 'Terror and Dream: Methodological remarks on the experience of time during the Third Reich', in *Futures Past: On the semantics of historical time*, trans. K. Tribe, Cambridge, Mass. MIT Press, 1985.

Lake, P. *Anglicans and Puritans*, London: Unwin Hyman, 1988.

Laslett, P. (ed.) *Philosophy, Politics and Society*, Oxford, Blackwell, 1957.

Laslett, P. and Runciman, W. G. (eds), *Philosophy, Politics and Society*, 2nd series, Oxford, Blackwell, 1962.

Laslett, P., Runciman, W. G. and Skinner, Q. (eds), *Philosophy, Politics and Society*, 4th series, Oxford, Blackwell, 1972.

Laver, M. *The Politics of Private Desires*, Harmondsworth and New York, Penguin Books and Penguin Viking, 1981.

Leca, J. 'Individualism and Citizenship' in P. Birnbaum and J. Leca (eds), *Individualism: Theories and Methods*, Oxford, Oxford University Press, 1990.

Lehmann, H. and Richter, M. (eds) *The Meaning of Historical Terms and Concepts: New studies on Begriffsgeschichte*, Washington, DC: German Historical Institute, 1996.

The Levellers: Overton, Walwyn and Lilburne, J. R Otteson (ed.) 5 vols, Bristol, Thoemmes Press, 2003.

The Leveller [1659] in *The Levellers*, vol. 5, J. R Otteson (ed.) Bristol, Thoemmes Press, 2003.

Levy Peck, L. *The Mental World of the Jacobean Court*, Cambridge, Cambridge University Press 1991.

Lilburne, J. *Lilburne's Ghost* [1659].

Lipton, M. 'The theory of the optimising peasant', *Journal of Development Studies*, 4 (1968).

List, C. 'A model of path-dependence in decisions over multiple propositions', *American Political Science Review*, 98 (2004).

Locke, J. *Selected Correspondence*, M. Goldie (ed.), Oxford, Oxford University Press, 2002.

— *A Letter Concerning Toleration* [1689], J. Horton and S. Mendus (eds), London, Routledge, 1991.

— *Two Tracts on Government*, P. Abrams (ed.), Cambridge, Cambridge University Press, 1967[1660].

Lodge, D. *Nice Work*, London, Secker and Warburg, 1988.

London Corresponding Society, *London Corresponding Society, 1792–1799*, M. T. Davis (ed.), 5 vols, London, Pickering, 2002.

— *Selections from the Papers of the London Corresponding Society 1792–1799*, M. Thale (ed.), Cambridge, Cambridge University Press, 1983.

Lovett, F. 'Rational choice theory and explanation', *Rationality and Society*, 18 (2006).

Macaulay, C. *An Address to the People of England, Scotland and Ireland*, Bath, 1775.

McDairmid, J. F. *The Monarchichal Republic of Early Modern England: Essays in response to Patrick Collinson*, Aldershot, Ashgate, 2007.

MacDonald, P. 'Useful fiction or miracle maker: the competing epistemological foundations of rational choice theory', *American Political Science Review*, 97 (2003).

MacIntyre, A. 'A Mistake about Causality in Social Science', in P. Laslett and W. G. Runciman (eds), *Philosophy, Politics and Society*, 2nd series, Oxford, Blackwell, 1962.

— *Whose Justice? Which Rationality?*, Oxford, Duckworth, 1988.

McLean, I. *Public Choice: An introduction*, Oxford, Wiley-Blackwell, 1987.

— *Rational Choice and British Politics: An analysis of rhetoric and manipulation from Peel to Blair*, Oxford, Oxford University Press, 2001.

Machiavelli, N. *The Prince*, London, Penguin Books, 1999.
Madison, J., Hamilton, A. and Jay, J. *The Federalist Papers*, Indianapolis, Liberty Fund, 2001.
Maitland, F. W. *Township and Borough*, Cambridge, Cambridge University Press, 1898.
Maltzman, F. and Wahlbeck, P. 'Strategic policy considerations and voting fluidity on the Burger Court', *American Political Science Review*, 90 (1996).
Mandeville, B. *The Fable of the Bees*, F. B. Kaye (ed.), Oxford, Oxford University Press, 1949; repr. Indianapolis, Liberty Fund, 1988.
Markus, R. *Saeculum, History and Society in the Theology of St Augustine*, 2nd edn, Cambridge, Cambridge University Press, 1989.
Martin L. and Vanberg, G. 'Coalition policymaking and legislative review', *American Political Science Review*, 99 (2005).
Mason, R. A. (ed.) *Scots and Britons: Scottish political thought and the Union of 1603*, Cambridge, Cambridge University Press, 1995.
Mendus, S. (ed.), *Justifying Toleration: Conceptual and historical perspectives*, Cambridge, Cambridge University Press, 1988.
Mendus, S. and Horton, J. (eds) *Toleration Identity and Difference*, London, Routledge, 1998.
Merkl, P. H. *Political Continuity and Change*, New York, Harper and Rowe, 1967.
de Mesquita, E. B. 'The quality of terror', *American Journal of Political Science*, 49 (2005).
Mill, J. *Essay on Government*, Indianapolis, Ind., Bobbs-Merrill, 1955.
Mill, J. S. *A System of Logic*, Location, Press, 1967.
Miller, D. 'Market neutrality and the failure of cooperatives', *British Journal of Political Science*, 11 (1981).
— *Market, State and Community: The theoretical foundations of market socialism*, Oxford, Oxford University Press, 1989.
Mintz, S. 'Pratik: Haitian personal economic relationships', *Proceedings of the American Ethnographic Association*, Seattle, Washington University Press, 1961.
Mintz, S. and Woolf, E. 'An analysis of ritual co-parenthood (Compadrazgo)', *South West Journal of Anthropology*, 6 (1950).
Mises, L. von, *Epistemological Problems of Economics*, Princeton, NJ., Von Nostrand, 1960.
— *Human Action: A treatise on economics*, New Haven, Yale University Press, 1949.
— *The Ultimate Foundation of Economic Science*, Princeton, N. J., von Nostrand, 1962.
Monroe, K. (ed.), *The Economic Approach to Politics: A critical reassessment of the theory of rational action*, New York: Harper Collins, 1991.
Montesquieu, C. L. de S., Baron, A. M., Cohler, B. S., Miller and H. S. Stone, (trans. and ed.), *The Spirit of the Laws*, Cambridge, Cambridge University Press, 1989.
Morgenthau, H. J. *Dilemmas of Politics*, Chicago, Chicago University Press, 1958.

Morill, J. S. (ed.), *Revolution and Restoration in England in the 1650s*, London, Collins and Brown, 1992.
Morris, C. *Political Thought in England from Tyndale to Hooker*, Oxford, Oxford University Press, 1953.
Mosher, M. 'The Deconstruction of Moral Personality in Rawls, Nozick, Sandel and Parfit', *Political Studies* 39 (2) (1991).
Mouffe, C. *The Democratic Paradox*, London, Verso, 2000.
Mueller, D. 'The future of public choice', *Public Choice* 77 (1993).
— *Public Choice II*, Cambridge, Cambridge University Press, 1989.
Muller, E. and Opp, K. 'Rational choice and rebellious collective action', *American Political Science Review*, 80 (1986).
Muller, E. and Opp, K. with Dietz, H. and Finkel, S. 'Discontent and the expected utility of rebellion: the case of Peru', *American Political Science Review*, 85 (1991).
Nef, Robert, 'Socialism, Envy and Redistribution', (consulted online at http://www.libinst.ch/?i=socialism-envy-and-redistribution--en
Norbrook, D. *Writing the English Republic: Poetry, rhetoric and politics 1627–1660*, Cambridge, Cambridge University Press, 1988.
North, D. and Thomas, R. *The Rise of the Western World: A new economic history*, Cambridge, Cambridge University Press, 1973.
— *Structure and Change in Economic History*, New York, Norton, 1981.
Nozick, R. *Anarchy, State and Utopia*, New York, Basic Books, 1974.
Oakeshott, M. *Experience and its Modes*, Cambridge, Cambridge University Press, 1933.
— *Selected Writings*, L. O'Sullivan (ed.), Exeter, Imprint Academic, 2004.
— 'The vocabulary of a modern European state', *Political Studies*, 23 (2–3) (1975).
O'Donnell, A. T. 'The Neutrality of the Market', in R. E. Goodin and A. Reeve (eds) *Liberal Neutrality*, London, Routledge, 1989.
Oldfield, T. B. *An Entire and Complete History ... of the Boroughs of Great Britain*, vol. 1, London, 1792.
Olsen, M. *The Logic of Collective Action*, Cambridge, Mass., Harvard University Press, 1965.
Onuf, P. S. 'Reflections on the founding: constitutional historiography in bicentennial perspective', *Wm. & Mary Quarterly*, XLVI, 2 (1989).
Oppenheim, P. 'Introduction' in N. Rescher (ed.), *Essays in Honour of Carl G. Hempel*, Dordrecht, Reidel, 1969.
Otteson J. R. (ed.) *The Levellers* 5 vols., Bristol, Thoemmes Press, 2003.
Ouchi, G. 'Markets, bureaucracies and clans', *Administrative Science Quarterly*, 25 (1980), and in G. Thompson *et al.* (eds), *Markets, Hierarchies and Networks*, London, Sage, 1991.
Pagden, A. *The Languages of Political Theory in Early Modern Europe*, Cambridge, Cambridge University Press, 1987.
Paine, T. *Complete Writings of Thomas Paine*, P. S. Foner (ed.), 2 vols., New York, Citadel Press, 1969.

— *Rights of Man*, Harmondsworth, Penguin Press, 1984.
— *First Principles of Government* [1795], in P. S. Foner (ed.), *Complete Writings of Thomas Paine*, vol. 2, New York, Citadel Press, 1969.
Palonen, K. 'The history of concepts as a style of political theorizing: Quentin Skinner's and Reinhart Koselleck's subversion of normative political theory', *European Journal of Political Theory*, 1 (2002).
Parfitt, D. *Reasons and Persons*, Oxford, Oxford University Press, 1986.
Parssinen, T. M. 'Association, convention and anti-parliament in British Radical Politics 1771–1848', *English Historical Review*, 88 (1973).
Peltonen, M. *Classical Humanism and Republicanism in English Political Thought 1570–1640*, Cambridge, Cambridge University Press, 1995.
Pennington, K. 'Law, legislative authority and theories of government, 1150–1300', in J. H. Burns (ed.), *The Cambridge History of Medieval Political Thought*, Cambridge, Cambridge University Press, 1988.
Picketty, T. *Capital in the Twenty-First Century*, Camb., Mass., Harvard, Belknap Press, 2014.
Pizzorno, A. 'On Rationality and Democratic Choice' in P. Birnbaum and J. Leca (eds) *Individualism: Theories and Methods*, Oxford, Oxford University Press, 1990.
Plamenatz, J. *Man and Society*, 2 vols., London, Longman, 1963.
Plattner, S. 'Economic custom in a competitive marketplace', *American Anthropologist*, 85 (1983).
Pocock, J. G. A. *The Ancient Constitution and the Feudal Law: A study of English historical thought in the Seventeenth Century*, Cambridge, Cambridge University Press, 1987.
— 'Burke's analysis of the political economy of the French Revolution', *Historical Journal* 25(2) 1982 and in J. G. A. Pocock, *Virtue, Commerce and History*, Cambridge, Cambridge University Press, 1985.
— 'The Concept of a Language and the *Metier d'Historien*: Some considerations on practice', in A. Pagden (ed.), *The Languages of Political Theory in Early Modern Europe*, Cambridge, Mass., Cambridge University Press, 1990.
— 'Concepts and discourses: a difference in culture? Comment on a paper by Melvin Richter', in H. Lehmann and M. Richter (eds) *The Meaning of Historical Terms and Concepts: New studies on Begriffsgeschichte*, Washington, DC: German Historical Institute, 1996.
— *The Discovery of Islands*, Cambridge, Cambridge University Press, 2005.
— 'The history of British political thought: the creation of a centre', *Journal of British Studies*, 24 (3) (1985).
— 'The History of Political Thought: A methodological enquiry' in P. Laslett and W. G. Runciman (eds), *Philosophy, Politics and Society*, 2nd series, Oxford, Blackwell, 1962.
— *The Machiavellian Moment: Florentine political thought and the Atlantic Republican tradition*, Princeton, N. J., Princeton University Press, 2003.

— 'Quentin Skinner: the history of politics and the politics of history', *Common Knowledge*, 10, 3 (August 2004), pp. 532–550.
— 'The State of the Art', in J. G. A. Pocock, *Virtue, Commerce and History*, Cambridge, Cambridge University Press, 1985.
— 'Time, history, and eschatology in the thought of Thomas Hobbes', in J. G. A. Pocock, *Politics, Language and Time*, London, Methuen, 1972.
— *Virtue, Commerce and History*, Cambridge, Cambridge University Press, 1985.
— 'Virtue, Rights and Manners: A model for the political theorist', in J. G. A. Pocock, *Virtue, Commerce and History*, Cambridge, Cambridge University Press, 1985.
Pocock, J. G. A. with Schochet, G. J. and Schwoerer, L. G. (eds) *The Varieties of British Political Thought, 1500–1800*, Cambridge, Cambridge University Press, 1996.
Pogge, T. *Realising Rawls*, Ithaca and London, Cornell University Press, 1989.
Popper, K. *The Spell of Plato*, Vol. 1, K. Popper, *The Open Society and its Enemies*, 2 vols., London, Routledge and Kegan Paul, 1945.
Potoski, M. and Prakash, A. 'Green Clubs and voluntary governance: ISO 14001 and Firms' Regulatory Compliance', *American Journal of Political Science*, 49 (2005).
Quine, W. V. 'On empirically equivalent systems of the world', *Erkenntnis*, 9 (3) (1975).
Rabin, J. 'Review of P. Blond, *Red Tory: How Left and Right Have Broken Britain and How We Can Fix it*', *London Review of Books*, 22 April, 2010.
Radcliffe Richards, J. 'Equality of opportunity', *Ratio* (new series), X (3), (1997).
Rawls, J. *Justice as Fairness: A restatement*, Cambridge, Mass., Belknap Press, 2001.
— 'Justice as fairness: political not metaphysical', *Philosophy and Public Affairs* 14, (summer 1985).
— *Political Liberalism*, New York, Columbia University Press, 1993.
— 'Some reasons for the maximin criterion', *American Economic Review* 64 (May 1974).
— *A Theory of Justice*, Oxford, Oxford University Press, 1971.
Raz, J. *The Morality of Freedom*, Oxford, Oxford University Press, 1986.
— 'Right-based morality' in J. Waldron (ed.), *Theories of Rights*, Oxford, Oxford University Press, 1984.
Reichardt, R. and Lüsebrink, H. J. (eds), *Handbuch politischsozialer Grundbegriffe in Frankreich 1680–1820*, Munich, Oldenburg, 1985.
Richter, M. *The History of Social and Political Concepts: A critical introduction*, Oxford, Oxford University Press, 1995.
— 'Pocock, Skinner and the *Geschichtliche Grundbegriffe*', *History and Theory*, 19 (1990), and in *History of Social and Political Concepts*, Oxford, Oxford University Press, 1995.
Ricoeur, P. *The Rule of Metaphor: The creation of meaning in language*, London, Routledge, 2003.

Riker, W. *The Art of Political Manipulation*, New Haven CT., Yale University Press, 1986.
Robertson J. C. (ed.) *A Union for Empire: The Union of 1707 in the context of British political thought*, Cambridge, Cambridge University Press, 1996.
Robinson R. and Gallagher, G. *Africa and the Victorians: The official mind of imperialism*, 2nd edn, London, Macmillan, 1981.
Roemer, J. *Free To Lose*, Cambridge, Mass., Harvard University Press, 1988.
Rottenberg, L. 'Organizational maintenance and the retention decision in groups', *American Political Science Review*, 82 (1988).
Rousseau, J.-J. *Social Contract and the Discourses*, London, Everyman, 1992.
— *Emile*, London, Everyman, 1911.
Russell, B. *A History of Western Philosophy*, London and New York, Allen and Unwin, 1946.
Ryan, A. 'Two Concepts of Politics and Democracy' in M. Fleisher (ed.), *Machiavelli and the Nature of Politics*, New York, Atheneum, 1972.
Sabine, G. H. *A History of Political Theory*, London and New York, Holt Rinehart and Winston, 1951 [1937].
Sahlins, M. *Stone Age Economics*, London, Tavistock Press, 1974.
Samuelson, P. 'Comment on E. Nagel's "Assumptions in Economic Theory"', in *The Collected Scientific Papers of Paul A. Samuelson*, 3 vols, Cambridge, Mass., MIT Press, 1966.
Satz, D. and Ferejohn, J. 'Rational choice and social theory', *Journal of Philosophy*, 91 (1994).
Schelling, T. *Micromotives and Macrobehaviour*, New York, Norton, 1978.
Schiemann, J. 'Meeting halfway between Rochester and Frankfurt: generative salience, focal points, and strategic interaction', *American Journal of Political Science*, 44 (2000), pp. 1–16.
Schmitt, C. *Political Theology*, Chicago, Chicago University Press, 2005.
Schochet, G. (ed.), *Proceedings of the Center for the Study of the History of British Political Thought*, 5 vols., Washington D.C., Folger Institute, 1990–1993.
— 'Quentin Skinner's method', *Political Theory*, 2 (1974).
— 'Why should history matter', in J. G. A. Pocock, G. J. Schochet and L. G. Schwoerer (eds), *The Varieties of British Political Thought, 1500–1800*, Cambridge, Cambridge University Press, 1996.
Scott, J. 'The English Republican Imagination' in J. S. Morill (ed.), *Revolution and Restoration in England in the 1650s*, London, Collins and Brown, 1992.
— *Commonwealth Principles*, Cambridge, Cambridge University Press, 2004.
Sen, A. 'Rational fools', *Philosophy and Public Affairs*, 6 (4) (1977); and in F. Hahn and M. Hollis (eds.), *Philosophy and Economic Theory*, Oxford, Oxford University Press, 1979.
Shagan, E. 'Two Republics: Conflicting views of participatory local government in early Tudor England', in J. F. McDiarmid (ed.), *The Monarchichal Republic of Early Modern England: Essays in response to Patrick Collinson*, Aldershot, Ashgate, 2007.

Shapiro, I. *The Flight from Reality in the Human Sciences*, Princeton NJ, Princeton University Press, 2005.
— 'Realism in the study of the history of ideas', *History of Political Thought*, 3 (1982).
Sharpe, A. (ed.) *The English Levellers*, Cambridge, Cambridge University Press, 1998.
Shepsle, K. 'Statistical political philosophy and positive political theory', *Critical Review*, 9 (1995).
Skinner, Q. 'Empirical theorists of democracy and their critics: a plague on both their houses', *Political Theory*, 1 (3) (1973).
— *Freedom and the Construction of Europe*, (ed. with M. van Gelderen), 2 vols., Cambridge, Cambridge University Press, 2013.
— *Foundations of Modern Political Thought*, 2 vols., Cambridge, Cambridge University Press, 1978.
— 'Meaning and understanding in the history of ideas', *History and Theory*, 8 (1969) and in J. Tully (ed.), *Meaning and Context: Quentin Skinner and his critics*, Polity, Cambridge, 1988.
— 'The Principles and Practice of Opposition: The case of Bolingbroke versus Walpole', in N. McKendrick (ed.), *Historical Perspectives on English Thought and Society: Essays in honour of J. H. Plumb*, London, Europa Press, 1974.
— 'A Reply to my Critics', in J. Tully (ed.), *Meaning and Context...*
— 'The Republican Idea of Political Liberty' in G. Bock, Q. Skinner and M. Viroli (eds), *Machiavelli and the Nature of Republicanism*, Cambridge, Cambridge University Press, 1990.
— *Republicanism: A shared European heritage*, (ed. with M. van Gelderen), 2 vols., Cambridge, Cambridge University Press, 2002.
— *On Method*, Vol. 1, *Visions of Politics*, Cambridge, Cambridge University Press, 2002.
Skorupski, J. 'Explanation and Understanding in Social Science', in D. Knowles (ed.), *Explanation and its Limits: Royal Institute of Philosophy Lectures: 27*, Cambridge, Cambridge University Press, 1990.
Smith, A. *The Wealth of Nations* [1776], R. H. Campbell and A. S. Skinner (eds.), 2 vols., Oxford, Oxford University Press, 1976.
Smith, Sir T. *De Republica Anglorum* [1583] M. Dewar (ed.), Cambridge, Cambridge University Press, 1982, [repr. 2009].
Snyder, J., 'Committee power, structure-induced equilibria and roll call votes', *American Journal of Political Science*, 36 (1992).
Sowell, T. *Markets and Minorities*, Oxford, Blackwell, 1980.
— *Race and Economics*, New York, McKay and Co., 1975.
Stiglitz, J. *The Price of Inequality*, London, Harmondsworth Press, 2012.
Stoppard, T. *Jumpers*, London, Faber, 1974.
Strauss, L. *History of Political Philosophy*, Chicago, Chicago University Press, 1963.
— *The Political Philosophy of Hobbes: Its basis and genesis*, Chicago, University of Chicago Press, 1936.

Strawson, P. F. *Individuals: An essay in descriptive metaphysics*, London, Methuen, 1959.
Swaan, A. de *In Care of the State*, Cambridge, Polity Press, 1988.
Sweet, R. 'Freemen and independence in English Borough Politics c. 1770–1830', *Past and Present*, 161 (1998).
Talmon, J. L. *The Origins of Totalitarian Democracy*, London and New York, Praeger, 1952.
Taylor, C. 'Atomism' in A. Kontos (ed.), *Powers Possessions and Freedom: Essays in honour of C. B. Macpherson*, Toronto, Toronto University Press, 1979.
— *The Explanation of Behaviour*, London, Routledge, 1964.
Taylor, M. *Anarchy and Cooperation*, New York and London, John Wiley and Sons, 1976.
— *The Possibility of Cooperation*, Cambridge, Cambridge University Press, 1987.
Thaler, R. H. and Sunstein, C. R. *Nudge: Improving decisions about health, wealth, and happiness*, New Haven, Yale University Press, 2008.
Thatcher, M. Candidacy Speech 1950, http://www.margaretthatcher.org/document/102777
Thelwall, J. *The Natural and Constitutional Rights of Britons*, London, 1795.
— 'On the Moral and Political Influence of the Prospective Principle of Virtue', *The Tribune* (1795), repr. in G. Claeys (ed.)
The Politics of English Jacobinism: Writings of John Thelwall, Pennsylvania, University of Pennsylvania Press, 1995.
Thies, M. 'Keeping tabs on partners: the logic of delegation in coalition governments', *American Journal of Political Science*, 45 (2001).
Thompson, E. P. *The Making of the English Working Class*, London, Gollancz, 1963; rev. ed., Harmondsworth, Penguin Press, 1968 and 1980.
Thompson G. et al.(eds), *Markets, Hierarchies and Networks*, London, Sage, 1991.
Toqueville, A. de *The Ancient Regime and the French Revolution*, trans. F. Gilbert, intr. H. Brogan, London, Fontana, 1966.
Trager, L. 'Customer and creditors: variations in economic personalism in Nigeria', *Ethnology*, 20 (1981).
Tucker, J. *A Treatise Concerning Civil Government*, London, [London, 1781], reprinted, New York, A. M. Kelley, Reprints of Economic Classics, 1967.
Tully J. (ed.), *Meaning and Context: Quentin Skinner and his critics*, Polity, Cambridge, 1988.
Tversky, A. 'A critique of expected utility theory: descriptive and normative considerations', *Erkenntnis* 9 (1975).
Veitch, G. S. *The Genesis of Parliamentary Reform*, London, Constable, 1913.
Voltaire, F.-M. A. *Lettres philosophiques sur les Anglais* (1734).
Waldron, J. *Liberal Rights*, Cambridge, Cambridge University Press, 1993.
— *Theories of Rights*, Oxford, Oxford University Press, 1984.
— 'Locke: Toleration and the Rationality of Persecution' in S. Mendus (ed.), *Justifying Toleration...*, Cambridge, Cambridge University Press, 1988.

— 'Rushdie and Religion', in J. Waldron, *Liberal Rights*, Cambridge, Cambridge University Press, 1993.
Walker, J. L. 'A critique of the elitist theory of democracy', *American Political Science Review*, 60, (1966).
Walsh, J., Haydon, C. and Taylor, S. (eds), *The Church of England, c.1689–c.1833*, Cambridge, Cambridge University Press, 1993.
Walwyn, W. 'Gold tried in the fire' [1647] in *The Levellers*, vol. 2, J. R Otteson (ed.) Bristol, Thoemmes Press, 2003.
Weale, A. 'Toleration, Individual Differences and Respect for Persons', in J. Horton and S. Mendus (eds), *Aspects of Toleration*, London, Methuen, 1985.
Weldon, T. D. *States and Morals*, London, John Murray, 1946.
Wende, P. '"Liberty" und "Property" in der politischen Theorie der Levellers', *Zeitschrift für Historische Forschung*, 1 (1974).
Wildman, J. *London's Liberties* [1650], [repr. Exeter, 1972].
Wilkinson, R. G. 'Income distribution and life expectancy', *British Medical Journal*, 304 (1992).
— *Unhealthy Societies*, London, Routledge, 1996.
Wilkinson, R. G. and Pickett, K. *The Spirit Level: Why more equal societies almost always do better*, London, Allen Lane, Penguin Books, 2009.
Winch, D. *Adam Smith's Politics*, Cambridge, Cambridge University Press, 1978.
Williams, B. 'Internal and External Reasons', in R. Harrison (ed.), *Rational Action*, Cambridge, Cambridge University Press, 1979.
Wilson, J. A. 'Adaptation to uncertainty and small numbers exchange: the New England Fresh Fish Market', *Bell Journal of Economics*, 11 (1980).
Winch, P. *The Idea of a Social Science and its Relation to Philosophy*, London, Routledge, 1958.
Withington, P. 'Two Renaissances: urban political culture in post-Reformation England', *Historical Journal*, 44 (2001).
Wittgenstein, L. *Philosophical Investigations*, Oxford, Blackwell, 1963.
Worden, B. 'Milton and Marchamont Nedham' in D. Armitage *et al.*, *Milton and Republicanism*, Cambridge, Cambridge University Press, 1995.
— 'Republicanism, Regicide and Republic: The English experience' in M. Van Gelderen and Q. Skinner, *Republicanism and Constitutionalism in Early Modern Europe*, vol.1, *Republicanism: A shared European history*, Cambridge, Cambridge University Press, 2005.

Index

actor's reasons 167ff *see also* explanation
Adams, J. 34
Adiaphora see also toleration
agency 40–1, 72
altruism 109, 123, 160
Al Qua'eda 149
American Journal of Political Science 138, 139–40, *141*
American National Election Studies 142
American Political Science Review 138, 139–40, *141*, 153
anarchy 97, 174
Anglicanism, establishment of 59
anomie 168
anthropology 162–3, 181–5
Aquinas, T. xxv
Arensburg, C. 185
Aristotle 9–11, 14, 78, 106, 115
   citizenship in 79, 86, 90
   and democracy 50
   on rhetoric 9–11, 19
Augustine, St. 7, 61
Austin, J. L. 26 n.18, 30, 31, 33 n.46, 46–7
   see also speech acts
authentic performance 13–14

Baker, K. 39
Barry, J. 85, 86
Begriffsgeschichte xxi–xxii, xxiii, 21, 23, 37–41, 73
   and Anglophone theory 37–8, 40
   diachronic dimension of 39, 40
   and social history 37, 38
   see also concepts

Belloc, H. 14
Benn, S. 53
Benn, T. 14
Bentham, J. 158
Berelson, B. R. 45
Berlin, I. 112
Berlusconi, S. 19
Bevir, M. xxiii
Bödeker, H. xxii
Bodin, J. 174–5
Boyle's Law 168
Bueno de Mesquita, E. 149
Burke, E. 7, 28, 53, 103 n.22, 113, 115
   and democracy 113
   reason, concept of 28
Butler, P. xvii, xviii

Cameron, D. 14
capitalism 32, 169–70, 179
   see also free markets
Cartwright, J. 50
Chesterton, G. K. 14
Chong, D. 138, 142 n.21
Christianity, non conformist 58 ff
   Catholic 62
Churchill, W. 124 n.14
cities 74, 74, 85, 86, 108 n.37, 151–2
   racial segregation study 151–2
'citizen', use of term 73, 74–5, 83–4, 87–8, 89–90
   and 'countryman' 75
   as 'freeman' 73–4, 75, 83, 84, 85, 90
   by London Corresponding Society 89–90
   as 'the people' 83, 84
   and 'subject' 87

Citizen's Charter 98 n.4
citizenship 73–93, 98 n.4, 125
   and civic identity 86, 89
   and cities 75, 85
   and Civil War republicanism 77, 81–5
      Levellers' active citizenship 82, 89
      vocabulary of citizenship in 83–4
      see also Civil War (1642–51)
   discourse/practice differences in 77, 78
      and Sir T. Smith's writings 77–80
      classical vocabulary and English practice of 77–80
   and equality 125–6
   in 18th C. England 85–87
      associational diversification in 85, 86–7
      and political liberty reform 87–8
      and the right to vote 88
   and freedom 75, 78, 90
   and liberty/rights 73, 88
   and office-holding 73, 76–7, 79–80, 84, 85
      civic identity of 86
      liberty in role of 91–3
      participatory 45ff, 82
   1790s reform movements 88–90
      and active citizenship 90
      French influence on 88, 90
      London Corresponding Society 88–9
   use of title, 'citizen' 89–90
civic, use of term 77ff, 85, 86
civic humanism 28
civic virtue 109
civil society, 116–8
Civil War (1642–51) 74, 75, 81–5
   the Levellers, role in xvi, 81–5
      citizenship, notion of in 83–4
      concept of freedom in 84–5
   republican vision in 75–7, 81–5
      notion of 'citizenship' in 76, 77, 81, 83

Coase, R. 107 n.36
Cohen, G. 7, 12
Coleman, J. xvii n.13, xxi
collectivism 97 n.1, 103, 179 n.5
   'bourgeoise' 85
   critique of Rawls 122
   and social goods 109
Collinson, P. 75–6, 77, 80
communism 99 n.12, 103
communitarian theory 109, 122, 131
community, conceptions of 109
Comparato, I. xxii
concepts xvii–xxii, 12–13, 14–15, 21–41
   and context 12–13, 37–41
      as linguistic 40
      see also language
   diachronic analysis of 39, 40
   essential contestability of xviii–xix
   history/historicity of xxi, xxiii, xxv, 37–41, 73
      concept/materiality tension in 38
      and political change 38–9
      see also Begriffsgeschichte
Condren, C. 92, 93
consciousness, xviii, 19, 53, 90, 101–2
Constant, B. 86
context 32
Crick, B. xvi, xxvii, 97–8, 99ff, 109, 110, 115
   In Defence of Politics 97–8, 99, 100, 101, 109, 110, 117
   and the new individualism 117
   and politics as freedom 98, 99

Dahl, R. 54
Davidson, D. 166, 187 n.28
Davis, W. G. 182, 184–5
Dawkins, R. 106 n.30
decision theory 164–5, 166, 187 n.28
Deleuze, G. 17
democracy 18, 45–7, 49–55, 99, 108
   apathy in 45, 51
   and citizen participation 45, 51
   developmental conception of 51–3, 54
      Godwin's case for 52–3

economic or market model 51, 54
empirical and classical theory 45–6, 49–50, 51, 53–4, 55
and equality 54
instrumental vs. value 54
meaning of xvi, xix, 40 n.81, 45–55
  and agreed criteria 46, 47
  historical development of 49–50, 51–2
  and politics 113
  as 'rule by the people' 46, 47, 49, 50
  use of the word 46–7, 49–51, 53–5
    as evaluative-descriptive word 47, 49
    and ideological redefinition 49–50
    as term of commendation 50–1, 53, 55
    as a speech act 51
  utilitarian/instrumental paradigm 54–55
de Swaan, A. 108 n.37
Dewan, T. 150
Diogenes 19
discrimination, racial xxviii, 186
Dowding, K. 150
Dunn, J. xvi
Durkheim, E. 168
Dworkin, R. 7

economic theory 100–1, 137, 157–75, 191–3
  critique of 160–75, 177
    and beliefs/perceptions network 170–5
    decision theory 164–5, 166
    and human choice-making studies 165
    preferences/motivations use in 164–5
  formation of a cultural norm in 161
  Friedman's test of 177
  and human behaviour 157–75, 187 n.28, 189–93
  predictability of 160, 161, 167
  rational utility maximiser hypothesis 164, 189–90
  rationality in xxvii, 104–7, 157–8, 159, 161, 165
  new economic history in 161, 167
    assumptions in 162–3, 167, 191–2
    hunter-gatherer to agrarian economy 161–4
  realism, rejection of in 160
  see also explanation; free markets; market-based society; rational choice theory
egalitarianism 119, 124, 126
  as an 'eligible' good (Rawls) 119
  and envy 120, 122, 123, 124
  and inequality consequences 127, 128–9
  as substantive or background 119
  see also equality; Rawls, J.
egoism 103–5, 107, 121, 123
  see also free markets; individuals, conceptions of; rational choice theory
Elton, G. 75
English Civil War see Civil War (1642–51)
English Revolution (1688) 39
equality 52, 54, 120–2, 123–4
  'difference principle' (Rawls) 120–2, 123
  as envy 121, 123, 125
  equality of opportunity principle 123, 128, 129
  as an ideal 119
  intrinsic value of 125–6, 133
  and public goods provision 123
  as a social relationship 124–5, 133
  see also egalitarianism; inequality; Rawls, J.
Erasmus 65
explanation 146, 155–75
  conditions of 156, 157
  covering law model 168–70

method of difference (Mill) in 168, 169, 170
and cultural meaning 155, 157–8, 169, 172, 175
economic model 155, 156, 157–75
and actor's reasons 155, 167, 170–5
and cultural values 157–8, 161, 172
and indeterminacy 166–7
and historical explanations 161–4
and the question of utility 158, 164, 189
see also rational choice theory
and *explanandum* 155
and intention 170–2, 173
beliefs, aims, ideals in 173
cultural shaping of 172
empirical identification of 171, 173
as social meaningful action 172
as satisfactory (criteria) 156, 157, 164, 167, 175
structural 143, 152, 162
see also economic theory; rational choice theory

facts, social xviii, xxiv, 127–8
Filmer, R. 50
Fish, S. 29
Fisher, R. xxii
Flew, A. xv, 24 n.11
Founders' Intent 14
Foxley, R. 78 n.20, 83
free markets 177
ideal and defence of 178, 181, 184, 185–6, 192
discrimination, erosion of 179–80, 185, 189, 190
libertarian argument 178–81, 184, 186, 190, 192
prices and demand in 186
and labour fragmentation 178
and neutrality 177, 184, 186–7, 190, 192
preferential relationships in 181–5
compadrazgo (Mexico) 185
ethnicity and kinship in 184–5
onibara (Nigeria) 182, 183–4
pratik-type (Haiti) 181, 182, 183, 184, 187
Soulard study (St. Louis) 183, 185, 187
suki (The Philippines) 181, 182, 184–5, 187
tolerance claim analysis xxviii, 70, 177, 179–81, 185–92
conceptual criticisms of 185–8, 192
criteria of discrimination used 188–9
market neutrality, issue of 186–7, 190, 192
methodological prescriptions in 190–2
rational egoism assumption in 190–1, 192
revealed preferences, language of 184, 187
and trust-based dyadic ties 184, 185, 187
and utility-maximisation 189–90, 192
freedom xix, 73–4, 83
and citizenship 75, 78, 83, 84
c1600 England 74, 81, 83, 84
and freedoms 90ff
and individual choice 111–12
of office 74ff, 91
and politics 98
republican/liberal conceptions of 99
see also liberty
freeman *see* citizen
French Revolution 39, 115
reinterpretive work on 39
Friedman, M. xxvii, 158–9, 177, 178 n.2, n.4, 179
discrimination erosion arguments 179, 186–7, 188, 189, 190
Furet, F. 39

Galileo 156
Gallagher, G. 173–4
Gauthier, D. 190 n.33
Gilder, G. 180 n.7, n.8
Godwin, W. 52–3
  case for democracy by 52–3
Goldie, M. 61 n.13, 76, 80, 85
Goldsmith, M. xvii
Goodin, R. E. 99 n.9
Green, D. 135, 136, 138, 140, 153–4
Greenleaf, J. xviii
Grotius, H. 26

Hahn, F. 103 n.23
Hampsher-Monk, I. 154
Hansson, B. 166
Harding, A. 74 n.5
Harrington, J. 29, 81
Hausman, D. 145
Hayek, F. A. 103 n.23, 106, 158, 159, 160, 162, 178–9, 191 n.35
Hegel, G. W. F. xviii, 118 n.60, 125
  consciousness in xviii, 102
  master-slave dialectic 101–2
Herodotus 3–4, 5, 10
history xviii, 3–6, 8, 12
  and linguistic agency 40–1
  philosophy, tensions with xviii, 5–6
    competing claims of 6
  see also philosophy
history of political thought xvii, xxiii, xxv n.33, 3, 8, 9–20, 38
  context, importance of in 26 n.17, 103–4
  influence on political theory of 12–16
  Pocock's topography 26–7
  and political discourse 9–12, 15–16, 20, 38
  and linguistic agency 40–1
  republican discourse, recovery of 73, 98 n.4
  see also concepts; philosophy; political theory; politics (political practice)

History of Political Thought xvii
Hobbes, T. xxv, 7, 13, 24, 26, 29, 32, 65, 184
  and *explanandum* 155, 164
  and liberty 92
  state of nature in 114
Hollis, M. 155 n.1, n.2, 158, 160, 177 n.1
Hope-Mason, J. 104
Hopkins, A. G. 174
Hughes, C. xvi
Hume, D. 106 n.34
Hunt, L. 39
Hurd, R. 87 n.56

identity, personal 70, 101–2, 104, 106
  civic, 89
  and market structures 104–7
  personality, shaping of 104–7
  political, linguistic construction of 15–16
  and professionalism 104–5
  social construction of 123
  and the social nexus 102
  see also individualism
ideology/ical redefinition 45ff
illocutionary acts 31, 38, 46–7, 50, 55
  see also speech acts
indifferency xx, 59
  see also adiaphora
individual, conceptions of 100–3, 122–3
  altruism in 123
  and community 123
  and egoistic motivation 123
  as rational-egoistic agent 104–6, 107, 160, 164
  in rational choice theory 143
  and social context 101–4
individualism 70, 85, 99, 103–17, 122
  and demise of collectivism 103, 116–18
  as distinct from communal identity 122–3
  libertarian 100, 107, 108

and public goods problem 107–9,
    111, 123
  and public health 108–9, 111,
    130–2
  and rational egoist model 104, 105,
    107 n.36, 116, 131, 160, 190
  see also liberty; market-based
    societies
inequality 127, 128–33
  and 'epidemiological transition'
    129–30
  and equality of opportunity 129
  health effects of 129, 130–2
  and life-expectancy 131–3
  and liberty 129
  social consequences of 128, 129,
    132–3
  see also egalitarianism; equality
intention 155, 171–2, 173, 175
  concept of 101 n.18m 172
  in explanation 155, 170–2, 175
    empirical identification of 171–2
  public character of 172
  as socially meaningful action 172
  see also explanation; Skinner, Q.
interest groups 117
Islam xix, 67

Jefferson, T. 34
Jones. E. 155, 161, 162, 169
Jordan, B. 155 n.1
judgement 47–8

Kant, I. 8, 41, 191 n.35
Keller, H. 13–14
Koselleck, R. xxii, 26, 37 n.61, n.64,
    38–9

language
  and agency 40–1
  concept of 27, 30
  and individual understanding 101 n.17
  langue/parole distinction 27, 28
  and social reality 38–9, 40
  see also speech; speech acts

Larrère, C. xxii
Laslett, P. xv, 26 n.17
Leca, J. 118 n.60
legitimacy, concept of 12, 13
Levellers, the see Civil War (1642–51)
liberalism xx, 24, 55, 98–9, 100 n.14
  individualistic concerns of 98,
    106, 107
libertarianism 16, 107, 108, 125 n.14,
    178 n.2
  free markets, defence of 178–81
  see also free markets
liberty 12, 74, 81, 84, 86, 87, 91–3, 99,
    110, 117, 120, 123
  and diversity 115
  economic 99
  as a legal condition 91
  and monarchy 87
  negative/positive distinction
    109, 112
  and new individualism 117
  in office and roles 91–3
  and politics 110, 117
  see also freedom; individualism;
    market-based society
life expectancy 129ff
Lighthouse example 107, 186
Lilburne, J. 83, 84, 85
logical positivism 7
Locke, J. xx, 7, 26, 32, 58–62, 64
  contextual understanding of 26
    n.17, 27 n.20,
  and concept of liberty 93
  and religious toleration xx, 58–62,
    64, 68
    as culturally localised 61–2
    conception of religion in 61
    see also religion; toleration
  theory of legitimacy 12
Lockyer, A. xvi, 98 n.4
Lodge, D. *Nice Work* 102
Lovejoy, A. O. 26

McAllister, I. 150
Macaulay, C. 88

Machiavelli, N. 31–2, 81, 106, 115, 117
MacIntyre, A. 138 n.12, 169–70
McLean, I. 123 n.13
Madison, J. 34, 35, 113, 115
Maitland, F. W. 73
Mandeville, B. 50, 106 n.33, 116, 172
Major, J. 67 n.26
market, the *see* economic theory; free markets; market-based society
market-based societies xxviii, 106–18, 123, 161
   associations, demise of in 115–17
   failure 107ff, 122ff
   and individual choice 111–12, 114–15, 123, 157–8
      non-monetary values in 157–8
   liberal individualist view of 106, 107
   and libertarian individualism 107
   and moral responsibility 112–14
   perfect information, assumption of 111
   and political personality 106–7
   privatisation policy in 116
   and public goods provision 107–9, 110, 123
   social goods provision in 109, 110–11, 116
   see also explanation, economic type of; free markets; individualism
Marsilius of Padua 24
Marten, H. 81
Martin, L. 139, 147–9, 152, 153
Marx, K. xvi, 18
Marxism 100–1
mass society 115
maxi-min strategy 121
Mennell, S. 155, 168, 173, 174
Mexico 185
Mill, J. 51, 54
   and democracy 54
Mill, J. S. 13, 51, 60, 178
   Essay on Liberty 60
   on toleration 60, 61
   A System of Logic 168–9
      method of difference in 168, 169, 170

Miller, D. 109, 110, 186 n.25, 190 n.33
Mintz, S. 182
monarchy 75, 78, 87, 92
   absolute 92
Montesquieu, C. de S. 34, 75, 115
Mosher, M. 70
Mouffe, C. 18
Mueller, D. xxv n.35, 123 n.13, 135, 153

nationalism 99
natural endowments 119
Nef, R. 124 n.14
Nell, E. 160, 177 n.1
Netherlands Institute for Advanced Study (NIAS) xxi
North, D. xxviii, 161–2
Nozik, R. 70, 99 n.9, 107, 120, 178

Obama, B. 14
O'Donnell, A. T. 186 n.24, n.27
Oedipus, 170
Olson, M. 115
ontology, social and political xxiv–xxv
Ouchi, G. 105 n.29

Paine, T. 63, 88, 91
Paisley, I. 172
Parfitt, D. 101, 102
peasants 80, 174, 184
Peters, R. S. 53
philosophy xviii, 3, 4, 18, 19
   academic teaching of 23–4
   continental 17
   of economics xxvi–xxix, 103–6, 157ff, 178–9, 189ff
   historical approach to 23–4
   history, distinction with 3, 4–6
      as belief distinction 5–6
      see also history
   and rhetoric 10, 18, 19
   and power 19
   practice of 24
   theory of forms 4
   and time 6–7
   see also political philosophy

Plato xv, xvi, 4, 7, 11, 19, 24, 49
  cave, idea of 11
Pocock, J. G. A. xvi, xxii, xxiii, 15 n.31, 21, 23, 24 n.12, 26–30, 35–6, 37ff, 40, 75
  historian, role of 28
  and historical meaning 26–30
    and interpretation 29
    language, role in 28–30
  and political language 8 n.18, 26–8
    langue/parole distinction 28
  and republican narrative 75, 98 n.8
  and sovereignty 15 n.31, 16
Pogge, T. 130
political, the 18
  discursive construction of 18, 19
  political-private divide 19
  religious space in 64
political action 38–9, 54–5, 76, 113–14
  decisions, making of in 113–14
  as linguistic action 38–9
  and moral responsibility 112–13
  see also political theory; politics (political practice)
political culture 14–15, 72, 153
  and individualism 117 n.57
political philosophy xvii, 6, 7–9, 12, 13, 15, 20
  as a career 11, 17
  and normative theory 8, 20
  and politics 18–19
    arena of rhetoric in 18–19
  see also history of political thought; politics (political practice)
political science xvii, xix, 97, Ch. 8 *passim*
political stability 99
political theory xv, 7, 8, 13–20, 23
  academic study of 23–4, 28
  action and belief in 136, 137, 139, 144–5, 148, 150–2, 155, 167–8, 170–5
    and economic explanations 155, 157,
    instrumental/structural approaches 138, 144, 146
    intention, identification of 170–3
    and interpretative evidence 136, 137, 138, 144, 146, 148, 150, 151, 153, 154
    and unintended consequences 151–2, 154
    see also explanation; intention; rational choice theory
  analytical approach xvii, xviii
  Cambridge school xv, 21–2, 25ff
  conceptual analysis xv, xvii, 23, 24
    see also Begriffsgeschichte; concepts
  and economic theory 100–1, 137, 157–75, 189–93
    and human behaviour 157–75, 189–93
    see also economic theory; explanation; rational choice theory
  Exeter chair in xvii
  historical texts, study of xv, xvi, 17
    see also history of political thought
  historical revolution (Anglophone) 24–41
    diachronic connections in 25–6, 39–40
    'eternal problems' in 24–5
    meaning/interpretation in 32–4
    see also concepts; Pocock, J.G.A.; Skinner, Q.
  as philosophy 7–8
  positivist tradition xvii, 136, 191 n.36
    see also political philosophy; politics (political practice)
politics (political practice) 8–9, 13–16, 109–10
  and academic discourse 11–12
  and diversity 115
  and importance of association 115, 117–18
  community, commitment to 109–10
  as freedom 98, 99, 110, 111
  and individual choice 111–12
  see also Crick, B.

and history of political thought
  13–20
ideal of liberty in 100, 110
and ideology 99
  ideological innovation 33ff
and language 9–12, 15–16, 18–19,
  20, 30, 35–6, 39
  as political identity 15–16
  as public discourse 15–16, 35–6
  three nodal points of 11–12
  use of rhetoric 9–11, 13, 18–19
and market politics 116, 118
  see also free markets; individualism; market-based society
and moral consensus 109
and moral responsibility 113–14
  in political decisions 113–14
and the private 19, 66–7
as a social good 109, 110, 114
topoi in 15
and truth 11
Popper, K. 49, 191 n.35
preferences, market shaping of 110
Price, R. 63
Priestley, J. 63, 88
private property 84, 162, 179–80
psychology 103ff, 121, 165ff
Public Choice 135
public choice theory xxv n.35, 123
  n.13, 135
  egoistic motivation in 123 n.13
  see also economic theory; rational choice theory
public good(s) 84, 86, 89, 107–9

Quine, W. V. 164 n.20

rational choice theory xxv–xxviii, 101,
  105, 110, 135–54, 157, 163
  action and reason in 138–9, 143,
    144, 146–7, 150
    interpretative evidence, use
      in 138–9, 141–2, 146, 147,
      148, 154
  as a realist theory 143, 144, 145,
    146, 150, 154

critique of 135–6, 138, 153
  external/internal evidence in 136
  as 'flight from reality' 135–6,
    138, 145
as economic explanation 157
  see also explanation
game theory, use in 149
historical origins of xxvi
individuals, conception of in 103–4,
  143, 144
moral hazard, notion in 105
rational chooser model xxvi–xxvii,
  107 n. 36
research value of 139, 145, 150–4
  assumptions, role of 150,
    152, 153
  and conflicting interpretative
    evidence 152–3, 154
  and empirical evidence 151
  and unintended consequences
    151–2, 154
as structural theory 143–4, 145
use in articles analysis 138–2,
  153–4
  interpretive evidence in 141–2
  percentages 1984–2005 *141*
  see also economic theory; free
    markets; market-based society
Rawls, J. xvii, xx–xxi, xxvi, xxvii, 7,
  70, 119–33
  critique of 122–3
  and decision-making xxvi
  'rational chooser' model
    xxvi–xxvii
  and religious liberty 65–6
  theory of justice 7, 66, 119–33
    difference principle in 120–2,
      123, 126, 128, 129, 132–3
    and egoism 120
    equality, notion of xxvi, xxvii,
      119–20, 123–5, 128
    free market premise in 128
    health in 129ff
    individual, concept of in 127
    liberty principle, priority in 129,
      130–1

notion of 'envy' in 123–5
social knowledge in 128
see also egalitarianism; equality; inequality
Rayner, J. 37 n.64
Raz, J. 109 n.38, 190 n.33
realist assumptions 159–61, *see also* Rational Choice
reason, conceptions of xxv–xxvi, 28
as explanation of actions 168
hermeneutic approaches xxv
Reichardt, R. 26
religion xx, 58–63, 64, 65–70, 71
and atheism 63–4, 65, 70
coercion/faith relationship 61, 62
1790s liberty campaign 88
Protestant Reformation period 63, 64
unbelievers, fate of 63
and toleration xx, 58–63, 64, 65–70, 71
claims of conscience in 61–2, 63, 64, 65
and Non-Anglicans 62, 63, 64
see also Locke, J.; toleration
rent seeking 116, 129
republic, meaning of 34–5, 'unacknowledged' 75–7
republicanism xxii, 8 n.18, 29, 75, 81, 98, 109
and collective concerns 98
in English Civil War period 81–5
and liberty 109 n.40
revival of 73, 98 n.4
revolution, interpretation of 39
rhetoric 9–11, 13–14, 17, 18–19, 20
and the enthymeme 10, 18
topos, concept of 10, 15
Richter, M. xxii, 23 n.8, 37
Ricoeur, P. 17
rights 88, 109, 110
to vote 88
Robinson, R. 173–4
Roman law 13
Rousseau, J.-J. 13, 24, 32, 98, 115, 125

Rushdie affair xix–xx, 67, 71 n.31
Ryan, A. 51

Sahlins, M. 163
typology of exchanges 182
Samuelson, P. 159, 191 n.34
Sandel, M. 70
Saussure, 27
Schelling, T. 151–2
secularisation, xx, 49
Searle, J. 30
segregation, 66, 152
Sen, A. xxvi n.36, 187 n.28
Shapiro, I. 135, 136, 138, 140, 153–4
Shearmur, J. 189 n.30
Shepsle, K. 140
Skinner, Q. xvi, xxii, xxiii, 6 n.11, n.12, 12, 21–2, 23, 25, 30–6, 37ff, 40, 109, 136 n.8
'Meaning and Understanding' 25–6, 46 n.5
and speech acts 30–2, 36
intention and meaning in 32, 46 n.5, 101 n.18
conventional/subversive levels 34, 35
Smith, A. 14, 87
Smith, T. 77–80
citizenship and freedom 78
social contract 13, 123
social democracy 121 n.9
social science
deductive *see* rational choice theory
interpretive xxiiiff, 136, 139ff
structuralist, 143, 152
socialism 117 n.58, 124 n.14
Socrates 19
sovereignty, concept of 16
Sowell, T. 180 n.7, n.8, 189 n.31
speech, normal xv, 30
evaluative-descriptive words 47, 48–9
meaning of a word xv, xviii, 101
moral terminology 47

use of a word 46–8
  change of meaning in 49
  see also language
speech acts 17, 19, 26 n.18, 30–1, 33 n.46, 40–1, 47–9
  illocutionary/perlocutionary acts 31, 48
  see also Skinner, Q.
state, the
  church/state separation 64, 66
  concept of 40 n.81
  as a democracy 45
    see also democracy
  English cultural continuities in 66
  and tolerance 57, 60, 62, 69–70
    as absence of persecution 62
    and individual autonomy 67, 68, 69–70
    and religious belief 60–2, 64, 66, 69–70
    see also religion; toleration
Stiglitz, J. 129
Stoppard, T. *Jumpers*, 49
Strawson, P. F. 101
subject 76, 80, 87

Tacitus 106
Taylor, C. xvi, 38 n.71, 101 n.18
Tebbit, N. 66
Thatcher, M. 14, 16, 70, 117 n.58, 124 n.14
Thelwall, J.
thick description 146
Thompson, E. P. xv
Tocqueville, A. de 66, 115
toleration xx–xxi, xxviii, 57–72, 110
  adiaphora, concept of xx–xxi, 59
  committed/instrumental conceptions 57–8
  English tradition/form of 59, 62–3, 65–7, 68, 71
    as an assimilationist view 65
    as claims of conscience 61–2, 63, 64, 65

political/religious boundaries in 66–7
and free markets xxviii, 70, 177–92
  see also free markets
historical arguments for 58, 71
as 'indulgence' 62–3
and individual autonomy 67, 69, 70
and legislation 57
and neutrality 57, 58, 62, 65, 66, 68–9, 72
  as principle of equal respect 69
and Rawls, 65
religious xx, 58–9, 60–4, 65–70, 71
  limits/boundaries of 64–5, 66–7, 71
  as sufferance 63
  and unbelief/atheism 63–4, 65, 70
  see also Locke, J.; religion
and a secular state 69–70
totalitarianism 24, 32, 115
Tribe, K. xxii, 37
Tversky, A. 165–6, 187 n.28
tyranny 92

United States 14
  Constitution 34
  Founder's Intent 14
  inequality in 129
  republic, meaning debate of 34–5
  toleration in 66
  War of Independence 34
utility, 158

Vanberg, G. 139, 147–9, 152, 153
van Gelderen, M. xxi, xxii
virtue, concept of 36, 47
Voltaire, F.-M. A. xxviii
Von Mises, L. 143, 158, 159, 160, 178 n.2, n.4, 179 n.6, 189 n.32, 191

Waldron, J. 60 n.8, 61 n.12, n.13, 66 n.24
Walwyn, W. 82, 83
Weale, A. 60 n.10, 68–9
Weber, M. 137 n.10,
    and the causes of capitalism 169–70
Wellington, N. 77
Wildman 83–4
Wilkinson, R. G. 127
Williams, R. 37 n.61
Winch, P. 101 n.18
Withington, P. 85
Witkins, B. 168
Wittgenstein, L. xv, 18, 101, 172